About the Author and the Photographer

. . . .

JEFFREY POMPE is a professor of economics at Francis Marion University in Florence, South Carolina, where he is the Nellie Cooke Sparrow Professor of Business and University Trustee Research Scholar. He is co-author of *Environmental Conflict: In Search of Common Ground*.

KATHLEEN POMPE is a professor of art at Francis Marion University. For the past thirty years her photography has been exhibited extensively in one-person, invitational, and juried art shows throughout the United States. In addition her photographs have appeared in many books and journals.

To receive a free catalog of Poisoned Pen Press titles, please contact us in one of the following ways:

Phone: 1-800-421-3976
Facsimile: 1-480-949-1707
Email: info@poisonedpenpress.com
Website: www.poisonedpenpress.com

Poisoned Pen Press
6962 E. First Ave. Ste 103
Scottsdale, AZ 85251

The Anthropology of Learning in Childhood

The Anthropology of Learning in Childhood

Edited by
David F. Lancy,
John Bock, and
Suzanne Gaskins

ALTAMIRA PRESS
A Division of
ROWMAN & LITTLEFIELD PUBLISHERS, INC.
Walnut Creek • Lanham • New York • Toronto • Plymouth, UK

AltaMira Press
A division of Rowman & Littlefield Publishers, Inc.
A wholly owned subsidiary of The Rowman & Littlefield Publishing Group, Inc.
4501 Forbes Boulevard, Suite 200
Lanham, MD 20706
www.altamirapress.com

Estover Road
Plymouth PL6 7PY
United Kingdom

British Library Cataloguing in Publication Information Available

Library of Congress Cataloging-in-Publication Data

The anthropology of learning in childhood / edited by David F. Lancy, John Bock, and
Suzanne Gaskins.
  p. cm.
Includes bibliographical references and index.
  ISBN 978-0-7591-1322-0 (cloth : alk. paper) — ISBN 978-0-7591-1324-4 (electronic)
  1. Educational anthropology. 2. Child development. 3. Learning. I. Lancy, David F.
II. Bock, John C. III. Gaskins, Suzanne.
  LB1125.A567 2010
  306.43—dc22   2009036462

Printed in the United States of America

CONTENTS

CONTENTS

FIGURES AND CREDITS

FOREWORD

Robert A. LeVine

Anthropological research on learning has advanced dramatically since the middle of the last century, and this book's chapters provide unique access to the scope, depth and theoretical power of that progress in scientific understanding. Learning has been fundamentally re-conceived and re-examined in terms of its evolution in humans and other primate species, its place in the life cycle, its forms and contents under diverse cultural and socioeconomic conditions, and its uses in unprecedented settings of the contemporary world. The anthropologists contributing to this volume have documented in depth the ways children learn in contexts hitherto unknown to Western science, and they have formulated generalizations about human learning by considering the evidence comprehensively rather than imposing theories of dubious relevance or extrapolating from restricted studies. The results reveal universals and variations in learning as a basic aspect of human adaptation.

The study of human learning has come a long way since the period, roughly 1935–60, when "learning theory" was the dominant paradigm in academic psychology and "the laws of learning" were thought of as having been set forth by Clark L. Hull, particularly in his *Principles of Behavior* (Hull, 1943). Hull's integration of the "classical" or associative conditioning of Pavlov with the "instrumental" conditioning of Thorndike in a unified stimulus-response theory of habit formation was likened to Newton's achievement in uniting terrestrial and celestial mechanics in the mathematical theory of gravitation. Having been established by rigorous experiments (largely with albino rats learning to run a maze after 22 hours of food deprivation), Hull's laws were not subject to revision by human evidence; instead, human learning was considered a field to which the laws were applied. Learning in vertebrates, including humans, consisted of the strengthening of stimulus-response bonds into habits through drive-reducing rewards—the reinforcement mechanism—and there was no need to involve "mental" processes even to conceptualize the abstract thinking of humans. Through the concepts of acquired or secondary drives, Hullian theory could encompass human learning and social behavior, and through the concept of stimulus generalization, the laws of learning could be seen to be at work in the childhood learning of particular human populations as far away as New Guinea and in comparative studies across the world.

This behavioristic theory was developed at Yale in the 1930s, attracted some of the best minds in psychology, became the orthodox position in the 1940s, and stigmatized opposing positions as unscientific. There were some early dissenters who proposed that rats formed "cognitive maps" of the mazes they ran, whether or not they were reinforced, and who questioned the "ecological validity" of experimental evidence. But it was only later that these arguments attained the credence they deserved. In the 1940s and 1950s "The Psychology of Learning" as Hull and his students had conceptualized it reigned supreme in the curriculum of American psychology. In the decade after Hull's death in 1952, behavioristic learning theory began its decline, hastened after 1960 by the "cognitive revolution" that had been gaining strength in psychology as an approach, or family of approaches, focused on the processes involved in human thought, experience and development.

Once the stigma wore off other approaches to human learning, the flaws of the Hullian position became evident if not downright obvious: In complex human environments, for example, identifying the "reinforcers" that were supposed to account for learning was often a matter of guesswork, highlighting the possibility that the rewards that acted as reinforcers in laboratory experiments had been arbitrarily selected (and amplified by the experimenter) from among those that occurred naturally in the rodent's environment. Furthermore, the continuity presumed between animal and human learning was credible only if you assumed that humans had no greater capacity for learning than rats. But that required blinding yourself to most of what we know about human thought outside the laboratory. The radical utilitarian premise of Hullian theory, that we learn only what is rewarded, did not stand up to close examination when the behavior of humans was examined as closely as that of rodents. Finally, there is the matter of Hull's grandiosity: In his quest for scientific prestige, Hull not only fashioned laws of learning mimicking Newton's laws of motion and adopted a strictly experimental method, he also used pseudo-mathematical formulae that looked like Newton's equations but were free of actual mathematics. This is of course not science but scientism, embarrassing psychology without providing enlightenment.

Hull's learning theory seems like ancient history now, some 50-60 years later, but the influence of its logical positivist model of science (based on an idealized history of physics), has not entirely worn off in academic psychology. In that discipline, experimental and reductionist approaches are given primacy over other forms of knowing, despite the example of Darwin's *field observations* as having generated the theoretical framework for modern biology.

Where are the field observations that will generate the theoretical framework for scientific research on human learning? Largely in anthropology, and they are well represented by this volume. Its editors and contributors are keenly aware of the plasticity in human development that permits learning under diverse conditions that investigators cannot imagine in advance (let alone simulate in experiments) but must discover through fieldwork. The results of their careful observations and analytic reflections in a wide variety of settings, informed by an understanding of evolution and behavioral development, provide the basis for a new and long awaited science of learning in the human species.

References

Hull, Clark L. (1943). *Principles of Behavior*. New York: Appleton and Century.

Part I

UNDERSTANDING THE ANTHROPOLOGICAL RESEARCH

CHAPTER ONE
PUTTING LEARNING IN CONTEXT

David F. Lancy, John Bock, and Suzanne Gaskins

Few topics in the social sciences have attracted as much attention as "learning," and that is certainly the case in anthropology—a history that will be detailed in chapter 3. However, anthropologists have not spoken with a single voice—more like the proverbial Babel of tongues. This book, for the first time, brings together in a single volume the varied perspectives of archeologists, cultural anthropologists, evolutionary anthropologists, linguists, and others who share a common bond as anthropologists. Our synthesis aims to represent these scholarly traditions and to find common denominators. In the process, we hope to provide a fresh look at learning in childhood.

The quintessential image of "learning" that some readers may retain from their undergraduate education is of a pigeon or a rat pecking or levering away for a reward in a "Skinner box." David Lancy, in fact, "ran" just such experimental trials as an undergraduate. Anthropologists in no way deny the validity of well-established ideas such as "operant conditioning," or more contemporary models of learning from the perspective of information processing, but do tend to see learning in more complex terms.

We began our collaboration on this book with each of us bringing a different conceptualization of learning in childhood from our own subdisciplinary perspective. We viewed this diversity in interest as strength. David Lancy, an ethnographer, draws inductive inferences from a corpus of ethnographic data. His perspective emphasizes the individual experience of enculturation and the commonalities and differences across the

Figure 1.1.   Skinner box: device used to study learning (A. Black graphic)

form and function of childhood in cultures varying in geographical and temporal dimensions. John Bock, an evolutionary anthropologist, focuses on the ways that the environment has shaped the basic human pattern, and how through the process of development individuals respond to their own social, ecological, and cultural contexts. Suzanne Gaskins, a psychological anthropologist, concentrates on the production and reproduction of culture by individuals' construction of meaning from experience.

Despite our differences, the editors are united on six general principles that we think inform the range of anthropological perspectives on learning and that have guided our editorial work on this volume. First, and most foundational, when anthropologists look at childhood through an evolutionary lens (chapter 2), they note some unique aspects, relative to other species. In particular, for humans, the *length* of the period of immaturity is elongated and this is accounted for, in some theories, by brain growth and the acquisition—via learning—of all that constitutes "culture." The flexible and powerful capacity of individuals to learn and

Figure 1.2. Shelling peas in Lesotho (B. Sypkerman photo)

the need for each new member to acquire a wide range of cultural knowledge are sometimes seen as two sides of the same coin, and the coin itself is unique to the human species.

The second principle is that while cultural information is universally transmitted between generations through teaching and learning, there is wide variation in the specific knowledge to be passed down. Humans are unique in that the end points of learning, "objectives" or "outcomes," are culturally defined. As anthropologists have recorded, there is considerable variation in what production skills children must learn in pastoralist, forager, and farming communities (chapter 15). And cultures vary widely in their belief systems, cultural institutions, and social practices. Learning objectives can vary within a culture, too. For instance, in many nonindustrial societies, gender is typically a powerful mediator of what children are expected to learn (chapter 12). Morality and character are often important socialization targets (chapter 11), and language is a powerful socialization medium for transmitting cultural ideas (chapter 10).

5

The third principle, often referred to as *parental ethnotheory*, is that a "culture," to support the transmission process, will always include well-established ideas on when and how the child can be expected to learn the behaviors and skills that are valued and which confer success (chapter 4). Equally important are notions about whom the child should look to for guidance and instruction—often a sibling (chapter 8). Dramatic variation exists in the ethnographic record on issues such as the age at which children become teachable or the appropriateness of corporal punishment to aid the learning process (chapter 7).

The fourth principle is that learning—at any age—is embedded in social processes that are not necessarily organized for learning. The societies that have attracted the greatest attention from anthropologists have usually lacked formal educational institutions (aside from initiation rites). To "find" learning, we have to follow children around rather than comfortably situating ourselves in a classroom. The locus for learning may be the home (chapter 16), the village, farm, or bush (chapters 13 and 14), and when we do study learning in schools (chapter 9), there is the predilection to focus on the ad hoc or socially constructed aspects of what may otherwise seem a decontextualized process.

The fifth principle is that children must take an active part in pursuing their own education. The single most important form of learning is through observation (chapter 5). Following the careful verbal instructions of a teacher, on the other hand, is rarely observed. Children are expected to negotiate a steady state in which they are learning what is expected in order to shoulder a larger and larger share of the household economy while also meeting personal needs and goals. Such a state might be achieved, for example, when a child is able to learn and/or complete chores while playing (chapter 6).

The sixth and last principle is that learning as a process is influenced by the fact that children are simultaneously being and becoming. Children can be seen as acting in the moment, behaving appropriately for their age, but also moving on a developmental trajectory toward adulthood. This duality is particularly evident when we look at children playing (chapter 6) or surviving in the streets (chapter 17). As culture is dynamic, any theory of learning in culture must address the impact of change on children as well as the potential impact on culture of children acting as agents of change. The last two chapters look at children in the midst of rapid

social change and include a survey of rural children learning in novel contexts—classrooms, in the midst of civil conflict, as immigrants to a foreign
country, and in the streets of large cities.

In sum, anthropology's perspectives suggest that learning in childhood occurs through participation in socially meaningful contexts over an
extended period of immaturity. It is organized by culturally specific ideas
about desirable learning outcomes and effective means to achieve them, as
well as children's individual abilities and motivations and their responses
to ecological conditions. Children actively pursue learning in the present in
order to be productive participants in their current everyday environments
and over time in order to become fully functional adult members of their
community, even as it might be undergoing cultural change or stress.

Overview of the Volume

In part I, we provide the essential background material for an understanding of anthropological research on learning in childhood. Chapter 2, by
John Bock, reviews evolutionary perspectives on children's learning. It
discusses views on the possible function of childhood as a distinct stage in
human development, and how natural selection has shaped childhood to
respond to social, cultural, and ecological features of children's environments. Much of the thinking on these issues is associated with a fairly new
perspective in anthropology, "life history theory." Chapter 3, by Robert
L. Munroe and Mary Gauvain, traces the trajectory of scholarship in anthropology from Malinowski and Mead in the late 1920s to contemporary
work on childhood among hunter-gatherers. The authors document the
alteration, over time, between concern for finding universals in children's
patterns of learning and development and concern for local variants. They
also reveal the continuing theoretical engagement between work in child
psychology—often claiming universality of a particular phenomenon—and
cross-cultural findings that undermine such claims. In chapter 4, by Sara
Harkness, Charles Super, and others, we learn of the importance of cultural models and parental ethnotheories in shaping the family's and community's treatment of the child as a learner. While the previous chapters
highlighted anthropological or scientific perspectives on children's learning
in village (and more recent studies of urban) settings, the Harkness et al.
chapter counters with folk or native views on the same subject.

As we indicated above, a highlight of the anthropological study of children's learning has been to acknowledge and document the profoundly social nature of the process. In part II, Learning as a Social Process, we explore these processes in depth. Suzanne Gaskins and Ruth Paradise, in chapter 5, unpackage an often invoked but rarely analyzed process—observational learning. Drawing on psychological theory and ethnographic accounts, they establish the basic elements that one can expect to find in any study of children's observational learning in culture. The anthropologists' initial field notes are often replete with instances of children playing and working and the interconnections between them—the subject of chapter 6, by Garry Chick. Chick shows that, despite this ubiquity, defining work and play and demonstrating how they are learned is not straightforward. But some things seem quite clear, including the consistent differentiation in play and work as a function of gender (for example, that girls transition from play to work earlier than boys). Chick also complements the chapter by Harkness and Super in discussing parental views on the value and functions of play in children's learning.

The next two chapters review work on the significant individuals who act as caretakers, role models, and teachers for children, particularly adults (chapter 7) and peers (chapter 8). In chapter 7, David Lancy and Annette Grove review research where the child's progress in learning is monitored or accelerated by watchful adults who rely on local theories of teaching and learning. These occasions include the teaching of kin terms and politeness conventions, locomotor skills, chores, craft skills, and adolescent rites of passage. In chapter 8, Ashley Maynard and Katrin Tovote contrast societies where parents are heavily involved with children's development with those in which siblings, as primary caretakers, fulfill the role of guide and teacher. Their chapter also explores the influence that schooling has on patterns of sibling interaction and instruction. The gulf between the informal teaching and learning which are characteristic of children maturing in the village and the more formal processes which are observed in schools is taken up by Leslie Moore in chapter 9. Moore notes the extensive reliance on rote memorization and learning in a second language that is characteristic of both Muslim and state-sponsored public schools. However, she expands our limited perspective on memorization, demonstrating its importance in conveying more subtle, value-laden aspects of the two modes of schooling.

The work reviewed in part III, Learning Cultural Meanings, falls under what has typically been referred to as socialization, defined as "the deliberate shaping of individuals to become adapted to the social environment" (Schönpflug and Bilz 2009, 213). Laura Sterponi, in chapter 10, reviews research in linguistic anthropology—in particular, studies of language socialization. She demonstrates that children's communicative competence is molded and organized by sociocultural processes and, when language refers to social relations, speaking is dependent on understanding the social system; conversely, socialization is often mediated through language. In chapter 11, Heidi Fung and Ben Smith look at the socialization of morals, values, and behavior. This chapter discusses studies of how children learn the cultural meaning of morals through everyday interactions and socialization practices such as play, teasing, and shaming. While there are a limited number of studies in this tradition, they span the history of anthropology's study of childhood and have been central to the cultural analysis of children's self-construction. In chapter 12, Heather Montgomery considers a sample of a larger corpus on this very important topic. She first looks at the ritual and customary actions associated with a newborn, revealing how much of this symbolic action is aimed at defining gender. Next she moves on to middle childhood, showing the sharp demarcation of gender roles that emerges at this time, and lastly she considers the role of initiation ceremonies in shaping gender identity.

Anthropology's unique value to scholarship in children's learning is particularly evident in part IV, Learning to Make a Living. On display in this section are rich, multifaceted reviews of learning in focused skill areas. Kerry Ossi-Lupo is a primatologist studying how juvenile monkeys learn from interacting with and observing adults. In chapter 13, she discusses research on the evolved patterns that shape the way juvenile primates develop social awareness and skills that pay off in terms of their learning to forage or learning to care for their offspring. Rebecca Zarger, in chapter 14, applies a cognitive anthropology lens to view children's learning in the natural world. The chapter discusses how children learn to name, use, and categorize natural kinds. Katharine MacDonald, in chapter 15, explores the central role hunting has played in human evolution and surveys the broad literature on children's learning to hunt. She develops a template or model of the life cycle of the successful hunter that she then applies to an analysis of fossil remains that suggest the origins of hunting in the Palaeolithic era. Patricia Crown, in chapter 16, also draws on both ethnographic cases as well as the archeological record to analyze Puebloan children's learning the skill of pottery-making. These analyses have yielded insights into the age at which ceramic work is first essayed, the task components as they were broken down and as evidence of emerging skill, the role of adults in children's pots, and children's contributions to adult-made pottery.

Part V, Learning in the 21st Century, examines the lives of children during a period of rapid cultural change. In chapter 17, Jon Wolseth draws on his fieldwork and experience working with a nongovernmental organization in Santo Domingo to describe how children adapt to street culture. In particular, he shows how children move among various "careers" or niches that are open to an enterprising child. Wolseth also discusses how an applied anthropological approach to the study of street children can be critical in the development of effective intervention programs. In chapter 18, David Lancy examines the transitional state in which many children can be found today. He first reviews the perilous state of classroom learning in third world communities that leads to heightened but ultimately unfilled expectations. He then reviews how socialization is radically altered when parents and other adult kin are largely absent from children's lives (as is the case with street children, orphans, and child soldiers) or become less relevant (as is the case with immigrant children).

Acknowledgments

The editors are extremely grateful to M. Annette Grove for her enormous contribution to this book. She copyedited and, working with individual authors, assembled the constituent elements of each chapter. We also acknowledge John Lucy's very helpful feedback on this chapter.

Bibliography

Schönpflug, Ute, and Ludwig Bilz. "The Transmission Process: Mechanisms and Contexts." Pp. 212–39 in *Cultural Transmission: Psychological, Developmental, Social, and Methodological Aspects*, edited by Ute Schönpflug. Cambridge: Cambridge University Press, 2009.

CHAPTER TWO

AN EVOLUTIONARY PERSPECTIVE ON LEARNING IN SOCIAL, CULTURAL, AND ECOLOGICAL CONTEXT

John Bock

The form and timing of human childhood (here I use the term to encompass the entire juvenile period: infancy, childhood, and adolescence) are products of evolution. That evolutionary foundation underlies both the consistency and variation we see in children's growth and development in physical and cognitive dimensions. The great behavioral flexibility and complexity children exhibit in negotiating the social, cultural, and ecological context of their lives are themselves evolved characteristics. Because childhood has been shaped by natural selection, it is not possible to fully comprehend or interpret the entirety of childhood without integrating an evolutionary perspective. Viewing childhood through an evolutionary lens leads to several insights. Features of childhood such as the long period of growth and development, post-weaning dependence, and the patterning of learning and skill acquisition are best identified and understood as products of a selective history. This selective history is the result of an accumulation of successful adaptations to the environments of our ancestors.

This chapter reviews the evolutionary ecology of childhood and discusses the ways in which that history of adaptation plays out in varied social, cultural, and ecological contexts of today. We begin with the evolved pattern of reproduction and parenting, or the life history of humans as seen as part of the order Primates. This leads to a more detailed analysis of how the maturational process in humans interacts with the evolutionary substrate of learning to produce the capacity to successfully function in varying social, cultural, and ecological contexts. We can develop a new understanding of children's learning in context through the analysis of the ways that growth and experience interact in the development and acquisition of skills and knowledge.

Differing Costs and Benefits to Different Patterns

Imagine a being without childhood. Such a being would emerge into the world fully formed and able to function as an adult. This creature would not grow or develop in the sense that we use these terms in discussing children. Such creatures do occur in nature. Many single-cell organisms separate from a parent and immediately function as almost identical copies—there is no period of time separating emergence and adulthood, there is no growth, there is no learning, and there is no development. A system like this works in an environment that does not change, and where it is possible to imbue an offspring with everything it needs to function without a developmental stage. An offspring emerges with full adult capacity without undergoing maturational processes.

What do such organisms gain by entering the world as adults? First, they are able to reproduce right away, virtually guaranteeing some reproductive output and avoiding the possibility that the individual could die (through predation, accident, or disease) before reproducing. Another way of saying this is that all of the energy that would have been devoted to growth and development is available for reproduction. This is important because all organisms face limited energy budgets. Energy allocated to one purpose is precluded from allocation to other purposes. Second, because they start reproducing right away, they can have more offspring compared to an organism that waits before reproducing.

These benefits, however, are counterbalanced by costs. An individual who is born as an adult has no time to shape physiology, morphology, or behavior to adjust to the environment. If the risk of mortality is quite high, then it makes evolutionary sense to start reproducing right away. If mortality is a little lower, then there is less risk of dying before reproducing if an individual spends some time growing and developing. But this comes at a cost to the parent, who must devote some energy away from its own further reproduction to ensuring the survival of the growing offspring. Because natural selection works in an economical fashion, the pattern of energy allocation to growth and reproduction will represent the optimal mix of benefits. The direction of natural selection is based on features of the environment such as the probability of mortality, so this pattern, or life history, of a taxon (a grouping of organisms such as family, genus, or species) is the best fit to the environment.

Trade-offs in Energy Allocation

In the aforementioned bacteria, an offspring buds off of a parent and emerges as a fully formed, functioning adult. In this case, any developmental period has been traded off for reproductive maturity, or current reproduction has been favored over future reproduction. But because all of the reproductive output has been put into one individual, that individual is large and fully capable. There is another trade-off that parents face, and this is between the *number* and *quality* of offspring (Stearns 1992). Here, quality is a synonym for the ability to survive to reproduce—the higher the quality, the more likely an offspring will survive to reproduce itself. Rather than putting all of her reproductive output into one or few individual offspring, it is also possible for a parent to spread reproductive output over large numbers of offspring. Because the energy available to parents is finite, however, spreading reproduction over more offspring results in having to "divide the pie" more ways. So organisms that have large broods usually have small offspring. In nature, small size equals increased vulnerability to predation and other threats, so the likelihood of surviving to reproduce is much lower in these organisms.

In an environment where mortality is high because of environmental unpredictability, there seem to be two ways to increase the likelihood that at least some will survive to reproduce themselves—have very few, high-quality offspring or have lots of low-quality offspring. Most or all of the high-quality offspring survive, but few of the low-quality offspring survive. In either case, usually enough survive to perpetuate the species, but this is because natural selection has led to the strategy that is the best fit with the environment for that taxon.

Life History Evolution

Within evolutionary ecology, we use life history theory to understand adaptation to a specific environment based on these two central trade-offs—

13

between current and future reproduction and between number and quality of offspring (Stearns 1992). The level of mortality within an environment and whether that mortality is more likely early or later in life are major determinants of this pattern (Charnov 1993). Features of the environment such as the number and distribution of predators, the temporal and spatial availability of food, and the physical environment all act as selective forces on life history patterns. Life history theory has been very effective in explaining the patterning of fertility, growth, reproduction, and mortality across different taxa, from the level of the family to the level of subspecies.

The Primates

If we look at the order Primates compared to other mammals, primate individuals tend to be long lived and slow growing (Charnov and Berrigan 1993). This indicates that the environment in which primates evolved had a lower level of extrinsic mortality (death due to outside forces such as predation or climate) than for other mammals. Through the primate lineage, it is clear that there has been consistent directional selection for longer life spans and slower growth (Leigh 2001). If we view the life history of an organism as having some distinct phases such as gestation, juvenility, and maturity, then it seems clear that among the primates these phases have stretched out in proportion to the longer life spans. Across the Primates order, from tiny prosimians to great apes, we see the same relative proportion of length of immaturity to life span (Charnov and Berrigan 1993).

There has clearly been another source of directional selection in the primate lineage—selection for increased brain size and behavioral complexity. The source of this selection will be more fully explored in chapter 13 by Kerry Ossi-Lupo, but there appear to be two: foraging in more complex niches and living in social groups. These two selection pressures interact because, for individuals within a social group, being able to find and extract food resources depends on the level of cooperation and competition with other members of the group (Johnson and Bock 2004). Within the Primates order, selection has acted on the benefits accrued to individuals who have more behavioral complexity and flexibility to successfully negotiate the challenges of food acquisition and sociality. In a very general sense, successive grade shifts of primates (prosimians to monkeys to apes to hominids) have moved into successively more complex subsistence and social ecologies. Each of these grades, in general, has longer lives, longer juvenile periods, and larger brains with increased behavioral complexity and flexibility.

The Maturational Process in Humans

In relation to the two central life history trade-offs, the human pattern favors future reproduction over current reproduction—that is, growing a long time before reproductive maturity—and favors quality of offspring over number—that is, having a few offspring who have a very high likelihood of surviving and reproducing (Kaplan et al. 2000). We grow more slowly than most other primates and we are apparently unique in having a long female post-reproductive period (Hawkes et al. 1998). We also have an extreme and unique level of behavioral complexity and flexibility compared to the other primates. The human life history pattern is one of slow growth, extended juvenility, relatively few offspring, and long life span (Bogin 1999). The phases of the maturational process can be demarcated by morphological changes. Some of these vary little across individuals and are relatively insensitive to environmental cues, such as the duration of gestation. One reason for this was that selection on the specific timing of these events was so strong that variation has been eliminated. The length of gestation and the helplessness of human newborns are an example of stabilizing selection resulting from two opposing selection pressures.

One of the first traits produced by natural selection that differentiated humans from our ancestors was upright bipedal posture and locomotion. There are several hypotheses about the emergence of this trait, but it seems that, in general, bipedality was a way to move more efficiently for long distances in a more open environment. Our earliest human ancestors were very apelike in terms of their brains but much like us in their hips, legs, feet, and other parts related to walking upright on two legs.

That same environment afforded advantages in acquiring resources and negotiating social relationships to those with flexible, problem-solving behavior. Over time, brain size increased in response to selective pressure in our hominid ancestors. At some point, these two traits came into conflict. There was selection for larger brains related to enhanced behavioral complexity and flexibility, but selection for upright posture and locomotion had drastically reshaped the pelvis. This resulted in opposing forces—the selective force to keep the pelvis the same was opposed by selection for the bigger brain.

As anyone who has experienced or witnessed childbirth knows, it's a tight fit when the baby emerges. The average baby's head is about as big as it can be and still make it through the birth canal. But natural selection has worked to maximize what can be done. Babies' heads compress as they twist their way around the bones in the pelvis in a corkscrew fashion.

This still is not enough to allow the brain to develop as much as it does in our ape relatives in utero. So humans are born with a lot of development to do outside the womb—development that occurs within the womb in our nonhuman primate relatives and many other mammals. These relatively undeveloped infants need a lot of care and can do much less for themselves than other primate newborns.

Other maturational markers such as teeth emergence have windows, sometimes overlapping, where these events occur (Bogin 1999). This may be due to underlying genetic variation coupled with some environmental sensitivity. Events such as the development of walking and language (Knudsen 2004) have sensitive windows where exposure to environmental stimuli not only paces development but, in the case of language, has a huge effect on the developmental outcome, that is, the language(s) spoken. In English, we speak of children "learning to walk" or "learning to speak," but we can think of these as developmental processes in which the outcome (walking, talking) is the result of physical maturation coupled with experience. As many who have attempted to learn to speak a foreign language as an adult can testify, once the underlying maturational process is completed, it is difficult to forge neural connections even in the context of substantial exposure and experience listening to another language.

Some maturational markers, however, are highly responsive to environmental cues, especially post-weaning growth and reproductive maturation. Children's bodies are very sensitive to the amount of resources, such as food energy, present in the environment. The level of resources available and protection from infection, mediated by the cultural, social, family/household, and ecological context, can advance or delay growth and maturation (Bogin 1999; Panter-Brick 1997). Infection uses resources to repair damage that otherwise would be devoted to growth. Girls with access to high levels of resources tend to reach menarche substantially earlier than girls who are in low-resource environments and/or subject to infectious disease (Eaves et al. 2004). Boys, while somewhat less responsive to the environment in terms of reproductive maturation are still highly sensitive to environmental conditions affecting growth (Eaves et al. 2004).

The Evolutionary Substrate of Learning

Of all of the body's systems such as musculoskeletal, dentition, endocrinological, and reproductive, the neurological system achieves maturity earliest (Bogin 1999). However, developmental processes continue within the brain and neurological system into adulthood. There are two major schools of thought regarding selection for increasing brain size through the hominin lineage. The complex social systems of primates may have conferred advantages in reproductive fitness (genetic representation in succeeding generations) to individuals who were better able to navigate social relationships through alliances, manipulation, and/or dominance (Joffe 1997; see chapter 13 for a thorough review). Clearly, many nonhuman primates that share ancestry with humans have dominance hierarchies, sometimes inherited through the matriline, as in many Old World monkeys. Studies have demonstrated advantages in access to resources, fertility, and the survivorship of offspring in several of these taxa (Johnson 2003; Silk 2007). It is also becoming increasingly clear that alliance formation may confer distinct advantages that translate into increased fitness (Nguyen et al. 2009). Other studies have demonstrated the capacity for manipulation and deception among nonhuman primates (Byrne and Whiten 1988).

Equally compelling arguments have been made for ecological competence as the major selective force on increasing brain size (Barrickman et al. 2008; Kaplan et al. 2000). Movement into increasingly complex, extractive foraging niches requires more cognitive abilities related to memory, such as the location of resources distributed patchily in space and/or time, identification of ripeness and other attributes of palatability, and extraction techniques. Hominid evolution in particular seems to have been marked by several shifts into increasing reliance on extracted and embedded resources (Kaplan et al. 2000) such as roots and tubers, nuts, and meat. Increased reliance on these sorts of resources confers fitness benefits on those with enhanced cognitive abilities related to the utilization of these resources. Within the hominid line, intensive tool manufacture and use may be a direct outcome of selection for these abilities (see chapter 15) which appear to be related to individuals' abilities to retain images in memory, operate in multiple dimensions, and coordinate precise movements. It has been argued that these manipulative abilities are not unlike some aspects of social manipulation (Tomasello et al. 2005). Because the large brain and advanced neurological system have increased metabolic demands, there may have been a feedback system where increased cognitive abilities led to greater harvesting of high-quality resources, such as animal products, which in turn provided more fuel for brain growth in an iterative process (Aiello and Wheeler 1995).

Social and ecological context, however, do not function independently of one another (Johnson and Bock 2004). Cognitive ability or the strength necessary to extract a high-quality resource does not guarantee access to that resource. Other individuals, often from the same social group, may be competing for the same high-quality resource. We can expect that there would be strong selection for the ability to navigate social relationships to successfully compete for resources within one's social group. But the ability to navigate social relationships has additional benefits with regard to foraging. Through observation and imitation, individuals can acquire the skills to be successful at complex foraging tasks. This may be through proximity to closely related individuals, such as mother-offspring dyads in chimpanzee termite fishing (Lonsdorf 2006). Or this may occur through observation of competent individuals in a social setting (King 1999). Disentangling the contribution of social and ecological context in the selective history of increasing hominin brain size will be an ongoing project for many researchers. While it may not be clear at this point whether the selection pressure from social relationships or foraging came first, it does seem to be the case that continued interaction between these domains would jointly push brain size to increase.

The large brain and advanced neurological system that has evolved in humans allows for great behavioral complexity and flexibility (Deaner et al. 2007). The selective history of this system provides the structure of that complexity and flexibility. Children become competent in languages in which they are exposed early in life, and easily become facile in several languages whose use varies by social context (see chapter 18). Children reach high levels of competency in understanding their physical environments at a young age (see chapter 14). People are adept at understanding complex social and political relationships regardless of the cultural setting (Henrich and McElreath 2003; Patton 2005). Children quickly acquire an understanding of their own familial and social relationships (Toren 1990) and even of the political structure of their community (Bridges 2009). Children are adept at understanding the norms and values of their community (McElreath 2004; see chapter 11). All of these abilities are learning strategies shaped by natural selection (McElreath 2004). The timing of acquiring these specific abilities is also the result of natural selection on the patterning of developmental trajectories (Bock 2002a, 2005; Bock and Johnson 2002), which will be discussed further below.

These learning strategies encompass many ways that children acquire information that will be explored in this volume, including through observation (chapter 5), guidance by adults (chapter 7) and siblings (chapter 8), active teaching (chapter 9), and trial and error. It is clear that most learning takes place within a social context, and that through a variety of means children seek out and retrieve information through their own devices. Even though parents and others may manipulate children's time and activities so that they are more likely to be exposed to certain types of information (chapter 7), learning arises from within the child.

The Development of Capacity

Two areas appear to be interacting in the development of adult competency (Bock 2002a). The first area is the growth and development of the body. Children have lower levels of ability than adults in certain tasks simply because they are smaller and weaker. Second is the development of the brain and neurological system and the concomitant changes in cognitive ability. These two interacting processes affect children's abilities to evaluate and negotiate ecological, social, and cultural contexts. Because these contexts vary so widely across time and place, the ways in which these processes interact have also shown great variation. Kaplan and colleagues (1995, 2000; Kaplan and Bock 2001), integrating human capital models from economics (Becker 1993) with life history models from biology (Charnov 1993; Stearns 1992) coined the term "embodied capital" to encompass all of the physical and cognitive attributes that are related to the development of adult capacity. The punctuated development model expanded this concept by more explicitly differentiating between attributes that increased with growth, or "growth-based embodied capital," such as physical strength, coordination, muscle memory, and size, and those that increase with experience, or "experience-based embodied capital," particularly cognitive functions and memory (Bock 2002a; Gurven and Kaplan 2006). Clearly, these interact at a most basic level, since experience affects growth as discussed above.

If we visualize any productive task, there is a certain amount of strength, size, coordination, and stamina, among other physical attributes, required to be successful. All of this constitutes growth-based embodied capital. At the same time, there are few activities that do not require specialized knowledge of technique or material that is gained through experience, whether learned from observation, teaching, or trial and error/practice. From the standpoint of efficiency, it makes little sense to engage in an activity unless an individual possesses the necessary combination of growth-based and experience-based embodied capital to be effective (see chapter 7).

An example is from my own fieldwork in a multiethnic community in the Okavango Delta of Botswana. About 400 people from five ethnic groups—Hambukushu, Dceriku, Wayeyi, ǁanikhoe, and Bugakhoe (see Bock and Johnson 2002 for a complete ethnographic description)—live in this community, engaging in a variety of subsistence pursuits. Farming (without irrigation and often without the aid of draught animals), fishing, hunting, and herding cattle and goats are the most common economic activities, with a very few people participating in wage labor and remitting funds to their families. Historically the San-speaking ǁanikhoe and Bugakhoe have been foragers, and the Bantu Hambukushu, Wayeyi, and Dceriku have been farmers, fishers, and herders, but today many families are involved in all economic pursuits to varying degrees. Still, the ǁanikhoe and Bugakhoe have very few cattle and emphasize foraging over other activities. At the time of our studies, there was no school in the community, and the few children attending school were boarded in another community.

We measured individuals' productivity at different tasks widely seen in the community as critical skills for adult competency. These included pounding grain in a mortar and pestle and processing mongongo nuts. The grain pounding and mongongo nut processing data were collected through experiments where individuals were given a set quantity of material and asked to process the grain or mongongo nuts in the usual way. We timed individuals and measured the amount they produced over a set amount of time. Because we had a representative age distribution for both males and females, we could see how age related to the ability to perform these tasks. We could see how long it took for children to achieve adult competency. Girls, who spend substantial amounts of time *pretending* to pound grain and observing adult women pound grain, achieved adult levels at about 14 years old. Boys, who did not have the same experiences,

Figure 2.1. Two girls process grain while their grandmother and a younger girl look on (S. E. Johnson photo)

never reached adult women's capability. We can conclude, then, that it takes until about age 14 to have both the necessary physical characteristics such as strength and coordination and the necessary experience to become a competent grain processor. A 14-year-old boy in this community might have equal or even greater strength and body size compared with a 14-year-old girl, yet because his experience has been different, he doesn't become competent. So we can say that it takes until about age 14 to learn to process grain (Bock 2002a).

Mongongo nut processing is another economically important activity for many families in this community. These wild nuts are collected by people of all ages, usually girls and women, and are usually processed by women. The processing consists of two stages—removing a very hard outer shell and then removing a softer inner shell. The goal in processing is to remove this hard outer shell leaving the inner shell intact, so that the nut stays protected but in an easy-to-use form. Removing the outer shell is done with an upward-facing axe held between the legs. A nut is placed on the axe blade and broken upward with a sharp downward blow with a piece of metal or wood. Community members explained that this is a hazardous job and is not appropriate for very young children. Most people agreed that about 10 years old was an appropriate age for girls to begin learning this task. In order to understand how long it took to become an effective processor, we asked males and females 10 years and older to participate. We found that women did not peak in their abilities until they were in their mid-30s. Men never reached women's capacities. Using the same logic as we used for the grain processing example, we concluded that mongongo nut processing was an extremely difficult activity that took over 20 years to master (Bock 2002a), considerably longer than the 10 years to learn effective grain processing.

In an efficient system, we would expect experience-based embodied capital to track growth-based embodied capital. In other words, it doesn't pay to acquire knowledge about how to do something too much before one has sufficient physical attributes to be successful. This is because the amount of time anyone can devote to all the activities he or she participates in is finite. Spending time on one activity means it can't be spent on another. Therefore, there is a cost to learning a skill without an immediate benefit. If that time could be spent learning a skill for which there is an immediate payoff, then it is more efficient to learn the skill with the present benefit. This is especially true if there will be further opportunities in the future to learn the aforementioned skill with future benefits. Of course, in reality there are delayed benefits to acquiring many skills, which will be discussed below. So it makes sense that the relationship between growth-based and experience-based embodied capital is one of incremental change in that one leads to incremental change in the other. One can visualize this as a series of steps. An increase in physical ability provides an opportunity to apply knowledge, with this pattern repeated until adult competency is achieved.

In our evolutionary history, the action of natural selection should have been operating on the timing of these "steps" so that sensitive windows for acquiring certain cognitive skills follow certain biological markers of maturation. The punctuated development model predicts the timing of these sensitive windows (Bock 2002a; Gurven and Kaplan 2006; see chapter 15). Since Piaget, there has been significant attention on the 5- to 7-year-old period, or middle childhood. Based on models from nonhuman primates, paleoanthropological data, and ethnographic descriptions of living foraging peoples, weaning seems to have occurred at 3–4 years old during our evolutionary history. The switch to post-weaning foods is accompanied by a plateau in growth. During this growth plateau, children take on a more independent role in their cultures (see Lancy and Grove 2009 for a complete review of changes in children's cultural roles related to maturational stages) and display rapid brain growth (Somsen et al. 1997). Another period of rapid cognitive development and brain growth occurs after the adolescent growth spurt at the onset of puberty (Sowell et al. 2001).

In some ecological contexts, the distribution and abundance of resources and the simplicity of the food production technology allows young children to function at near adult competence (Lancy 1983). There are subsistence ecologies that do not rely heavily on complex tasks, such as some forms of farming (Kramer 2005). Bliege Bird and Bird (2002) found that Merriam Island children reached adult competency at very young ages in gathering marine resources such as shellfish. In subsistence ecologies that rely more heavily on skills that take long periods of time to acquire—the case in many foraging societies—children do not become competent food procurers until late in childhood or even into adulthood (Bock 2002a; also see chapters 14 and 15). Among Ache foragers in

Paraguay, hunting ability, as measured by returns, does not peak for men until the late 30s (Gurven et al. 2006; Walker et al. 2002). This is an indicator that, even after the body stops growing, men are acquiring knowledge and skills that improve their ability. While the ability to shoot a projectile accurately can be acquired relatively quickly (Blurton-Jones and Marlowe 2002), the cognitive abilities related to tracking are extremely complex and take many years to develop (Liebenberg 1990). Hunting is not unique in these characteristics. Our study of mongongo nut processing (Bock 2002a), demonstrated that other tasks in foraging societies have these intense cognitive demands. The selective force that has driven the human pattern of development is, in a larger sense, *ecological* competence. Industrial society may represent an extreme case, where most information is hidden and difficult to access and many activities require mastery of a complex sequence of skills.

Children's ability to navigate social contexts also is the result of the interaction of growth and experience. Small body size may limit an individual's abilities to act in many social situations, and greater cognitive development allows more complex and flexible responses to social context (Flinn and Ward 2005; Locke and Bogin 2006). Variation in social complexity also affects the age at which the child can reach adult competency. It is common in many societies for ability at productive tasks to be used as a marker of social status (Henrich and McElreath 2003; also see chapter 7).

Trade-offs between Skill Acquisition and Productivity

The extended juvenile period in humans—the period prior to reproductive maturity—may be the result of two separate selection pressures, selection for a long life and selection for greater behavioral complexity and flexibility (Kaplan et al. 2000). It may be that these two selection pressures have been interacting in a synergistic fashion, so that longer life allows for greater behavioral complexity and flexibility that in turn are used to increase the life span (Kaplan et al. 2000). This long juvenile period is characterized by dependence on other individuals. Part of this is due to the smaller body size of juveniles (Janson and van Schaik 1993) and part of this is due to the lower level of skill that juveniles exhibit in obtaining food (Johnson and Bock 2004). This period of dependence is characterized by its own set of trade-offs that will be explored below and in more detail in chapters 6, 13, and 15. One of the most important is the trade-off between immediate productivity and preparation for the future (Bock 2002a). When children invest time acquiring new skills, as opposed to practicing well-learned skills, they are *not* producing food and other resources or producing at a lower level (Bock 2002a). This deficit must be compensated for by other individuals (Kaplan 1994). In essence, parents or others must finance the development of children's competencies. In different ecological contexts, people have responded to this in many different ways, including biparental care or allocare and other forms of cooperative parenting (Hrdy 2009).

Examples of this trade-off can be seen in our Botswana studies. An activity we called "play pounding" was one of the most common activities of girls under 10 years old. This consisted of pretending to process grain, usually using sticks and sand as stand-ins for the real things. We found that girls peaked at the amount of time per day spent at this activity at about 8 years old, after which age they spent increasing amounts of time per day at actually processing grain. Our supposition is that the play-pounding activity helped girls acquire the skills necessary to be a successful grain processor, and at about age 8 they were ready to move into working with the actual tools and grain. Prior to that age, parents actively discouraged children from using the pounding material and grain to avoid loss or damage. In this example, we see a trade-off between productivity and skill acquisition. When girls are acquiring the skills, they cannot be productive, but as they become more skillful, they are able to increase their productivity (Bock 2002a; see also chapter 6).

Since most families rely on processing grain and mongongo nuts to meet their nutritional requirements, there is substantial incentive to efficiently allocate labor in the household. At first glance, it seems that the best thing to do is to have younger girls process grain so that women can process mongongo nuts. However, doing so means that young girls will never get the experience necessary to become a competent mongongo nut processor. Parents and other household decision-makers face a trade-off—use girls' labor now and have more resources available immediately, or have girls spend some of their time learning mongongo nut processing so that there will be a future benefit. By pursuing the latter course, productivity in the present is sacrificed for increased productivity in the future. Of course, reality is more complex than this example, which focuses on only two of the many possible activities that girls participate in. These trade-offs exist in multiple dimensions across many activities and many individuals. Further complicating the issue is that parents and children do not necessarily have the same interests. Immediate productivity gives parents and households resources to use in the present, while acquiring skills provides the child with resources in the future which may or may not come to benefit the parents and household.

In a continuum from collectivism to individualism, as a culture emphasizes individual attainment more, we can expect this conflict to become more apparent (Caldwell 2004). An example of this comes from our Botswana studies. First-born girls were far more likely to be spending their time in household chores than attending school. The more older sisters and other girls living in a household, the more likely that the youngest girls would attend school (Bock 2002b). While older girls might have benefited just as much from schooling as the younger girls, their own formal education was traded-off, or sacrificed, because their parents wanted the proceeds of their labor. These proceeds were used to finance further reproduction by the parents (Kramer 2005) and the formal education of younger girls in the household. One can imagine the parents receiving benefits in the future from having some children with formal education. Rather than parents acting to make sure that each child's future is the best for that particular child, the pattern of investment and time allocation is based on the parents' interests. This pattern is certainly not unique—19th-century American children were involved in forms of wage labor highly detrimental to their own interests, as are many children in the developing world today. And it is common for older children in immigrant families in the United States to work in the family business or at wage labor so that their younger siblings can acquire an education. As seen in the examples above, these trade-offs can affect one gender preferentially depending on social, cultural, and ecological conditions (see chapter 12 for an extensive review).

These trade-offs have been seen in other cultures as well. Kaplan and colleagues (2000) found that among the Ache foragers of Paraguay, the Machiguenga of Peru, and Hiwi of Venezuela (forager/horticulturists) males did not begin to meet their own nutritional needs until their late teens to mid-20s. For females, this period of dependence was even longer because productivity was traded-off for child care. Among the Hadza of

Tanzania, who are foragers, this period of dependence is shorter because their subsistence ecology offers more opportunity for high productivity among females, And through the collection of easy to obtain and process baobab fruits, children can make a substantial contribution to their own provisioning (Blurton-Jones and Marlowe 2002). Kramer found that among Yucatec Maya, who are horticulturists, this period of dependence is shorter for both genders because, in their subsistence system, people can be highly productive at younger ages. The clear implication is that the types of resources people use in a specific time and place affect the duration of skill acquisition. Where resources are easy to extract, either because they are highly abundant or because a relatively low level of skill is necessary, children become competent at earlier ages and there is a shorter period of provisioning. Conversely, when resources are difficult to extract because of scarcity or a hazardous environment, or because high levels of skill are necessary, the period of learning is much longer, requiring consequently a longer period of provisioning. In industrial societies, it seems that this period of dependence can be quite long because the duration of skill acquisition is so extended (see chapter 18). In fact, borrowing against future returns is the most common form of financing a college education in the United States (Chapman 2006).

Cultural Transmission

Culture is often cited as a distinguishing characteristic of humans (Boyd and Richerson 2005), but the term "culture" is nebulously defined and there is far from universal agreement on what constitutes culture. Children are variously described as already culturally competent and active *agents*, as sponges soaking up the cultural information necessary to be competent adults, or as vessels into which culture is poured during *child-rearing*. This seeming paradox actually makes sense when we think of children as both "being" and "becoming." Even with their small body size and developing cognition, children must navigate their current cultural, social, and ecological contexts, and we should expect natural selection to have acted to shape brains and behavior to be successful at learning how to navigate successfully. At the same time, they are acquiring information that may not be of current use but will be important when they reach adult physical and cognitive capacity.

It is difficult to conceive of nonhuman primates as having culture, especially when culture includes attributes like meaning, norms, and values. However, we can gain some insight into the selective history of our adaptation of culture acquisition from the spread and maintenance of "traditions" among nonhuman primates. Perhaps the most widely known example is that of fruit washing among Japanese macacques (Nakamichi et al. 1998). In one troop of these animals, one individual began "washing" fruit prior to eating it, and over a period of time, other individuals began to adopt this behavior. Washing gradually became established among all of the monkeys in this particular group and was transmitted between generations. Although there is no obvious function to the washing behavior, it became part of the behavioral repertoire of that group of individuals and survived beyond the lifetime of the individual who initiated the practice. Similar kinds of practices have been documented among capuchin monkeys. Researchers have noted the emergence and horizontal (within a generation) and vertical (between generations) transmission of these behaviors (Perry 2008). For instance, capuchins engage in a behavior called "eyeball poking." A pair of individuals sit facing one another while one pushes its fingers into the eye sockets of the other individual. There is no obvious physical function to this activity, yet in one group of capuchins it became common. It may be that this is a way of establishing trust within a social relationship, and for that reason it became a regular part of that groups' behaviors (Perry 2008). Many other traditions have been documented among our closer relatives, the chimpanzees, including using specific materials for tools and employing differing techniques for resource extraction and processing (McGrew 1998). These examples illuminate the possibility that the selective history that shaped humans' adaptation to culture predates the emergence of the hominids. It may be that as humans became adapted to increasingly complex social systems and ecological niches, what we view as culture expanded from the kinds of traditions seen in nonhuman primates to include the elements common to human cultures today.

Culturally transmitted information, whether it consists of traditions, roles, values, and/or meaning, is a very effective way of communicating about what "works" in specific social and ecological contexts (Boyd and Richerson 2005). As our ancestors adapted to more complex social and ecological conditions, the amount of information needed to live continued to grow. We can imagine that the elements of information stored in a specific culture built up over a long period of time. At some point, the benefits of storing this information outside the brain and developing the necessary cognitive mechanisms to use and transmit this information among individuals outweighed the costs. Transmitting information this way is especially effective in stable environments, where current social and ecological conditions remain similar across generations. It may be much more effective to develop specific strategies for storing and transmitting information than letting each new learner flounder around with trial and error. Trial and error is an especially costly form of learning, especially in complex contexts where there is much information to acquire. On the other hand, if social and ecological conditions are in flux, the cost of relying on culturally transmitted information may be higher than the cost of trial and error. The stability of a specific environment (social and physical) should be a major influence on the mix of information obtained firsthand through trial and error and information obtained through cultural transmission (Bock 1999). In very unstable environments (see chapters 17 and 18), information obtained through cultural transmission between generations may not be useful, and since people are having to discover many new coping strategies in unprecedented environmental conditions, horizontal transmission becomes much more important. Since our ancestors evolved in environments marked by periods of environmental instability (Potts 1998), humans have the capacity to effectively respond to both stability and instability by drawing on cultural information or developing new information that can be transmitted to other individuals.

Learning in Context

The set of characteristics that comprise the human capacity to learn about and navigate social, cultural, and ecological contexts is the result of natural selection in our ancestors. Our physical maturation and cognitive development are interactively responsive to social, cultural, and ecological influences. This interaction has consistent effects on the pace of skill acquisition and learning. The environment simultaneously shapes the pattern of learning and provides the opportunities to apply that learning for either immediate or delayed benefits. The form and patterning of childhood are the direct result of that shaping, and as such, childhood and learning are inextricably linked. Rather than establishing a set of rigid universal characteristics of learning, our selective history has led to learning in childhood that is broadly patterned but highly responsive to children's environments.

Acknowledgments

I would like to thank the people of two communities in the Okavango Delta, Botswana, who welcomed me as a friend and fellow community member for over a decade. Fieldwork in Botswana was supported by the LSB Leakey Foundation, the National Science Foundation, the University of New Mexico, the Australian National University, and the James Swan Fund of the University of Oxford. I would also like to thank the Office of the President of Botswana for approving the research. Sara Johnson, Hillard Kaplan, Jane Lancaster, Kim Hill, Nick Blurton-Jones, Pat Draper, Jack Caldwell, Barry Bogin, David Lancy, and Suzanne Gaskins have all been deeply influential in my thinking about childhood. Of course, all errors and omissions are solely my responsibility.

Bibliography

Aiello, Leslie C., and Pater Wheeler. "The Expensive-Tissue Hypothesis: The Brain and the Digestive System in Human and Primate Evolution." *Current Anthropology* 36, no. 2 (April 1995): 199–221.

Barrickman, Nancy L., Meredith L. Bastian, Karin Isler, and Carel P. van Schaik. "Life History Costs and Benefits of Encephalization: A Comparative Test Using Data from Long-term Studies of Primates in the Wild." *Journal of Human Evolution* 54, no. 5 (May 2008): 568–90.

Becker, Gary S. "Nobel Lecture: The Economic Way of Looking at Behavior." *Journal of Political Economy* 101, no. 3 (June 1993): 385–409.

Bliege Bird, Rebecca, and Douglas W. Bird. "Constraints of Knowing or Constraints of Growing? Fishing and Collecting by the Children of Mer." *Human Nature* 13, no. 2 (June 2002): 239–67.

Blurton-Jones, Nicholas G., and Frank W. Marlowe. "Selection for Delayed Maturity: Does It Take 20 Years to Learn to Hunt and Gather?" *Human Nature* 13, no. 2 (June 2002): 199–238.

Bock, John A. "Evolutionary Approaches to Population: Implications for Research and Policy." *Population and Environment* 21, no. 2 (November 1999): 193–222.

———. "Learning, Life History, and Productivity: Children's Lives in the Okavango Delta of Botswana." *Human Nature* 13, no. 2 (June 2002a): 161–98.

———. "Evolutionary Demography and Intrahousehold Time Allocation: Schooling and Children's Labor among the Okavango Delta Peoples of Botswana." *American Journal of Human Biology* 14, no. 2 (March/April 2002b): 206–21.

———. "What Makes a Competent Adult Forager?" Pp. 109–28 in *Hunter-Gatherer Childhoods: Evolutionary, Developmental, and Cultural Perspectives*, edited by Barry S. Hewlett and Michael E. Lamb. Somerset: Aldine Transaction, 2005.

Bock, John A., and Sara E. Johnson. "The Okavango Delta Peoples of Botswana." Pp. 151–69 in *Endangered Peoples of Africa and the Middle East*, edited by Robert K. Hitchcock and Alan J. Osborne. New York: Greenwood, 2002.

Bogin, Barry. *Patterns of Human Growth*. New York: Cambridge, 1999.

Boyd, Robert, and Peter J. Richerson. *The Origin and Evolution of Cultures*. New York: Oxford, 2005.

Bridges, M. "The Acquisition of Sociopolitical Skills in an Egalitarian Society." Master's thesis, California State University, Fullerton, 2009.

Byrne, Richard W., and Andrew Whiten, eds. *Machiavellian Intelligence: Social Expertise and the Evolution of Intellect in Monkeys, Apes, and Humans*. New York: Oxford University Press, 1988.

Caldwell, John C. "Demographic Theory: a Long View." *Population and Development Review* 30, no. 2 (June 2004): 297–316.

Chapman, Bruce. "Income Related Student Loans: Concepts, International Reforms, and Administrative Challenges." Pp. 79–103 in *Cost-Sharing and Accessibility in Higher Education: A Fairer Deal?* edited by Pedro N. Teixeira, D. Bruce Johnstone, Maria João Rosa, and Hans Vossensteyn. Amsterdam: Springer, 2006.

Charnov, Eric L. *Life History Invariants*. New York: Oxford University Press, 1993.

Charnov, Eric L., and David Berrigan. "Why Do Female Primates Have Such Long Lifespans and So Few Babies?" *Evolutionary Anthropology* 1, no. 6 (1993): 191–94.

Deaner, Robert O., Karin Isler, Judith Burkart, and Carel P. van Schaik. "Overall Brain Size, and Not Encephalization Quotient, Best Predicts Cognitive Ability across Non-Human Primates." *Brain, Behavior, and Evolution* 70, no. 2 (2007): 115–24.

Eaves, Lindon, Judy Silberg, Debra Foley, C. Bulik, Hermine Maes, A. Erkanli, Adrian Angold, E. J. Costello, and C. M. Worthman. "Genetic and Environmental Influences on the Relative Timing of Pubertal Change." *Twin Research* 7 (October 2004): 471–81.

Flinn, Mark V., and Carol V. Ward. "Ontogeny and Evolution of the Social Child." Pp. 19–44 in *Origins of the Social Mind: Evolutionary Psychology and Child Development*, edited by Bruce J. Ellis and David F. Bjorklund. New York: Guilford, 2005.

Gurven, Michael, and Hillard Kaplan. "Determinants of Time Allocation across the Lifespan: A Theoretical Model and an Application to the Machiguenga and Piro of Peru." *Human Nature* 17, no. 1 (March 2006): 1–49.

Gurven, Michael, Hillard Kaplan, and Maguin Gutierrez. "How Long Does It Take to Become a Proficient Hunter? Implications for the Evolution of Extended Development and Long Life Span." *Journal of Human Evolution* 51, no. 5 (November 2006): 454–70.

Hawkes, Kristin, James F. O'Connell, Nicolas G. Blurton-Jones, Helen Alvarez, and Eric L. Charnov. "Grandmothering, Menopause, and the Evolution of Human Life Histories." *Proceedings of the National Academy of Sciences, USA* 95, no. 3 (February 1998): 1336–39.

Henrich, Joseph, and Richard McElreath. "The Evolution of Cultural Evolution." *Evolutionary Anthropology* 12, no. 3 (2003): 123–35.

Hrdy, Sarah Blaffer. *Mothers and Others: The Evolutionary Origins of Mutual Understanding*. Cambridge, Mass.: Belknap, 2009.

Janson, Charles H., and Carel P. van Schaik. "Ecological Risk Aversion in Juvenile Primates: Slow and Steady Wins the Race." Pp. 57–74 in *Juvenile Primates: Life History, Development, and Behavior*, edited by Michael E. Pereira and Lynn A. Fairbanks. New York: Oxford University Press, 1993.

Joffe, Tracey H. "Social Pressures Have Selected for an Extended Juvenile Period in Primates." *Journal of Human Evolution* 32, no. 6 (June 1997): 593–605.

Johnson, Sara E. "Life History and the Competitive Environment: Trajectories of Growth, Maturation, and Reproductive Output among Chacma Baboons." *American Journal of Physical Anthropology* 120, no. 1 (January 2003): 83–98.

Johnson, Sara E., and John A. Bock. "Trade-offs in Skill Acquisition and Time Allocation among Juvenile Chacma Baboons." *Human Nature* 15, no. 1 (March 2004): 45–62.

Kaplan, Hillard S. "Evolutionary and Wealth Flows Theories of Fertility: Empirical Tests and New Models." *Population Development Review* 20, no. 4 (December 1994): 753–91.

Kaplan, Hillard S., and John A. Bock. "Fertility Theory: The Embodied Capital Theory of Human Life History Evolution." Pp. 5561–68 in *The International*

Encyclopedia of the Social and Behavioral Sciences, edited by Neil J. Smelser and Paul B. Baltes. Oxford: Elsevier Science, 2001.

Kaplan, Hillard S., Kim Hill, Jane B. Lancaster, and A. Magdalena Hurtado. "A Theory of Human Life History Evolution: Diet, Intelligence, and Longevity." *Evolutionary Anthropology* 9, no. 4 (2000): 156–83.

Kaplan, Hillard S., Jane B. Lancaster, John A. Bock, and Sara E. Johnson. "Does Observed Fertility Maximize Fitness among New Mexican Men? A Test of an Optimality Model and a New Theory of Parental Investment in the Embodied Capital of Offspring." *Human Nature* 6, no. 4 (December 1995): 325–60.

King, Barbara J., ed. *The Origins of Language: What Nonhuman Primates Can Tell Us*. Santa Fe, N.M.: SAR Press, 1999.

Knudsen, Eric I. "Sensitive Periods in the Development of Brain and Behavior." *Journal of Cognitive Neuroscience* 16, no. 8 (October 2004): 1412–25.

Kramer, Karen L. *Maya Children: Helpers at the Farm*. Cambridge, Mass.: Harvard University Press, 2005.

Lancy, David F. *Cross-Cultural Studies in Cognition and Mathematics*. New York: Academic, 1983.

Lancy, David F., and M. Annette Grove. "Getting Noticed: Middle Childhood in Cross-Cultural Perspective." *Human Nature* (2009 in press).

Leigh, Steven R. "The Evolution of Human Growth." *Evolutionary Anthropology* 10, no. 6 (2001): 223–36.

Liebenberg, Louis. *The Art of Tracking: The Origin of Science*. Capetown: David Philip, 1990.

Locke, John L., and Barry Bogin. "Language and Life History: A New Perspective on the Development and Evolution of Human Language." *Behavioral and Brain Sciences* 29, no. 3 (June 2006): 259–80.

Lonsdorf, Elizabeth V. "The Role of the Mother in the Acquisition of Tool-Use Skills in Wild Chimpanzees." *Animal Cognition* 9, no. 1 (January 2006): 36–46.

McElreath, Richard. "Social Learning and the Maintenance of Cultural Variation: An Evolutionary Model and Data from East Africa." *American Anthropologist* 106, no. 2 (June 2004): 308–21.

McGrew, William C. "Culture in Nonhuman Primates?" *Annual Review of Anthropology* 27 (1998): 301–28.

Nakamichi, Masayuki, Eiko Kato, Yasuo Kojima, and Naosuke Itoigawa. "Carrying and Washing of Grass Roots by Free-Ranging Japanese Macaques at Katsuyama." *Folia Primatologica* 69, no. 1 (1998): 35–40.

Nguyen, Nga, Russell C. van Horn, Susan C. Alberts, and Jeanne Altmann. "'Friendships' between New Mothers and Adult Males: Adaptive Benefits and

Determinants in Wild Baboons (*Papio cynocephalus*)." *Behavioral Ecology and Sociobiology* 63, no. 9 (July 2009): 1331–44.

Panter-Brick, Catherine. "Seasonal Growth Patterns in Rural Nepali Children." *Annals of Human Biology* 24 (1997): 1–18.

Patton, John Q. "Meat Sharing for Coalitional Support." *Evolution and Human Behavior* 26, no. 2 (March 2005): 137–57.

Perry, Susan. *Manipulative Monkeys: The Capuchins of Lomas Barbudal*. Cambridge, Mass.: Harvard University Press, 2008.

Potts, Richard. "Variability Selection in Hominid Evolution." *Evolutionary Anthropology* 7, no. 3 (1998): 81–96.

Silk, Joan B. "The Adaptive Value of Sociality in Mammalian Groups." *Philosophical Transactions of the Royal Society* 362, no. 1480 (2007): 539–59.

Somsen, Riek J. M., Ben J. van't Klooster, Maurits W. van der Molen, Harry M. P. van Leeuwen, and Rob Licht. "Growth Spurts in Brain Maturation during Middle Childhood as Indexed by EEG Power Spectra." *Biological Psychology* 44, no. 3 (January 1997): 187–209.

Sowell, Elizabeth R., Paul M. Thompson, Kevin D. Tessner, and Arthur W. Toga. "Mapping Continued Brain Growth and Gray Matter Density Reduction in Dorsal Frontal Cortex: Inverse Relationships during Postadolescent Brain Maturation." *Neurosci* 21, no. 22 (November 2001): 8819–29.

Stearns, Stephen C. *The Evolution of Life Histories*. New York: Oxford University Press, 1992.

Tomasello, Michael, Malinda Carpenter, Josep Call, Tanya Behne, and Henrike Moll. "Understanding and Sharing Intentions: The Origins of Cultural Cognition." *Behavioral and Brain Sciences* 28, no. 5 (October 2005): 675–91.

Toren, Christina. *Making Sense of Hierarchy: Cognition as Social Process in Fiji*. London: Athlone, 1990.

Walker, Robert, Kim Hill, Hillard Kaplan, and Garnett McMillan. "Age Dependency of Strength, Skill, and Hunting Ability among the Ache of Paraguay." *Journal of Human Evolution* 42, no. 6 (June 2002): 639–57.

CHAPTER THREE

THE CROSS-CULTURAL STUDY OF CHILDREN'S LEARNING AND SOCIALIZATION: A SHORT HISTORY

Robert L. Munroe and Mary Gauvain

[T]he habit of comparison leads to generalization.

— Charles Darwin, *The Voyage of the Beagle*

There are great sources of error in the comparative method.

— William James, *The Principles of Psychology*

In the epigraphs above, two eminent thinkers were positing opposite views about the scientific value of comparison. One saw the promise, the other the pitfalls—and both men, we believe, were right. Darwin's point was conceptual: There is power, even scientific necessity, in investigating similarities and differences, in comparing *to* and comparing *with*. James, in the quoted passage, was concerned about methodology, and about the consequent difficulty of interpretation if several dimensions of comparison were treated at once. This was decidedly true of the early 20th-century investigators who studied children in non-Western settings, for they not only were trying to trace the trajectory from child to adult but were doing so in cultural contexts markedly different from their own. It did not diminish their hope that comparative evidence would support or rebut generalizations that were being based on the study of Western peoples alone. Ultimately, though, as the century went on and a variety of methodological controls was introduced, the grand goal of understanding socialization[1] (or enculturation) was seen for the immense undertaking that it was, and aspirations became more modest. In the present chapter, we will try to trace the main projects and traditions in this important subdiscipline.[2]

At the outset, we need to make a distinction between child training practices and the processes of learning. The two are obviously intertwined, but for a long time, cross-cultural researchers tended to assume that the acquisition of culture was an unproblematic matter of detecting and describing the rearing of children, and that the outcomes were ultimately adults of the same makeup as those who were carrying out the child training. This did not mean that those who raised children were believed to understand the full consequences of their actions—to the contrary, in many cases—but it did indicate, as we shall see, that early investigators were making assumptions about the nature of children and childhood that only later were brought under scrutiny.

Pioneers: Margaret Mead and Bronislaw Malinowski

Fragmentary information about childhood could often be found in the cultural descriptions of 19th- and early 20th-century ethnographers, but seldom was there any focus on the pre-adult life phases. Then, during the 1920s, two influential anthropologists took issue with certain ambitious statements about human development that were common among social scientists. In Polynesia, Margaret Mead (1928/1973) failed to find the *Sturm und Drang* that American psychologist G. Stanley Hall (1904) had claimed was typical of adolescent life. She located the Samoan adolescent girl's innocuous, little-troubled existence in an atmosphere of diffuse affective life, which was rooted, she thought, in the early experience of repeated exposure to many caretakers both in the extended household and beyond. Probably stretching a point, Mead declared that "a baby whose mother has gone inland to work on the plantation is passed from hand to hand for the length of the village" (23). (One of the present authors participated in a much later study of infants in Mead's Samoan village and saw no such behavior [Munroe and Munroe 1984].) Around the same time, Bronislaw Malinowski (1927/1955, 1929) argued that the Oedipal conflict, which was central to Freud's theorizing about the "natural" course of human development, was a culture-bound phenomenon resting not on father-son sexual conflict but on a family structure in which the father was the disciplinarian, or authority figure. Looking to his matrilineal Trobrianders of New Guinea, Malinowski concluded that there, the authority of the mother's brother—not that of the father, who was without power over his son—was what generated a boy's hostility. Unfortunately for Malinowski's hypothesis, the Trobriander boy did not begin to come under his uncle's authority until about age six, and by this time, according to orthodox Freudian theory, the Oedipal conflict would have been resolved (Hall and Lindzey 1957). Yet, in attacking the Oedipal construct, Malinowski may have identified a particularly weak point in Freudian thought (Sears 1951), and in Mead's case, the idea of general adolescent stress in America has not held up well against the long-term empirical evidence (Steinberg 1996). As LeVine (2007) points outs, these studies launched anthropology as the cultural critic of developmental ideas introduced by psychologists and based largely on Western samples.

In questioning Western-based theory, Mead and Malinowski were early formulators of an anthropological perspective concerning the enormous plasticity of human beings. Their work also helped lay to rest the 19th-century parallelisms that had been drawn among "primitive" peoples, children, the mentally ill, and even animals, views that reflected the Social Darwinism of the time. As late as 1939, however, Irving Hallowell (1939/1955) found it necessary to refute the argument that "aboriginal peoples that still survived represented arrested stages of cultural development that the more advanced races had passed through" (15). Bateson and Mead (1942; Mead 1930/1973, 1932; Mead and Macgregor 1951), in trips to New Guinea and Indonesia, went on to consider other generalizations about human development, and these efforts always resulted in one conclusion about the causes of human behavior: "It's not human nature, but . . . our culture" (as phrased by Singer 1961, 17). Child-rearing was given a favored place in this scheme by Mead and others, but only in the sense that it was the initial phase of a persisting, self-replicating system that underlies human personality and behavior, including their organization and motive forces. Reflecting in later years on her ideas, Mead (1930/1973) conceded, "We knew very little—in 1930—about differences in upbringing among different peoples; we knew still less about the importance of character formation . . . in terms of the precise learning experiences of the infant and the young child" (6). The assessment is accurate, but it was her own and Malinowski's contributions that were the first to depict in rich ethnographic detail the settings and experiences of children in non-Western cultures.

Early Descriptive Approaches

As of the 1930s, thorough accounts of children in non-Western societies started to appear with some regularity (e.g., Dennis 1940; Firth 1936; Fortes 1938/1970; Hogbin 1931, 1943, 1946; Leighton and Kluckhohn 1947; Little 1951; Raum 1940; Richards 1932, 1956; Wedgwood 1938; J. Whiting 1941). These ethnographies represented a broad range of cultural settings geographically and in terms of social structure and community size. For the most part, the "theory-testing" mode of Mead and Malinowski was eschewed; the focus was instead on detailed descriptions of socialization practices and child behavior. These descriptions made clear the diversity of child-rearing and children's experiences around the world. From a society in sub-Saharan Africa, we give an example that implicitly illustrates the difference between Western child-rearing and the situation in a typical rural village:

> Nothing in the universe of adult behaviour is hidden from [Tallensi] children or barred to them. They are actively and responsibly part of the social structure, of the economic system, the ritual and ideological system. . . . Hence the children need not be coerced to take a share in economic and social activities. They are eager to do so. (Fortes 1938/1970, 18–19).

Of the many reports, some were full-fledged ethnographies of childhood; some constituted one element in a general ethnographic study; still others took up specific aspects of child experience such as task responsibilities, play activities, status and behavioral changes with age, "bush" schooling, and initiation ceremonies. Little attempt was made to delineate the learning process itself, aside from the assumption that child training practices led to successful outcomes. However, there were suggestions of explicit efforts in some cultures to convey important lessons to children, such as accounts of putting young adolescent boys in settings with men so that they would learn behaviors expected of them (e.g., Hogbin 1970). Distinctively, these researchers were working prior to the very great changes soon introduced almost everywhere by formal schooling and other forces of modernization, including the prolonged absence of many adult males due to extensive migratory wage labor. The early work also helped to establish socialization, education, and the life cycle as standard topics for ethnography, and these continued to appear throughout the remainder of the 20th century (for coverage of socialization research through the 1960s, see Draper 1974 and Williams 1972; for case studies of education and the life cycle, see volumes in the Holt, Rinehart, and Winston series edited by George Spindler and Louise Spindler, e.g., Huntington and Hostetler 1971; Williams 1969).

One exception to the generally atheoretical orientation of the early descriptive approaches was the work of neo-Freudian Abram Kardiner (1939, 1945). In association with anthropologist Ralph Linton, Kardiner produced a series of ethnographic vignettes—for example, on the Native American Comanche and the Marquesans, a Polynesian island culture—and interpreted the varying sets of child training practices as generating *basic personality structures*, which were then said to be projected, as "secondary institutions" (meaning outside the person), onto folklore, magico-religious observances, and value systems. Anthropologist Cora Du Bois participated in Kardiner and Linton's seminars at Columbia University, absorbed the Kardinerian model, and then applied it in her Indonesian fieldwork. In a landmark study (Du Bois 1944), she portrayed the level of basic-need satisfaction given to Alorese children, even neonates, as very low and irregular, and she related this to a widespread pattern of lengthy temper tantrums and rages among 2- to 5-year-olds. Indeed, in Alorese folklore, a common motif was, fittingly, frustration engendered by the parents. The neglect and inconsistency in children's treatment led, according to Du Bois, to an adult personality rife with suspicion, mistrust, and deception. Du Bois brought to her analysis extensive life-history interviews, Rorschach protocols, and children's drawings, which represented a broadening of methods beyond observational techniques.

Holocultural or Whole-World Research

In the early 1950s, John W. M. Whiting and colleague Irvin L. Child (1953) made a new and bold attempt to investigate the long-term effects on personality of early experiences, especially those revolving around the Freudian oral, anal, and genito-phallic systems. This approach helped reignite a focus on theory testing. Others (e.g., Erikson 1950; Spiro 1958) were also basing their research on Freud's psychosexual stages, but what made Whiting and Child's study unique was its use of an archived ethnographic survey, the Human Relations Area Files (then the Cross-Cultural Survey; Ember and Ember 2001a; Murdock et al. 2000; see also chapter 7, this volume). Whiting and Child compiled and analyzed the (usually meager) child-rearing information available from a world sample of 75 societies, each culture being considered as a unit. This innovative technique, termed *holocultural*, helped prompt a small industry of similarly oriented "childhood determinism" research that continues today (Ember and Ember 2001b), though most of these studies were carried out by about 1975. The dependent variables ranged across aggression (Allen 1972), drunkenness (Bacon et al. 1965), explanations for illness (Whiting and Child 1953), types of games (Roberts and Sutton-Smith 1962), and initiation ceremonies (Brown 1963; Whiting, Kluckhohn, and Anthony 1958).

In a review of this research genre, Levinson and Malone (1980, 189) concluded, "Many of the holocultural studies of . . . the effects of child rearing practices on adult personality . . . *are not direct tests of the hypotheses they claim to test* [emphasis in original]. . . . The [hypothesized] cause and effect are measured, the mediating variable [e.g., fixation] is not." Still, successful examples of this type of research can be given. In research on games, John Roberts and colleagues (Roberts, Arth, and Bush 1959; Roberts and Sutton-Smith 1962) found that socially complex societies (high political integration, social stratification) practiced frequent games of strategy. Roberts reasoned that societies with games of strategy would emphasize obedience training in their socialization, and this proved correct. Such emphasis, he thought, probably contributed to the learning of command, management, and the giving and taking of orders necessary to the functioning of any complex society. Another strong finding in relation to socialization was that societies with frequent games of physical skill emphasized achievement training for children. Then Roberts, in a significant extension of these results, showed that (a) on a worldwide basis, girls were given more consistent obedience training, and boys higher levels of achievement training; that (b) "these differences in socialization correspond to the general differences between male and female roles over the world" (Roberts and Sutton-Smith 1962); and that (c) in a sample (N = 1900) of American children, game preferences followed the gendered pattern of cross-cultural results, with girls favoring games of strategy (e.g., checkers) and boys favoring games of physical skill (e.g., bowling).

Holocultural inquiry was most successful when it avoided trying to specify adult outcomes and simply surveyed socialization practices and childhood experiences in the large.[3] Weisner and Gallimore (1977), tabulating holocultural ratings for socialization (Barry and Paxson 1971) on more than 150 small-scale societies, found that care of infants exclusively by the mother occurred in just 3 percent of the cases, dropping to zero for older children—a finding directly contradictory to the Western assumption that exclusive care by the biological mother is essential. Although the specific consequences of these varying patterns of child care are not known,[4] it seems clear that children can be successfully raised via a multiplicity of caretaking options in small-scale as well as complex societies such as India (Seymour 2004).

Holocultural surveys have also established that food accumulators (agriculturalists with heavy stock-raising) are much more likely to set tasks for young children than are food collectors (hunter-gatherers, fishers) (Barry, Bacon, and Child 1967; Barry, Child, and Bacon 1959). These tasks, including housekeeping chores, errands, food preparation, subsistence activities, and care of young siblings, typically begin at about age 3 and grow thereafter in frequency, intensity, and complexity (Rogoff et al. 1975). The lower level of tasks among hunter-gatherer children is probably due to their smaller store of material goods (thus minimal maintenance activities and related chores) and to subsistence techniques that require near-adult strength and endurance. The difference in task loads between children in the two types of societies implies varying interests and levels of skill, but these have not been looked into. Nor is it known whether adults in food-accumulating societies are directly training children in anticipation of psychological styles and economic patterns (Barry et al. 1959), or whether, on the basis of current need, they are inducting children into the economy at an early age (Whiting and Whiting 1971).

The Whitings' Comparative Field Projects

John Whiting's experience in trying to construct valid measures from the unstandardized reportage in the ethnographic archive left him convinced that new fieldwork, directed toward specific goals and organized around the study of human development, was appropriate for his next large research project. Together with colleagues Child and Lambert, he launched, in the mid-1950s, the Six Cultures Study of Socialization (SCS), the largest comparative field study of child-rearing and child behavior that had been undertaken in anthropology. With six field teams spread over four continents and a clearinghouse at Harvard University led by Beatrice Whiting, the project eventually was to publish a methodological guide for developmental inquiry (Whiting, Child, and Lambert 1966), monographs on each culture with detailed descriptions of socialization practices (B. Whiting 1963), an analysis of standardized mother interviews (Minturn and Lambert 1964), and a volume on the relations between sociocultural contexts and children's behavior in daily settings (Whiting and Whiting 1975). A later work by Beatrice Whiting and Carolyn Edwards, *Children of Different Worlds* (1988), incorporated data from the SCS and added comparable materials from seven additional culture groups.

The SCS and related research can be discussed in terms of theoretical orientation, methodology, and a few of the main findings. The original plan, as described in the Field Guide (Whiting et al. 1966), was to test hypotheses derived from both psychoanalytic and behaviorist psychology, and to use child tests and interviews,[5] but these techniques proved difficult to apply and were abandoned, as were the accompanying hypotheses. But the project led the way in illuminating the broader contexts (technoeconomic, social-organizational) within which development occurs, and concomitantly, the effects of those contexts on children's social behavior. The Whitings' emphasis on documenting the varied environments in which culture is learned has been taken up broadly in developmental psychology and can be seen in such concepts as the developmental niche (Super and Harkness 1986), ecocultural theory (Weisner 1997), and bioecocultural models (Worthman in press).

Methodologically, the repeated observational protocols gathered on the 3- to 11-year-old children proved the most significant feature of the SCS (Whiting and Whiting 1975). These running narratives, which were transcribed by the anthropologists as they followed the children ($n = 24$ per community) in their daily activities, generated a set of 12 "summary act categories" (e.g., seeking help, reprimanding, assaulting) that occurred commonly but with differential frequency across the communities. Offering quantitative comparability both within and among cultures, the method, or a kindred technique, was taken up by many others (Borgerhoff, Mulder, and Caro 1985; Ember 1973; Harkness and Super 1985; Hewlett 1991; LeVine et al. 1994; Nerlove et al. 1974; Rogoff 1981a; Seymour 1983; Weisner 1979). One drawback of this approach, an absence of interobserver reliability, was overcome with "spot observations" (Munroe and Munroe 1971; Rogoff 1978), which focus on the recording of a targeted individual's activity at the initial moment of observer-participant contact.[6]

The great majority of the culture groups studied via Whiting-style observations were subsistence-level agricultural communities. Unlike both urban-industrial peoples and technologically simple foragers, these mid-level societies tend to assign their children numerous tasks, all the way from passive sibling care to intensive subsistence activities (Johnson 1980). Generalizing about social styles among children in such societies, Beatrice Whiting (1980) argued that "the habits of interpersonal behavior that one learns and practices in the most frequented settings may be overlearned and may generalize [transfer] to other settings" (103). In a four-culture study involving 3- to 9-year-old children, Ruth Munroe and colleagues (Munroe, Munroe, and Shimmin 1984) found a pattern supportive of Whiting's statement. Those children who worked frequently, even when not engaged in tasks, were involved in a pattern of interaction that itself seemed worklike. They made responsible suggestions and reprimanded others who broke the rules: "The picture [was] one of businesslike, purposeful social behavior" (375). But among those who did relatively little or no work, "there was almost a sense of 'fooling around,' of playfulness " (375). These children engaged in frequent horseplay and attention-seeking behavior, and they appeared to treat interaction as an end in itself. Yet even the children who worked at high levels, approaching half of their daylight hours, found time for leisure activities. As Lancy (2007) has indicated, "Children are observed playing in every society studied by anthropologists" (274). This proposition is consistent with Whiting and Edwards's characterization of their naturalistic behavioral observations on "yard children": "healthy 4- and 5-year-olds in all cultures are always on the move. They are characterized by a high level of activity and by an intense interest in the physical and social environments" (1988, 203).

Building further on the SCS, Whiting and Edwards (1988) noted a widespread same-sex preference in children's play. Developmentalist Eleanor Maccoby (1998) described the tendency as a "strong bias in every society for children to be drawn toward members of their own sex" (29). Such a pervasive pattern would obviously afford opportunities for the learning of appropriate sex-role behaviors and attitudes (see also chapter 12, this volume). How much, if any, of this regularity might be located in biologically predisposed responses was even-handedly discussed but not answered by these researchers (see also Draper 1975).

Aware that the SCS, for all its influence, had been short on both the overall number of culture groups and the within-group sample sizes, the Whitings imaginatively tried to greatly expand their project (J. Whiting 1970). In the event, a more modest effort led to the establishment of research headquarters in Kenya, another briefly in Nigeria. Basic data were collected on some 13 communities and reported on in numerous individual studies.[7] While much was still to learn, the Whitings' explicitly comparative approach set the standard for the following decades of cross-cultural fieldwork in child study.

Childhood among Hunter-Gatherers: Lessons from Human Evolution?

Realizing that viable hunter-gatherer societies would not be sequestered from modernizing forces for much longer, anthropologists began in the late 1960s to study the few remaining groups. Foraging groups were seen as important for more than their scarcity: Their subsistence style had characterized the adaptive life pattern of every human society until the emergence of agriculture about 10,000 years ago, and they therefore promised insight into long-term evolutionary processes. The hunter-gatherer research teams were the first to bring neo-Darwinian ideas into cultural anthropology (Lee and DeVore 1968), and they tested the degree to which an understanding of human behavior was enhanced by concepts like "prepared responses," "reproductive success," and "fitness enhancing strategies" (Draper and Harpending 1982; Hawkes, O'Connell, and Blurton-Jones 1997; Konner 1977b). Theorists also tried to probe the applicability of evolutionary paradigms to children's learning (Hewlett and Cavalli-Sforza 1986; LeVine 1982). But Darwinian ideas were seen by most anthropologists as threatening the central tenet that culture should be studied autonomously, without resort to biological concepts (Caton 1990; Sahlins 1976). For the greater part, this antireductionist paradigm held sway. The evolutionary perspective, however, continues to make progress, taking seriously the critiques leveled at its claims (see chapter 2, this volume). Human behavioral ecology has become a specialized subfield of anthropology with growing importance in child study. We now turn to that body of work.

The small number of intensively studied foragers, about 10 culture groups altogether, have displayed some notable variability in their child socialization practices, but they can nonetheless be said to exhibit a distinctive style. Breastfeeding by women besides the child's mother occurs among many hunter-gatherers, but such a practice is seldom found in other types of societies (Hewlett and Lamb 2005; Tronick, Morelli, and Winn 1987). And almost universally, the unweaned hunter-gatherer child receives a higher level of indulgent care—whether from mothers or others—than is to be found elsewhere (Hewlett and Lamb 2005). Also, hunter-gatherer fathers tend to participate in infant care somewhat more frequently than do fathers in either urban-industrial or agricultural groups (Fouts 2008; Katz and Konner 1981), though this generalization requires careful qualification. For one specific hunter-gatherer society, the Central African Aka, Hewlett (1992) found that fathers were within reaching distance of their infants 50 percent of the time, and they held their babies "at least five times more than fathers in [all] other human populations" (153). Hewlett interpreted the finding as reflective not of "parental effort" per se but as part of a pattern in which Aka fathers and mothers help each other in a host of different contexts. Aside from the Aka, Konner's (1977a) statement about fathers continues to hold: "In all known human cultures, males exhibit an extremely minor role in relation to small children and especially to infants, and human hunter-gatherers may be included in this generalization" (95–96). It is worth noting, too, that even in the Aka infant case, the level of the father's caretaking does not match that of the mother.

From a Western perspective, a pattern of care characterized by extensive physical contact and proximity might suggest a notable degree of play with infants. This would be especially true of fathers in the urban-industrial world; as Lamb (1987) phrased it, "[North American] fathers are behaviorally defined as playmates" (10). But hunter-gatherer fathers, and other adult caretakers, do little or no playing with children (Fouts 2008; Lancy 2009, personal communication). Altogether, the style of hunter-gatherer child-rearing is best seen as one of physical protection, unhurried pace, and lack of urgency in "training." There seems to be little emphasis on "facilitating or speeding up skills" (Hewlett and Lamb 2005, 415). This generalization is consistent with what has been found on the basis of holocultural research, wherein food collectors (hunter-gatherers) do not involve their children in work as frequently as do food accumulators. Importantly also, the hunter-gatherer research teams have documented their findings via the same systematic observational techniques as were introduced by the Whiting teams during the Six Cultures Study of Socialization (above).

The anthropologists and other social scientists undertaking intensive research with these hunter-gatherer peoples over the final decades of the 20th century accumulated an inventory of materials that will permanently enrich the ethnographic record. They continue to work with these foraging peoples who, though increasingly encroached upon, often retain central patterns that illuminate a style of adaptation which was once worldwide in its distribution.

Cognitive Studies

Beginning in the 1960s, inspired both by the "cognitive revolution" in psychology and by Jean Piaget's (1970) description of universal stages of intellectual development,[8] behavioral scientists began to look carefully at children's cognitive performance in cross-cultural settings (Cole et al. 1971; Cole and Scribner 1974; Dasen 1977; Dasen et al. 1978; Greenfield 1966, 1974; Irwin and McLaughlin 1970; Price-Williams 1962). Some of this research was motivated by the need for deeper understanding of learning in the hope that it could help explain the increasing and increasingly worrisome issue of school failure in Western and Western-type schools (Gay and Cole 1967; Serpell 1979; Stevenson et al. 1978; Wagner 1978). Up to that time, as we have seen, most inquiry had focused on children's behavior (play, skills, social interaction, and work contribution) and their socioemotional development. It was quickly found that children in traditional societies did not perform as well as those in urban-industrial environments. The differences appeared on a wide variety of tests, including Piagetian "stage" attainment, logical reasoning, level of moral reasoning, memory, and even on nonverbal, hypothetically culture-free tests (for a discussion of these results, see Dasen 1974; Edwards 1981; Goodnow 1976; Lloyd 1972; Scribner 1979; Wagner 1981).

The many reasons advanced for the poorer performance included unfamiliarity with test materials, emphasis on rote learning, low tolerance of questioning of authority figures (i.e., adults), inferior educational levels, inexperience with the forms of discourse and modes of representation associated with formal schooling, nonliteracy, and different understandings of the meaning of an activity, how to solve a particular problem, and even what a good solution entails (Rogoff, Gauvain, and Ellis 1984). Attempts to compensate or control for the discrepancies often involved a complex series of adjustments (types of tests and methods of testing) that, in the end, did not abolish many differences in performance (e.g., Cole et al. 1971; Lancy 1983). As cultural study of learning and cognition advanced, a comparative approach seemed, for many, far less interesting than delving deeper into the specific cognitive competencies expressed in particular cultural contexts. This research not only resulted in better descriptions and appreciation of human cognition in its various forms but also helped lead anthropologists and psychologists alike to the realization that cognition itself is a contextualized process.

Traditional peoples were observed to possess unusual cognitive skills and to use elegant reasoning (Gladwin 1970; Hutchins 1983; Lave 1977; Scribner 1976). As well, children in non-Western settings were found to have impressive expertise reflective of their everyday experiences, such as relational and spatial knowledge, classification systems, number and measurement concepts, and pattern representation, and their expertise sometimes surpassed similar behaviors observed among children in Western communities (e.g., see Greenfield and Childs 1977; Kelly 1977; Saxe 1981; Serpell 1979). Among both Western and traditional samples, a common theme emerged: cognitive performance is better on the activities and skills that are practiced and valued in a culture, and the more an assessment or test deviates from the familiar context, the poorer is the performance. This observation introduced new ways of thinking about learning and cognition, specifically as a highly contextualized or situated set of practices. But now an age-old question in psychology about transfer, or comparable performance on similar tasks, became paramount. That is, although these everyday cognition studies, as they were called, demonstrated that children both in traditional and Western societies could display high levels of functioning, such competence was not easily transferrable to classroom performance or to Western-style testing situations. For instance, children in Brazil who sell candy and fruit on the streets engage in complicated mathematical calculations while trading their wares, yet when these same children are asked to perform similar calculations in a schoollike form, they do quite poorly (Carraher, Carraher, and Schliemann 1985). Findings such as these led to closer examination of how formal schooling contributes to cognitive development (Rogoff 1981b), and whether schooling itself is a specialized form of cognitive training with its own benefits and limitations (Lancy 1983; Lave 1988; Saxe 1991; Serpell 1993).

Despite extensive research, the exact relation between cultural values and practices and children's learning and cognitive development remains unknown. As stated, not all cultural variation in cognitive performance is explained by differences in societal institutions such as schooling. Even when schooling is taken into account, the cognitive consequences of this experience vary significantly across cultures (Stevenson and Stigler 1992). The original aim to discover universal features of cognitive development has yet to be achieved, and whether this aim is valid continues to be debated. As Michael Cole (1989) wrote: "an approach that begins its analysis with everyday human practices in their cultural-historical contexts experiences great difficulty in arriving at global characteristics of our mental lives that generalize broadly across contexts" (329). Yet this research, for all its limitations, was the first tradition to try to specify some of the processes of learning that define and support cultural socialization.

The Learning of Language: Acquisition and Socialization

Noam Chomsky (1957, 1959, 1965) has been charged both with accelerating (Bowerman 1981) and retarding (Mohanty and Perregaux 1997) the cross-cultural study of language acquisition in children. Whichever the case, his fundamental claims—too complex to be more than limned here—were that the human brain contains an innate ability, or language instinct, entailing the specific knowledge needed to learn any language; that children are born with this capability; and that a universal grammar underlies the vast differences in specific languages, meaning that "all languages are basically the same, though they differ in many superficial characteristics" (Macaulay 2006, 54). In the 1960s, early cross-linguistic data indicated, as Chomsky had predicted, that all "normal" children begin to speak before the age of 2. Children seemed also to acquire language in patterned (rule-governed) ways, even to spontaneously produce comprehensible but unusual utterances they wouldn't have heard before (e.g., in English, "Him have glasses on him eyeball"). With the emphasis on commonalities across languages, Chomsky's ideas echo Piaget's views on the universality of mental functions.

For Chomsky, such regularities were supportive of his fundamental assumption that structures in the brain underlay the comprehension and production of all languages. Certain other expected regularities, however, failed to appear in some languages (Everett 2005), and a number of researchers—using inductively derived arguments—began to ask whether children's speech productions could be analyzed adequately using Chomsky's general ideas. The cross-cultural study of children's language thus began to change direction, heading into what may be called a post-Chomskyan era[9] (Bowerman 1981). For a brief period, a "cognition-first" hypothesis was entertained. Prior to their ability to express something verbally, children could often convey understanding of a concept by nonlinguistic means. However, the proposition that cognitive growth preceded language development, and even was relatively independent of the acquisition of language, was a strong position that did not robustly withstand all critiques,[10] and the empirical evidence was mixed. In some languages, the linguistic devices for encoding a given meaning were difficult and therefore slow to develop (e.g., expressing location by means of prepositions), and in others the development was more rapid (expressing location with suffixes), the difference being due to children's general propensity to attend to the ends of words (Slobin 1973). In these cases, one could perhaps see the primacy of a cognitive prerequisite. But then, in a Mayan (Central American) language, Tzeltal Maya, a highly specific set of verbs about location seemed to influence children's ideas about the kinds of spatial meanings those verbs could have, and here we had an apparent instance of the opposite, with the linguistic categories affecting cognition (Brown and Levinson 1993). Also, in a comparative study, Lucy and Gaskins (2001) showed that differences between English and Yucatec Maya in the use of plural and numeral classifiers—that is, in use of certain linguistic categories—affected cognition beginning in middle childhood, long after children had mastered the rules of their language.

Because language differences as well as possible universals were now being explored, a major feature of the newer research was its close attention to language-specific patterns of development. What this meant in practice was that language-acquisition studies were looking at the varying sociocultural contexts of language learning, including the communicative practices that parents and others engaged in with young children (Blount 1981). Probably the most salient result of these studies, considered together, was the discovery of immense cultural variety: in rates of language acquisition, in children's agency in learning, in the degree to which more mature individuals "teach" language to young children, in the use (or nonuse) of special baby talk or motherese, and in the explicit pressure applied to the learning of culturally appropriate usage (Schieffelin and Ochs 1986; Watson-Gegeo and Gegeo 1986). Moreover, realization of the centrality of language acquisition to all socialization meant that subsequent work on children's learning would require not only competent but also subtle language command by the researcher. What was now demonstrated, in other words, was a need to study both "socialization to use language" and "socialization through the use of language" (Schieffelin and Ochs 1986, 163)[11] (see also chapter 10, this volume).

Conclusion

We have seen that through much of the 20th century, there were considerable shifts of focus as a variety of interests in children's learning arose and then subsided. But there was also a pattern to the changes. Early on, in the 1920s, Margaret Mead and Bronislaw Malinowski asked questions concerning the validity of certain generalizations about children's development. This was followed by a flourishing period of careful descriptive work, without much regard to theoretical issues.[12] Then, beginning in the 1950s, a number of research cycles—holocultural inquiry, the Whitings' comparative projects, the hunter-gatherer studies, cognitive research programs, language-learning studies—all followed a common trajectory: After an initial phase in which principles or strong regularities were sought, and were sometimes found, each of these mini-traditions tended either to experience a downturn of interest or to find a different emphasis. Yet, in the process of uncovering the complexities of their special problems, they consistently evoked a theoretically informed appreciation of the great cultural range of adaptive paths in childhood learning.

The Euro-American model of human development has been based on a program of so much depth and wealth of reportage that cross-cultural studies have almost necessarily played off some aspect of it.[13] In effect, then, as noted in our introduction, every cross-cultural investigation of children's learning was, and is, comparative. When carried out well, such studies have served as indispensable complements to the developmentalist's emphasis on laboratory-based research. Naturalistic studies can also capture changes over time, as when recent research has involved revisits to field sites, and even decades-long dedication to the continuing study of culture groups (e.g., Gaskins 2003; Greenfield 2004; LeVine et al. 1994; Seymour 1999). Along with this have come new technologies providing researchers with a suite of methodological and measurement-related improvements in data collection.[14]

In both historical and contemporary cross-cultural research on children's learning and socialization, a tension exists between two competing views of children and childhood. Theory suggests that children are active and constructive agents in their own development. However, learning and socialization are often studied in ways that depict children as passive in these processes, as recipients of culture rather than as contributing and vital forces in both individual and cultural development. Rarely do we see the child's own perspective taken into account: for example, adults, principally caregivers, are asked about children (how they rear children, what they think and believe about them), and child interviews, when they occur, are often based on the scientist's views of what is important about childhood. A more child-centered approach would describe the full scope of children's learning and socialization. Important questions include what children choose to learn in the myriad socialization efforts presented to them by adults and cultural institutions, and how children themselves, both individually and with other children, shape these learning and socialization experiences to meet their own needs and goals and, thereby, change culture.

In ending, we may reconsider our epigraphs and the opposed statements of James and Darwin. We should always keep in mind James's claim about the likelihood of error when the classical experimental method is not adopted. To remember this is to aid in the reduction of error, an accomplishment that has been slowly but increasingly achieved in comparative child research. On the other side, Darwin's "habit of comparison" has indeed led to generalizations, though many of them have been weak and others unfulfilled. Still, we continue to search for them, as the chapters in the present volume show. And it is probably not too much to hope that the cultural paths to successful human development, while various and plentiful, are not without limit and can ultimately be understood.

Acknowledgments

The authors are indebted to editors David Lancy and Suzanne Gaskins for their many helpful comments on preliminary versions of this chapter.

Notes

1. The term *socialization* is used broadly here to refer to cultural transmissions during childhood, and thus, depending on context, may indicate either child training practices or cultural-acquisition processes.

2. A chapter that is historical should avoid the temptation to update the field by citing current literature. Although we have not been entirely successful in this regard, our 21st-century references amount to fewer than 10 percent of all citations.

3. Ronald Rohner (1975) showed a holocultural connection between what he termed "parental acceptance-rejection" and adult outcomes (degree of emotional stability and responsiveness). He and colleagues have since followed up with a large number of intracultural studies, and as he has summarized the results, early negative treatment tends to have long-lasting deleterious effects (Rohner 2004). For the opposite pole, parental acceptance, it is likely that positive treatment interacts with numerous processes, including many that occur after childhood, and acceptance is therefore associated with a variety of developmental outcomes.

4. How do the Indonesian Alorese, described above as neglectful and inconsistent in their treatment of children, fit into this picture? Retrospectively, LeVine (2007, 252) sees the ethnography of Du Bois (1944) as having a "judgmental cast" and as "psychiatrically inspired," but the fact is that Du Bois made detailed documentation of both the irregular care given Alorese children and their rages, which were "so consistent, so widespread, and of such long duration that they

were one of [her] first and most striking observations" (51). This apparently low level of care is quite different from the concept of multiple caretaking.

5. Interviews with the mothers about child-rearing practices provided a separate set of results which, though published (Minturn and Lambert 1964), were only tangentially integrated into subsequent analyses (Whiting and Whiting 1975).

6. But the specificity of the spot-observation technique, while facilitating adequate reliability and enabling a profile of activities and social behavior to be built up through repeated sampling, virtually disallows the measurement of ongoing sequences of behavior. Although the use of both approaches would be optimal, the needed resources in research time and effort have seldom been available.

7. For a list of the names of the primary Kenyan and American participants in the University of Nairobi's Child Development Research Unit, see John Whiting (1994, 40). Numerous doctoral dissertations by Americans came out of the program. Several Kenyan students received their master's degrees or doctorates from Harvard.

8. Piaget (1974) revised his position in later writing to acknowledge that the highest stage of his theory, that of "formal operations" (or the logic of scientific reasoning without the aid of any concrete content), might apply only to individuals in societies with complex systems of technology and science and even in these settings in particular contexts.

9. Chomsky himself began to insist on the importance of his universal grammar for "the investigation of the structure and predispositions of the human mind" (Lyons 1970, 91). In a trenchant critique, Macaulay (2006; see appendix) discusses how Chomsky has promulgated an ever evolving model for which "[t]here is no direct evidence" (199). This has led Chomsky, and those who continue to follow him, outside the realm of ordinary science, which depends on evidence to evaluate competing hypotheses.

10. Bowerman (1981) discussed the evidence and several of the problems associated with this position.

11. The surge of overseas applicants to anthropology departments in the United States in recent years will help meet this need for high competence in languages other than English.

12. As noted above in the text, after this period and since, there have always been some cultural anthropologists whose interests were never theoretical but whose monographs contributed to a growing ethnographic record on child life and learning.

13. This reliance has occurred despite the fact that the Western model has been changing over time—Freudian, behaviorist, social learning, cognitivist (LeVine 2007).

14. At the same time, the accelerating pace of change, particularly the near global adoption of new technologies, has posed some novel challenges to our understanding of how children are learning their cultures.

Bibliography

Allen, Martin G. "A Cross-Cultural Study of Aggression and Crime." *Journal of Cross-Cultural Psychology* 3, no. 3 (September 1972): 259–71.

Bacon, Margaret K., Herbert Barry III, and Irvin L. Child. "A Cross-Cultural Study of Drinking II: Relations to Other Features of Culture." *Quarterly Journal of Studies on Alcohol, Supplement*, no. 3 (1965): 29–48.

Barry, Herbert, III, Margaret K. Bacon, and Irvin L. Child. "Definitions, Ratings, and Bibliographic Sources for Child-Training Practices of 110 Cultures." Pp. 293–331 in *Cross-Cultural Approaches*, edited by Clellan S. Ford. New Haven, Conn.: HRAF Press, 1967.

Barry, Herbert, III, Irvin L. Child, and Margaret K. Bacon. "Relation of Child Training to Subsistence Economy." *American Anthropologist* 61, no. 1 (February 1959): 51–63.

Barry, Herbert, III, and Leonore M. Paxson. "Infancy and Early Childhood: Cross-Cultural Codes 2." *Ethnology* 10, no. 4 (October 1971): 466–508.

Bateson, Gregory, and Margaret Mead. *Balinese Childhood: A Photographic Analysis*. New York: New York Academy of Sciences, 1942.

Blount, Ben G. "The Development of Language in Children." Pp. 379–402 in *Handbook of Cross-Cultural Human Development*, edited by Ruth H. Munroe, Robert L. Munroe, and Beatrice B. Whiting. New York: Garland, 1981.

Borgerhoff Mulder, Monica, and T. M. Caro. "The Use of Quantitative Observational Methods." *Current Anthropology* 26, no. 3 (June 1985): 323–36.

Bowerman, Melissa. "Language Development." Pp. 93–185 in *Handbook of Cross-Cultural Psychology*, vol. 4, edited by Harry C. Triandis and Alastair Heron. Boston: Allyn and Bacon, 1981.

Brown, Judith K. "Cross-Cultural Study of Female Initiation Rites." *American Anthropologist* 65, no. 4 (August 1963): 837–53.

Brown, Penelope, and Stephen C. Levinson. "Linguistic and Nonlinguistic Coding of Spatial Arrays: Explorations in Mayan Cognition" (Working Paper Number 24). Nijmegan: Cognitive Anthropology Research Group, Max Planck Institute for Psycholinguistics, 1993.

Carraher, Terezinha, David W. Carraher, and Analucia D. Schliemann. "Mathematics in the Streets and in Schools." *British Journal of Developmental Psychology* 3 (1985): 21–29.

Caton, Hiram, ed. *The Samoa Reader: Anthropologists Take Stock*. Lanham, Md.: University Press of America, 1990.

Chomsky, Noam. *Syntactic Structures*. The Hague: Mouton, 1957.

———. "Review of Skinner (1957)." *Language* 35 (1959): 26–58.

———. *Aspects of the Theory of Syntax*. Cambridge: MIT Press, 1965.

Cole, Michael. "Cultural Psychology: A Once and Future Discipline." Pp. 279–335 in *Nebraska Symposium on Motivation: Cross-Cultural Perspectives*, edited by John J. Berman. Lincoln: University of Nebraska Press, 1989.

Cole, Michael, John Gay, Joseph Glick, and Donald W. Sharp. *The Cultural Context of Learning and Thinking*. New York: Basic Books, 1971.

Cole, Michael, and Sylvia Scribner. *Culture and Thought*. New York: Wiley, 1974.

Dasen, Pierre R. "The Influence of Ecology, Culture, and European Contact on Cognitive Development in Australian Aborigines." Pp. 381–408 in *Culture and Cognition: Readings in Cross-Cultural Psychology*, edited by John W. Berry. London: Methuen, 1974.

———. *Piagetian Psychology: Cross-Cultural Contributions*. New York: Gardner, 1977.

Dasen, Pierre R., Barbel Inhelder, Margot Lavallée, and Jean Retschitzki. *Naissance de l'intelligence chez l'enfant Bauolé de Côte d'Ivoire*. Berne: Hans Huber, 1978.

Dennis, Wayne. *The Hopi Child*. New York: Appleton-Century, 1940.

Draper, Patricia. "Comparative Studies in Socialization." *Annual Review of Anthropology* 3 (1974): 263–78.

———. "Cultural Pressure on Sex Differences." *American Ethnologist* 2, no. 4 (November 1975): 602–16.

Draper, Patricia, and Henry Harpending. "Father Absence and Reproductive Strategy: An Evolutionary Perspective." *Journal of Anthropological Research* 38, no. 3 (Autumn 1982): 255–73.

Du Bois, Cora. *The People of Alor*. Minneapolis: University of Minnesota Press, 1944.

Edwards, Carolyn Pope. "The Comparative Study of the Development of Moral Judgment and Reasoning." Pp. 501–28 in *Handbook of Cross-Cultural Human Development*, edited by Ruth H. Munroe, Robert L. Munroe, and Beatrice B. Whiting. New York: Garland, 1981.

Ember, Carol R. "Feminine Task Assignment and the Social Behavior of Boys." *Ethos* 1, no. 4 (Winter 1973): 424–39.

Ember, Carol R., and Melvin Ember. *Cross-Cultural Research Methods*. Lanham, Md.: AltaMira, 2001a.

———. "Father Absence and Male Aggression: A Re-Examination of the Comparative Evidence." *Ethos* 29, no. 3 (September 2001b): 296–314.

Erikson, Erik H. *Childhood and Society*. New York: Norton, 1950.

Everett, Daniel L. "Cultural Constraints on Grammar and Cognition in Pirahã." *Current Anthropology* 46, no. 4 (August/October 2005): 621–34.

Firth, Raymond. *We, the Tikopia*." London: Allen and Unwin, 1936.

Fortes, Meyer. "Social and Psychological Aspects of Education in Taleland." 1938. Pp. 14–74 in *From Child to Adult*, edited by John Middleton. Garden City: Natural History Press, 1970.

Fouts, Hillary N. "Father Involvement with Young Children among the Aka and Bofi Foragers." *Cross-Cultural Research* 42, no. 3 (August 2008): 290–312.

Gaskins, Suzanne. "From Corn to Cash: Change and Continuity within Mayan Families." *Ethos* 31, no. 3 (September 2003): 248–73.

Gay, John, and Michael Cole. *The New Mathematics and an Old Culture*. New York: Holt, Rinehart, and Winston, 1967.

Gladwin, Thomas. *East Is a Big Bird*. Cambridge, Mass.: Harvard University Press, 1970.

Goodnow, Jacqueline J. "The Nature of Intelligent Behavior: Questions Raised by Cross-Cultural Studies." Pp. 169–88 in *The Nature of Intelligence*, edited by Lauren B. Resnick. Hillsdale, N.J.: Erlbaum, 1976.

Greenfield, Patricia Marks. "On Culture and Conservation." Pp. 225–56 in *Studies in Cognitive Growth*, edited by Jerome S. Bruner, Rose R. Olver, and Patricia Marks Greenfield. New York: Wiley, 1966.

———. "Comparing Dimensional Categorization in Natural and Artificial Contexts: A Developmental Study among the Zinacantecos of Mexico." *Journal of Social Psychology* 93, no. 2 (April 1974): 157–71.

———. *Weaving Generations Together: Evolving Creativity in the Maya of Chiapas*. Santa Fe: School of American Research Press, 2004.

Greenfield, Patricia Marks, and Carla P. Childs. "Understanding Sibling Concepts: A Developmental Study of Kin Terms in Zinacantan." Pp. 335–38 in *Piagetian Psychology: Cross-Cultural Contributions*, edited by Pierre R. Dasen. New York: Gardner, 1977.

Hall, Calvin S., and Gardner Lindzey. *Theories of Personality*. New York: Wiley, 1957.

Hall, G. Stanley. *Adolescence*. 2 vols. New York: Appleton, 1904.

Hallowell, A. Irving. *Culture and Experience*. 1939. Philadelphia: University of Pennsylvania Press, 1955.

Harkness, Sara, and Charles M. Super. "The Cultural Context of Gender Segregation in Children's Peer Groups." *Child Development* 56, no. 1 (February 1985): 219–24.

Hawkes, Kristin, James F. O'Connell, and Nicholas G. Blurton-Jones. "Hadza Women's Time Allocation, Offspring Provisioning, and the Evolution of Long Postmenopausal Life Spans." *Current Anthropology* 38, no. 4 (October 1997): 551–77.

Hewlett, Barry S. *Intimate Fathers: The Nature and Context of Aka Pygmy Paternal-Infant Care.* Ann Arbor: University of Michigan Press, 1991.

———. "Husband-Wife Reciprocity and the Father-Infant Relationship among Aka Pygmies." Pp. 153–76 in *Father-Child Relations*, edited by Barry S. Hewlett. New York: Aldine de Gruyter, 1992.

Hewlett, Barry S., and Luigi L. Cavalli-Sforza. "Cultural Transmission among the Aka Pygmies." *American Anthropologist* 88, no. 4 (December 1986): 922–34.

Hewlett, Barry S., and Michael E. Lamb. "Emerging Issues in the Study of Hunter Gatherer Children." Pp. 3–18 in *Hunter Gatherer Childhoods*, edited by Barry S. Hewlett and Michael E. Lamb. New Brunswick, N.J.: Transaction, 2005.

Hogbin, H. Ian. "Education at Ontong-Java, Solomon Islands." *American Anthropologist* 33, no. 4 (October-December 1931): 601–14.

———. "A New Guinea Infancy." *Oceania* 13 (1943): 285–309.

———. "A New Guinea Childhood." *Oceania* 16 (1946): 275–96.

———. *The Island of Menstruating Men.* Scranton, Pa.: Chandler, 1970.

Huntington, Gertrude Enders, and John Andrew Hostetler. *Children in Amish Society.* New York: Holt, Rinehart, and Winston, 1971.

Hutchins, Edwin. "Understanding Micronesian Navigation." Pp. 191–225 in *Mental Models*, edited by Dedre Gentner and Albert L. Stevens. Hillsdale, N.J.: Erlbaum, 1983.

Irwin, Marc H., and Donald H. McLaughlin. "Ability and Preference in Category Sorting by Mano Schoolchildren and Adults." *Journal of Social Psychology* 82, no. 1 (1970): 15–24.

Johnson, Allen. "Comment on 'Does Labor Time Decrease with Industrialization? A Survey of Time-Allocation Studies' by Wanda Minge-Klevana." *Current Anthropology* 21, no. 3 (June 1980): 292.

Kardiner, Abram. *The Individual and His Society.* New York: Columbia University Press, 1939.

———. *The Psychological Frontiers of Society.* New York: Columbia University Press, 1945.

Katz, Mary Maxwell, and Melvin J. Konner. "The Role of the Father: An Anthropological Perspective." Pp. 155–85 in *The Father's Role in Cross-Cultural Perspective*, edited by Michael E. Lamb. New York: Wiley, 1981.

Kelly, Max. "Papua New Guinea and Piaget: An Eight-Year Study." Pp. 169–202 in *Piagetian Psychology: Cross-Cultural Contributions*, edited by Pierre R. Dasen. New York: Gardner, 1977.

Konner, Melvin. "Evolution of Human Behavior Development." Pp. 69–109 in *Culture and Infancy*, edited by P. Herbert Leiderman, Steven Tulkin, and Anne Rosenfeld. New York: Academic, 1977a.

———. "Infancy among the Kalahari Desert San." Pp. 287–328 in *Culture and Infancy*, edited by P. Herbert Leiderman, Steven Tulkin, and Anne Rosenfeld. New York: Academic, 1977b.

Lamb, Michael E. "Introduction: The Emergent American Father." Pp. 3–25 in *The Father's Role*, edited by M. E. Lamb. Hillsdale, N.J.: Erlbaum, 1987.

Lancy, David F. *Cross-Cultural Studies in Cognition and Mathematics*. New York: Academic, 1983.

———. "Accounting for Variability in Mother-Child Play." *American Anthropologist* 109, no. 2 (June 2007): 273–84.

Lave, Jean. "Cognitive Consequences of Traditional Apprenticeship Training in West Africa." *Anthropology and Education Quarterly* 8, no. 3 (August 1977): 177–80.

———. *Cognition in Practice: Mind, Mathematics, and Culture in Everyday Life*. Cambridge: Cambridge University Press, 1988.

Lee, Richard B., and Irven DeVore, eds. *Man the Hunter*. Chicago: Aldine, 1968.

Leighton, Dorothea, and Clyde Kluckhohn. *Children of the People*. Cambridge, Mass.: Harvard University Press, 1947.

LeVine, Robert A. *Culture, Behavior, and Personality*. 2nd ed. New York: Aldine, 1982.

———. "Ethnographic Studies of Childhood: A Historical Overview." *American Anthropologist* 109, no. 2 (June 2007): 247–60.

LeVine, Robert A., Suzanne Dixon, Sarah LeVine, Amy Richman, Constance H. Keefer, P. Herbert Leiderman, and T. Berry Brazelton. *Child Care and Culture: Lessons from Africa*. New York: Cambridge University Press, 1994.

Levinson, David, and Martin J. Malone. *Toward Explaining Human Culture*. New Haven, Conn.: HRAF Press, 1980.

Little, Kenneth. *The Mende of Sierra Leone*. London: Routledge and Kegan Paul, 1951.

Lloyd, Barbara B. *Perception and Cognition: A Cross-Cultural Perspective*. Harmondsworth: Penguin, 1972.

Lucy, John A., and Suzanne Gaskins. "Grammatical Categories and the Development of Classification Preferences: A Comparative Approach." Pp. 257–83 in *Language Acquisition and Conceptual Development*, edited by Melissa Bowerman and Stephen C. Levinson. Cambridge: Cambridge University Press, 2001.

Lyons, John. *Noam Chomsky*. New York: Viking Press, 1970.

Macaulay, Ronald K. S. *The Social Art: Language and Its Uses.* 2nd ed. Oxford: Oxford University Press, 2006.

Maccoby, Eleanor E. *The Two Sexes.* Cambridge, Mass.: Harvard University Press, 1998.

Malinowski, Bronislaw. *The Sexual Life of Savages in North Western Melanesia.* London: Routledge, 1929.

———. *Sex and Repression in Savage Society.* 1927. New York: Meridian, 1955.

Mead, Margaret. "An Investigation of the Thought of Primitive Children, with Special Reference to Animism." *Journal of the Royal Anthropological Institute of Great Britain and Ireland* 62 (January–June 1932): 173–90.

———. *Coming of Age in Samoa.* 1928. New York: Morrow, 1973.

———. *Growing Up in New Guinea.* 1930. New York: Morrow, 1973.

Mead, Margaret, and Frances C. Macgregor. *Growth and Culture.* New York: Putnam, 1951.

Minturn, Leigh, and William W. Lambert. *Mothers of Six Cultures: Antecedents of Child Rearing.* New York: Wiley, 1964.

Mohanty, Ajit, and Christiane Perregaux. "Language Acquisition and Bilingualism." Pp. 217–53 in *Handbook of Cross-Cultural Psychology*, vol. 2, 2nd ed., edited by John W. Berry, Pierre R. Dasen, and T. S. Saraswathi. Boston: Allyn and Bacon, 1997.

Munroe, Ruth H., and Robert L. Munroe. "Household Density and Infant Care in an East African Society." *Journal of Social Psychology* 83, no. 1 (February 1971): 3–13.

———. "Household Density and Holding of Infants in Samoa and Nepal." *Journal of Social Psychology* 122, no. 1 (February 1984): 135–36.

Munroe, Ruth H., Robert L. Munroe, and Harold S. Shimmin. "Children's Work in Four Cultures: Determinants and Consequences." *American Anthropologist* 86, no. 2 (June 1984): 369–79.

Murdock, George P., Clellan S. Ford, Alfred E. Hudson, Raymond Kennedy, Leo W. Simmons, and John W. M. Whiting. *Outline of Cultural Materials.* 5th ed. revised. New Haven, Conn.: HRAF Press, 2000.

Nerlove, Sara B., John M. Roberts, Robert E. Klein, Charles Yarbrough, and Jean-Pierre Habicht. "Natural Indicators of Cognitive Development: An Observational Study of Rural Guatemalan Children." *Ethos* 2, no. 2 (Summer 1974): 265–95.

Piaget, Jean. *Genetic Epistemology.* New York: Columbia University Press, 1970.

———. "Need and Significance of Cross-Cultural Studies in Genetic Psychology." Pp. 299–309 in *Culture and Cognition*, edited by J. W. Berry and P. R. Dasen. London: Methuen, 1974.

Price-Williams, D. R. "Abstract and Concrete Modes of Classification in a Primitive Society." *British Journal of Educational Psychology* 32 (1962): 50–61.

Raum, Otto F. *Chaga Childhood*. London: Oxford University Press, 1940.

Richards, Audrey I. *Hunger and Work in a Savage Tribe*. London: George Routledge and Sons, 1932.

———. *Chisungu: A Girl's Initiation among the Bemba*. London: Faber and Faber, 1956.

Roberts, John M., Malcolm J. Arth, and Robert R. Bush. "Games in Culture." *American Anthropologist* 61, no. 4 (August 1959): 597–605.

Roberts, John M., and Brian Sutton-Smith. "Child Training and Game Involvement." *Ethnology* 1, no.2 (April 1962): 166–85.

Rogoff, Barbara. "Spot Observation: An Introduction and Examination." *Quarterly Newsletter of the Institute for Comparative Human Development* 2, no. 2 (April 1978): 21–26.

———. "Adults and Peers as Agents of Socialization: A Highland Guatemalan Profile." *Ethos* 9, no. 1 (Spring 1981a): 18–36.

———. "Schooling and the Development of Cognitive Skills." Pp. 233–94 in *Handbook of Cross-Cultural Psychology*, vol. 4, edited by Harry C. Triandis and Alastair Heron. Boston: Allyn and Bacon, 1981b.

Rogoff, Barbara, Mary Gauvain, and Shari Ellis. "Development Viewed in Its Cultural Context." Pp. 533–71 in *Developmental Psychology: An Advanced Textbook*, edited by Marc H. Bornstein and Michael E. Lamb. Hillsdale, N.J.: Erlbaum, 1984.

Rogoff, Barbara, Martha Julia Sellers, Sergio Pirrotta, Nathan Fox, and Sheldon H. White. "Age of Assignment of Roles and Responsibilities to Children: A Cross-Cultural Survey." *Human Development* 18, no. 5 (July/August 1975): 353–69.

Rohner, Ronald P. *They Love Me, They Love Me Not*. New Haven, Conn.: HRAF Press, 1975.

———. "The Parental 'Acceptance-Rejection Syndrome': Universal Correlates of Perceived Rejection." *American Psychologist* 59, no. 8 (2004): 830–40.

Sahlins, Marshall D. *The Use and Abuse of Biology*. Ann Arbor: University of Michigan Press, 1976.

Saxe, Geoffrey B. "Body Parts as Numerals: A Developmental Analysis of Enumeration among a Village Population in Papua New Guinea." *Child Development* 52, no. 1 (March 1981): 306–16.

———. *Culture and Cognitive Development: Studies in Mathematical Understanding*. Hillsdale, N.J.: Erlbaum, 1991.

Schieffelin, Bambi B., and Elinor Ochs. "Language Socialization." *Annual Review of Anthropology* 15 (1986): 163–91.

Scribner, Sylvia. "Situating the Experiment in Cross-Cultural Research." Pp. 310–26 in *The Developing Individual in a Changing World*, vol. 1, edited by Klaus F. Riegel and John A. Meacham. Chicago: Aldine, 1976.

———. "Modes of Thinking and Ways of Speaking: Culture and Logic Reconsidered." Pp. 223–43 in *New Directions in Discourse Processing*, edited by Roy O. Freedle. Norwood, N.J.: Ablex, 1979.

Sears, Robert R. *Survey of Objective Studies of Psychoanalytic Concepts*. New York: Social Science Research Council, 1951.

Serpell, Robert. *Culture's Influence on Behavior*. London: Methuen, 1979.

———. *The Significance of Schooling: Life-journeys in an African Society*. Cambridge: Cambridge University Press, 1993.

Seymour, Susan. "Household Structure and Status and Expressions of Affect in India." *Ethos* 11, no. 4 (December 1983): 263–77.

———. *Women, Family, and Child Care in India: A World in Transition*. Cambridge: Cambridge University Press, 1999.

———. "Multiple Caretaking of Infants and Young Children: An Area in Critical Need of a Feminist Psychological Anthropology." *Ethos* 32, no. 4 (December 2004): 538–56.

Singer, Milton. "A Survey of Culture and Personality Theory, in Studying Personality Cross-Culturally." Pp. 9–90 in *Studying Personality Cross-Culturally*, edited by Bert Kaplan. New York: Harper, 1961.

Slobin, Dan I. "Cognitive Prerequisites for the Development of Grammar." Pp. 175–208 in *Studies of Child Language Development*, edited by Charles A. Ferguson and Dan Isaac Slobin. New York: Holt, Rinehart, and Winston, 1973.

Spiro, Melford E. *Children of the Kibbutz*. Cambridge, Mass.: Harvard University Press, 1958.

Steinberg, Laurence D. *Adolescence*. New York: McGraw-Hill, 1996.

Stevenson, Harold W., Timothy Parker, Alex Wilkinson, Beatrice Bonnevaux, and Max Gonzalez. "Schooling, Environment, and Cognitive Development: A Cross-Cultural Study." *Monographs of the Society for Research in Child Development* 43, Serial No. 175, 1978.

Stevenson, Harold W., and James W. Stigler. *The Learning Gap: Why Our Schools Are Failing and What We Can Learn from Japanese and Chinese Education*. New York: Summit Books, 1992.

Super, Charles M., and Sara Harkness. "The Developmental Niche: A Conceptualization at the Interface of Child and Culture." *International Journal of Behavioral Development* 9, no. 4 (December 1986): 545–69.

Tronick, Edward Z., Gilda A. Morelli, and Steve Winn. "Multiple Caretaking of Efe (Pygmy) Infants." *American Anthropologist* 89, no. 1 (March 1987): 96–106.

Wagner, Daniel A. "Memories of Morocco: The Influence of Age, Schooling, and Environment on Memory." *Cognitive Psychology* 10, no. 1 (January 1978): 1–28.

———. "Culture and Memory Development." Pp. 178–232 in *Handbook of Cross-Cultural Psychology: Developmental Psychology*, vol. 4, edited by Harry C. Triandis and Alastair Heron. Boston: Allyn and Bacon, 1981.

Watson-Gegeo, Karen Ann, and David W. Gegeo. "The Social World of Kwara'ae Children: Acquisition of Language and Values." Pp. 109–27 in *Children's Worlds and Children's Languages*, edited by Jenny Cook-Gumperz, William A. Corsaro, and Jurgen Streeck. New York: Mouton de Gruyter, 1986.

Wedgwood, Camilla H. "Life of Children in Manam." *Oceania* 9 (1938): 1–29.

Weisner, Thomas S. "Urban-Rural Differences in Sociable, Aggressive, and Dominant Behaviors of Kenya Children." *Ethnology* 18, no. 2 (April 1979): 153–72.

———. "The Ecocultural Project of Human Development: Why Ethnography and Its Findings Matter." *Ethos* 25, no. 2 (June 1997): 177–90.

Weisner, Thomas S., and Ronald Gallimore. "My Brother's Keeper: Child and Sibling Caretaking." *Current Anthropology* 18, no. 2 (June 1977): 169–90.

Whiting, Beatrice B., ed. *Six Cultures: Studies of Child Rearing*. New York: Wiley, 1963.

———. "Culture and Social Behavior: A Model for the Development of Social Behavior." *Ethos* 8, no. 2 (Summer 1980): 105–16.

Whiting, Beatrice B., and Carolyn P. Edwards. *Children of Different Worlds*. Cambridge, Mass.: Harvard University Press, 1988.

Whiting, Beatrice B., and John W. M. Whiting. "Task Assignment and Personality." Pp. 33–45 in *Comparative Perspectives in Social Psychology*, edited by William W. Lambert and Rita Weisbrod. Boston: Little, Brown, 1971.

———. *Children of Six Cultures*. Cambridge, Mass.: Harvard University Press, 1975.

Whiting, John W. M. *Becoming a Kwoma*. New Haven, Conn.: Yale University Press, 1941.

———. *Progress Report: Child Development Research Unit*. Nairobi: University College, Nairobi, 1970.

———. *Culture and Human Development: The Selected Papers of John Whiting*. Edited by Eleanor Hollenberg Chasdi. Cambridge: Cambridge University Press, 1994.

Whiting, John W. M., and Irvin L. Child. *Child Training and Personality*. New Haven, Conn.: Yale University Press, 1953.

Whiting, John W. M., Irvin L. Child, and William W. Lambert. *Field Guide for a Study of Socialization*. New York: Wiley, 1966.

Whiting, John W. M., Richard Kluckhohn, and Albert Anthony. "The Function of Male Initiation Ceremonies at Puberty." Pp. 359–70 in *Readings in Social Psychology*, 3rd ed., edited by Eleanor E. Maccoby, Theodore M. Newcomb, and Eugene L. Hartley. New York: Holt, Rinehart, and Winston, 1958.

Williams, Thomas Rhys. *A Borneo Childhood*. New York: Holt, Rinehart, and Winston, 1969.

———. *Introduction to Socialization: Human Culture Transmitted*. St. Louis, Mo.: C. V. Mosby, 1972.

Worthman, Carol M. "The Ecology of Human Development: Evolving Models for Cultural Psychology." *Journal of Cross-Cultural Psychology*, in press.

CHAPTER FOUR

PARENTAL ETHNOTHEORIES OF CHILDREN'S LEARNING

Sara Harkness, Charles M. Super,
Moisés Ríos Bermúdez, Ughetta Moscardino,
Jong-Hay Rha, Caroline Johnston Mavridis, Sabrina Bonichini,
Blanca Huitrón, Barbara Welles-Nyström, Jesús Palacios,
On-Kang Hyun, Grace Soriano, and Piotr Olaf Zylicz

Picture yourself, for a moment, as an American visitor who has the privilege of spending a morning in a pleasant middle-class Dutch home observing the normal routine of a mother and her 6-month-old baby. The mother made sure you got there by 8:30 to witness the morning bath, an opportunity for playful interaction with the baby. The baby has been dressed in cozy warm clothes, her hair brushed and styled with a tiny curlicue atop her head. The mother has given her the mid-morning bottle, then sung to her and played patty-cake for a few minutes before placing her in the playpen to entertain herself with a mobile while the mother attends to other things nearby. Now, about half an hour later, the baby is beginning to get fussy. The mother watches her for a minute, then offers a toy and turns away again. Soon, the baby again begins to fuss. "Seems bored and in need of attention," you think. But the mother looks at the baby sympathetically and in a soft voice says, "Oh, are you tired?" Without further ado, she picks up the baby, carries her upstairs, tucks her into her crib, and pulls down the shades. To your surprise, the baby fusses for a few more moments and then is quiet. The mother looks serene. "She needs plenty of sleep in order to grow," she explains. "When she doesn't have her nap or go to bed on time, we can always tell the difference—she's not so happy and playful."

This scenario—based on an actual observation—illustrates how parents' cultural beliefs, or "parental ethnotheories," are expressed in the daily lives of families. The Dutch mother we observed interpreted her child's behavior in the context of culturally shared beliefs about the nature of infants (perhaps you, for your part, interpreted the baby's fussiness in an American cultural framework). In the Dutch case, some of these ethnotheories have been encoded as the "three R's" of good parenting, a set of beliefs passed down through generations of parents and formalized in guidelines by the national health care system (Super, Harkness, et al. 1996).

We discovered the "three R's" of Dutch child-rearing—*rust* (rest), *regelmaat* (regularity), and *reinheid* (cleanliness)—while doing research on how Dutch parents in a typical mid-sized town think about the development of their infants and children, and how these ideas guide the way they organize children's lives from day to day. We found that the "three R's" were powerfully represented in differences in the amount that babies slept, as well as how they were cared for while awake. At 6 months, the Dutch babies were sleeping more than a comparison group of American babies—a total of 15 hours per day versus 13 hours for the Americans. While awake at home, the Dutch babies were more often left to play quietly in their playpens or infant seats. A daily ride in the baby carriage provided time for the baby to look around at the passing scene or to doze peacefully. If the mother needed to go out for a time without the baby, she could leave it alone in bed for a short time, or time her outing with the baby's nap time and ask a neighbor to monitor with a "baby phone." Many families also had grandparents or grown siblings nearby who would be glad to baby-sit. The important thing was to protect the baby's regular schedule, especially time for sleeping.

Understanding parents' ethnotheories about their children is key to understanding the strategies parents use to help their children grow up to become successful members of their communities. In particular, parental ethnotheories about children as learners provide a foundation for the ways that parents think about children's environments for learning. These ideas, in turn, are related to parental ethnotheories of children's intelligence and personality, a topic that Harkness and Super first studied in a rural Kipsigis community of western Kenya in the 1970s (Harkness and Super 1992; Harkness, Super, et al. 2009; Super 1983). Mothers in this community identified six different groupings of words used to describe children. The first group referred to children's helpfulness and obedience, and it included phrases denoting a child who is respectful, polite, hospitable to visitors, and responsible. Particularly interesting in this group was the term *kaseit*, derived from the verb *kase*, to understand, describing a child who understands quickly what needs to be done—and does it. The second group referred specifically to cognitive qualities, including *ng'om* (intelligent), *utat* (clever, or wise and unselfish), and *kwelat* (sharp, clever, sometimes devious). The word *ng'om* was used only in describing children and was typically used to describe intelligent behavior at home. As one mother said:

> For a girl who is *ng'om*, after eating she sweeps the house because she knows it should be done. Then she washes dishes, looks for vegetables [in the garden], and takes good care of the baby. When you come home, you feel pleased and say: "This child is *ng'om*." Another girl may not even clean her own dishes, but just go out and play, leaving the baby to cry. For a boy, if he is *ng'om*, he will watch the cows, and take them to the river without being told. He knows to separate the calves from the cows and he will fix the thorn fence when it is broken. The other boy will let the cows into the maize field and will be found playing while they eat the maize.

As the Kokwet mothers explained further, the term *ng'om* could also be applied to academic intelligence. However, they stressed that being intelligent in school and at home were two different things: a child might do well in school despite often forgetting to be responsible and helpful at home. In summary, the Kokwet parents' concept of intelligence highlighted aspects of social competence, including responsibility and helpfulness, that have been documented throughout traditional cultures in sub-Saharan Africa (Serpell and Jere-Folotiya 2008), and that have tended to be overlooked in Western formal theories of children's intelligence (Nsamenang and Lamb 1993; Sternberg et al. 1981).

Parental Ethnotheories and the Developmental Niche

As illustrated in these examples, parental ethnotheories are cultural models that parents hold regarding children, families, and themselves as parents. The term *cultural model*, drawn from cognitive anthropology, indicates an organized set of ideas that are shared by members of a cultural group (D'Andrade and Strauss 1992; Quinn and Holland 1987). Like other cultural models related to the self, parental ethnotheories are often implicit, taken-for-granted ideas about the "natural" or "right" way to think or act, and they have strong motivational properties for parents.

Parental ethnotheories are related to each other both across domains and in hierarchical fashion. The top of the hierarchy contains implicit, linked models of child, family, and parent; further down the hierarchy we find more specific and consciously held ideas about particular aspects of child development, parenting, and family life. These ideas inform parents' perceptions of their own children, as well as providing a basis for evaluating oneself and others as parents. Mediating the relationship between parents' cultural beliefs and behavior are other factors such as the child's own individual characteristics, competing cultural ideas, and situational factors such as parents' work and the composition of the family.

Parental ethnotheories are closely related to other aspects of the child's culturally constructed environment. This environment is not a random collection of unrelated social customs, aesthetic values, interpersonal interactions, physical situations, and beliefs about the world (Harkness and Super 2005). Rather, the various components of the child's environment together constitute a developmental niche (Super and Harkness 1986, 2002), which is conceptualized as three interactive subsystems. First, the physical and social settings provide places and people that constitute the child's learning environment. Second, customs and practices of care offer opportunities to acquire various competencies, from reading to self-regulation, from playing baseball to caring for an infant sibling. Finally, the psychology of the caretakers, particularly parents' ethnotheories of the child and of development, shape the choices that parents make in relation to the settings that their children inhabit and the competencies they acquire; parents' ethnotheories are also evident in parent-child interactions.

Parental Ethnotheories of Infants' Learning and Development

Cultural learning starts early in life, as the universal strands of the infant's developmental agenda are interwoven with the cultural agenda for normative development communicated by the infant's developmental niche (Super and Harkness 2009, see also chapter 12, this volume). A study of parental ethnotheories in five cultures (Harkness, Super, et al. 2007) indicated that mothers' ideas and practices related to infant development vary substantially, even among middle-class, post-industrial Western communities. The samples for the study were drawn from the International Baby Study (IBS), a longitudinal study of caretaking ideas and practices for infants from the prenatal period to 2 years of age in the United States and the Netherlands, augmented with partial replications in Spain, Italy, and Korea. Study sites in each country were chosen to be broadly representative of a local middle-class population in a city or region. The goal of the study was not to establish national profiles, much less capture intracultural variability within increasingly multicultural populations, but rather to identify shared parental ideas and their relationship to parenting practices and child outcomes within somewhat homogeneous groups in each cultural site.

Semistructured interviews with the mothers when their infants were 2 months old indicated that parental ethnotheories of infant care and development were characterized by a relatively small number of themes and associated practices. Based on detailed coding of the transcribed interviews, a "salience index" of themes and practices was derived for each of the five samples. Cultural variability in the occurrence of these themes and practices suggests that infants in each place were learning distinctive sets of skills.

The themes of cognitive processing and stimulation of cognitive development, for example, were emphasized most by the U.S. mothers. When asked what they thought their baby's most important development need was at this time, the U.S. parents tended overwhelmingly to mention stimulation. As one mother said:

> I think he needs to be warm, to be fed, to be clean, dry, that kind of thing, but I also think he definitely needs some stimulation. There are times when he is in a chair and we're not paying attention to him or, you know . . . he needs some stimulation, something of interest to look at, something to, you know, just for him to play with.

These mothers had plenty of resources that could be incorporated into the baby's settings of daily life in order to provide stimulation, as one mother described:

> Somebody got us a video. It's Baby Einstein. It works a lot with colors and music and just stimulating, so we play that for him. Not every day, but almost every day. Just, there's a whole different range of things. One of

them is colors. One is language. The other one is just, you know, shapes
and . . . it's stimulating to him. We try to stimulate him in some way.

The mothers also had strong direction from professional, "expert"
sources of advice about the importance of stimulation, as one mother
commented:

> You hear about studies of brain development and having the brain make
> certain connections at certain points so early on, and if they're not ex-
> posed to music or things like that, that certain parts of their brain won't
> develop as well . . . things in my baby magazines that they give you in
> the OB/GYN office, books that you buy that tell you how to raise your
> kids. Experts, I guess.

The Korean mothers were also concerned about stimulating their
babies' cognitive development, and they approached this task in terms of
early academic training. As one mother said:

> I play music to her or I play tapes with a recorded story so she can listen
> to them. The stories are recorded in Korean and in English. The earlier
> she starts the better.

Like the U.S. mothers, the Korean mothers also added special sources of
stimulation to the baby's settings of daily life; as one mother observed:

> My baby looks at new things very intensively for a long time. I think he
> recognizes things and he is thinking . . . I like it. It is his brain develop-
> ment. I would like to show him lots of things to help and encourage his
> brain development. . . . I put some pictures on the wall to show him
> things. . . . I would like to do more for him.

In contrast to both the U.S. and Korean mothers, the Italian mothers
spoke about stimulation more in terms of social relationships and socio-
emotional intelligence, both related to the theme of emotional closeness.
In response to the interviewer's question about stimulating the baby, one
mother responded:

> Yes, we stimulate him. . . . Actually, my husband makes him jump, he
> is the "baby skier," the "baby pilot." His father makes him do all these

things and he is crazy about that, I mean he seems to understand, it sounds impossible, but he really gets crazy, as soon as he sees his dad he really brightens up. He smiles at me when I talk to him, if he hears my voice or I stand in front of him and say "Marco!" then he smiles.

For these Italian mothers, the most important opportunities for the baby's learning and development seemed to be through social interaction with others:

In my opinion he is a demanding little boy, I mean he wants to see, to do things. I don't think he likes being alone, at least now, maybe because he gets bored . . . and also because he is used to having me or other people around talking to him: aunt, grandpa or this woman who takes care of my father. There's always somebody talking to him, perhaps he's more used to seeing faces than to playing. . . . He has so much fun when somebody talks to him, puts him on the couch, plays with him, or on his bed. . . . When he's in the mood, he has more fun than with his toys!

Among the Spanish mothers, the themes of socio-emotional closeness and social intelligence were also frequently expressed. For these mothers, stimulation was described as available from the wider social and physical environment:

I believe that it is important for the baby to go out to get some fresh air and sunshine and . . . so that she relates to her environment. . . . There are some things that she doesn't see in the house. The trees, the branches, she looks at them and she likes looking at the children in the street. . . . All these are different kinds of stimulation that she doesn't see in the house.

Finally, the Dutch mothers were unique in their emphasis on the importance of rest and regularity of routines as a necessary foundation for all aspects of development. Taking the baby out for a walk in the carriage, for example, could either stimulate or calm the baby, as one mother described:

Now, I have the idea that it's healthy to be outside and he really likes it . . . also when he's restless like yesterday evening . . . and then I just go about a block with him . . . and then often he just goes to sleep.

In contrast to their concern with the baby's healthy development through rest and regularity, two cornerstones of the traditional Dutch "three R's of child-rearing (see Super, Harkness, et al. 1996), these mothers had relatively low expectations for stimulating early cognitive development, instead emphasizing the importance of maintaining a calm, positive state of arousal in the baby. As one mother responded to a question about what activities or experiences she wanted her baby to have:

> It's not that I take him to baby swimming lessons [a typical activity in this community], but we have little outings with my husband, the three of us go out and have a nice time. When he's had his bath, I give him a little massage with lotion. You know, I do what he enjoys. Or I read books with him, or he likes pictures, showing him pictures, that kind of thing. . . . You notice that he likes it, and it makes him calm.

As these examples suggest, the mothers in our five samples viewed the development of their young infants through distinctively different cultural lenses. Their ethnotheories of early care and development assigned differential importance to the acquisition of various kinds of competence, including cognitive competence, socio-emotional intelligence, and self-regulation of state of arousal. "Learning" according to these mothers could be accomplished through various different means; this in turn implied different roles for mothers.

For the U.S. mothers in our study, "stimulation" was considered the basis for learning, and it could be provided through objects in the environment, including the latest video technology. The mother's role, according to this implicit parental ethnotheory, was primarily to provide "stimulation" by making sure that the infant's immediate environment included plenty of interesting objects that would stimulate the baby's "brain development," thus equipping him for a successful transition to school and beyond.

The Korean mothers were also concerned about their babies' early brain development but they assigned themselves a more proximal role in providing stimulation. This is evident in the quotes: "*I* play music to her or *I* play tapes with a recorded story" and "*I* would like to show him lots of things to help and encourage his brain development." The mothers' proximal role was also evident in the ways that they set up the baby's environment: for example, in one home, pictures for the baby to look at were put on the wall over the sofa, where the baby could only see them while being held by the mother or other caretaker.

The Italian mothers also saw themselves as direct providers of stimulation for the baby. But in their implicit model, "stimulation" meant social interaction, not providing interesting objects or instructional materials. Speaking within the framework of this model, the mother points to social expressiveness—a smile—as evidence that the baby "understands" (exactly what he understands is not made explicit). According to this ethnotheory, it would appear that no amount of social stimulation is too much—the baby is accustomed to having people around talking to him all the time, and thrives on it.

Similarly for the Spanish mothers, the baby was perceived as an essentially social creature who demanded attention and interaction. Taking the baby outside to "the street," as it was often expressed, was a way to vary the baby's environment, thus providing various kinds of stimulation—sensory, visual, auditory, as well as social. The importance of the daily walk was emphasized by doctors, relatives—"everyone" (as one mother said)—as beneficial to both baby and mother.

Finally, the Dutch mothers' talk about their babies recalls the emphasis on rest and regularity seen in our opening vignette. We have dubbed this ethnotheory, with its focus on maintaining health and well-being through a regular and restful routine, the "horticultural model" of child-rearing, in an allusion to the flower bulb fields surrounding this community. Just provide the right conditions and monitor the child's state carefully, according to this model, and the child will develop nicely and learn what she needs along the way. Showing pictures to the baby, in this framework, was an activity intended to calm, not to educate.

Thematicity in Parental Ethnotheories of the Child

As the above examples illustrate, parental ethnotheories about their children are apparent from early on in the ways that parents talk about their infants. Indeed, some parental ethnotheories are already in evidence during pregnancy: as one American mother recounted to us, "Of course, I read to him before he was born." A striking aspect of these ethnotheories is their consistency across domains as well as across developmental time. As with cultural models more generally (Quinn and Holland 1987), it appears that parental ethnotheories are characterized by a small number of themes that can be used for many different purposes. This quality of thematicity is captured by a study of parents' descriptions of their children, a component of the International Study of Parents, Children, and Schools (ISPCS) (Harkness, Blom, et al. 2007; Harkness and Super 2005). In each of the seven cultural sites for this study, researchers recruited a sample of 60 families with target children divided evenly into five age groups balanced for birth order and sex: 6 months, 18 months, 3 years, 4.5 years, and 7–8 years. The sample families again were broadly middle-class, with one or both parents employed and no major health problems; most of them were nuclear families with both parents present in the home; and parents in each sample were all native-born to that culture. The study sites were located in communities in Sweden, Poland, the Netherlands, Italy, Spain, Australia, and the United States. The samples of children did not overlap with those of the later International Baby Study; in addition, they were older. Nevertheless, there is remarkable continuity in the cultural themes expressed by parents from the same cultural communities that were represented in both studies (Spain, Italy, the Netherlands, and the United States).

Parents' descriptions of their children were elicited in the semistructured interviews carried out in the ISPCS; in addition, the parents' perceptions of their children's characteristics were interwoven throughout the interviews. As we listened to these accounts, we came to recognize them as not only individual perceptions but also cultural constructions that framed parents' experiences of their own child. In these constructions, we could see evidence for a cultural model of "the child," to which a particular child was implicitly compared. Although such cultural models are by definition as unique as the culture to which they belong, they can be indexed by patterns of descriptive words or phrases found to varying extents in parents' descriptions in various settings. Parents from all six samples described their children as sociable, loving, active, and strong willed: frequencies of each of these descriptors varied from at least 5 percent to over 14 percent of all descriptors and were among the top 10 most frequently used. Beyond this common core of parental perceptions of young children, however, group differences emerged in the particular kinds of qualities that engaged parents' attention.

Among the American parents, the attention to cognitive abilities seen in the IBS was typical: the highest frequency American descriptors included "intelligent" and "cognitively advanced" as well as "asks questions." Along with these qualities, the American parents described their children as "independent" and even "rebellious." At the opposite extreme were the Italian parents, who rarely described their children as intelligent and never characterized them as cognitively advanced. Instead, these parents talked about their children as being even tempered, well balanced, and *simpatico*—a group of characteristics suggesting social and emotional competence further supported by the characterization "asks questions," which for these families was an aspect of being sociable and communicative (see also chapter 10, this volume). The Italian parents also described their children as "knowing what they want," a less aggressive version of strong will than the American "rebellious." Like the Italian parents, the Dutch parents also focused more on their children's social qualities, describing them as "agreeable" and "enjoying life." The attribution of having a "long attention span" is a high-frequency descriptor only for the Dutch parents, as is being "regular"—not surprisingly given these parents' concern with rest and regularity and its benefits. For the Dutch parents, the descriptor "asks questions" may be linked with "seeks attention," two aspects of dependent behavior. The profile of descriptors for these parents, then, indicates a child who is positive in mood, regular in habits, and able to entertain himself for periods of time although needing attention every so often. The Swedish parents were similar to the Dutch parents in describing their children as "persistent," a quality closely related to having a long attention span. However, the most frequently used descriptors of the Swedish parents—agreeable, well balanced, even tempered, secure, and (most frequently of all) happy—indicated what may be a cultural ideal for these parents. The Spanish parents' descriptions again focus on social qualities, indexed by terms for social maturity and "good character"; these descriptions suggest a cultural model of the child centered on an ideal of the good citizen and family member. This conceptual cluster of attributes was balanced by attention to the child's cognitive abilities as expressed by the descriptors "intelligent" and "alert."

The Australian parents appeared similar to the U.S. parents in their focus on cognitive competence as indicated by the descriptors "intelligent" and "asks questions." For these parents, "happy" was also a frequent descriptor. Unlike all other samples, however, the Australian parents seemed to focus more on the child's emotional state and reactivity, as suggested by the descriptors "calm" and "sensitive."

In summary, the patterns of both cross-cultural similarity and difference in parents' descriptions of their own children suggest that these descriptions are culturally constructed in the sense that there are locally shared ideas about what child qualities are most important, most worthy of note. Comparing across the six cultural samples, there is evidence of commonality in the group of descriptors that were among the most frequent in all of the samples. At the same time, the particular ways that these are combined with other, more culture-specific profiles of descriptors suggests that each community has its own unique perspective on the nature of the child. Within the four cultural communities that were sampled for both the ISPCS and the IBS, there is evident continuity of themes: from a focus on cognitive stimulation through toys and videos to "remarkable" intelligence in the U.S. samples, from social stimulation to socio-emotional competence in the Italian studies, from the "three R's" of rest, regularity, and good hygiene to the calm, happy and well-regulated child in the Dutch studies, and from social creature to good citizen in the Spanish studies.

Parental Ethnotheories and Children's Learning: Three Challenges

The developmental niche framework makes evident the kind of systematic regularity that culture provides—environmental organization that emphasizes repeatedly or with singular salience the culture's core "messages." As Super and Harkness have suggested elsewhere (Super and Harkness 1999), it is through such cultural thematicity that the environment works its most profound influences on development. This quality of "contemporary redundancy" is important for the acquisition of skills and competencies, as it offers multiple opportunities for learning the same thing, whether that "thing" is reading, sibling caretaking, or the communication of emotions. Similarly, the elaboration of themes across stages, over the course of developmental time, reinforces lessons learned earlier and recasts them in a more adequate format for meeting the challenges of increasing maturity.

Despite its qualities of redundancy and thematicity across development, however, parental ethnotheories are not always easily translated into action. Other factors mediate the relationship between ideas and behavior and contribute to the challenges of parenting in any culture. One frequent dilemma for American parents, for example, is the issue of competing cultural models related to family time and time for children's activities. In one such situation, the two senior authors of this paper were confronted with their daughter's invitation to join a prestigious indoor soccer team. There was only one drawback—the team would practice on Saturday evenings from 6:00 to 8:00 p.m., exactly the time when the family would otherwise be sitting down to dinner together. Fortunately for the parents, the issue was easily settled since the family was about to leave for a period of research in the Netherlands. More typically, however, parents must prioritize the importance of various cultural models, often derived from different sources, as they choose which one to instantiate.

Individual qualities of the child also may alter the ways that parental ethnotheories are used in practice. Research about parents' perceptions of their children's temperaments in the seven cultural samples of the ISPCS, however, suggests that even this adaptation to individual variability is culturally structured (Super, Axia, et al. 2007). Parents of children aged 3 years, 4.5 years, and 7–8 years in each of the seven cultural samples filled out the Behavioral Style Questionnaire (McDevitt and Carey 1978) to assess their children's temperaments in the framework of the nine-dimensional model developed by Thomas and Chess (Thomas and Chess 1977). They also made a global rating of their child's overall "difficultness." Although parents in most of the cultural samples tended to associate difficultness with low adaptability and negative mood, there were important exceptions. The Italian parents, for example, did not associate negative mood with difficultness; on the other hand, they did find being slow to warm up in new social situations to be a difficult aspect of young children's temperament. As they explained in interviews, the ability to move quickly and gracefully into new social situations was considered an important skill for navigating various gatherings of family and friends from a young age. This emphasis on the importance of social competence, as we have seen previously with regard to Italian mothers' talk about their infants and Italian parents' descriptions of their children, underlines the point that "difficult" behavior—behavior that requires an uncomfortable change of parenting practices—varies across cultures.

When families move from their culture of origin to a new environment, parents face a different kind of challenge: how to preserve the most meaningful aspects of the children's developmental niches while incorporating necessary changes. Research on Asian immigrant families in the United States suggests that parental ethnotheories travel relatively well, and that they are at least partially instantiated in parenting practices in the new environment. For example, Parmar, Harkness, and Super (2004, 2008) found that Asian immigrant parents of preschoolers thought that they should be teachers rather than playmates to their young children, and that they actually did engage in more educational activities with their children than did a Euro-American comparison group. Likewise, Raghavan, Harkness, and Super (2009) found that Asian Indian mothers focused more on qualities such as being hospitable and responsible when describing their daughters, in contrast to the Euro-American comparison group of mothers who described their daughters more in terms of independence and being athletic. Relatedly, the Indian immigrant daughters spent more time at home with their families and entertaining guests, whereas the Euro-American girls spent more time in sports.

Parenting Ethnotheories and Children's Successful Development

As our beloved friend and colleague the late Harry McGurk used to say, there are many ways to bring up children successfully. Nevertheless, as Harry noted, the literature on parenting is replete with studies of parents "at risk" and failures of parenting; there is little research to be found on successful parenting. Perhaps it was Harry's energetic and optimistic approach to life that led him to suggest there is something important to be learned by focusing on the positive, and his own experiences working closely with colleagues from other countries that directed him to cross-cultural interests. It was his opinion that cross-cultural studies of normal, well-functioning families can illuminate different pathways to successful parenting, thereby making it possible to see our own culturally designated routes in a new light as well.

Parental ethnotheories provide a framework for understanding the ways that parents think about their children, their families, and themselves, and the mostly implicit choices that parents make about how to bring up the next generation. Parents' cultural beliefs about children's learning, as we have seen in this chapter, vary widely even within the Western world, both in terms of what children need to learn and how parents can help them in this process. Likewise, cultural models of children's successful development—as reflected in the qualities parents implicitly choose to highlight when they describe their children—also vary in subtle but profound ways. Understanding these ideas, and their instantiation in the child's developmental niche of everyday life, can yield new perspectives on children's learning for the benefit of both research scientists and children's most ardent fans—their parents.

Bibliography

D'Andrade, Roy, and Claudia Strauss. *Human Motives and Cultural Models.* Cambridge: Cambridge University Press, 1992.

Harkness, Sara, Marolijn J. M. Blom, Alfredo Oliva, Ughetta Moscardino, Piotr O. Zylicz, Moïses Ríos Bermúdez, Xin Feng, Giovanna Axia, and Charles M. Super. "Teachers' Ethnotheories of the 'Ideal Student' in Five Western Cultures." *Comparative Education* 43, no. 1 (February 2007): 113–35.

Harkness, Sara, and Charles M. Super. "Parental Ethnotheories in Action." Pp. 373–92 in *Parental Belief Systems: The Psychological Consequences for Children*, 2nd ed., edited by Irving Sigel, Ann V. McGillicuddy-DeLisi, and Jacqueline J. Goodnow. Hillsdale, N.J.: Erlbaum, 1992.

——. "Themes and Variations: Parental Ethnotheories in Western Cultures." Pp. 61–79 in *Parental Beliefs, Parenting, and Child Development in Cross-Cultural Perspective*, edited by Kenneth H. Rubin and Ock-Boon Chung. New York: Psychology, 2005.

Harkness, Sara, Charles M. Super, Oumar Barry, Marian Zeitlin, Jennifer Long, and Semou Sow. "Assessing the Environment of Children's Learning: The Developmental Niche in Africa." Pp. 133–55 in *Assessment of Abilities and Competencies in the Era of Globalization*, edited by Elena Grigorenko. New York: Springer, 2009.

Harkness, Sara, Charles M. Super, Ughetta Moscardino, Jong-Hay Rha, Marjolijn J. M. Blom, Blanca Huitrón, Caroline A. Johnston, Mary Sutherland, On-Kang Hyun, Giovanna Axia, and Jesus Palacios. "Cultural Models and Developmental Agendas: Implications for Arousal and Self-Regulation in Early Infancy." *Journal of Developmental Processes* 2 (Spring 2007): 5–39.

McDevitt, Sean D., and William B. Carey. "The Measurement of Temperament in 3- to 7-Year-Old Children." *Journal of Child Psychology and Psychiatry* 19, no. 3 (July 1978): 245–53.

Nsamenang, A. Bame, and Michael E. Lamb. "The Acquisition of Socio-Cognitive Competence by Nso Children in the Bamenda Grassfields of Northwest Cameroon." *International Journal of Behavioral Development* 16, no. 3 (September 1993): 429–41.

Parmar, Parminder, Sara Harkness, and Charles M. Super. "Asian and Euro-American Parents' Ethnotheories of Play and Learning: Effects on Pre-School Children's Home Routines and School Behavior." *International Journal of Behavioral Development* 28, no. 2 (March 2004): 97–104.

———. "Teachers or Playmates? Asian Immigrant and Euro-American Parents' Participation in Their Young Children's Daily Activities." *Social Behavior and Personality: An International Journal* 36, no. 2 (2008): 163–76.

Quinn, Naomi, and Dorothy Holland. "Culture and Cognition." Pp. 3–42 in *Cultural Models in Language and Thought*, edited by Dorothy Holland and Naomi Quinn. Cambridge: Cambridge University Press, 1987.

Raghavan, Chemba, Sara Harkness, and Charles M. Super. *Parental Ethnotheories in the Context of Immigration: Asian Indian Immigrant and Euro-American Mothers and Daughters in an American Town.* Submitted for publication, 2009.

Serpell, Robert, and Jacqueline Jere-Folotiya. "Developmental Assessment, Cultural Context, Gender, and Schooling in Zambia." *International Journal of Psychology* 43, no. 2 (2008): 88–96.

Sternberg, Robert J., Barbara E. Conway, Jerry L. Ketron, and Morty Bernstein. "People's Conceptions of Intelligence." *Journal of Personality and Social Psychology* 41, no. 1 (1981): 37–55.

Super, Charles M. "Cultural Variation in the Meaning and Uses of Children's Intelligence." In *Expiscations in Cross-Cultural Psychology*, edited by Jan G. Deregowski, Suzanne Dziurawiec, and Richard C. Annis. Lisse: Swets and Zeiglinger, 1983.

Super, Charles M., Giovanna Axia, Sara Harkness, Barbara Welles-Nyström, Piotr Olaf Zylicz, Moïses Rios Bermudez, Sabrina Bonichini, Parminder Parmar, Ughetta Moscardino, Violet Kolar, Jesus Palacios, and Harry McGurk.

"Culture, Temperament, and the 'Difficult Child' in Seven Western Cultures." *European Journal of Developmental Science* 2 (2007): 136–57.

Super, Charles M., and Sara Harkness. "The Developmental Niche: A Conceptualization at the Interface of Child and Culture." *International Journal of Behavioral Development* 9, no. 4 (December 1986): 545–69.

———. "The Environment as Culture in Developmental Research." Pp. 279–323 in *Measurement of the Environment in Developmental Research*, edited by Theodore Wachs and Sarah Friedman. Washington, D.C.: American Psychological Association, 1999.

———. "Culture Structures the Environment for Development." *Human Development* 45, no. 4 (2002): 270–74.

———. "The Developmental Niche of the Newborn in Rural Kenya." Pp 85–97 in *The Newborn as a Person: Enabling Healthy Infant Development Worldwide*, edited by J. Kevin Nugent, Bonnie Petrauskas, and T. Berry Brazelton. New York: Wiley, 2009.

Super, Charles M., Sara Harkness, Natalie Van Tijen, Ellen Van Der Vlugt, Jarissa Dykstra, and Marinka Fintelman. "The Three R's of Dutch Child Rearing and the Socialization of Infant Arousal." Pp. 447–66 in *Parents' Cultural Belief Systems: Their Origins, Expressions, and Consequences*, edited by Sara Harkness and Charles M. Super. New York: Guilford, 1996.

Thomas, Alexander, and Stella Chess. *Temperament and Development*. New York: Brunner/Mazel, 1977.

Part II
LEARNING AS A SOCIAL PROCESS

CHAPTER FIVE

LEARNING THROUGH OBSERVATION IN DAILY LIFE

Suzanne Gaskins and Ruth Paradise

Learning through observation in daily life is a universal learning strategy in childhood and beyond. Observational learning typically occurs in familiar contexts in which one person performs an activity while another person, who knows less, watches them do it. In the case of children, they might intentionally watch because they want to learn, but they might also watch for the fun of watching or just for the pleasure of the company of the person who is working, such that learning then becomes an incidental byproduct of social life. Learning through observation, however, involves more than just picking up a discrete skill; it is complex and culturally situated.

After two examples to illustrate the enormous range of behaviors that fall within the category of learning through observation, the chapter provides an overview of recent thinking about this learning strategy by reviewing underlying theoretical accounts and identifying two key characteristics that have been consistently recognized in the literature. We then introduce a new characteristic we believe is central to an understanding of observation that previously has not been widely recognized. Finally, we address two areas where there is a risk of underestimating the power of observational learning, first exploring how observational learning is coordinated with but distinct from other learning strategies, and then highlighting the wide range of content that can be learned with this strategy. While learning through observation is clearly a universal characteristic of our species, we argue that some cultures, because of their understandings of childhood and learning, provide environments that maximize the opportunities for this kind of learning and lean more heavily on it as a tool of cultural transmission. In these cultures, the potential to learn through observation may be amplified. Because of the wealth of documentation and our own research interests,[1] many of the extended examples in this chapter are drawn from New World indigenous cultures, but examples from other parts of the world are also included to demonstrate that many cultures around the world share a serious commitment to learning through observation.

Examples of Learning through Observation of Everyday Life

We begin with an example of adult learning, to illustrate the capacity of "full-throttle" observational learning and to emphasize this is not an age-specific form of learning. Nash (1958) describes how Mayan workers in a new factory in Guatemala were trained to use a complex foot loom to weave "in a manner similar to learning situations in the home and throughout childhood":

> For five or six weeks . . . most of the time is spent in observing the op-
> erations of the person running the machine. . . . In one case a girl . . .
> watched the operator go through the motions of running the loom. She
> neither asked questions nor was given advice . . . at the end of this time
> she announced that she was ready to run a loom. . . . [T]he machine
> was turned over to her and she operated it, not quite as rapidly as the
> girl who had just left it, but with skill and assurance. What went on in
> the "training" period? . . . She observes and internally rehearses the set
> of operations until she feels able to perform. (26)

This example contains some of the more striking characteristics of learning through the observation of others: (1) the learning process takes place in the culturally structured context of ongoing work, and the model's primary motivation during the activity was the weaving itself, that is, to get something done *other than teaching or demonstrating*; (2) the learner was *not expected to contribute* to the work in any significant way while learning; and (3) the learner was given *primary responsibility for organizing the learning task*, including structuring the learning problem, directing and sustaining attention, and assessing when enough learning had occurred for her to be ready for her own competent performance. This example shows how effective observational learning can be. It does not, however, illustrate the complications of studying learning through observation in the less structured everyday environments more typical for learning in childhood. Those will be taken up in the next example.

While this example is of adult learning, it reflects a broad cultural commitment in Mayan culture to just this sort of learning. As in many indigenous cultures in the Americas, as well as others throughout the world, the socialization of Mayan children relies intentionally on their learning through observation of others, including learning how to weave. Not only does Nash report that weaving is learned at home in the same way the girl learned to weave in the factory, but Childs and Greenfield (1980) report a virtually identical process for Zinacanteco Mayan girls learning to weave in Chiapas, Mexico.

Weaving is only one of a wide range of skills, behaviors, and responses that children learn through observation, but not all of them are so easy to recognize. Young children learning through observing everyday activities do not show the same compact learning strategy seen in the weaver above who is learning a new commercial skill. The most difficult challenge for studying this kind of learning is that it is often an unmarked, fully integrated, almost invisible, part of everyday interactions. It often occurs when a caregiver or other "teacher" has no specific intention to teach, and sometimes even when the child has no specific intention to learn. For this reason, it may appear that learning happens through a kind of osmosis. For example, every Yucatec Maya girl learns tortilla-making before she is of marriageable age. However, it is rare to see a girl of any age spending concentrated periods of time intentionally observing others making tortillas, even though they regularly spend time around the hearth, and since the corn dough is considered sacred, children are not allowed to use it to practice. But one day, the girl will offer to help, sit down at the hearth with her mother, and begin to make tortillas. With no evidence of verbal instructions and no encouragement, she has learned the complicated and subtle art of turning a sticky wad of dough into a well-formed circle and thus takes, by virtue of her competence, a giant step toward full participation in the shared social world of women. Because learning does not occur in marked events, there are more retrospective descriptions of such learning in ethnographic reports than direct observations of it.

The following example, captured on videotape, demonstrates how subtle and fleeting learning through observation can be, and therefore why it is often difficult to see, let alone to measure.

> Adi, five-years-old, was at home with her mother, who was making tortillas in the kitchen alcove attached to the one-room house. Adi walked in to talk to her mother for a few minutes, and in the course of conversation, watched her mother at work, forming each tortilla on a small piece of plastic through (1) gentle pressure applied while simultaneously rotating the dough stuck to the plastic (much like a potter shaping clay on a wheel), (2) a few quick pats of the dough paired with turns of the plastic to smooth it out, and then (3) rotation of the tortilla to apply an even edge. (It is the second, "patting" movement that is the most dramatic and iconic motion, which also makes a loud, distinctive sound of beating on the table.) Soon, Adi returned to the main room and looked around for something to do. A fragment of a plastic bag was nearby on the floor, and she picked it up and stretched it. She licked her knee, then stretched the plastic over it, and explored how stuck the plastic was to her body by trying to wiggle it. As the plastic dried, it no longer stuck, and when she saw this, she rotated the plastic several times on her knee by hitting and twisting it with her open palm, *a movement very similar to what she had just observed in the kitchen.* After a few turns of the plastic, she returned to exploring the stretchy and sticky properties of the material, repeating the patting motion as the plastic again became movable. Soon, she abandoned the plastic and moved on to some other activity.

This example shares almost nothing substantive with the example of the mature learner of weaving, yet it is also very typical of how children who are beginning to learn everyday tasks learn through observation of others. Not only was Adi's mother unaware of any learning, but also quite likely Adi herself was making no conscious effort to learn. If it had not been caught on tape, neither would the researcher have made the connection between the visit to the kitchen and the brief, playful exploration of the plastic sheet's stickiness and how to rotate it.

The same emphasis on observational learning seen among the Maya has been particularly well documented for other Native American groups,

Figure 5.1. During a celebration, a Yucatec Mayan girl watches as the cook serves the meal (photo by S. Gaskins, copyright 2009)

where learning through observation takes place in settings where adults and children of all ages are present and can be observed. For example, Don Talayesva, in recalling his own Hopi childhood, reports, "Learning to work was like play. We children tagged around with our elders and copied what they did" (Simmons 1942, 51). Philips (1972) noted that Warm Springs Indian children "are present at many adult interactions as silent but attentive observers . . . [and] that there are many adult conversations to which children pay a great deal of silent, patient attention" (385). Wilbert (1979) noted that among South American Warao canoe makers, "By the time a child can hold a paddle in his hands, he has observed his elders on so many occasions that paddle shaft and handle slide into the small fists almost naturally" (317). Although observational learning refers to learning that often depends on using all of the senses (Paradise and Rogoff 2009), it has probably come to be identified as "observational" because of the apparent centrality of the visual aspect of this learning. Children are expected and told to "use their eyes" (e.g., Briggs 1970; Cazden and John 1971; Chisholm 1996). Yet children are also expected to get "close" to their surroundings with all of their senses (Maurer 1977, 94).

This kind of learning is found in virtually every ethnographic description of children's lives from around the world and their socialization into patterns of cultural meaning and everyday activities. As we will see, observational learning incorporates the full range of cultural content. In many of these cultures, it is the primary teaching/learning strategy: for example, "No formal instruction is practiced among the [!Kung] . . . learning . . . comes from the children's observation of the more experienced" (Marshall 1958, 286). Ethnographic accounts beyond those of indigenous societies in America that point to observation playing an important role in learning span the globe and include, among others, Polynesia (Ritchie and Ritchie 1979), Borneo (Williams 1969), Tahiti (Levy 1973), Punan Bah of Sarawak (Nicolaisen 1988), Meriam of Torres Straits (Bird and Bird 2002), Bantu (Read 1960), Mbuti Pygmies (Turnbull 1965), and the Kpelle of Liberia (Lancy 1996). Even in those cultures where there is a strong commitment to school-based learning, much of what children learn comes from the observation of others in shared, everyday activities (see, e.g., Corbett 2004; Harper 1987), although it is often not given much weight in those adults' cultural understanding of learning.

Theoretical Perspectives on Learning through Observation in Daily Life

This capacity to make cultural meaning from observing others' contextually grounded behavior seems to be unique to our species, even though primates also appear to be evolutionarily adapted to learn in social contexts (Boyd and Richerson 1996; Byrne 1995). In particular, humans' capacity to evaluate their social partners' intentions and understandings has been identified as a critically important development by humans over other primates, one that is used not only to coordinate social activities but also to facilitate the transmission of cultural knowledge from one generation to the next (Tomasello 1999). Importantly for this chapter, Tomasello (1999) argues that human "imitative learning" is made possible by "the ability of individual organisms to understand conspecifics as beings *like themselves* who have intentional and mental lives like their own" (5). This capacity—sometimes called "theory of mind"—allows humans to "copy" unobservable intentions and mental states in addition to observable actions. (See chapters 2 and 13, this volume, for more on the evolution of the capacity for learning.)

Recent work by developmental psychologists has identified the timing of onset for two related capacities. Both the awareness of others' intentions and the emergence of joint attention begin around the human infant's first birthday (Carpenter, Akhtar, and Tomasello 1998; Gergely, Bekkering, and Ildiko 2002; Meltzoff 1995). The additional ability to evaluate others' knowledge or other mental states as different from one's own begins around the age of 4 or 5 (Astington, Harris, and Olson 1988; Wellman 2002) and leads to the child's anticipation and interpretation of others' behaviors in social interaction given their current knowledge (including false beliefs).

Many theorists have recognized the importance of the capacity to recognize similarities between *self* and *other* for the development of a sense of membership in a social group and learning within that group. From the perspective of these theories, as children observe and participate in everyday activities with others, they use their capacity to see others as *like themselves* to motivate their mapping of cultural knowledge, practices, values, and attitudes of others to themselves, and thereby become culture-bearing members. This process has been considered universal (Redfield 1979, 91), but the resulting cultural knowledge and understanding of self depend on particular cultural traditions.

Three theories that have contributed significantly to this argument are those of Mead, Bandura, and Lave and Wenger. G. H. Mead (1962) focuses on children's observing and participating in everyday social interaction as being the means by which they develop a social self. A child "takes over" a particular organized set of responses that Mead identifies as "the generalized other," the integrated meaningful behavior or "attitudes" of other members of the social group with whom the child interacts over time (144–64). In his social learning theory, Bandura (1977, 1986) argues that humans learn a great deal vicariously through watching others, accompanied or not by imitation. Bandura's theory also recognizes that the social relations between observer and model influence the learning process, through the process of *identification* with a model, which motivates children to learn. Building on Bourdieu's (1977) theory of practice, Lave and Wenger (1991) argue that a community of practice is "an intrinsic condition for the existence of knowledge" (98) and that learning is "an integral and inseparable aspect of social practice" (31). Similar to Mead and Bandura, they claim that "learning and a sense of identity are inseparable" (Lave and Wenger 1991, 15). That is, through *legitimate peripheral participation*, learners are in fact learning to participate "in a community of practitioners as well as in a productive activity" (110). All these theorists propose that children must identify with those they are observing if they are to learn from them. When children's learning is embedded in the familiar everyday activities, this condition is usually fulfilled.

Previously Recognized Characteristics of Observational Learning

Despite its centrality in theories of human social learning, instances of observational learning are often hard to separate out from the inherent complexity of daily life activity, and descriptions of it tend to spread indiscernibly into a discussion of *all* everyday learning strategies. The phenomenon is often described in the ethnographic record, but previous accounts, and even reviews of observational learning, frequently fail to analyze it or formally identify its core characteristics. Our first step in providing such an analysis is to extract from the existing literature and then to clarify two important characteristics of learning through observation: the learner observes while participating in meaningful social activities, and the learner is actively engaged. This review will be followed by our introduction of a third characteristic that we believe is equally important but that has not been widely discussed.

Children Learn While Participating in Meaningful Social Activities

One of the earliest characteristics of observational learning to be recognized and described by anthropologists is its embeddedness in the everyday life of family and community (e.g., Fortes 1934/1970). Ethnographic reports provide numerous concrete examples of the theoretical claim that human learning depends on identifying with those around you. For observational learning to have its full power, not only must children be present but they must also be involved in the adult world—in other words, they must *belong* there.

Bolin (2006) describes how children share adults' world in the case of Highland Andes Quechua communities. "Children's culture . . . is not separated from that of adults. Children feel proud as they learn adult tasks little by little, as they sing the same songs and dance the same dances as do adults" (43). Gaskins (1999) similarly describes how Yucatec Mayan children's "engagement in their world" is grounded in adult activities: "children's daily activities are primarily structured by adult work activities. These in turn revolve around the immediate work needs of the household and the families' participation in social and religious events within the household and the larger community" (33).

Children's ongoing presence and integration in adult activities is related to the society's mode of economic production. If adults are engaged in work that is organized at the level of the home or community, rather than at the level of an institutionalized workplace outside the home, then children are likely to be around, helping out and learning effectively through observation. In the family-centered economic systems typical of most nonindustrialized societies, children are highly valued as current and potential labor. The culture's "chore curriculum" (Lancy 2008, 235) is present in their everyday lives and available for observation, much as the "social interaction curriculum" is in all cultures (LeVine and White 1986). Thus, family-based activities seem relevant and interesting to children, and they are motivated to pay attention to them.

Equally important, as children learn to do the activities that surround them, those activities become a constitutive part of their own way of seeing the world. Even when children separate themselves from adults, they continue to share the same world. For example, a group of Mazahua children eating together in the marketplace are separate from the adults, yet they recreate the same social and cultural reality observable in a nearby group of adults and babies. They are similarly seated in a circle on the ground, the food is prepared and distributed by the children as the adults do, and they evince the same calm and mature social communication and warmth during their meal. Through observation and practice, not only have they learned how to eat in this way with all the appropriate subtle social attitudes and behaviors involved, but they choose to do so even when they are in a group composed solely of children (Paradise and de Haan 2009). Holland and colleagues (1998) describe this as an ongoing learning experience by means of which one becomes a member of a figured world: "expertise, salience, and identification co-develop in an interrelated process" (122).

In their review article, Paradise and Rogoff (2009) also point to how identifying with others—wanting to belong and be like them—is an integral part of observational learning. A particularly good example of this comes from a middle-class American social and cultural setting: a family-run auto repair shop—the principal source of economic support for the family—where the majority of the family as well as other community members are regularly involved (Harper 1987). The shop owner's preteen daughter engaged in observational learning by choosing to hang around the workshop, sticking close to her father as he worked, and watching. In addition, she helped out when she could, taking on assigned tasks, and taking initiative in finding her own repair projects with which she could practice and learn. Through the coordination of observing and practicing, she learned to use automotive tools, diagnose mechanical problems, and speak the shop lingo used by the workers. This example illustrates that observational learning practices can be found in any society in those contexts where children belong, participate, and are continually present.

Children Are Active Learners

Observational learning is sometimes dismissed as insignificant because of a commonsense understanding that it is basically a passive activity—"just looking"—in contrast to the "hands-on participation" that is valued by many educational perspectives (including the constructivist approach based on Piagetian theory). Although observational learning is a meaningful way of engaging with the immediate social and physical environment, intentional physical action that is directly related to that learning often is absent. So it is especially important to clarify how observational learning is in fact an active learning strategy. Three distinct but interrelated ways show how observational learning is an active learning process: children are intrinsically motivated, take initiative to learn, and direct their attention actively to what is going on around them.

Intrinsic Motivation

Intrinsic motivation to become competent (White 1959) leads children to learn through observing without regular feedback from others beyond what the activity itself provides. In many cultures, children rarely receive direct feedback from others while observing or even while participating together in an activity or event. When children take part in activities where they belong, they have an intrinsic motivation to learn and a desire to take initiative in carrying out these activities, and therefore they are able to learn with little or no regular systematic feedback. According to Howard (1970), who observed the islanders of Rotuma, "In contrast to American parents, who seem to feel that knowledge is something like medicine—it's good for the child and must be crammed down his throat even if he does not like it—Rotuman parents acted as if learning were inevitable because the child *wants* to learn" (37). Their motivation to take part in everyday adult activities is not a simple response to the attractiveness of the activity, nor is it explained satisfactorily by a basic desire for sociality or an appreciation of immediate social companionship. Rather the intrinsic motivation children display in their readiness to become involved in and to learn about everyday adult activities appears to be born out of a deep, even if unnoticed, desire to be useful and a recognition that in order to help (or "pitch in," cf. Paradise and Rogoff 2009), they need to learn. Fiske (1997, 11) has characterized the prevalence of observational learning as evidence that "there is less child-rearing than there is 'culture-seeking.'"

However, children do not operate in a social vacuum: caregivers may encourage or even manipulate children's motivation. For instance, if children do not take what is seen as age-appropriate responsibility to be aware of ongoing activities, or if they are particularly slow in mastering some task, they may be criticized, either directly or indirectly through a report to a third party about the child (sometimes neutral, but sometimes judgmental, teasing, or sarcastic) that is intended to be overheard (Rogoff et al. 2003). Positive feedback also exists, when children learn something precociously or particularly well, but it may take a form more subtle than direct praise; for instance, their accomplishment may be reported proudly to a third party, or they may simply be allowed to participate in the activity, which by itself serves as strong positive feedback (Gaskins 2009). The goal of such indirect feedback, negative or positive, is not only to provide children with useful information about their performance but also to encourage them to be responsible for their learning.

Taking Initiative

Intrinsic motivation to learn is closely related to the capacity to take initiative and make things happen. The capacity for taking initiative that is characteristic of children's learning through observation is not, however, limited to their physical involvement with specific activities. Children display initiative even when they quietly and intently observe ongoing activities in order to find out more about them. They show initiative when they get close to or choose to remain present as "interesting" activities take place, such as the small Muslim village in Lebanon described by Williams (1968), where great numbers of children "congregate to watch a trivial but slightly out of the ordinary event" (37).

Children also take initiative when they organize activities with which they can practice and gain expertise in some partially mastered task or activity. Philips (1972) described how "in many areas of skill, the [Warm Springs Indian] child takes it upon himself to test the skill unsupervised and alone, without other people around" (386). Although children may not explicitly be encouraged to practice specific skills on their own, neither are they discouraged from doing so, even when things can go seriously wrong, as illustrated in the following example of a Quechuan boy in Peru practicing how to make a fire by himself.

> When little Marcos was five-years-old, he practiced making a fire with the use of two stones, as he had seen his parents and older siblings do. But now, instead of remaining outdoors, he sat in the doorway of a small shed used for storage. When he finally sparked a flame, it caught the dry grass spread on the floor and within a short time the roof and some objects in the shed were burning. Family and neighbors rushed to the site, helping to put out the fire with buckets of water. The little boy was scared and ashamed of what he had done. (Bolin 2006, 39)

Marcos's feeling of shame indicates that a sense of responsibility accompanies his taking initiative. He is not, for instance, simply playing with fire. His initiative is directed toward finding a way to practice a mature skill that he wants to master. Given the relative absence of feedback during the learning process, children rely more heavily on their personal disposition to become involved; they take initiative in directing their attention and finding or creating activities to practice on their own skills they have not yet mastered.

Paying Attention and Making Meaning

When observation is intentional, children may be in complete stillness but watching carefully, as in the case of Tzeltal Maya described by Maurer (1977). Here "stillness" does not imply that children are inactive but rather that children are focused on their surroundings in order to perceive them better. Rogoff and colleagues (2003) have coined the term "intent participation" to capture this kind of attention. When children's observation is less intentional, they may appear to be just hanging around, fiddling with some object, or helping others carry out specific activities, yet they may still be absorbing information.

In addition to directing their attention, they are internally processing what it is they are "taking in" (Bandura 1986). Faced with a "sea of information," (Hall 1991), they must categorize and remember what they observe. While much of the mental processing children engage in while they observe may be outside of their conscious awareness, such processing can nevertheless be crucial to their evolving understanding. Observing and making meaning of what they observe imply full, active involvement in the learning process, even when it may seem to an outsider that nothing much is happening.

While children in all cultures actively make meaning from their experiences, there is cultural variation in how much responsibility children are given for organizing the details of their everyday world (Gaskins 1999). In those societies where adult mediation of activities is highly valued, children receive much more input about structuring and assigning meaning to their experiences (see Vygotsky 1978) compared to those where they are allowed to operate more as individual agents. In the latter case, in the absence of adult guidance, children are more likely to be consistently active learners in the sense that they are intrinsically motivated to learn, taking initiative, and organizing their observing and making sense of it.

Observational Learning and Open Attention

In addition to the two previously recognized characteristics discussed above—embeddedness and active learning—we believe that observational learning often is accompanied by a unique kind of attention that has not been fully described in past accounts, called here *open attention*. In this section, we make a case for recognizing this distinct attentional stance. Based on our own ethnographic research and a reading of other accounts, we believe that this pattern of attention is regularly found in many cultures that highly value observation as a more general source of knowledge for everyone in the community, but that it has been overlooked or underreported in the past. We hope that by identifying open attention as a core characteristic of learning through observation, we will encourage others to look for it, observe it more carefully, and explore its implications.

In our view, open attention is a distinct, habitual way of taking in information from the present environment that is strikingly different from the common Euro-American way of observing. We begin with an illustration of how ways of attending can greatly differ in their effectiveness in seeing details in the physical world:

> Three Mayan brothers from Chamula, Mexico, were visiting me in Southern California, and I suggested we go hiking in the nearby foothills where I often walk. At the trailhead, we met an agitated group coming down the trail, who urged us to be careful because there was a large rattlesnake on the path just ahead. Hearing the alarm in their voices, the Chamulas asked me what was wrong. Trying not to scare them, I told them about the sighting, but added that they should not worry since I had never seen a snake on this trail. To which one of the Chamulas responded calmly, "Really? I see three right now." He then picked up some rocks and threw them at the snakes to make them move, so I could see them, too. (Rus personal communication)

We see here how the Chamula men, used to maintaining an awareness of their environmental conditions, are able to see more than the American could, despite the fact that the setting was novel for them and familiar to him. Even more strikingly, when the snakes were pointed out to the American, he could not see them until they were made to move. This example underscores the potential development of acuity of observation when it is culturally valued. (Chapter 14 in this volume provides another, extended example of the importance of observation for understanding and using the plant world.)

Likewise, adults use such careful attention to discover and interpret events that occur in the community, both to know in general what is happening and to develop the immediate "common ground" needed for conversation. In Yucatec Maya villages, for instance, the default greeting is either "Where are you going?" or "Where are you coming from?" depending on whether the addressee is heading away from or toward home. But almost as likely is a statement by the speaker that "guesses" at the answer to one of the two questions, having attended to situational clues (dress, companions, objects present, time of day). This type of greeting demonstrates the cultural importance placed on an ability to discern social intent from careful observation.

To participate in this immediate use of observation in everyday life, children need to develop strong observation skills and practice them consistently in the here and now. They also need to learn how to draw conclusions by integrating new bits of information just observed with basic knowledge about the physical and social environment. In those cultures that emphasize paying careful attention to physical conditions and social events, children are expected to master these observational and integrative skills in order to be participants in everyday activities (e.g., Chavajay 1993), and as they do so, "open attention" becomes increasingly effective as a culturally honed tool for learning as well.

Open Attention Defined

Open attention is defined here as attention that is both *wide angled* and *abiding*. In open attention, the scope of attention is distributed across a wide field, in contrast to most models of attention that presume a narrow focus applied sequentially to a number of objects or events. This way of "openly" attending to what is happening in the immediate environment is not commonly valued in Euro-American culture. For example, a student in a U.S. classroom whose gaze travels around the room is likely to be accused of not paying attention. Just this sort of cultural difference in the scope of attention is reported by Chavajay and Rogoff (1999) in their study of European American and Guatemalan Maya mothers and infants. The

European American mothers and infants attended to multiple objects and events serially, in short but discrete time segments, while the Guatemalan Mayan mothers and infants distributed their attention across multiple objects/events simultaneously. This wide-angled, distributed attentional stance has several advantages for learning through observation, including event detection, awareness of contextual information, and a broader range of information processed.

In addition to being wide angled, open attention is *abiding*, that is, it is sustainable over time. Most models of attention presume that attention will be applied selectively and sporadically, brought to bear when there is something specific to be attended to. However, in culturally amplified observation during familiar everyday activities, children and adults apply their wide-angled, distributed attention skills consistently across time, whether or not they are intentionally observing something specific in order to learn, as seen in the example of Rus's Chamula visitors mentioned above.

One significant implication of this abiding, open attentional stance is that children are expected to always be observing and to keep their attention in the here and now. This allows them to observe something in the course of participating in social life and process it even before they know exactly why they need to understand it. Their attention is "on duty" by default, but in a manner that requires minimal effort. In contrast, in cultures where learning depends in large part on others' directing children's attention to specific objects and events, short-term, focused attention is more common and more valued but harder to sustain. As a result, children learning with this kind of attention more often "tune out" and sometimes fail to notice even the most obvious events occurring around them.

Concentration and Open Attention

In addition to being wide angled and abiding, open attention has a third and final characteristic that has often been noted in cases of observational learning, especially among American indigenous people: the learner's ability to sustain a high level of concentration while observing over long periods of time. Maurer (1977) describes such concentration in the case of Tseltal Mayan children: "Even a young child can stay for long periods of time in almost absolute immobility, watching attentively what the adults are doing" (94). This characteristic has been referred to as "keen" or "intense" observation by Rogoff and colleagues (2003). While it is not a defining characteristic of open attention, it is a compelling one when it is present, and it is often the key behavior that causes ethnographers to notice the existence of open attention.

Concentrated open attention is seen most often in cases where learners intentionally direct their attention toward an activity in order to learn. The central difference between the two extended examples given in the introduction is that the young woman learning to weave was concentrating intentionally on the weaving, but Adi, the young girl playing with the sheet of plastic, was *not* concentrating intentionally while watching her mother making tortillas nor later while playing with the sheet of plastic. We would argue, however, that while the two girls differ in their level of concentration and in the level of intentionality to learn, both were observing with open attention as described above. That is, even as the woman is concentrating on the weaving, she does not lose the "peripheral awareness" characteristic of open attention; likewise, while the girl shows no intentional concentration while observing her mother making tortillas, she is nonetheless fully tuned in to what is going on around her. Observational learning, then, includes both intentional and unintentional observation, but *highly focused concentration* comes into play only during intentional observation. (See Strauss 1984 for a discussion of intentional vs. incidental learning.)

Perhaps another reason intentional, concentrated observation has been emphasized in ethnographic descriptions of observational learning is that it shares with other existing models of learning the characteristic of intense focus or absorption. Concentration is central to the ideal attention aimed for in school-like learning where children are encouraged to focus on discrete, narrow, building-block lessons, one at a time, and to filter out other information from the environment (see, e.g., Diamond et al. 2007, on how to improve preschoolers' cognitive control). Concentration is also found in Csíkszentmihályi's (1990) notion of "flow," a state in which people become so absorbed in a specific activity that they lose track of time and the surrounding environment: for example, a writer at work on a manuscript or a rock climber during an assent. But while intentional open attention shares the quality of concentration with these other models of attention, the quality of that concentration differs in that it is always contextually grounded rather than detached from the setting. It appears doubtful that children and adults engaged in open attention ever lose track of time or place, even when they are concentrating intently.

The focus found in open attention has intriguing similarities to the Buddhist practice of *mindfulness* (Hanh 1987). The goal of mindful meditation is to bring awareness to the present moment. Mindfulness can involve concentrating on one's breath or other object, or on releasing one's inner thoughts, but it also can include being fully aware of (i.e., paying attention to or noticing) what is happening in the world in the present moment, in an open, nonjudgmental way. This sense is well captured in the title of a book by Kabat-Zinn (1995) about the use of mindfulness for pain management and other therapeutic uses in the West: *Wherever You Go, There You Are*. The continuous openness and full awareness of the here and now promoted by mindfulness seem closely related to the wide-angled, abiding attention that is described here as open attention.

Implications of Open Attention

Recent research by Silva, Correa-Chávez, and Rogoff (Correa-Chávez and Rogoff 2009; Silva, Correa-Chávez, and Rogoff in press) shows how Guatemalan and U.S. Mexican-heritage children are better able to learn by paying attention to interactions directed toward others, as compared to European American children who do not follow others' interactions as attentively. These researchers designed a structured learning task (how to build a simple toy) that took place in the presence of the target child but that involved an instructional activity between an adult and a different child; the target child could (but was not encouraged to) observe while "waiting for a turn." In this task, Mexican American and Guatemalan Mayan target children were more likely than European American target children to observe the instructional activity directed to the other child; European American children often "killed time" while waiting rather than observing the instruction. The Mexican American and Guatemalan children were also more likely to know how to make the other child's toy in an unannounced post-test done a week later. Ellis and Gauvain (1992) report a similar finding for Navajo children, who paid more attention to interactions when they were not participating than did their European American counterparts.

These studies show that, in contrast to European American children, children with cultural experiences rooted in Native American cultures (which value open attention) approached events happening around them as something to attend to, even when they were excluded from these events, and observation was an effective learning strategy for them. Such experimental evidence, when paired with the ethnographic evidence, suggests that there are important cultural differences in attentional stance and that open attention is an important construct for understanding the potential of learning through observation. However, much of the available evidence is often circumstantial and, by psychological research standards, imprecise. It would be useful to have additional studies that document more fully the presence and characteristics of open attention, and a survey of cultures to identify how widespread it is and where it occurs. Future research also needs to focus on identifying the specific cognitive and neuropsychology correlates of open attention, similar to the growing body of research addressing the psychological correlates of meditation (Lutz, Dunn, and Davidson 2007). In the hopes of attracting more work on the concept, our effort here is to describe open attention, as we understand it from our fieldwork among two indigenous groups in the Americas, as a distinct attentional stance whose impact on learning through observation has not fully been appreciated.

Understanding the Potential of Learning through Observation

While observational learning has long been recognized as a universal learning strategy used by children in their daily lives and has been reported in many ethnographic accounts, we argue that its unique potential as a primary learning strategy has been underestimated both because it is hard to see happening in children's everyday experience and because other learning strategies, especially verbal ones, are more central to Euro-American ethnographers' own ethnotheories of learning. As a result, learning through observation is often confounded with complementary and more discernible learning strategies rather than being considered as a legitimate learning strategy on its own that can be coordinated with other strategies. Further, the range of knowledge that can be learned with observation has often been underestimated. In this section, we take up these two topics with the goal of demonstrating more clearly how it operates in cultures where it is fully embraced as a principal learning strategy.

The Coordination of Observation with Other Kinds of Learning

In the first part of the chapter, we intentionally isolated observation as a learning strategy in order to better understand its characteristics. We turn now to showing how it is found in the child's natural world, seamlessly integrated with other learning strategies. While children can and do learn many things through observation alone, observational learning is often coordinated with both teaching strategies (primarily under the control of adults or other "guides") and other learning strategies (primarily under the control of the learner). As Howell (1988) says about Chewong children, "It is up to each individual to absorb knowledge of all kinds from watching, listening, participating, and by asking questions" (162).

While learning through observation requires an active learner, four complementary teaching strategies can co-occur with observation when the "teacher" has an explicit desire for the child to learn something in particular. (See chapter 7, this volume, for a more extended discussion of adult-guided learning.) First, we can identify *direct instruction* of children's learning, either verbal or nonverbal, including demonstration, directing attention to some aspect of the activity, or more rarely, verbal explanation. For example, Pettitt (1946) shows how "Yurok-Karok children played at weaving while the elders worked, but if any showed more than passing interest special instruction was given; . . . [since] imitation on the part of a child would hardly suffice to acquire the necessary knowledge" (46). Next is *learning while working*, which occurs when children have already partially mastered an activity and can learn more by observing while being a "legitimate peripheral participant" with an assigned responsibility. Third, children are taught through *narrative*, or storytelling, although the child must take responsibility for extracting the lesson, thus relying on cognitive skills similar to those of observation. For example, Read (1960) describes Bantu children having to work at figuring out on their own if a proverb had been said for their benefit. Lastly, children are expected to learn from *feedback* that provides an evaluation of the competency and appropriateness of their behavior. When employed alongside observation, these teaching styles yield a co-construction of knowledge transmission between teacher and learner, where the learner's behavior retains the same three characteristics seen in more independent examples of observation: a sense of social belonging, a commitment to take responsibility for learning, and an open attentional stance.

Children themselves also coordinate learning through observation with other learning strategies that fall under their own control. Again, in such cases, the primary characteristics of observational learning are not lost. Children often produce a *reproduction of a behavior as practice*, which can take three different forms. First, it sometimes occurs *during an activity*, in which case what is practiced is usually a specific component of what they have just observed, and the switching between observing and practicing can become very frequent. Children may be discouraged or ignored; they may receive timely feedback as correction; or if their attempt is good enough, they may even be allowed to enter into the activity as a legitimate participant.

Second, discrete skills also get individual or social *practice outside the original context*. Sometimes, children practice and explore a specific physical component of a previously observed activity with no evidence of playfulness. "[In the Andes,] they learn by copying their parents or whomever else they are in contact with, watching them work and then practicing by trying out the task or some aspect of it for themselves. Sometimes, this practice may be a useful act in itself, such as sweeping the floor or grinding some food" (Sillar 1994, 50). But specific components of social or cultural performance can also be practiced out of context, as seen in, for example, the description by Göncü and colleagues (1999) of preschool-aged African American boys working to perfect their performances of the extreme intonations of a popular radio disk jockey.

Such practice away from the original context, and often away from adults in general, helps explain how children can learn without their caregivers knowing it. De León (2005) describes a young Tzotzil Maya boy's efforts to practice surreptitiously things he has observed: "[he is observed] 'stealing' his Grampa's knife to peel fruit and putting it back surreptitiously . . . embroidering his sister's appliqués [while] hiding under beds . . . 'heating up' tortillas in a cold *comal* (pan), or experimenting with the waist loom" (3–4). (See also Reichard 1934 for an account of a young Navaho girl surreptitiously learning how to weave.)

Finally, children might engage in yet another kind of practice, a more *global reenactment of activities*, focusing on roles and scripts. Global reenactments can occur when children adopt an adult interactional stance as they work alongside adults. Watson-Gegeo (2001) describes Samoan children who at times take on adult roles in ongoing activities: "Like

105

collages, children's dramatic scripts in adult mode are strips from interactions they have heard or heard about. They often build their performances on historically real events and interactions, creatively linking them together with explanatory or interpretive detail of their own" (145).

But global reenactments are more often accomplished through pretend play. Reality-based pretend play scripts appear to be found in some form in all cultures (Schwartzman 1978), and as they pretend to process and prepare food, go to the store, get married, and so on, children both practice and interpret what they have observed (see also chapter 6, this volume). Bock and Johnson (2004) have demonstrated that the more frequently Botswana children are exposed to a daily activity, the more frequently it appears in their pretend reenactments. This kind of reality-based pretend play is complementary to learning through observation because it gives an opportunity to practice culturally organized activities that children have seen. From this vantage point, such pretense is more about understanding and interpretation than imagination, and it is often cited as evidence of observational learning in the ethnographic literature.

It should be noted that even when children concentrate on practicing particular activities or get caught up in co-constructing a world of real-world–inspired pretend, open attention is not set aside. An open attentional stance maintained during practice or play derives not only from a general cultural expectation to always pay attention to the world or from children's just being in the habit of doing so; it stems as well from the immediate practical demands of children's everyday lives that are not suspended during these activities. Even during play, children are not free of responsibilities (e.g., the care of younger siblings) in the here and now. Under these circumstances, they know they do not have *permission* to leave the here and now and enter into an inner world of imagination and fantasy, nor do they appear to have the *inclination* to do so.

What Can Be Learned through Observation?

In cultures throughout the world that emphasize and amplify learning through observation, parents have confidence in the effectiveness of observational learning, and they therefore leave much of the initiative to the children as learners, relying on their observation of ongoing activities and events to be a central mechanism for cultural transmission. For example, among the Inuit, there is "remarkably little meddling by older people in this learning process. Parents do not presume to teach their children what they can as easily learn on their own" (Guemple 1979, 50). Their confidence appears to be well placed. When observation in daily life co-occurs with other complementary learning strategies, failure to learn is rarely reported. Virtually all children seem to master a wide range of specific cultural content along the way as they strive to become competent and confident participants in their social world (Spindler and Spindler 1989). We review some of the evidence in support of our argument that when culturally amplified—through children's regular presence during daily activities, the assumption of an active learning stance, and the development of open attention—learning through observation is a powerful learning strategy. This review demonstrates that the content to be learned is far broader than just physical skills and specific tasks; in fact, all kinds of knowledge can be acquired through observation, including language, social interaction behaviors, expression of emotion, situational scripts, and even spiritual beliefs and other abstract knowledge.

For those familiar with the ethnographic socialization literature, the examples of observational learning that most often come to mind are cases of children learning everyday work skills. Often these skills take place on a regular basis in the children's presence, involve repetitive behaviors and the use of simple tools, and represent common knowledge shared across all adult members of a particular society. Examples include water carrying in Kpelle culture (Lancy 1996), manual arts and songs in adolescent males in Tapirape' Indians, Central Brazil (Wagley 1977), and sabar drumming in Griot culture (Tang 2006).

But skill-learning is by no means the only information that can be learned by watching others. Even more ubiquitous but less often labeled as a case of observational learning is language learning—not only the acquisition of vocabulary and grammar as such, but also the subtle social uses of language. Accounting for how language is learned has posed significant problems for developmental psycholinguists who have tried to explain it within the framework of existing theories of learning at their disposal, in part because they do not assign observational learning a significant role in the process. For example, most do not consider the role of speech directed to others that a child may overhear (Akhtar, Jipson, and Callanan 2001; Blum-Kulka and Snow 2002). Language socialization studies, on the other hand, have consistently demonstrated the role of observing others' talk for learning language and how to use it (Ochs and Schieffelin 1984; see also chapter 10, this volume).

At the same time they are learning how to communicate and use language appropriately, children are also learning culturally structured rules about social behavior and social roles, in large part by observing the interactions that go on around them. Learning social customs occurs in part through talk, either directed to them or to others (again, see chapter 10, this volume). For example, social categories, such as kinship relations, can also be learned by overhearing conversations among adults (Beverly and Whittemore 1993, on Mandinka children). But modeling behavior also conveys important information. This can be as basic as Zinacatecan Mayan girls learning how to sit properly, by observing that women regularly use a kneeling position (Maynard, Greenfield, and Childs 1999). They can also observe the consequences of certain social acts in their particular social worlds—what Bandura (1977) called *vicarious reinforcement*—by observing others who share a social category with them and are seen therefore to be "like me" (e.g., gender, age, race, or class). For instance, a Makiritare girl comes to understand her gendered social position through observing the ceremonial use of space by others: "She will observe that the center of the *atta* is reserved for men, that the world is made up of two concentric circles with the outer serving as support for the inner" (Guss 1982, 261). Similarly, Toren (2001) describes how children adopt a subordinate politeness posture through observation and imitation as early as 4 years old.

Many rules about emotions must be learned, including how and when to express emotions and how they are managed, labeled, and interpreted. These rules can be observed by attending to people's facial expressions, body language, speech and other audible expressions of emotion, and actions directed toward others and the physical environment. For example, Miller and Sperry (1987) report that very young girls living with their mothers in a neighborhood in South Baltimore, Maryland, learn how and when to express anger in part by watching and listening as their mothers tell stories to others about personal experiences. Moral socialization can also be learned through children's observation of the reactions of others to their behaviors (see chapter 11, this volume). Garcia-Rivera (2007) tells of how Peruvian Quechua children learn to listen to and understand the songs of specific birds as moral messengers:

> These birds have different songs that are codified from a human per-spective as forms of communication between the birds and humans. Some birds announce bad news, good news, or express collaboration with a mother in her task of raising her children. For example, if chil-dren refuse to eat, mothers often say that they can hear well the dove's song that says *punyay punyay warmachaykita punyay* [hit him, hit him, hit your little child]. According to the mothers, the dove is singing telling them to hit the child if he or she doesn't obey their mother. As children we heard this dove song and it seemed to us that it certainly did sound like *punyay punyay warmachaykita punyay*, although that phrase is an onomatopoeic adaptation of the dove's song. Normally, after hearing this song children believe that the dove knows of their disobedience and they eat up their dinner without resistance. (90)

When children accompany others to events as observers, they also learn cultural scripts, that is, events made up of predictable strings of activities motivated by shared understandings. Political and legal fo-rums, economic exchange, and religious ceremonies all have events with specific scripts that children must learn. Those cultures where children belong in most contexts offer the most opportunities for script learn-ing through observation, because they are present. For example, Lancy (1996) reports that some Kpelle children were always present, watching from the sidelines, during the presentation of legal cases to the chief, even though the talk was in "high Kpelle" that they could not easily un-derstand. Some cultures rely heavily on children's observational learning of abstract ideas. Nicolaisen (1988) describes how complex cultural ideas are learned by Punan Bah children of Sarawak: "Children, even the older ones, are rarely offered straightforward explanations on social matters, beliefs, ideas, values, or rituals. They must use their eyes and ears and reason a great deal" (205).

Such scripts are based on abstract beliefs and values that are not di-rectly observable but whose meaning is implicitly present in the cultural artifacts used, the types of participants and their assigned roles, and the symbolic enactments that occur. Talk among participants during the event, either as formal performance, informal negotiation about how to conduct the event, or commentary, can also provide important information about abstract cultural understandings. For example, Fernea (1991) describes how children's understanding is shaped from a very young age when they attend Muslim weddings and therefore observe the ritual display of a blood-stained sheet that demonstrates the bride's virginity as well as hear the accompanying discussion about honor. And Astuti and Harris (2008) report that among the Vezo, a fishing people in Madagascar, adults intentionally avoid teaching children about ancestral spirits in order to protect them from being victims of the anger of the spirits, even as they ensure that children are present for ancestral worship events since it pleases the ancestors to see their descendents. They demonstrate that children by age 9 have acquired a culturally accurate understanding of the afterlife, based on no information beyond what they observe at these events and funerals.

From this short review of ethnographic evidence, it is clear that much specific content knowledge as well as general cultural understanding can be learned through observation if and when children are present and participating in activities and events, ready to take responsibility for their learning, and bring the ability to learn through open attention. When children are not present, and therefore do not participate regularly in such activities and events, or even when they are present but are waiting to be told what to do or are paying little attention, then the effectiveness of learning through observation is substantially reduced.

Conclusion

Learning through observation in daily life is a universal human capacity. When coordinated with other teaching and learning skills, observation plays an important role in facilitating mastery of the full range of cultural knowledge and understanding children must learn to become full members of their society. When used intentionally, observational learning is easy to identify by the accompanying high level of concentration. However, it also can, and often does, occur unintentionally when a child is "simply" present and participating in everyday life, in which case it is much harder to recognize that observational learning is taking place.

Effective learning through observation of daily life depends in large measure on the quality of children's involvement with and commitment to be part of activities and settings that constitute the contexts in which such learning is accomplished, based on an identification with others who are engaged in those activities. When the quality of involvement and commitment is high, then children actively seek, organize, and digest information and experiences. They bring to these activities also an open attentional stance, anchored in the present. When its importance and potential are culturally *amplified* through these three characteristics, observational learning matures into an *expert* skill that has remarkable power.

Acknowledgments

Support for the writing of this chapter was provided to the first author by the National Science Foundation under Grant No. 0837898.

Note

1. Gaskins has done continuous fieldwork among the Yucatec Maya of Mexico for 30 years, focusing on children's everyday lives and their development from infancy through middle childhood. Paradise has studied the learning practices of Mazahuas in family, community, and primary school in Mexico City and a Mazahua community in the State of Mexico since the 1980s.

Bibliography

Akhtar, Nameera, Jennifer Jipson, and Maureen A. Callanan. "Learning Words through Overhearing." *Child Development* 72, no. 2 (March 2001): 416–30.

Astington, Janet W., Paul L. Harris, and David R. Olson, eds. *Developing Theories of Mind*. New York: Cambridge University Press, 1988.

Astuti, Rita, and Paul L. Harris. "Understanding Mortality and the Life of the Ancestors in Rural Madagascar." *Cognitive Science* 32, no. 4 (2008): 713–40.

Bandura, Albert. *Social Learning Theory*. Oxford: Prentice Hall, 1977).

———. *Social Foundations of Thought and Action: A Social Cognitive Theory*. Englewood Cliffs, N.J.: Prentice Hall, 1986.

Beverly, Elizabeth, and Robert D. Whittemore. "Mandinka Children and the Geography of Wellbeing." *Ethos* 21, no. 3 (September 1993): 235–72.

Bliege Bird, Rebecca, and Douglas W. Bird. (2002). "Constraints of Knowing or Constraints of Growing? Fishing and Collection by the Children of Mer." *Human Nature* 13, no. 2 (June 2002): 239–67.

Blum-Kulka, Shoshana, and Catherine E. Snow. *Talking to Adults: The Contribution of Multiparty Discourse to Language Acquisition*. Mahwah, N.J.: Erlbaum, 2002.

Bock, John, and Sara E. Johnson. "Subsistence Ecology and Play among the Okavango Deltas People of Botswana." *Human Nature* 15, no. 1 (March 2004): 63–82.

Bolin, Inge. *Growing Up in a Culture of Respect: Child Rearing in Highland Peru*. Austin: University of Texas Press, 2006.

Bourdieu, Pierre. *Outline of a Theory of Practice*. Cambridge: Cambridge University Press, 1977.

Boyd, Robert, and Peter J. Richerson. "Why Culture Is Common, but Cultural Evolution Is Rare." *Proceedings of the British Academy* 88 (1996): 77–93.

Briggs, Jean. *Never in Anger: Portrait of an Eskimo Family*. Cambridge, Mass.: Harvard University Press, 1970.

Byrne, Richard. *The Thinking Ape*. Oxford: Oxford University Press, 1995.

Carpenter, Melinda, Nameera Akhtar, and Michael Tomasello. "Fourteen-through Eighteen-Month-Old Infants Differentially Imitate Intentional and Accidental Actions." *Infant Behavior and Development* 21, no. 2 (1998): 315–30.

Cazden, Courtney, and Vera P. John. "Learning in American Indian Children." Pp. 252–72 in *Anthropological Perspectives on Education*, edited by Murray L. Wax, Stanley Diamond, and Fred O. Gearing. New York: Basic Books, 1971.

Chavajay, Pablo. "Independent Analyses of Cultural Variations and Similarities in San Pedro and Salt Lake." Afterword to Rogoff, Barbara, Jayanthi Mistry, Artin Göncü, and Christine Mosier. "Guided Participation in Cultural Activity by Toddlers and Caregivers." *Monographs of the Society for Research in Child Development* 58, no. 7 (1993): 162–5.

Chavajay, Pablo, and Barbara Rogoff. "Cultural Variation in Management of Attention by Children and Their Caregivers." *Developmental Psychology* 35, no. 4 (1999): 1079–90.

Childs, Carla P., and Patricia M. Greenfield. "Informal Modes of Learning and Teaching: The Case of Zinacanteco Weaving." Pp. 269–316 in *Studies in Cross-Cultural Psychology*, vol. 2, edited by Neil Warren. London: Academic, 1980.

Chisholm, James S. "Learning 'Respect for Everything': Navajo Images of Development." Pp. 167–83 in *Images of Childhood*, edited by C. Philip Hwang, Michael E. Lamb, and Irving E. Sigels. Mahwah, N.J.: Erlbaum, 1996.

Corbett, Michael. "'It Was Fine If You Wanted to Leave': Educational Ambivalence in a Nova Scotian Coastal Community 1963–1998." *Anthropology and Education Quarterly* 35, no. 4 (December 2004): 451–71.

Correa-Chávez, Maricela, and Barbara Rogoff. "Children's Attention to Interactions Directed to Others: Guatemalan Mayan and European American Patterns." *Developmental Psychology* 45, no. 3 (2009): 630–41.

Csíkszentmihályi, Mihaly. *Flow: The Psychology of Optimal Experience.* New York: Harper and Row, 1990.

de León, Lourdes. "Intent Participation and the Nature of Participation Structures: A Look from a Chiapas Mayan Community Everyday Life." Presented at the Presidential Workshop on Intent Participation, Santa Cruz, California, June 2005.

Diamond, Adele, W. Steven Barnett, Jessica Thomas, and Sarah Munro. "Preschool Program Improves Cognitive Control." *Science* 318 (2007): 1387–8.

Ellis, Shari A., and Mary Gauvain. "Social and Cultural Influences on Children's Collaborative Interactions." Pp. 155–80 in *Children's Development within Social Context*, edited by Lucien T. Winegarand and Jaan Valsiner. Hillsdale, N.J.: Erlbaum, 1992.

Fernea, Elizabeth. "Muslim Middle East." Pp. 447–70 in *Children in Historical and Comparative Perspective*, edited by Joseph M. Hawes and N. Ray Hiner. Westport, Conn.: Greenwood, 1991.

Fiske, Alan Page. Learning a Culture the Way Informants Do: Observing, Imitating, and Participating. Unpublished manuscript, University of California, Los Angeles, 1997.

Fortes, Meyer. "Social and Psychological Aspects of Education in Taleland." Pp. 14–74 in *From Child to Adult*, edited by John Middleton. 1934. Garden City, N.Y.: Natural History, 1970.

Garcia-Rivera, Fernando. Runa Hina Kay. "Imágenes de la Educación Familiar y Comunitaria Orientada al Respeto en una Comunidad Quechua." Doctoral dissertation, Departamento de Investigaciones Educativas, Centro de Investigación y de Estudios Avanzados, Mexico City, 2007.

Gaskins, Suzanne. "Children's Daily Lives in a Mayan Village: A Case Study of Culturally Constructed Roles and Activities." Pp. 25–61 in *Children's Engagement in the World*, edited by Artin Göncü. Cambridge: Cambridge University Press, 1999.

———. "Work before Play for Yucatec Maya Children." In *The Child: An Encyclopedic Companion*, edited by Richard A. Shweder et al. Chicago: University of Chicago Press, 2009 (in press).

Gergely, Gyorgy, Harold Bekkering, and Király Ildiko. "Rational Imitation in Preverbal Infants." *Nature* 415, no. 6873 (2002): 755.

Göncü, Artin, Ute Tuermer, Jyoti Jain, and Danielle Johnson. "Children's Play as Cultural Activity." Pp. 148–72 in *Children's Engagement in the World*, edited by Artin Göncü. Cambridge: Cambridge University Press, 1999.

Guemple, D. Lee. "Inuit Socialization: A Study of Children as Social Actors in an Eskimo Community." Pp. 39–71 in *Childhood and Adolescence in Canada*, edited by Ishwaren Karigoudar. Toronto, Canada: McGraw-Hill Ryerson, 1979.

Guss, Daniel M. "The Enculturation of Makiritare Women." *Ethnology* 21, no. 3 (July 1982): 259–69.

Hall, Edward T. "Unstated Features of the Cultural Context of Learning." Pp. 37–41 in *Reflections on American Education: Classic and Contemporary Readings*, edited by James A. Johnson, Victor L. Dupuis, and John H. Johansen. Boston: Allyn and Bacon, 1991.

Hanh, Thich Nhat. *The Miracle of Mindfulness*. Boston: Beacon, 1987.

Harper, Douglas. *Working Knowledge: Skill and Community in a Small Shop*. Chicago: University of Chicago Press, 1987.

Holland, Dorothy, William Lachicotte Jr., Debra Skinner, and Carole Cain. *Identity and Agency in Cultural Worlds*. Cambridge, Mass.: Harvard University Press, 1998.

Howard, Alan. *Learning to Be Rotuman*. New York: Teachers College Press, 1970.

Howell, Signe. "From Child to Human: Chewong Concepts of Self." Pp. 147–68 in *Acquiring Culture: Cross-Cultural Studies in Child Development*, edited by Gustav Jahoda and Ioan M. Lewis. London: Croom Helm, 1988.

Kabat-Zinn, Jon. *Wherever You Go, There You Are: Mindfulness Meditation in Everyday Life*. New York: Hyperion, 1995.

Lancy, David F. *Playing on the Mother Ground: Cultural Routines for Children's Development*. New York: Guilford, 1996.

———. *The Anthropology of Childhood*. Cambridge: Cambridge University Press, 2008.

Lave, Jean, and Etienne Wenger. *Situated Learning: Legitimate Peripheral Participation*. Cambridge: Cambridge University Press, 1991.

LeVine, Robert, and Merry L. White. *Human Conditions: The Cultural Basis of Educational Development*. London: Routledge & Kegan Paul, 1986.

Levy, Robert. *Tahitians: Mind and Experience in the Society Islands*. Chicago: University of Chicago Press, 1973.

Lutz, Antoine, John D. Dunn, and Richard J. Davidson. "Meditation and the Neuroscience of Consciousness: An Introduction." Pp. 499–551 in *The Cambridge Handbook of Consciousness*, edited by Phillip David Zelazo, Morris Moscovitch, and Evan Thompson. Cambridge: Cambridge University Press, 2007.

Marshall, John. "Man as Hunter." *Natural History* 67, no. 6 (1958): 291–309; 67, no. 7 (1958): 376–95.

Maurer, Eugenio. "¿Aprender o Enseñar?: La Educación en Takinwits, Poblado Tseltal de Chiapas (México)." *Revista del Centro de Estudios Educativos (México)* 7, no. 1 (1977): 84–103.

Maynard, Ashley E., Patricia M. Greenfield, and Carla P. Childs. "Culture, History, Biology, and Body: Native and Non-Native Acquisition of Technological Skill." *Ethos* 27, no. 3 (September 1999): 379–402.

Mead, George Herbert. *Mind, Self, and Society.* 1934. Chicago: University of Chicago Press, 1962.

Meltzoff, Andrew. "Understanding the Intentions of Others: Re-enactment of Intended Acts by 18-Month-Old Children." *Developmental Psychology* 31 (1995): 838–50.

Miller, Peggy J., and Linda Sperry. "The Socialization of Anger and Aggression." *Merrill-Palmer Quarterly* 33, no. 1 (1987): 1–31.

Nash, Manning. "Machine Age Maya," memoir no. 87. *American Anthropologist* 60, no. 2.2 (1958).

Nicolaisen, Ida. "Concepts and Learning among the Punan Bah of Sarawak." Pp. 193–221 in *Acquiring Culture: Cross-Cultural Studies in Child Development*, edited by Gustav Jahoda and Ioan M. Lewis. London: Croom Helm, 1988.

Ochs, Elinor, and Bambi B. Schieffelin. "Language Acquisition and Socialization: Three Developmental Stories and Their Implications." Pp. 276–320 in *Culture Theory: Essays on Mind, Self, and Society*, edited by Richard A. Shweder and Robert A. LeVine. Cambridge: Cambridge University Press, 1984.

Paradise, Ruth, and Mariëtte de Haan. "Responsibility and Reciprocity: Social Organization of Mazahua Learning Practices." *Anthropology and Education Quarterly* 40, no. 2 (June 2009): 187–204.

Paradise, Ruth, and Barbara Rogoff. "Side by Side: Learning by Observing and Pitching In." *Ethos* 37, no. 1 (March 2009): 102–38.

Pettitt, George A. *Primitive Education in North America.* University of California Publications in American Archaeology and Ethnology, vol. 43, no. 1. Berkeley: University of California Press, 1946.

Philips, Susan. "Participant Structures and Communicative Competence: Warm Springs Children in Community and Classroom." Pp. 370–94 in *Functions of Language in the Classroom*, edited by Courtney Cazden, Vera P. John, and Dell Hymes. New York: Teachers College Press, 1972.

Read, Margaret. *Children of Their Fathers: Growing Up among the Ngoni of Malawi.* New Haven, Conn.: Yale University Press, 1960.

Redfield, Robert. *The Primitive World and Its Transformations.* Ithaca, N.Y.: Cornell University Press, 1979.

Reichard, Gladys. *Spider Woman: A Story of Navaho Weavers and Chanters.* New York: Macmillan, 1934.

Ritchie, Jane, and James Ritchie. *Growing Up in Polynesia.* Sydney: Allen and Unwin, 1979.

Rogoff, Barbara, Ruth Paradise, Rebeca M. Arauz, Maricela Correa-Chávez, and Cathy Angelillo. "Firsthand Learning through Intent Participation." *Annual Review of Psychology* 54, no. 1 (2003): 175–203.

Schwartzman, Helen. *Transformations: The Anthropology of Children's Play.* New York: Plenum, 1978.

Sillar, Bill. "Playing with God: Cultural Perceptions of Children, Play, and Miniatures in the Andes." *Archaeological Review from Cambridge* 13 (1994): 47–63.

Silva, Katie G., Maricela Correa-Chávez, and Barbara Rogoff. "Mexican-Heritage Children's Attention and Learning from Interactions Directed to Others." *Child Development* (in press).

Simmons, Leo W., ed. *Sun Chief: The Autobiography of a Hopi Indian.* New Haven, Conn.: Yale University Press, 1942.

Spindler, George, and Louise Spindler. "There Are No Dropouts among the Arunta and the Hutterites." Pp. 7–15 in *What Do Anthropologists Have to Say about Dropouts?* edited by Henry T. Trueba, George Spindler, and Louise Spindler. New York: Falmer, 1989.

Strauss, Claudia. "Beyond 'Formal' versus 'Informal' Education: Uses of Psychological Theory in Anthropological Research." *Ethos* 12, no. 3 (October 1984): 195–222.

Tang, Patricia. "Memory, Childhood, and the Construction of Modern Griot Identity." Pp. 105–20 in *Musical Childhoods and the Culture of Youth*, edited by Susan Boynton and Roe-Min Kok. Middletown, Conn.: Wesleyan University Press, 2006.

Tomasello, Michael. *The Cultural Origins of Human Cognition.* Boston: Harvard University Press, 1999.

Toren, Christina. "The Child Mind." Pp. 155–79 in *The Debated Mind: Evolutionary Psychology versus Ethnography*, edited by Harvey Whitehouse. Oxford: Berg, 2001.

Turnbull, Colin M. *Wayward Servants: The Two Worlds of the African Pygmies.* Garden City, N.Y.: Natural History, 1965.

Vygotsky, Lev. *Mind in Society: The Development of Higher Psychological Processes.* Cambridge, Mass.: Harvard University Press, 1978.

Wagley, Charles. *Welcome of Tears: The Tapirapé Indians of Central Brazil.* New York: Oxford University Press, 1977.

Watson-Gegeo, Karen. "Fantasy and Reality: The Dialectic of Work and Play in Kawara'ae Children's Lives." *Ethos* 29, no. 2 (June 2001): 138–58.

Wellman, Henry M. "Understanding the Psychological World: Developing a Theory of Mind." Pp. 167–87 in *Blackwell Handbook of Childhood Cognitive Development*, edited by Usha Goswami. Oxford: Blackwell, 2002.

White, Robert W. "Motivation Reconsidered: The Concept of Competence." *Psychological Review* 66, no. 5 (1959): 297–333.

Wilbert, Johannes. "To Become a Maker of Canoes: An Essay on Warao Enculturation." Pp. 303–58 in *Enculturation in Latin America*, edited by Johannes Wilbert. Los Angeles: University of California, Los Angeles, Latin American Publications, 1979.

Williams, Judith, R. *The Youth of Haouch El Harimi, a Lebanese Village*. Cambridge: Cambridge University Press, 1968.

Williams, Thomas Rhys. *A Borneo Childhood*. New York: Holt, Rinehart, and Winston, 1969.

CHAPTER SIX

WORK, PLAY, AND LEARNING

Garry Chick

Children's Work and Play

It is often claimed that play is the work of the child. However, children in much of the world spend considerable time engaged in productive work and often contribute substantially to the family larder. During field research in the late 1970s in a small community of approximately 1,100 in the rural highlands of central Mexico, I watched boys as young as 4 or 5 breaking up clods of soil as they followed their fathers plowing their small fields with mule- or ox-drawn plows. This may not seem like much, but since the farmers lacked harrows, the task was crucial before seeding. Had the children not done the work, adults would have had to. When the seeds—always maize—were planted, the boys became live scarecrows, chasing birds from the fields with sticks or stones. Little girls of the same age commonly assisted their mothers or older sisters with house cleaning, food preparation, infant care, and washing clothes at a nearby creek.

Play melded with these productive activities, however. Boys chased each other, played simple games, clearly enjoyed throwing sticks or stones at marauding birds, and occasionally at each other, while they guarded fields. Washing clothes was generally a pleasant activity for village women and their daughters as it was time outside the home away from its routine and an opportunity to socialize with others engaged in the same chore.

There were opportunities for unadulterated play as well. Children attended a small elementary school (grades 1–6) in the village while older children went to middle school or high school in nearby, larger communities. The village school had a small playground, and children engaged in typical playground activities during recesses and at other times when the playground was available (it was gated and closed during most nonschool hours). Community festivals, which occupied a total of about 10 weeks during the year, also afforded children numerous play opportunities (Chick 1991; Roberts et al. 1981).

Scenes similar to those I observed in Mexico are common in anthropological studies of nonindustrial societies. A problem with many such studies, however, is that work and play are inconsistently defined, if defined at all. For example, are "make-believe," "pretend," and "imaginative" play distinct subtypes or the same thing with different labels attached (Fisher 1992, 164)? Defining work is not much easier. For subsistence activities such as hunting or gathering, work can be defined in terms of calories produced, but that is not especially useful for most other kinds of work. Money earned provides a measure for market-sector labor but does not work well for housework or child care.

Child work is usually differentiated from child labor. Nieuwenhuys (1996) claimed that children in modern societies are ideologically distinguished from people who are economically productive, and child labor is seen as a reflection of underdevelopment. She argued, however, that this view of children as passive and dependent is a Western concept largely associated with the exploitation of poor children via factory work and wage labor. Progressive legislation in Western countries established a distinction between exploitative wage labor for children under a certain age and "morally desirable and pedagogically sensible activities," such as "housekeeping, child minding, helping adults for no pay on the family farm and in small shops, domestic service, street selling, running errands, delivering newspapers, seasonal work on farms, working as a trainee in a workshop, etc. [Activities] lauded for their socializing and training aspects" (Nieuwenhuys 1996, 239). Such legislation has typically used chronological age to distinguish exploitative child labor from legitimate adult work but usually disregards local or cultural markers of life stages. It may be useful to differentiate child labor from child work by viewing the former in terms of its exchange value and the latter in terms of its use value, but this distinction is not always clear.

Observers usually must also determine the primary activity when children are doing more than one thing at a time. That is, even if children appear to be playing while guarding a seeded field from birds, their primary activity is generally characterized as work. This problem is at least partly the result of the cultural definitions of work and play but also the common adult valuation of work over play. Moreover, children's perceptions of what is work and what is play may not match those of adults (Wing 1995). For example, Briggs (1998, 5) observed Inuit parents "playing" with their children by posing questions that involved "emotionally powerful problems that the children could not ignore," such as "Why don't you kill your baby brother?" While the adults always knew that such questions were being asked in a playful manner and for the purpose of educating children about important cultural values, the children did not. The questioning generally related to transitions the child might be undergoing, such as weaning or the birth of a sibling. As soon as the child was able to disentangle the playful from the serious with respect to a particular issue, the parents stopped questioning on that topic. Despite these problems, many, probably most, ethnographic studies of children's work and of play have identified them using what might be called the "Justice Potter Stewart Criterion," that is, "I know it when I see it."[1] Since both work and play are difficult to define free from context but seem to be rather easily and consistently known when observed,[2] this may not be a major problem in individual cases but may complicate comparative studies.

Studies reviewed below describe the work and play of children and address their value and consequences. Ethnographers of children's work usually evaluate it in terms of its immediate worth to the family unit and for the child's preparation for his or her future life. For its part, play is generally defined in terms of its lack of immediate consequences. On the other hand, play may have long-term developmental effects although empirical evidence for them is often hard to come by (Caro 1988). Hence, relating children's work and especially children's play to learning ideally requires long-term research. Ethnographic studies are often protracted but lack features of experimental design such as the control group; hence, one can never be certain that observed effects, such as learning, are due to hypothesized causes. This increases the value of comparing multiple case studies carried out in different contexts, as they can serve, in some measure, as controls for each other.

Trade-offs in Children's Work and Play

How should we think about children, work, play, and learning? With respect to work, it seems important to know the extent to which children contribute, particularly in terms of the amount of time they spend working, the kinds of work they do, and the degree to which their work contributes to their households. Additionally, what do children learn from work? Questions related to play are similar. How much time do children spend in play, and what is the nature of their play activity? Since play is presumably nonproductive in the short term, it doesn't make much sense to think about its immediate contribution to the household. However, since play is often regarded as a means to prepare children for their roles as adults, we can ask how, and how effectively, does play prepare them?

Children's work and play have generally been considered from two broad theoretical perspectives. First, children's work and play can be examined in terms of their evolutionary and economic determinants and consequences. Second, children's work and play can be studied in terms of psychosocial determinants and consequences. Although they may appear distinct, these perspectives are complementary and ultimately dovetail with respect to learning at least to some extent.

The economic value of children was taken for granted until Cain and Nag produced quantitative analyses, based on time allocation data, of children's contributions to the domestic economy in villages in south Asia. Cain (1977) showed that, among males age 10 and older in a village in Bangladesh, those from landless households worked more than those from landowning households, while those below age 10 worked less. Moreover, male children of landed parents worked most at animal care and crop production, while those of the poor spent the greatest amount of their work time in paid employment and fishing. Cain (1977) found that for female children from richer households, work time often was equal to or even exceeded that of female children from poor households. Most of the work done by female children in rich households consisted of housework, while those from poor families did more productive (wage) work. Finally, while there were class differences in hours worked, the total work input of both boys and girls increased with age, with male children becoming net producers (e.g., brought in more resources than they consumed) between the ages of 10 and 13. Because the mean age of marriage for female children was 13.5, Cain estimated that girls never became net producers for their households, a finding consistent with the practice of selective female infanticide.

Nag, White, and Peet (1978), in their study of villages in Java and Nepal, held that children can contribute labor to the household economy and can provide economic support for elderly parents. Based on family time use, food consumption, income, and expenditure data, they concluded, "Children in both villages spend an increasing amount of time in work activities as they grow older" (294). And at any given age, females usually worked longer hours than males, primarily due to their extra contribution to household maintenance activities such as food preparation. The researchers also found that Javanese households with higher children's work input and more child producers were more successful economically.

These results were incorporated in Caldwell's (1976) demographic transition theory, which held that in societies where wealth flows upward, from children to parents, parents should maximize the number of offspring who can then work and provide additional wealth, take care of aged parents, and enhance family status. In industrial societies, where wealth flows downward from parents to children, parents should limit their fertility. The theory explains the contrasting low fertility rates in industrial Europe and North America and high fertility noted in traditional agrarian societies. More recently, the theory has been modified. Kaplan (1994) and Kaplan and Bock (2001) showed that even where resources can flow both upward and downward, the net flow is down, from parents and grandparents to children and grandchildren. However, the size of the net flow varies with ecological, demographic, and economic variables. For example, in a comparison of two groups of savannah hunter-gatherers of sub-Saharan Africa, Blurton-Jones, Hawkes, and Draper (1994) showed that Hadza children are far more productive economically than !Kung children, particularly during certain seasons. This difference appears to be explained, in part, by the fact that the environment for !Kung children is more dangerous (e.g., longer distance to resources and the presence of dangerous animals) than for Hadza children. For groups with different subsistence strategies, two other factors are important. Among subsistence farmers or herders, children's labor can often be relatively productive, as their tasks do not require adult physical strength or extensive learning (Bock 2002a; Kramer 2002). In contrast, the complexities of foraging as a subsistence strategy usually means that forager children are less productive than agrarian children. Also, there is usually a trade-off between present and future productivity such that children can either spend time developing skills to use in the future or spend time on productive tasks they're already proficient in (Bock 2002a, 2002b).

As discussed in chapter 2 of this volume, life history theory addresses the purpose of the juvenile period. A recent interpretation is referred to as "embodied capital theory" (Kaplan 1997; Kaplan and Bock 2001; Kaplan, Lancaster, et al. 1995; Kaplan, Hill, et al. 2000). Integration of the physical and functional aspects of embodied capital characterizes competent adults. Bock (2002a) distinguished two versions of embodied capital: growth based and experience based. The former includes things such as "body size, strength, balance, and general coordination" while the latter involves "attributes such as cognitive function, memory function, task-specific skills, learned knowledge, endurance, and specific coordination" (164). He referred to this as "punctuated development" and suggests that adaptation to particular subsistence strategies, such as hunting and gathering or agriculture, may "mean that when growth-based forms of embodied capital reach certain levels, experience-based forms are acquired. Punctuating the acquisition of embodied capital in this way could have the effect of 'ratcheting' an individual's ability level along. In this way competency could build by depositing new embodied capital, whether growth-based or experience-based on top of that previously acquired" (166).

Embodied capital theory, with the addition of the punctuated development model, permits predictions about life history development, including time allocated to work, play, and learning among individuals who differ in terms of age, gender, status, subsistence strategy and household economy, and family demography (Bock 2002a, 2002b, 2005). The balance of work and play among children entails both short-term and long-term costs and benefits. Children's work may produce resources that contribute to the household economy and/or develop growth-based embodied capital in the short term. In the long term, children's work may develop experience-based, embodied capital. In the short term, certain productive tasks prevent resource acquisition from others while, in the long term, participation in one array of activities precludes the acquisition of skills relevant to others (Bock 2002a). All of this means that competent parents should channel children's activities in ways that maximize both short- and long-term gains while minimizing costs. Hence, children's activities, including the distribution of work and play, will vary with context as well as individual differences.

Play is commonly thought to develop growth- and experience-based capital. Physical play among juvenile animals and humans is usually good exercise, although it can also lead to injury and commonly involves social learning and other skill acquisition (Bekoff and Byers 1981; Burghardt 1998, 2005; Fagen 1981; Smith 1982, 1995). However, while numerous functions of play have been proposed, there has not been a great deal of empirical support for them (Bekoff and Byers 1981; Smith 1995). A virtue of the punctuated development model of embodied capital theory is that it permits the development of numerous testable hypotheses relevant to the functions of play. In general, the punctuated development model suggests that the distribution of children's time to work and play should reflect trade-offs between present and future productivity. Moreover, parental interest and guidance, in terms of the allocation of children's time to work and to play, should reflect their goals in maximizing immediate and/or future returns (Bock 2002a, 2002b, 2005).

Bock (2002a, 2002b, 2005) and Bock and Johnson (2004) tested hypotheses derived from the punctuated development model using time allocation data collected in a community of approximately 400 people in the Okavango Delta area of northwestern Botswana. They showed that skill development involves alternation between growth- and experience-based embodied capital and that time allocated to types of play associated with adult skills substitutes for the actual task. For example, pounding is part of grain processing and involves both strength and skill. Girls between the ages of 3 and 18 participated in an activity that Bock called "play pounding," with a stick representing the pestle and, usually, an imaginary mortar of grain. Bock (2002a) showed that as time allocated to actual grain processing increases with age, and presumably skill, the amount of time spent in play pounding decreases in proportion.

Bock and Johnson (2004) found it more difficult to measure the trade-offs between productivity and boys' play in what they called the "cow game" and the "aim game." The "cow game" involves role-playing, with some children acting as oxen yoked to a sledge (either a toy sledge or an object used to represent one). The "driver" must control the "oxen" while hauling the load. In the "aim game," boys throw sticks at a target area on the ground. Boys also participate in ball games, usually governed by flexible rather than fixed rules (Bock 2005). Bock and Johnson (2004) note that while the relationship of the "aim game" to hunting is clear, it is unclear whether it actually results in more successful hunting (or fishing). Hence, there may be other skills learned in the game. Smith (1982) argued that play may serve as training when more direct practice or actual practice in activities may be dangerous or otherwise disadvantageous, a point made by Roberts and Sutton-Smith (1962) 20 years earlier. In their study of child training and involvement in games, they concluded that games provide arenas for "buffered learning." These may help assuage childhood conflicts introduced by parents and other adults over things such as obedience, responsibility, and achievement training but also permit learning about real-life activities or situations modeled by the games. In the game context, however, players are safe from the dangers—both physical and social—that can occur in real life.

Psychosocial Perspectives on Children's Work, Play, and Learning

Research on the psychosocial effects of work and play developed in the culture and personality school of anthropology that arose during the 1920s and blossomed during the 1930s and 1940s. Under the influence of Freudian psychoanalytic theory, the culture and personality school held that adult personality characteristics are largely determined by childhood socialization practices, such as feeding, weaning, toilet training, obedience training, responsibility training, and aggression control. Because different societies have different socialization practices, they therefore produce different personality types. Moreover, culture itself can be described in personality-like terms. For example, Benedict (1934) used the terms *Apollonian* and *Dionysian* to contrast the allegedly placid and restrained Pueblo Indians of the American Southwest versus the Indians of the Great Plains who purportedly lived with abandon and valued sensory escape. Although now out of the mainstream, culture and personality studies are incorporated in the field of psychological anthropology. Current issues of concern include comparative concepts of the self in non-Western societies. Additionally, the idea that work and play are rooted in socialization provides a link to anthropological studies of children's learning.

That early socialization affects such things as attitudes, values, beliefs, and behavior in later life is difficult to dismiss, but it is also difficult to demonstrate empirically. In most cases, researchers have attempted to show that early socialization through work, play, and other child-rearing practices is consistent with attitudes, values, beliefs, personality, or behavior exhibited by older group members. Margaret Mead (1935), in *Sex and Temperament in Three Primitive Societies*, mentions the congruence between child's play and adult behavior. Among the putatively cooperative Arapesh, children played few games, none of which were competitive. Among the Mundugumor, a group that she described as competitive, hostile, and aggressive, she reported that children's play involved competitive, aggressive activities.

In the *Six Cultures* project of the 1950s (Whiting 1963; see also chapter 3, this volume), the teams of researchers recorded the child's dominant activity during each observation as play, work, or learning. If none of these fit the circumstance, the observers coded the activity as casual social interaction. Results showed that young children (between the ages of 3 and 11) in the six communities were engaged in play during 273 observations, in work during 85, in learning during only 39, and in casual social interaction during 198 (Whiting and Whiting 1975, 48). What the children thought they were doing was not determined. Also, because the communities differed in a variety of ways, the number of observations in similar settings was not the same. For example, in Nyansongo (in Kenya), 31 percent of observations were recorded in "adjacent pasture or garden" but none in "school and school playground" (43). Observation location probably influenced the number of learning activities versus work or play activities recorded.

Several general conclusions resulted from the *Six Cultures* study. First, girls spent more of their time in productive work, including housework, gardening, and child care, while boys spent more time playing. Girls were observed interacting and holding infants more frequently than boys. During middle childhood, defined as ages 6–10, boys spent more of their time away from their mothers and more distant from their homes than did girls.

Edwards (2005) reexamined the *Six Cultures* data in order to look at play in more detail. The original coding scheme (Whiting 1963) included four categories for play: fantasy play, creative play, role-play, and games with rules. Each five-minute observational period could be scored with only one type, so what observers thought to be the *dominant* form of play was recorded. Fantasy play involved pretending to be some imaginary animal or character. Creative play included such things as drawing in or building things of sand or mud, whittling or carving, and playing creatively with a store-bought toy. Role-play was defined as acting out an adult activity, such as cooking, shopping, parenting, or hunting. Games with rules involved the familiar types described by Roberts, Arth, and Bush (1959), that is, games of physical skill such as running races, games of strategy such as tick-tack-toe, or games of chance such as dice or cards. Edwards found that children in Nyansongo (Kenya) and Khalapur (India) played the least, while those in Taira (Okinawa) and Orchard Town (United States) played the most. Edwards found games with rules to be more common in the three more complex communities (Orchard Town, Khalapur, and Taira). Role-play was common in all of the communities but lower in Nyansongo (also the only community where boys were as involved in role-play as girls) "because children there participated earliest and most heavily in real adult work and therefore did not need to 'practice' through acting out" (Edwards 2005, 94). Moreover, role-play appeared to diminish dramatically as children reached the age where they could contribute to the household, except for Taira, where it did not diminish and there was no expectation that children would engage in work. Edwards concluded, "Both play and work seemed to allow children to build their repertoire of skills and schemes and to exercise and extend their knowledge and control over their environments" (95). Edwards's analyses seem to support hypotheses proffered by Sutton-Smith and Roberts (1971), who suggested that competitive games would be most common when children played with peer groups, more characteristic of communities with formal schools, rather than in mixed-age groups, and by Sutton-Smith (1974), who held that children, especially girls, learn adult tasks and responsibilities in the context of role-play.

The Whitings' culture and personality model (Whiting 1963) did not specifically address the role of play as an agent of socialization and enculturation but, instead, viewed it as an outcome of these processes.

The model also did not propose feedback loops whereby either work or play influenced maintenance systems or child-rearing practices. Wenger (1989) augmented the *Six Cultures* study framework in her examination of work, play, and social relationships in Kaloleni, a rural Giriama community in Kenya. She claimed that the amount of time spent contributing to the household economy is strikingly different between American and Giriama children. Further, while American children may regard chores as undesirable assignments at the prerogative of parents, Kaloleni children regard their work as "necessary to the well-being of household members" (Wenger 1989, 92). Moreover, for the children of Kaloleni, "work provides a context for learning meaningful cooperation around a goal that benefits the domestic group" (92). Children in Kaloleni learn both responsibility and mutuality through their chores.

Wenger noted that work increases dramatically with age. She looked at children in the 2–3, 4–5, 6–7, and 8–11 age ranges and found, using spot observations, that the percentage of children's work activities ranged from 1 percent in the youngest group, through 8 percent and 18 percent in the two middle groups, to 38 percent in the oldest group, claiming that these percentages are considerably higher than for children in the United States. Research in other nonindustrialized societies (e.g., Rogoff 1981; Rogoff et al. 1975; Whiting and Edwards 1988; Whiting and Whiting 1975) shows similar patterns.

The kinds of work done by children in Kaloleni differ by gender. Among children in the 8–11 age range, Wenger found girls to be working about 51 percent of the time while boys were working during only 26 percent of observations. Moreover, boys performed fewer types of tasks than girls. Boys do not do "women's work" such as carrying water, produce, or firewood, and they do little child care. Boys' most common chore is running errands, although they do spend some time in gardening. Girls, on the other hand, divide most of their work time between collecting and retrieving firewood and water, transporting produce and palm wine, and housework, such as food processing, housecleaning, and laundry. Their remaining time is divided among running "errands, child care, and gardening" (Wenger 1989, 100).

Wenger showed that, after about 8 years of age, boys are generally involved in less structured and supervised activities than girls. For example, girls were engaged in chores during 74 percent of observations while boys were working in only 49 percent. When both girls and boys were working, girls were outside the *mudzi* (extended family households in the dispersed Kaloleni community) during 54 percent of observations while boys were outside for 82 percent, meaning that girls were far more supervised than boys. Wenger concludes that girls are being trained, by their mothers, in work that will prepare them for adult roles as wives and mothers. In contrast, boys' work activities have little to do with what will be their adult roles. This may reflect the fact that homesteads in Kaloleni are patrilineal and virilocal; that is, wives marry into their husbands' *midzi* (the plural of *mudzi*) and are expected to be competent at women's tasks.

Play routines in Kaloleni mirror and reinforce those from work. Older boys play outside their *mudzi* more than girls, hence, more often with children either related by marriage, rather than blood, or who are unrelated. Boys spend more time with peers while girls spend more time with infants and/or adults, and play takes place most commonly when children are in peer groups. This means that boys engage in social play more than girls. Wenger interprets the patterning of both work and play among children in Kaloleni as marking the "divergent paths of preparation for female and male adulthood in Giriama society" (1989, 111). While girls' activities mirror the productive activities of adult females, those of boys usually do not. Instead, the relatively greater freedom afforded boys to structure their own time doing chores as well as in social play allows them to learn to deal with others in cooperative and dominance relationships, something that they may ultimately be required to do as patriarch of their own *mudzi*.

Munroe, Munroe, and Shimmin (1984) examined children's work in four societies: the Logoli of Kenya, the Garifuna of Belize, the Newars of Nepal, and American Samoa. Their study adopted the position that childhood experience affects adult temperament and used some of the Whitings' coding scheme. They assumed that "(a) children will be expected to work where they are of economic value, and (b) the experience of working will have implications for their developing character" (369). They examined 48 children in each of the four societies, 12 at the ages of 3, 5, 7, and 9, respectively. Trained native investigators observed each child about 30 times over a six-week period using a spot observation method. Children in each of the four societies spent about 10 percent of their time doing chores by the age of 3; by age 9, they were working about one-third of their waking nonschool time. Closer analysis revealed that children worked mostly when they were members of domestic units or families that were "relatively low in the proportion of workers present, and when their domestic units possess an infant requiring care" (375). More important, the researchers concluded that children's work influences their social behavior. They used the labels "nurturant/responsible" and "sociable/intimate," derived from the Whitings' (1975) work, to describe the behaviors of the more hardworking children versus those who work less. They did not determine whether these effects are permanent, or whether work among adolescents has similar effects.

Moving still further from the Whitings' model, ethnographers have examined many of these issues in great depth. Lancy (1974, 1996) gathered both linguistic (i.e., Kpelle words for work [*tii*] and play [*pele*]) and ethnographic evidence in order to examine if, and how, play operates as a mechanism for socialization and how play and work interact among the Kpelle. He looked at this interaction in the context of make-believe activities, including playing at being a blacksmith, a hunter, a warrior, and newer occupations such as a driver, a rubber tapper, or a soldier. Boys from age 9 on engage in story-telling as another play form. Lancy (1976) also discussed a type of game called *kolong* where a member of a team gives the first phrase of a pair and a member of the opposing team must supply the corresponding phrase. If successful, the responding team scores a point and challenges the first team with a phrase. The game, along with story-telling, appears to relate to adult litigation in courts, which is fairly common. Winning these court cases is related more to skill in presenting one's case than to the elucidation of facts. Lancy (1976) notes that the *kolong* response phrases are actually parts of proverbs and that children learn skills as debaters in the game. And in story-telling, "children are exposed to important underlying beliefs or ethos of the culture" (Lancy 1976, 88).

In his 1996 book *Playing on the Mother-Ground*, Lancy again addressed play and development. For Kpelle children, "the mother-ground" is the public area where they can be seen by adults who may, or may not, be involved in their activities. This is where children engage in either "playforms" or "adult-guided activities" that prepare them for adulthood. Playforms include make-believe, story-telling, and games, as described earlier, wherein children imitate adult activities but are not adult directed. Lancy concluded that the Kpelle case provides evidence for the role of play in learning adult roles and cultural values.

Figure 6.1. Amazigh (Berber) girl with her self-made clay utensils, Igîsel village, Morocco (Jean-Pierre Rossie photo)

In a second in-depth ethnography but with somewhat contrasting results, Jane Fajans (1997) determined the core of Baining socialization to be in their concepts of work and play. The Baining, who live in the Baining Mountains on the Gazelle Peninsula of East New Britain (part of Papua New Guinea), are well known in Melanesian ethnography because of their practice of discarding or destroying very elaborate costumes after ceremonies, as well as their failure to adapt to a market economy like their neighbors, the Tolai. According to Fajans, the Baining "make themselves" by socializing children into adults, largely through work. Spontaneous children's play is strongly discouraged, and children appear to have few games. The Baining have a noun and a verb that translate to English as "play" and "to play" (Fajans 1997, 168). These apply, however, not only to children's play but also to the adult dances for which they are famous, as well as to sorcery. According to Fajans, the Baining "regard children's play as the antithesis of proper social activity" (168). They contrast children's play to adult work, the former being something done by a "natural" or unsocialized person. "Play is not considered the work of children; eating and learning to work are" (168). For the Baining, the transformation from a child being "natural" at birth to a social "person" as an adult is achieved via "activities such as the ingestion of garden produce, adoption, and productive labor" (85).

"The Baining do not consider that children learn from play. Parents do not make toys for their children. They do not give them miniatures of adult objects such as spears, baskets, tools, etc. They rarely play with their children in either a verbal or active way" (Fajans 1997, 92); instead, "parents proceed from the principle that children learn from work. Consequently, they teach children to work in the garden as soon as they show the interest and capability" (92). Socialization of children is not accomplished merely through their being fed and looked after but is more explicit. Baining teach their children "how to work, and how they should eventually reciprocate the food they are presently receiving" (98).

Toys as Models

"Play is the work of children, and toys are their tools" has been something of a standard refrain from many child development experts for years (Cross 1997). However, Sutton-Smith (1986) disputed the common wisdom that play is children's work, claiming instead that in their first two years, children are "too busy being intelligent (exploring, mastering, imagining, and performing) to play most of the time" (244). As for toys, he asserted that we give children toys and refer to children's manipulation of them as play "in order to disguise from ourselves how much we are concerned with and driven by our own needs for our children's achievement and progress," and "most toys are more clearly parental signals of anxiety about children's achievement than they are assurances of child progress" (244). However, Sutton-Smith's claim does not seem to encompass toys made by children themselves (e.g., Rossie 2005).

Many toys are miniatures of adult tools, implements, and activities, and in the case of dolls and figurines, of people. But many are not. American children have played for years with wood building blocks, for example. While blocks can be used to make simple constructions, they are not obvious miniatures of adult building materials, given that alphabet blocks, for example, have letters, numbers, and representations, often of animals, on them. For this reason, *model*, rather than *miniature*, seems a more encompassing term for most toys.

Models and miniatures differ from the real thing in three basic ways. First, they usually, although not always, differ in terms of size or scale. Models tend to be smaller than the real object (e.g., a model Boeing 747), but can also be larger (e.g., a model of an atom). Second, models differ from their real-life counterparts in terms of complexity. Some toys, such as model airplanes or electric trains, are quite complex, but others often fashioned by children themselves are very simple. Finally, models differ in terms of verisimilitude, or true-to-lifeness. A child's bow and arrow may be very true to life and only differ in scale from their adult counterparts. Barbie and Cabbage Patch dolls and dolls carved from wood have different degrees of true-to-lifeness.

E. B. Tylor (1881), one of the founders of anthropology, claimed, "All through civilization, toy weapons and implements furnish children at once play and education; the North American warrior made his boy a little bow and arrow as soon as he could draw it, and the young South Sea Islander learnt by throwing a reed at a rolling ring how . . . to hurl his spear" (304–5). Hawkes (1916) described toy use among the Inuit:

> The girl helps her mother around the house, or plays with her dolls and miniature house and utensils. Admiring relatives provide small children with small ivory carvings of animals and birds with which they play by the hour, arranging them for various plays and hunts. The boys early receive small harpoons and bows and arrows, and try their skill on small birds and floating pieces of wood. The sling is a favourite amusement in summer when myriads of waterfowl visit the shores. When the "young ice" forms on the shore-line, the boys delight in making a miniature boat out of one of the cakes and paddle around with a little oar. (113)

Based on this and similar evidence, Laugrand and Oosten (2008) claim, "Obviously playing with miniature images implied a learning process for later life. . . . By handling the miniatures, the children would acquire the skills that would enable them to become good mothers and hunters" (71). They further assert that in Inuit societies, "teaching skills was done through learning experience, observation, and imitation. Miniatures were considered to be real tools for children, and it was assumed that if a child were able to make a small object, he or she would then be able to make the corresponding object for her or his own use in the future. It was held that toys and dolls would transform the children into fully autonomous adults" (71). However, these assertions about the importance of toys and play for acquiring vital skills (accepted as well-proven scientific fact in contemporary child-rearing manuals) must be tempered by the frequent notation by ethnographers, including Fajans (1997) and Lancy (2001; see also Gaskins, Haight, and Lancy 2007), of a paucity of toys and adult suppression of play.

Games as Models

Like his claim about toys, Tylor (1881) thought that learning takes place in games as well: "One class of games is spontaneous everywhere, the sports in which children imitate the life they will afterwards have to act in earnest" (304). While there were quite a few accounts of games published in the late 19th and early 20th centuries (e.g., Culin 1899; Dorsey 1891; Kroeber 1920), the focus was on games as folklore rather than as social interaction or opportunities for learning (Chick and Donlon 1992). In 1959, Roberts, Arth, and Bush published their classic cross-cultural study that provided a definition and a classification scheme, both of which remain standards for the discipline. They also described games as models of real-world activities, including war (see also Chick, Loy, and Miracle 1997), social organization (Roberts and Barry 1976), and religion (Roberts et al. 1959). Roberts and Sutton-Smith (1962) also proposed a "conflict-enculturation hypothesis" of game involvement, later generalized to other expressive activities. They hypothesized that the existence of games of physical skill, strategy, and chance relate to variations in child training. This theory is rooted in the culture and personality perspective described earlier in the chapter. They proposed:

(1) that there is an over-all process of cultural patterning whereby society induces conflict in children through its child-training processes; (2) that society seeks through appropriate arrays and varieties of ludic models to provide an assuagement of these conflicts by an adequate representation

135

of their emotional and cognitive polarities in ludic structure; and (3) that through these models society tries to provide a form of buffered learning through which the child can make enculturative step-by-step progress toward adult behavior. (183–4)

Roberts and Sutton-Smith used both archived ethnographic data (see chapter 7, this volume, for a discussion of this method) and data from U.S. children to test their conflict-enculturation hypothesis of game involvement. They found games of physical skill to be associated with achievement training, games of chance with obedience training, and games of strategy with responsibility training. In a later cross-cultural study, Roberts and Barry (1976) related combinations of game types to cultural complexity and to 13 traits inculcated during child training. In the cross-cultural data, they found evidence that where all three game types are present, obedience was emphasized over self-reliance or honesty. Similarly, in contemporary American sports, coaches have all but completely usurped decision-making. Hence, there is little need to be self-reliant. However, coaches value obedience and self-restraint. As for honesty, coaches teach how to shade the rules without getting caught. Roberts and Barry (1976) concluded, "If games build character, that character may be less than ideal" (59). As socialization research suggests, "in games, children learn all those necessary arts of trickery, deception, harassment, divination, and foul play that their teachers won't teach them, but that are most important in successful human interrelationship in marriage, business, and war" (Sutton-Smith 1973, 356–7).

Conclusion

Anthropological research on children's work, play, and learning can be approached from at least two general perspectives, as shown in the studies reviewed above. Fortunately, results from these perspectives largely agree, lending support to the validity of both, and several claims appear to be well supported. These include the following:

- Children work where and when they can be of economic value and play when and where they cannot.

- The amount of time spent playing decreases with age while the amount of time spent working increases for both girls and boys.

- Play is often sequentially ordered with work when children are learning complex adult tasks. Play with representations of adult tools precedes actual work with those tools.

- Girls work more at all ages than boys.

- Boys tend to be less supervised than girls in both work and play.

- Girls' chores appear to be more directly related to their adult roles than do boys' chores.

- Children work more when their domestic units have relatively fewer capable workers.

- Children's work often contributes to their household economy, but in general, net productivity is downward from parents and grandparents to children.

- Children appear to learn cultural values and skills needed to be competent adults in both work and play.

- There is a trade-off between present and future productivity of children. Parents channel children's work and play in ways that maximize short- and long-term benefits while minimizing costs.

- The productivity of children's work varies with subsistence type. In general, children in agricultural societies are more productive than those in foraging or herding societies, since tasks in the former usually require less strength and skill.

- Children's productivity in foraging societies varies with the potential danger (of getting lost, encountering dangerous animals, etc.) of foraging.

- Play affords a safe or buffered learning context where participation in the actual adult activity may be productively unsound or dangerous.

- Toys are often miniatures of adult tools, and play with them involves learning about adult activities.

- The punctuated equilibrium model of growth- and experience-based embodied capital theory appears to account for differences in work and play based on gender, household subsistence strategy, family demographics, and other variables in foraging and preindustrial agricultural societies.

The authors of most of the reports reviewed above conclude that learning takes place in the context of both work and play, although how much learning of useful adult skills can be attributed to children's work and play or to direct instruction is not yet clear.

It appears that much of the learning for adult roles, especially for boys, takes place outside of the context of work for those living either in foraging or industrial societies, as both have extended periods of adolescence. Learning through play may fill the gap. For children living in agrarian societies, especially where children are cognitively and physically able to do productive tasks, more of the learning necessary to be an adult appears to take place in the context of work. Again, this seems to be especially true for females.

Given their complementary nature, studies from both the evolutionary/economic and the psychosocial perspectives appear to have value, although the latter probably trails the former in terms of theory. They also tend to differ in method, with the former in many cases being more quantitative, especially in terms of time allocation, than the latter. Since both perspectives appear to have merit, using both in future studies may offer even greater insight into the roles of work and play in children's learning than we presently possess.

Notes

1. In an opinion concurring with the majority ruling on an obscenity case in 1964, U.S. Supreme Court Associate Justice Potter Stewart wrote that "hard-core pornography" was difficult to define but "I know it when I see it." See *Jacobellis v. Ohio*, 378 U.S. 1984 (1964), http://www.enfacto.com/case/U.S./378/184/.

2. Connor (1989) found that different groups of adults and children, after viewing a video of 14 incidents of apparent conflict in war toy play among 4- and

5-year-olds, systematically disagreed over what they thought was happening. Other children saw only two of the incidents as aggressive and the rest as play. Adult females regarded about nine as aggression, and adult males about six. However, the children's three nursery school teachers saw all 14 incidents as aggression. So play and aggression, like beauty, may be in the eye of the beholder. See also Boulton (1993) and Schafer and Smith (1996) for similar results.

Acknowledgments

I wish to express my thanks to the editors for inviting me to contribute to this volume, and especially to David Lancy and John Bock for their valuable suggestions during preparation of my chapter.

Bibliography

Bekoff, Marc, and John A. Byers. "A Critical Reanalysis of the Ontogeny and Phylogeny of Mammalian Social and Locomotor Play: An Ethological Hornet's Nest." Pp. 296–337 in *Behavioral Development*, edited by Klaus Immelmann, George W. Barlow, Mary Main, and Lewis Petrinovich. Cambridge: Cambridge University Press, 1981.

Benedict, Ruth. *Patterns of Culture*. Boston: Houghton Mifflin, 1934.

Blurton-Jones, Nicholas G., Kristin Hawkes, and Patricia Draper. "Differences between Hadza and !Kung Children's Work: Original Affluence or Practical Reason?" Pp. 189–215 in *Key Issues in Hunter-Gatherer Research*, edited by Ernest S. Burch and Linda J. Ellanna. Oxford: Berg, 1994.

Bock, John. "Learning, Life History, and Productivity: Children's Lives in the Okavango Delta of Botswana." *Human Nature* 13, no. 2 (June 2002a): 161–98.

———. "Evolutionary Demography and Intrahousehold Time Allocation: Schooling and Children's Labor among the Okavango Delta Peoples of Botswana." *American Journal of Human Biology* 14, no. 2 (March/April 2002b): 206–21.

———. "Farming, Foraging, and Children's Play in the Okavango Delta, Botswana." Pp. 254–81 in *The Nature of Play: Great Apes and Humans*, edited by Anthony Pellegrini and Peter K. Smith. New York: Guilford, 2005.

Bock, John, and Sarah E. Johnson. "Subsistence Ecology and Play among the Okavango Delta Peoples of Botswana." *Human Nature* 15, no. 1 (March 2004): 63–81.

Boulton, Michael J. "A Comparison of Adults' and Children's Abilities to Distinguish between Aggressive and Playful Fighting in Middle School Pupils." *Educational Studies* 19 (1993): 193–204.

Briggs, Jean L. *Inuit Morality Play: The Emotional Education of a Three-Year-Old.* New Haven, Conn.: Yale University Press, 1998.

Burghardt, Gordon M. "The Evolutionary Origins of Play Revisited: Lessons from Turtles." Pp. 1–26 in *Animal Play: Evolutionary, Comparative, and Ecological Perspectives*, edited by Mark Bekoff and John A. Byers. Cambridge: Cambridge University Press, 1998.

———. *The Genesis of Animal Play: Testing the Limits.* Cambridge, Mass.: MIT Press, 2005.

Cain, Mead T. "The Economic Activities of Children in a Village in Bangladesh." *Population and Development Review* 3, no. 3 (September 1977): 201–27.

Caldwell, John C. "Toward a Restatement of Demographic Transition Theory." *Population and Development Review* 2, no. 3/4 (September–December 1976): 321–66.

Caro, Timothy M. "Adaptive Significance of Play: Are We Getting Closer?" *Trends in Ecology and Evolution* 3, no. 2 (February 1988): 50–53.

Chick, Garry. "Acculturation and Community Recreation in Rural Mexico." *Play and Culture* 4 (1991): 185–93.

Chick, Garry, and John G. Donlon. "Going Out on Limn: Geertz's 'Deep Play: Notes on the Balinese Cockfight' and the Anthropological Study of Play." *Play and Culture* 5 (1992): 233–45.

Chick, Garry, John W. Loy, and Andrew W. Miracle. "Combative Sport and Warfare: A Reappraisal of the Spillover and Catharsis Hypotheses." *Cross-Cultural Research* 31, no. 3 (May 1997): 249–67.

Connor, Kathleen. "Aggression: Is It in the Eye of the Beholder?" *Play and Culture* 2 (1989): 213–7.

Cross, Gary. *Kids' Stuff: Toys and the Changing World of American Childhood.* Cambridge, Mass.: Harvard University Press, 1997.

Culin, Stewart. "Hawaiian Games." *American Anthropologist* 1, no. 2 (April 1899): 201–47.

Dorsey, James Owen. "Games of Teton Dakota Children." *American Anthropologist* 3, no. 4 (October 1891): 329–45.

Edwards, Carolyn Pope. "Children's Play in Cross-Cultural Perspective: A New Look at the Six Cultures Study." Pp. 81–96 in *Play: An Interdisciplinary Synthesis*, edited by Felicia Faye McMahon, Donald E. Lytle, and Brian Sutton-Smith. Lanham, Md.: University Press of America, 2005.

Fagen, Robert. *Animal Play Behavior.* New York: Oxford University Press, 1981.

Fajans, Jane. *They Make Themselves: Work and Play among the Baining of Papua New Guinea.* Chicago: University of Chicago Press, 1997.

Fisher, Edward P. "The Impact of Play on Development: A Meta-Analysis." *Play and Culture* 5, no. 2 (1992): 159–81.

Gaskins, Susan, Wendy Haight, and David F. Lancy. "The Cultural Construction of Play." Pp. 179–202 in *Play and Development: Evolutionary, Sociocultural, and Functional Perspectives*, edited by Artin Göncü and Suzanne Gaskins. Mahwah, N.J.: Erlbaum, 2007.

Hawkes, Ernest William. *The Labrador Eskimo*. Anthropological series no. 14, Memoir 91: 71–73. Geological Survey, Department of Mines. Ottawa: Government Printing Bureau, 1916.

Kaplan, Hillard. "Evolutionary and Wealth Flows Theories of Fertility: Empirical Tests and New Models." *Population and Development Review* 20, no. 4 (December 1994): 753–91.

———. "The Evolution of the Human Life Course." Pp. 175–211 in *Between Zeus and Salmon: The Biodemography of Longevity*, edited by Kenneth Wachter and Caleb Finch. Washington, D.C.: National Academy of Sciences, 1997.

Kaplan, Hillard, and John Bock. "Fertility Theory: The Embodied Capital Theory of Human Life History Evolution." Pp. 5561–5568 in *The International Encyclopedia of the Social and Behavioral Sciences*, vol. 3.3, edited by Niel J. Smelser and Paul B. Bakes. Oxford: Elsevier Science, 2001.

Kaplan, Hillard, Kim Hill, Jane Lancaster, and A. Magdalena Hurtado. "A Theory of Human Life History Evolution: Diet, Intelligence, and Longevity." *Evolutionary Anthropology: Issues, News, and Reviews* 9, no. 4 (2000): 156–85.

Kaplan, Hillard, Jane B. Lancaster, John A. Bock, and Sara E. Johnson. "Does Observed Fertility Maximize Fitness among New Mexican Men? A Test of an Optimality Model and a New Theory of Parental Investment in the Embodied Capital of Offspring." *Human Nature* 6, no. 4 (December 1995): 325–60.

Kramer, Karen. "Variation in Duration of Juvenile Dependence: Helping Behavior among Maya Children." *Human Nature* 13, no. 2 (June 2002): 299–325.

Kroeber, Alfred L. "Totem and Taboo: An Ethnologic Psychoanalysis." *American Anthropologist* 22, no. 1 (January 1920): 48–55.

Lancy, David F. "Work, Play, and Learning in a Kpelle Town." Doctoral dissertation, University of Pittsburgh, 1974.

———. "The Play Behavior of Kpelle Children during Rapid Cultural Change." Pp. 72–79 in *The Anthropological Study of Play: Problems and Prospects*, edited by David F. Lancy and B. Allan Tindall. Cornwall, N.Y.: Leisure, 1976.

———. *Playing on the Mother-Ground: Cultural Routines for Children's Development*. New York: Guilford, 1996.

———. "Cultural Constraints on Children's Play." *Play and Culture Studies* 4 (2001): 53–62.

Laugrand, Frederic, and Jarich Oosten. "When Toys and Ornaments Come into Play: The Transformative Power of Miniatures in Canadian Inuit Cosmology." *Museum Anthropology* 31, no. 2 (September 2008): 69–84.

Mead, Margaret. *Sex and Temperament in Three Primitive Societies.* New York: Morrow, 1935.

Munroe, Ruth H., Robert L. Munroe, and Harold S. Shimmin. "Children's Work in Four Cultures: Determinants and Consequences." *American Anthropologist* 86, no. 2 (June 1984): 369–79.

Nag, Moni, Benjamin N. F. White, and R. Creighton Peet. "An Anthropological Approach to the Study of the Economic Value of Children in Java and Nepal." *Current Anthropology* 19, no. 2 (June 1978): 293–306.

Nieuwenhuys, Olga. "The Paradox of Child Labor and Anthropology." *Annual Review of Anthropology* 25 (1996): 237–51.

Roberts, John M., Malcolm C. Arth, and Robert B. Bush. "Games in Culture." *American Anthropologist* 59, no. 3 (June 1959): 497–505.

Roberts, John M., and Herbert Barry III. "Inculcated Traits and Game-Type Combinations: A Cross-Cultural View." Pp. 5–11 in *The Humanistic and Mental Health Aspects of Sport, Exercise, and Recreation*, edited by Timothy T. Craig. Chicago: American Medical Association, 1976.

Roberts, John M., Garry Chick, Marian Stephenson, and Laurel Lee Hyde. "Inferred Categories for Tennis Play: A Limited Semantic Analysis." Pp. 181–95 in *Play as Context*, edited by Alyce T. Cheska. West Point, N.Y.: Leisure, 1981.

Roberts, John M., and Brian Sutton-Smith. "Child Training and Game Involvement." *Ethnology* 2, no. 1 (February 1962): 166–85.

Rogoff, Barbara. "The Relation of Age and Sex to Experiences during Childhood in a Highland Community." *Anthropology UCLA* 11 (1981): 25–41.

Rogoff, Barbara, Martha Julia Sellers, Sergio Pirrotta, Nathan Fox, and Sheldon H. White. "Age of Assignment of Roles and Responsibilities to Children: A Cross-Cultural Survey." *Human Development* 18, no. 5 (1975): 353–69.

Rossie, Jean-Pierre. *Toys, Play, Culture, and Society: An Anthropological Approach with Reference to North Africa and the Sahara.* Stockholm: International Toy Research Center, Royal Institute of Technology, 2005.

Schafer, Mechthild, and Peter K. Smith. "Teachers' Perceptions of Play Fighting and Real Fighting in Primary School." *Educational Research* 38, no. 2 (Summer 1996): 173–81.

Smith, Peter K. "Does Play Matter? Functional and Evolutionary Aspects of Animal and Human Play." *Behavioral and Brain Sciences* 5 (1982): 139–84.

———. "Play, Ethology, and Education: A Personal Account." Pp. 3–21 in *The Future of Play Theory*, edited by Anthony D. Pellegrini. Albany, N.Y.: SUNY Press, 1995.

Sutton-Smith, Brian. *Child Psychology*. New York: Appleton-Century Croft, 1973.

———. "Towards an Anthropology of Play." *Newsletter of the Association for the Anthropological Study of Play* 1, no. 2 (1974): 8–15.

———. *Toys as Culture*. New York: Gardiner, 1986.

Sutton-Smith, Brian, and John M. Roberts. "The Cross-Cultural and Psychological Study of Games." *International Review of Sport Sociology* 6 (1971): 79–87.

Tylor, Edward B. *Anthropology*. New York: D. Appleton, 1881.

Wenger, Martha. "Work, Play, and Social Relationships among Children in a Giriama Community." Pp. 91–115 in *Children's Social Networks and Social Supports*, edited by Deborah Belle. New York: Wiley, 1989.

Whiting, Beatrice B., ed. *Six Cultures: Studies of Child Rearing*. New York: Wiley, 1963.

Whiting, Beatrice, and Carolyn P. Edwards. *Children of Different Worlds*. Cambridge, Mass.: Harvard University Press, 1988.

Whiting, Beatrice B., and John W. M. Whiting. *Children of Six Cultures: A Psychocultural Analysis*. Cambridge, Mass.: Harvard University Press, 1975.

Wing, Lisa A. "Play Is Not the Work of the Child: Young Children's Perceptions of Work and Play." *Early Childhood Research Quarterly* 10, no. 2 (1995): 223–47.

CHAPTER SEVEN

THE ROLE OF ADULTS
IN CHILDREN'S LEARNING

David F. Lancy and M. Annette Grove

Anthropologists who study children in traditional societies almost universally note the absence or great rarity of adults *teaching* children in the village setting. Children are encouraged to learn on their own. This chapter teases out those instances where, in the view of adults, independent learning is not sufficient. In some situations, adult intervention—usually falling short of "teaching"—is deemed necessary. The chapter focuses on four very general issues. At *what age* is the child targeted for a course correction or intervention to facilitate his or her development and socialization? What is the *substance* or goal of this intervention? What should the child be doing that he or she isn't doing already? As we shall see, two very broad goals are to socialize children to "fit in" and to facilitate the child's becoming a contributor to the family, providing a return on the family's investment. *How* does the adult intervene? What strategies are used to change the child's behavior? Lastly, what general principle or *theory* guides these course corrections in the individual's path through childhood? These themes are woven throughout the chapter, which is organized to follow the child from infancy through adolescence.

The Absence of Teaching

Early ethnographic studies of childhood (Fortes 1938; Raum 1940) noted, with some degree of wonder, the near total absence of children being taught (in the explanatory, didactic sense) by adults.[1] Gaskins and Paradise (chapter 5, this volume) elaborate on what anthropologists *do* see—observational learning—but one has no difficulty finding many pointed examples from the literature of adults denying the efficacy of teaching, including:

- Among Nyaka foragers, in southern India, "parents do not feel the need to 'socialize' their children and do not believe that parents' activities greatly affect their children's development" (Hewlett and Lamb 2005, 10). Young people learn their skills from direct experience, in the company of other children or other adults" (Bird-David 2005, 96).

- On Sarawak, the Punan Bah "see little point in any systematic teaching of small children, due to the belief that only from the age of about five . . . will children have the ability to reason. . . . Still even from that time on socialization practices are rather incidental. Adults rely more on setting children a good example than on formal instruction" (Nicolaisen 1988, 205).

The view that children will become competent adults largely through their own initiative is accompanied by a fairly consistent "ethnotheory" of developmentally appropriate actions on the part of children and their caretakers. A key component of that ethnotheory is to match intervention or teaching to the family's needs and ability level of the child. Hence, adults may intervene *early* in a child's development to persuade him or her to behave in a socially acceptable manner, but they may wait until quite *late* in a child's development to ensure that he or she can make a useful contribution to the family garden. In the first case, the family may *accelerate* learning, while in the latter, they are content to wait until the child is *ready* to learn. We begin our explication of this theory with infancy.

Infants Are Not Seen as Learners

The educated elite in modern, industrialized societies share an ethno-theory of development specifying that teaching and learning should begin at birth or even *in utero*[2] (Keller 2007, 127; Kim and Choi 1994).

In other societies, and indeed in Western cultures until recently, these nascent capacities of the infant have been ignored or denied. In fact, the most common model of infant care in the ethnographic record prescribes isolation (Munroe 2005) and quiet (Reichel-Dolmatoff 1976, 277), immobility (Leighton and Kluckhohn 1948; Friedl 1997, 83), a constantly full tummy, and lots of restful repose (Tronick, Thomas, and Daltabuit, 1994). Not surprisingly then, playing with, talking to, or stimulating infants in the interest of awakening their capacity as learners is specifically rejected.

- Among the Liberian Kpelle, "mothers carry their babies on their backs and nurse them frequently but do so without really paying much direct attention to them; they continue working or . . . socializing" (Erchak 1992, 50).

- The Bonerate baby "is handled in a relaxed . . . manner . . . but also at times unemotional, almost apathetic . . . mothers do not establish eye contact with their nursing babies. . . . Toddlers are nursed quickly, without overt emotional expression. . . . [Since] 60 percent of all children die . . . the major goal . . . is to keep them alive [not] enculturation" (Broch 1990, 19, 31).

This period of quiescence and passivity does not always or even usually end once the infant begins crawling. While current thinking in developmental psychology sees this as a critical period for learning and exploration, villages or camps are not "child proofed." There are too many hazards in the environment—many of which could be fatal—to permit the infant free range (Draper and Cashdan 1988, 342; Hill and Hurtado 1996, 154). "Crawling and toddling are not periods of exploration and learning for a Baining (New Britain Island) child; they are periods of passivity" (Fajans 1997, 89; see also Toren 1990, 172).

The general picture, then, is one in which the very young are not stimulated, played with, or talked to (Lancy 2007); they are not "ready" to learn and, indeed, might be harmed by any attempt to invade what is often seen as a fragile psyche. However, in the majority of societies, the *end* of infancy is accompanied by the first overt and often painful "lesson." Almost without exception, infants are nursed on demand until the mother becomes pregnant. Hence, the child must be quickly transitioned from this state of extreme dependency to give way to a new baby. This first lesson[3] is examined in the next section.

Facilitating Independence

Infants constitute an enormous burden on their caretakers. Nursing is energetically costly, as is the toll taken by having to carry the infant—especially for far-ranging foragers. These costs are primarily borne by the child's mother, who not incidentally is usually the prime breadwinner and, perhaps, pregnant with the next infant (Wiley 2004). The Yoruba are quite typical in averring "mothers and grandmothers [prefer] wiry and agile babies who learn to walk early" (Zeitlin 1996, 412). Not surprisingly, we do find societies that sanction strategies designed to lessen this burden. "Kogi [Columbia] children are prodded and continuously encouraged to accelerate their sensory-motor development" (Reichel-Dolmatoff 1976, 277). A Ugandan baby at 3 months old is bundled in a cloth and placed in a hole in the ground to support the baby's spine "for about fifteen minutes a day, until able to sit unsupported" (Ainsworth 1967, 321). The Nso of the Cameroons believe that a "standing baby . . . makes less work for the mother" (Keller 2007, 124). Another practice is to dandle an infant on one's lap while the child pushes off vigorously (Takada 2005). Studies show that the "stepping" reflex is accentuated by such practices and leads, reliably, to the child walking at an earlier age (Zelazo, Zelazo, and Kolb 1972).[4] *Failure* to intervene in this fashion may be seen as threatening the child's motor development[5] (Harkness and Super 1991).

Weaning that is sometimes early—long before the child might initiate it—and severe is widely reported. "A [Luo] woman who is pregnant is supposed to stop breastfeeding, since it is believed that . . . the milk will be poisonous to the nursing baby and will cause it to get the illness *ledho*" (Cosminsky 1985, 38). Numerous ethnographic accounts show mothers imposing early and abrupt termination of breastfeeding (Fouts 2004, 138). On the other hand, extended nursing may be condemned as prolonging the infancy stage, resulting in a "weak, simpering" adult (Turner 1987, 107).

One widespread tactic to hasten independence is a phenomenon referred to as "toddler rejection" (Weisner and Gallimore 1977, 176;

see also Howard 1972, 117; Levy 1973, 454). Essentially, the toddler is "shooed away" from adult company; for example, Hawaiian "children are expected to function in a separate sphere that only overlaps that of adults at the peripheries" (Gallimore, Boggs, and Jordan 1974, 119). "With the arrival of the next sibling, *dénanola* (infancy) is over. Now, play begins . . . and membership in a social group of peers is taken to be critical to . . . the forgetting of the breast to which the toddler has had free access for nearly two years or more. As one [Mandinka] mother put it, 'Now she must turn to play'" (Whittemore 1989, 92).

Aside from freeing up the mother for other pursuits, sending toddlers off in the company of sibling caretakers and playmates is seen as an essential component of their socialization. For example, in rural Bengal, "Little girls accompany older girls in gathering, and they gradually learn the needed skills" (Rohner and Chaki-Sircar 1988, 33). Marquesan mothers see toddlers as developing skills because they *want* to hang out with and emulate their older siblings. By imitating their sibling caretakers, "toddlers learn to run, feed and dress themselves, go outside to urinate and defecate, and help with household chores" (Martini and Kirkpatrick 1992, 124). Similarly, in the eastern New Guinea highlands, Fore children are expected to focus their attention as learners on older children, not adults (Sorenson 1976).

It follows that if mothers must "evict" their weanlings,[6] they must have some hope that others will take up the slack. Indeed, Sarah Hrdy (2009) argues persuasively that humans are "cooperative breeders," meaning that our success as a species has depended on the distribution of child care over a cohort of relatives—alloparents. Hence, the next important lesson—after independence—is how to behave properly toward those of higher rank (e.g., everyone else). Many societies take quite deliberate steps to prepare children for their debut in adult company.

Teaching Speech, Kin Terms, and Manners

In the highlands of Papua New Guinea, Kaluli mothers do not hold their babies *en face* to elicit a response, as direct eye contact is associated with the practice of witchcraft. Rather, they hold their babies in front of themselves and, ventriloquist-like, make them "speak" to passersby (Schieffelin 1990). This pragmatic attitude toward making the child socially acceptable is often magnified by concerns that an "ignorant, willful" child threatens the family's social standing. Baining parents "claim to be ashamed of their children's public behavior" (Fajans 1997, 54). As we survey the ethnographic record, we find that the most frequent mention of explicit *teaching* occurs in conjunction with preparing the child to function within a complex web of social obligations (Demuth 1986, 75). Illustrative examples include the following:

- "The Rotuman child is subtly instructed in kin relations: 'Why don't you go outside and play with Fatiaki, he is your *sasigi*.' or 'You must show respect to Samuela, he is your *o'fa*'" (Howard 1970, 37).

- The Javanese mother repeats "polite" kin terms over and over and corrects her child's mistakes, urging proper etiquette. Hence, "children little more than a year old . . . go through a polite bow and say an approximation of the high word for good-bye" (Geertz 1961, 100).

- Kwara'ae caregivers "tell the child what to say, line by line. . . . Encoded in repeating routines is information on kin terms and relationships and on polite ways of conversing" (Watson-Gegeo and Gegeo 1989, 62).

- "From an early age, [West African Beng] children are taught the words for all of their relatives. Everyone must be addressed properly and greeted every morning and evening" (Gottlieb 2000, 83).

Aside from learning about kin terms and relations, the young child is subject to a variety of lessons on manners. Instruction "in Tikopia in matters of etiquette and decorum begins almost before the child can fully understand what is required of it" (Firth 1970, 79). These injunctions range from the proper hand for eating versus ablution to table manners to sharing. For example, Papel (West Africa) children are offered a desirable item and then immediately told to pass it on to another, particularly a sibling (Einarsdottir 2004, 94). Failure to relinquish the treat will lead to teasing and ridicule (Loudon 1970; Riesman 1992; Schieffelin 1986). The

!Kung display remarkable affection and indulgence toward their children, tolerating violent temper tantrums, for example. But they go to considerable lengths to teach even the very young the basic system of reciprocity and exchange (*hxaro*) (Bakeman et al. 1990, 796).

Nevertheless, these examples of rather direct instruction are uncommon. Other, more indirect teaching tactics are widely employed. A number of societies—particularly in the Pacific and Asia—stimulate the development of a package of emotions, including shame, shyness, and guilt (Fung 1999, 203; Martini and Kirkpatrick 1992, 203) to better control the child's behavior (see chapter 11, this volume). Javanese cultivate the emotion of "*isin* . . . (shame, shyness, embarrassment, guilt) [so] that at any formal public occasion [children] are exceedingly quiet and well-behaved and will sit docilely . . . through hours and hours of formal speeches" (Geertz 1961, 113). On Fiji, the same emotions "are inculcated in the child by ridicule, mockery, laughter, or plain disapproval" (Toren 1990, 183). To get a Japanese child to stop doing something, the mother will claim to be saddened by the behavior (Fogel, Stevenson, and Messinger 1992). Far from harming the child emotionally—a view held in the West—Chinese parents, for example, believe that "shame is an essential social and moral emotion, a virtue" (Li, Wang, and Fischer 2004, 794).

As the child matures, community members may subtly invoke shame (and an alteration in the child's behavior) via the use of an apt proverb (Messing 1985, 207–8; Raum 1940, 218; Read 1960, 44–45). Folktales also send not-so-subtle warnings. The Piaroa live along the tributaries of the Orinoco in the highlands of Venezuela and share an ethos of nonviolence. Among the duties of the shaman, or wizard, is the telling of folktales, which "have high pedagogical value for the Piaroa . . . the tales tell of characters whose out-of-control behavior leads to their own unhappiness and personal disaster, and sometime to danger for others" (Overing 1988, 179). Indonesian puppet theater takes this kind of pedagogy to a higher level where the objectives and means of instruction are taken very seriously (Hobart 1988, 134).

Folklore offers to children idealized models of citizenship by showing the awful things that happen to those who transgress (Lancy 1996, 125). But there are harsher means of controlling behavior. Among the Navajo, "children are told that if they misbehave the big gray *Yeibichai* will carry them off and eat them," and in children's autobiographies there is evidence that these threats are effective (Leighton and Kluck-hohn 1948, 51). Among Bena-Bena tribesmen in Papua New Guinea, "both boys and girls are threatened 'in fun' with axes and knives and they run crying in terror" (Langness 1981, 16).

Corporal punishment represents an escalation in the severity with which a child's error or waywardness is treated. A broad survey of the Human Relations Area Files (HRAF) found that corporal punishment of children "occurs as a frequent or typical technique of discipline in societies in all major regions of the world" (Ember and Ember 2005, 609). A few foraging societies specifically condemn it (Endicott 1992, 286), but most adults would endorse the Wogeo practice of beating children "only so they can learn" (Hogbin 1970, 144). So central is corporal punishment in folk theories of child-rearing that parents are considered too closely attached and sentimental toward their children to function as their teachers (Alber 2004, 41; Lutz 1983, 252). On Fiji, a doting, affectionate mother will delay her child's development, and children "brought up by their [ador-ing] grandmothers . . . are often said to be *either* presumptuous and 'too inquisitive' *or* 'childish' and unable to take on the tasks proper to their age" (Toren 1990, 172). It is widely believed that, at least for certain skills or certain recalcitrant children, learning will not occur without the ap-plication of punishment.[7] Given this rather fearsome arsenal of behavior modification tactics, it shouldn't surprise us to learn that on Tonga and elsewhere, children may prefer to "show respect by remaining on the pe-riphery of adult activities" (Morton 1996, 90).

Ideally then, with some prodding, or deliberate instruction in a few cases, the child learns to behave in a way that won't embarrass his or her parents and to stay unobtrusively in the background. Beyond the obvi-ous goal of shaping children to fit in, Bobbi Low's (1989) ethnology, aggregating over numerous studies such as those just cited, reveals broad relationships between child-rearing practices and preferred mating and reproduction patterns.

Native Theories of Learning and Intelligence

A central reason for the evident reluctance to *teach* children—aside from what might be termed "social survival" skills—is that, even at 4 years old, they may be viewed as uneducable. It is not until 5 or later that children are assumed to acquire *sense*. "The child before he is five or six is said to be *durung djawa* . . . not yet Javanese . . . not yet civilized, not yet able to control emotions . . . not yet able to speak with the proper respectful circumlocutions . . . he does not yet understand, therefore . . . there is no point in forcing him to be what he is not" (Geertz 1961, 105).

Examples of young children treated as being essentially uneducable are legion in the ethnographic record. For Fulani (West African) pastoralists: "It is when children begin to develop *haYYillo* (social sense) that adults in turn change their expectations and behavior" (Riesman 1992, 130). Kipsigis children aren't expected to demonstrate *ng'omnotet* (intelligence) until the age of about 6 (Harkness and Super 1985, 223). Interestingly, *sense* is not signaled by the child's display of knowledge or through questioning adults—in marked contrast to popular notions of intelligence in middle-class Euro-American society.[8] "In a Mayan community . . . children are taught to avoid challenging an adult with a display of greater knowledge by telling them something" (Rogoff 1990, 60). Tongan children who "interrupt or offer advice to adults without being asked may be accused of being *fie poto* (thinking themselves clever)" (Morton 1996, 90).

"Intelligence" in the village is associated with qualities like self-sufficiency, obedience, respect toward elders, attention to detail, willingness to work, and effective management of younger siblings and livestock (Wober 1972). For the Kipsigis (Kenya), children are said to have sense when they not only can take care of themselves but can undertake certain routine chores—watering the cows, sweeping the house—without supervision (Harkness and Super 1985). A child who has demonstrated such initiative around the house may be tested by being sent on a distant errand—such as delivering a message. In one foraging society—the Huaorani—adults are delighted when the child begins carrying a basket to gather food she or he will later share (Rival 2000, 116). A study in several Guatemalan villages showed that children could be reliably ranked on the basis of this native theory of "IQ" (Nerlove et al. 1974, 265).

Of course, initiative on the child's part may not always be welcomed. For foraging people, Draper and Cashden (1988) note, "the nature of adult work is such that children cannot easily be incorporated into it" (348). Foraging requires arduous treks through difficult terrain, and accompanying children would be an insuperable burden. In fact, one finds a surprising number of anecdotes in the literature suggesting that children may as likely be discouraged in attempting certain tasks as supported in their fledgling efforts.[9] These range from cases of girls making attempts to weave (Lancy 1996, 149–53; Pope-Edwards 2005, 91; Reichard 1934, 38), children prevented from handling grain for fear they'll let it spill on the ground (Bock and Johnson 2004), children prevented from messing up planted rows in the garden (Polak 2003, 126), Inuit boys kept some distance from the prey during a hunt so they won't scare it off (Matthiasson 1979, 74), to Bonerate children discouraged from "helping" with fishing activities because their rambunctiousness frightens the fish away (Broch 1990, 85).

The cases just mentioned highlight unwelcome precocity. But children who take the initiative to carry out tasks that are useful, within their competence level, and unlikely to cause damage or harm are appreciated. As we discuss in the next section, most domains of adult work have an inherent hierarchical structure—affording children a stepwise curriculum to work their way through.

The Chore Curriculum

It is striking how much of the culture, the village "curriculum," is laid out for all children to observe. This contrasts dramatically with the U.S. "core" curriculum concealed in classrooms, textbooks, and lessons taught by "certified" teachers. The second and closely related point is that a child's initial steps on the road to mastery of the village chore curriculum often pass through play (see chapter 6, this volume):

- "The social role play of [Guatemalan village] girls most frequently involves the mundane daily routine work of their mothers" (Nerlove et al. 1974, 275).

- A Yanomamö boy at age 5 "plays with a small bow and a reed-like arrow that his father or brother has made for him" (Peters 1998, 90).

- Touareg boys, who will eventually learn to herd camel, first care for a young goat that they treat like a playmate (Spittler 1998, 343).

- A young Conambo girl "plays with clay, making coils, pinch pots, and miniature animals while her mother builds . . . vessels" (Bowser and Patton 2008, 110).

Adults contribute to this initial stage primarily by serving as willing role models and only occasionally go further, for example, by supplying the child with scaled-down tools. This might include giving a little girl a tiny basin and setting it on a coiled "cheater" on top of her head so she might fetch water (Read 1960, 85). The "advantage of the miniature vessel used is that from an early age girls are able to perform all the necessary manipulations without help" (Raum 1940, 196).

As suggested earlier, adults are probably casually observing these play scenes for evidence of persistence, appropriate social interaction, leadership, and emotional stability—in short, signs of emerging *sense*. They will act on their assessment by sending the child on an errand: "Run and fetch me" is one of the commonest phrases heard addressed to young children in Tikopia" (Firth 1970, 80). Kpelle adults speak approvingly of child messengers. Little children were always welcome in other people's homes and no suspicion would attach to them. A well-behaved, polite child earned the attention of potential foster parents and praise for the family's diligence in curbing asocial tendencies (Lancy 1996, 76). Delivering messages and presents (and bringing back gossip!) segues easily into marketing. The "errand" curriculum incorporates many "grades," from carrying messages at age 5 to marketing produce, hard bargaining, and making change for customers by age 11 (Lancy 1996, 156). There is an obvious trade-off here between the child's age and maturity and the consequences for his or her failure to carry out the task.

Tasks that are graded or scaled in difficulty are a core feature of the chore curriculum. Among the island-dwelling Bonerate of southwest Sulawesi, "When children are from five to six years old they are delegated their first chores. . . . The assignments are, however, always adjusted to their physical age and mental maturity. . . . The children are still not regarded as capable of heavy work such as most agricultural labor, [or] netfishing, and other activities that require physical strength" (Broch 1990, 79).

Scaling in the chore curriculum depends on four factors. First, that all other things being equal, children reliably grow into greater strength,

155

dexterity, and intellectual prowess. Second, children eagerly pursue more challenging undertakings without prompting. Third, they spend most of their time in the proximity of slightly older children who act simultaneously as caretakers, role models, and teachers (see chapter 6). Fourth, the village task environment is sufficiently complex so that a scaling from easier to harder is readily apparent. If, for example, we unpackage the following description, we can readily envision a scale of difficulty with many levels: "[Bengali] girls often roam around the village area, collecting mushrooms and greens from the edges of ponds . . . collecting fuel, wood, twigs, and cow dung for home consumption and for sale" (Rohner and Chaki-Sircar 1988, 31). And there is ample evidence that young learners benefit from closely observing the next higher skill levels; for example, Amhara boys are said to trail after young males "like retainers follow a feudal lord" (Messing 1985, 213). On the other hand, these same boys may find a chilly welcome in the vicinity of adults. Among the Touareg, for a boy to query an adult male, even about something as highly valued as camels, would be seen as a breach of etiquette and sign of disrespect (Spittler 1998, 247).

Girls are kept in closer proximity to their mothers, where they can observe the women's work, emulate their behavior, and lighten their burdens (see chapter 12, this volume). As they "pitch in," girls can expect to be engaged in conversation with their mother that provides strategic information regarding the task at hand (Paradise and Rogoff 2009, 117). Their errands take them (usually in company) to the village water source to obtain water, or to the bush to gather firewood. But errand runners are more likely to be boys than girls, not because girls are any less reliable, on the contrary, but because girls' "radius of movement shrinks rapidly, for propriety's sake" (Friedl 1997, 7–8). A girl's most valuable contribution to the household is her care for younger siblings; this is less often a son's contribution. In a careful survey of nearly 200 societies, Weisner and Gallimore (1977) found that infants and toddlers were in the care of siblings as much as and sometimes more than they were under their mother's care. A 3-year-old will seek to hold her newborn brother and be permitted to do so, under supervision, for short periods. As the two age, she will become responsible for longer periods of care and meet a wider array of needs, including dressing, feeding, delousing, and above all, entertaining (Rindstedt and Aronsson 2003, 8). At age 8, we might find her caring for several younger siblings, out of sight of her mother, perhaps taking them to a pond to bathe them and clean off any urine or excrement (Rohner and Chaki-Sircar 1988, 70–71). Years later, she may be "proudly possessive of the achievements and exploits of younger brothers and sisters who had been [her] special responsibility" (Elmendorf 1976, 94).

Gardening also incorporates the stepwise character of the chore curriculum, as meticulously documented by Barbara Polak (2003) in her study of Bamana (Mali) bean cultivation. She describes the discrete roles of 3- to 11-year-old siblings, which range from picking a few beans to place in a calabash—at age 3—to harvesting an adult portion and supervising younger siblings—at 11 (130–2). While adults are absent from this scene, in another study of planting—this time sorghum—Polak (n.d.) shows that, in a complex sequence of component skills, an adult intervenes only when the learners get hung up on the most difficult submaneuver. Among the Warao, where canoe-making is the *sine qua non* of survival, and boys expect to be mentored by their fathers, "there in not much verbal instruction . . . but the father does correct the hand of his son and does teach him how to overcome the pain in his wrist from working with the adze" (Wilbert 1976, 323). This very limited, strategic instruction is most commonly seen during the craft apprenticeship (see below).

Adults may also serve a *motivating* role. A child's initial attempts at doing useful work, like gardening, may attract a parent's attention: "Praise is probably the most effective spur to industry, and I was constantly hearing zeal rewarded with approval" (Hogbin 1970, 148). Kaoka men "may allocate plots to their sons and speak of the growing yams as their own harvest" (Hogbin 1969, 39; see also Whiting 1941, 47). In the Sepik area of Papua New Guinea, we learn: "Children's initial efforts at subsistence work are recognized by giving them food. . . . enthusiastic praise and by calling other people's attention to [the] child" (Barlow 2001, 86). Hopi girls who've learned to grind corn with a nice smooth rhythm are "shown off" to visitors (Hough 1915, 63). "Whenever a [Netsilik] girl catches her first salmon or sews her first pair of socks, [or] a boy kills his first goose or traps his first fox, the community is given notice" (Balikci 1970, 45).

On the other hand, a child's *failure* to complete assigned chores will earn rebuke. If the Kaoka boy neglects the young pig he's been assigned to care for, he will be severely chastised (Hogbin 1969, 39). A Sebei mother condemns a daughter who isn't up to the mark by saying, "I hope that you have stomach pains and dysentery" (Goldschmidt 1986, 259). The daughter's failure redounds on the mother, who is charged by the community with overseeing the girl's development into a competent, hard-working, and marriageable woman. A Kwoma youngster will come under increased scrutiny when approaching middle childhood. Ordered to carry out household chores, the child will be beaten and scolded by the parents and other adults "for being lax about them" (Whiting 1941, 56). If a child is permitted to shirk responsibility, she or he will "inevitably emerge as an adult with few prospects and without the respect of the community" (Wenger 1989, 93). Consequently, a child who neglects chores or seems slow to master the chore curriculum is subject to community-wide censure, hazing by peers, barbed proverbs, and targeted folktales. On Java, the tale of two girls—*Bawang Putih* "Red Onion" and *Brambang Abang* "White Garlic"—may be used strategically. When Red Onion grew up, she turned out fine, but White Garlic "grew up stupid, unable to do anything useful, because all she had done all her life was play" (Geertz 1961, 43).

Nevertheless, because children are usually keen to help out and to demonstrate their nascent skill, and because somewhat older role models are usually available, "students" master the various chore curricula with very little adult intervention. However, as children tackle more complex tasks—such as those involved in crafts—they may need more explicit adult role models and guides.

Facilitating Craftsmanship

Among the Tapirapé forest dwellers of Brazil, a pre-adolescent boy will move into the men's quarters and is expected "to learn the male manual arts—how to weave baskets, how to make a bow and straight arrows, how to fabricate the spirit masks that the men wear in different ceremonies, and other handicrafts. However, [there is never] any express attempt on the part of an older man to teach a young boy such pursuits. On the other hand, the *takana* is the place where adult men generally work, and a boy has ample chance to watch them at it" (Wagley 1977, 150).

In the high Andes, Bolin (2006) reports that weaving is very much a part of the village curriculum: "Children are not taught to spin or weave. Rather, they observe family members who have mastered these crafts and imitate them directly" (99). Studies of the acquisition of a potter's repertoire among the Bella of southwestern Niger reveal that "learning is not a particularly visible process. One is seldom confronted with situations where knowledge is explicitly transmitted from a teacher to an apprentice" (Gosselain 2008, 158). These cases reflect what Lave and Wenger (1991) refer to as "legitimate peripheral participation." There is the tacit recognition by competent adults that children need opportunities to observe skilled work and, through trial and error and lots of practice, attempt to replicate it. The adults, if they think the child is mature and motivated sufficiently, may supply materials or the loan of tools to assist this effort. On the other hand, a busy adult may as well chase the aspirant basket-maker away (Gladwin and Sarason 1953, 414). In any case, active instruction is not evident.

Photo 7.1 shows one step in the construction of a felt textile common to Kyrgyztan. At this point, the mother is engaged in some finish work and is aided by her elder daughter while younger ones observe. Earlier in the process, all three girls (sans mother) completed the task of crushing the wool and expressing water; still earlier, the mother created the design while the three girls observed.

In a few cases, craft production may be transmitted through a more formal *apprenticeship*. Dioula (Côte d'Ivoire) apprentice weavers will be supervised by their father or uncle through a long, multistage process. An

Figure 7.1. Shyrdak construction, Tamchy village, Kyrgyzstan (D. Lancy photo)

159

important distinction is that in an apprenticeship, an adult has made a specific, contractual commitment to transmit his or her skill—for remuneration. At age 8, the apprentice weaver will wind thread onto bobbins for hours at a time. Next he will stretch the warp on the ground before it is transferred to the loom. He may also be permitted to weave plain, undyed strips. After about three years of this more menial work, actual *instruction* begins in earnest when the master sits beside the boy at the loom and begins to demonstrate some simple patterns, which the novice copies. By the time the novice is deemed proficient enough to learn how

Figure 7.2. Apprentice coppersmith, Fez, Morocco (D. Lancy photo)

to prepare the warp, he may be 18 years old and have produced a great many woven goods. These are appropriated by the master as payment for the training (Tanon 1994). Indeed, one of the main reasons that the apprenticeship is so lengthy is the opportunity to take full advantage of the novice's uncompensated labor.

Among the Tukolor of Senegal, "Some fathers prefer that another weaver should train their sons after they have acquired some basic skills since they feel that they will not exert enough discipline in training" (Dilley 1989, 188). The notion that parents may not be stern enough to function as their child's teacher is common in the literature (Goody 2006, 254). Another common theme, well illustrated among the Tukolor, is the existence of a body of secrets and lore parallel to the more mechanical skill inventory. This material is closely guarded and the clever apprentice is expected to winkle it out of the master or other senior craftsmen (Dilley 1989, 190; McNaughton 1988, xvi).

There is, in short, a tension inherent in the apprenticeship because, we would argue, adults are so loath to serve as teachers and youngsters resist playing a subordinate's role. Singleton's (1989) ethnography of a Japanese pottery workshop portrays a relationship rife with the hauteur of rank: "When an apprentice presumes to ask the master a question, he will be asked why he has not been watching the potter at work, or the answer would be obvious" (Singleton 1989, 26). Similarly, in the training of master minaret builders in Yemen, "Curses and derogatory remarks—as opposed to explanation—were the most common form of communication from 'teacher' to 'learner'"(Marchand 2001, 144).

Another theme in the literature on apprenticeship concerns the amount of freedom novices have to exercise innovation and creativity. Among Dii potters of Cameroon, girls are apprenticed to their mothers. "Initiative and trial and error are forbidden; every gesture must follow the mother's pattern. Corporal punishments (spanking, forced eating of clay) are used to ensure that rules are respected, and verbal humiliations are very common. . . . Good behavior is rarely noticed, but errors are always pointed out in public. This treatment puts a lot of pressure on the apprentices, who tend to be quite nervous when working in their mothers' company" (Wallaert-Pêtre 2008, 190–1).[10]

As with the Dii potters, the Hausa weaving apprenticeship "is very rigid and conservative. The apprentice is not expected to innovate, alter, change or improve upon anything. He is to copy the master's techniques . . . exactly" (Defenbaugh 1989, 173). Similar rigidity is observed in the training of West African blacksmiths (Coy 1989; McNaughton 1988) and in the production of grater boards by Baniwa tribesmen in northwest Amazonia (Chernela 2008, 145). Contrasting cases can be found among Conambo (tropical eastern Ecuador) potters, where creativity is valued and young potters are free to acquire styles and decorative ideas from others (Bowser and Patton 2008). Likewise younger Fali (Cameroon) potters are always trying out new ideas and aren't afraid to fail. "Personal gratification is important and overrides the judgment of other potters . . . leading to a diversity of production and style" (Wallaert-Pêtre 2001, 483, 489). In the Chiapas Highlands of Mexico, there has been a transition in the handwoven products over the last 30 years as daughters learning traditional patterns under their mother's tutelage now learn on their own and produce novel market-driven designs (Greenfield 2004). In fact, there is growing evidence that the more conservative apprenticeship programs actually lead to the decline of the craft as demand for traditional products wanes (Friedl 1997, 4; Wallaert-Pêtre 2008, 187).

While formal apprenticeships are not common, they are striking in both the wide commonality of their structure and in the fact that they reflect *formal* means of instruction. As children develop, the community continues to rely largely on the *informal* interaction inherent in family life and group work to transmit skills and values. We have seen how children as young as 3 readily accept their assignments in the chore curriculum and, later, apprentice themselves to acquire more complex skills. The transition to adulthood is fairly seamless. Learning social conventions is stressed from an early age and "fitting in" is rarely a problem.

Managing Adolescence

Earlier in the chapter, we identified a period in the child's life when, in some societies, the child's behavior is quite deliberately shaped to conform to a more "proper" or mature form of social interaction. Adolescence is the second point in the life cycle where we may see this very deliberate, even coercive intervention to bend the youth to social expectations. In most societies, as they mature physically and acquire the gender-appropriate repertoire of adult competencies, children pass briefly through adolescence and settle comfortably into the roles of spouse, parent, and provider. However, in approximately half of the societies in the ethnographic record, adolescents must pass through a rite of passage (Schlegel and Berry 1979) which, in effect, certifies them as ready to begin mating and forming their own family (Vizedom and Zais 1976). Montgomery discusses initiation as a rite of passage from a gender socialization perspective (chapter 12, this volume), but we touch on it briefly here because it represents a significant investment by the community in children's socialization.

Like apprenticeship, the rite of passage is one of the very few cases of *formal* education (Lancy 1996, 163–78) in the village setting. Not that these rites incorporate the transmission of practical skills. Rather, they force adolescents through dramatic and usually painful experiences (circumcision, clitoridectomy, body scarification, penetration of the nasal septum or ear lobe) designed to impress on them respect for the legal and spiritual authorities in the community and the values they espouse (Lancy 1975). "The dominant theme of the initiation is that of an ordeal—trial and proof of maturity" (Goldschmidt 1986, 95–96).

Among West African Mende farmers, the girls' initiation is organized by the Sande women's secret society, and a few, important lessons are conveyed: "One of the most dramatic ritual elements . . . is clitoridectomy. . . . Sande women explain that this makes women 'clean' . . . [also] the pain . . . is a metaphor for the pain of childbirth. . . . [Another] important element in the ritual process of Sande initiation is fattening. Beauty, prosperity, health and fertility are explicitly linked to fatness" (MacCormack 1994, 111–2). Similarly, the Bemba (Zimbabwe) girls' initiation process, *chisungu*, is replete with sexual imagery, to underscore the woman's role as breeder (Richards 1956, 65). Another common theme is the role of the woman as provider (Guss 1982, 264).

Historically, pastoralist societies in Africa were noted for their readiness to attack neighboring groups in raids to secure cattle and women. This may lead to the creation of warrior subcultures which young men are inducted into (Gilmore 2001, 209). The process of joining the Masaai warrior elite, becoming a *moran*, includes circumcision where a "flinch or even the bat of an eyelid as primitive razor sears into flesh is interpreted . . . as a desire to run away and [this loss of] honour . . . can never be redeemed" (Spencer 1970, 134). Throughout central and northern Papua New Guinea, elaborate rites of passage separate boys from their mothers and make them "manly," and teach them to despise and lord it over women and enemy tribesmen. The first stage in this initiation includes days of hazing, fasting, beating, sleeplessness, and sudden surprises. This is followed by forced nose-bleeding to remove female contaminates. The process is violent, painful, and frightening (Herdt 1990, 376). The senior males assert their superiority over the youth while inculcating the moral imperative of male dominance. To this end, they will make use of "secrets," including sacred terms, rituals, locations, and objects such as masks. These "secrets" are denied to women on pain of death (Tuzin 1980, 26).

In the absence of a warrior subculture, adults may yet feel the necessity of curbing or taming their obstreperous and "self-centered" adolescents (Weisfeld 1999, 106). Canela tribesmen from Brazil publicly chastise and humiliate wayward youth (Crocker and Crocker 1994, 37). Don Talayesva—who grew up in a conservative Hopi village—confesses in his autobiography to being quite "naughty" as a boy. So, when he was initiated into the Katchina society with his age group, his father arranged for him to be taught a lesson by having the Whipper Katsinas give him extra blows with the sharp-spined ocotillo whips to "drive the evil from [his] mind, so that he may grow up to be a good and wise man" (Simmons 1942, 80).

Because childhood is a time of relative freedom, societies have evolved mechanisms to guide youth onto the straight and narrow path of sober, responsible adulthood. A secondary theme in the ethnographic literature is that boys, associating exclusively with women throughout childhood, are weak and contaminated and must be forcibly strengthened and purged. Both motives can be found embedded in the rites of passage that serve to correct the youth's trajectory. The teaching/learning process is better described as indoctrination than education (Lancy 1975). The lessons may be few but they are deeply learned.

Summing Up

Before shifting focus to the contemporary scene, we'd like to review what might be concluded from a survey of children's *guided* acquisition of cultural practices. The common elements found in ethnotheories of child socialization include that children learn best on their own and that this initiative frees up adults from serving as teachers. The entire community

164

and its surroundings are seen as the "classroom," and the "curriculum" is displayed as an "open book." It also includes the core idea of "readiness"—that at certain times in the life cycle, intervening to assist the child to greater knowledge or skill will be most efficient. Four periods are at least loosely demarcated in the ethnotheories that people use to structure socialization, namely infancy, toddlerhood or early childhood, middle childhood, and adolescence. Not much cultural learning is expected to occur in infancy; rather, steps are taken to secure and shelter the child. In early childhood, limited and very strategic intervention is called for in *some* societies, to accelerate independence and/or to accelerate the child's assuming "correct" social behavior, including appropriate language. Otherwise, toddlers are expected to learn from emulating peers, through observation, and in play. Adults don't feel the need to intervene nor even to monitor closely the child's progress in personal hygiene, motor development, or speech, to name a few examples.

In middle childhood, through various changes in behavior (e.g., greater maturity and common sense), children signal two things to adults. First, they indicate they are ready to deploy the broad knowledge they have been independently acquiring in early childhood in carrying out useful activities such as errand running or baby minding. Second, they indicate they are ready to learn new skills, skills heretofore beyond their capacity or that required some degree of intervention by a busy adult. Again, however, the onus to acquire these skills rests primarily on the child.

In adolescence, there may arise the need for more deliberate instruction by adults. There are two general areas where this might occur: apprenticeship in the production of craft items and the initiation rite. In both situations, children must subordinate themselves to a master or senior member of the same sex. In both situations, obedience and the learning of lore are important, and some degree of verbal and physical abuse is considered essential in the teaching process, which is why parents aren't favored as teachers.

Contemporary Challenges to the Village Learning Model

Throughout this chapter, we have used the ethnographic present and tried to distill the patterns widely recorded by anthropologists who've observed childhood in non-Western societies beginning with Malinowski in 1914 (LeVine 2007). However, those patterns have been rudely shattered in many cases. Here we will briefly review the major disruptive forces and how they have affected what children are learning and from whom.

Most obviously, overpopulation, poverty, environmental degradation, civil strife, and epidemic disease (HIV/AIDS, tuberculosis) have conspired to force even very young children to fend for themselves and/or earn a meager wage to support their families. In undertaking work that pays a wage, however meager, children may lose the opportunity to observe and learn from adults carrying on traditional subsistence activities. We can only assume that if children are picking coffee or weaving rugs for hours each day, their opportunities to acquire the full panoply of the village curriculum are, therefore, limited. On the other hand, the obviously innate ability of children to learn through observation and from slightly older peers is certainly adaptive for survival in the streets (see chapter 17, this volume).

Schooling was thought to be the elixir that would transform and modernize village life, but this has rarely happened. The practices that worked so effectively to transmit the traditional culture don't transfer well to the school (Philips 1983). For example, the villagers' ethnotheory dictates that parents grant children autonomy to learn on their own, which leads them to a posture of "noninterference" in their children's schooling (Dehyle 1992; Levin 1992; Matthiasson 1979). Children are ill prepared to cope with the demands of classroom learning while also removed for most of the day from the community. Peruvian Shipbo children are kept "from learning their environment and own culture, [while acquiring] only minimal skills for life in town" (Hern 1992, 36). Inuit children "whose parents at the same age were already hunters or wives now continue to carry their books to school daily, awaiting the time when they can step into the 'real' world of adulthood" (Matthiasson 1979, 73).

Modernization often means that the skills of adults are no longer viewed as relevant (Friedl 1997, 4). Hence, their stature in the eyes of youth is diminished (Goody 1989, 239). This "drift" from conformity with the village social structure has been arrested in the past by a rite of passage. But these rites have also gone by the boards (Biersack 1998, 87). Among the Bumbita Arapesh, village youth have rebelled against the hegemony of senior males, refusing to subject themselves to the customary initiation rites. Their exit from the traditional socialization pattern has had a broad impact on the life of the community (Leavitt 1998, 178). During the long civil war in Angola, among the Tchokwe, "children were abducted . . . to fight [hence] the initiation rituals and systematic preparation of young people to become responsible adults ceased. A whole generation was seriously affected" (Honawana 2006, 43).

Social change is accelerating in the world's rural communities, and children are most affected. Their fate is uncertain. The migration of manufacturing in search of the lowest wage scale has dramatically increased demand for child labor (Kenny 2007) and the number of formerly village-resident children earning a wage from such labor is vastly greater than the tiny fraction earning a living from skills learned in school (Serpell 1993, 10). However, children's ability to learn unaided may be a boon in rapidly adapting to new opportunities, and they may be in a position to assist their kin in adjusting to change (Orellana 2009).

A Note on Methodology

The methodology we have employed in surveying the ethnographic record, assembling illustrative cases, and teasing out broad patterns is referred to as *ethnology*. As a scientific method, ethnology is the comparative analysis of data compiled from the hundreds of in-depth ethnographic studies of individual societies. These analyses often focus on the search for biologically based or universal aspects of cultural patterns, *cultural invariants* (Voget 1975).

Franz Boas, as director of the American Ethnological Association, is often credited with the founding of the U.S. ethnological tradition. While Boas had demonstrated the value of an inductive approach where broad patterns of human behavior could be discerned from the ethnographic record, accessing that record was a challenge. George Murdock was among those at the Yale Institute of Human Relations who recognized the need for a better organizational system for the growing body of ethnographic material. In 1950, he announced the creation of the Human Relations Area Files, or HRAF. HRAF provides access to a systematic compilation of ethnographic material, initially on index cards, then on microfiche, CD-ROM, and now wholly online. Organized into nine geographic regions, it includes thousands of documents (Roe 2007, 48).

An indexed classification system of subjects or Outline of Cultural Materials (OCM) enables searches of full-text documents within the collection. Each paragraph within each text has been cross-referenced with a three-digit OCM, which enables the user to search a large range of topics across and within texts (HRAF 2008; Roe 2007).[11] HRAF not only provides a comprehensive and searchable archive but, through the painstaking efforts of many scholars, it also includes "codes" or variables that have been reliably assigned to large, standardized samples or subsets of the larger corpus. Barry and Paxon's (1971) efforts are exemplary in this regard. Working with a sample of 168 societies, they were able to reliably code for systematic comparison dozens of child-care practices such as sleeping proximity, bodily contact, carrying technique, and postpartum sex taboo. Data coders found that some ethnographers were thorough in providing accounts relating to infancy and childhood while others were mute on the subject.

Several landmark studies in the anthropology of childhood have utilized the HRAF archive, such as the Weisner and Gallimore (1977) study cited above. Barbara Rogoff and colleagues selected 50 cases from the HRAF archive that provided extensive information about childhood in an effort to illuminate the transition points in children's development and the age ranges at which children were assigned various roles and responsibilities. Roles and responsibilities were assigned to 27 categories, and they found that "a modal cultural assignment of social responsibility" occurred in the 5–7 age range (Rogoff et al. 1975, 365). Other transitions occurred at puberty (e.g., sexual attraction and complete adoption of adult clothing). As a last example, we would cite Katharine MacDonald's (2007) seminal study on children learning to obtain game from hunting and trapping, described more fully in chapter 15 of this volume. Like MacDonald's study, our own research has used both the "thumbing through books and journals in the library approach" (Roe 2007, 50) and HRAF (Lancy 2007, 2008; Lancy and Grove 2009).

Acknowledgments

We are grateful to Suzanne Gaskins and John Bock for trying to keep us in check. They didn't always succeed.

Notes

1. We have only found three examples in the literature of teaching with a capital T. They are (1) the quite explicit and elaborate system for teaching kin relations and etiquette found on Kwara'ae in the Solomon Islands (Watson-Gegeo and Gegeo 1989); (2) the similarly explicit and mandatory transmission of food taboos by parents to offspring among the Ituri people in the Congo (Aunger 2000); and (3) the training of navigators in the Caroline islands (Gladwin 1970).

2. The "Baby Plus" prenatal education system describes the womb as the "perfect classroom." See www.babyplus.com.

3. As Montgomery discusses in chapter 12 of this volume, there nevertheless may be quite subtle and implicit lessons conveyed to the infant regarding gender and status.

4. I'm grateful to Suzanne Gaskins (personal communication) for pointing out the conflict between hastening the child's independence in order to unburden caretakers versus exposing the mobile but not yet sufficiently cautious child to environmental hazards, as noted in the previous section.

5. This emphasis on accelerated motor development in many East African societies can be contrasted with a complete indifference toward speech development (Harkness and Super 1991, 227).

6. While independence is universally valued, there is considerable variability in the child's "territory." Marquesan children are encouraged to range far from home (Martini and Kirkpatrick 1992), whereas Mayan children are expected to remain within the mother's hearing (Gaskins 2006).

7. This emphasis on scare tactics and corporal punishment to control the child's behavior probably accounts, in part, for the paucity of evidence for children learning directly from adults. This assertion arises from one of the earliest conclusions about the way humans learn (Yerkes and Dodson 1908). This 100-year-old notion is described as: "animals seem to learn more when they are in a state of moderate arousal than when they are in states of either low arousal or high arousal (an inverted-U-shaped learning curve)" (Byrnes 2001, 86). In other words, the high arousal associated with scaring or punishing children does not—in spite of folk wisdom to the contrary—create ideal conditions for learning.

8. "American middle-class parents are very proactive about encouraging their children to talk, and to talk early. . . . We put such emphasis on talking early, presumably because we view this as a sign of intelligence" (Quinn 2005, 479).

9. We concur with Goodnow's (1990, 279–80) skeptical review of Vygostkian models that show adults patiently reorganizing tasks and assisting unskilled children in their attempts at learning complex skills. The ethnographic record

contains many more instances of would-be child "apprentices" being rebuffed than invited.

10. We would argue that the harsh, punitive tone of the apprenticeship makes sense as a means of quickly weeding out novices who lack the skill and motivation to persist. The time available for a craftsperson to invest in teaching is extremely limited and they are loath to waste it.

11. For a listing of HRAF OCM codes, see www.yale.edu/hraf/outline.htm.

Bibliography

Ainsworth, Mary D. *Infancy in Uganda: Infant Care and the Growth of Love*. Baltimore: Johns Hopkins University Press, 1967.

Alber, Erdmute. "'The Real Parents Are the Foster Parents': Social Parenthood among the Baatombu in Northern Benin." Pp. 33–47 in *Cross-Cultural Approaches to Adoption*, edited by Fiona Bowie. London: Routledge, 2004.

Aunger, Robert. "The Life History of Culture Learning in a Face-to-Face Society." *Ethos* 28, no. 3 (September 2000): 445–81.

Bakeman, Roger, Lauren B. Adamson, Melvin Konner, and Ronald G. Barr. "!Kung Infancy: The Social Context of Object Exploration." *Child Development* 61, no. 3 (June 1990): 794–809.

Balikci, Asen. *The Netsilik Eskimo*. Garden City, N.Y.: Natural History Press, 1970.

Barlow, Kathleen. "Working Mothers and the Work of Culture in a Papua New Guinea Society." *Ethos* 29, no. 1 (March 2001): 78–107.

Barry, Herbert, III, and Lenora M. Paxon. "Infancy and Early Childhood: Cross-Cultural Codes 2." *Ethnology* 10, no. 4 (October 1971): 466–508.

Biersack, Aletta. "Horticulture and Hierarchy: The Youthful Beautification of the Body in the Paiela and Porgera Valleys." Pp. 71–91 in *Adolescence in Pacific Island Societies*, edited by Gilbert Herdt and Stephen C. Leavitt. Pittsburgh: University of Pittsburgh Press, 1998.

Bird-David, Nurit. "Studying Children in 'Hunter-Gatherer' Societies: Reflections from a Nayaka Perspective." Pp. 92–101 in *Hunter-Gatherer Childhoods: Evolutionary, Developmental, and Cultural Perspectives*, edited by Barry S. Hewlett and Michael E. Lamb. New Brunswick, N.J.: Transaction/Aldine, 2005.

Bock, John, and Sara E. Johnson. "Subsistence Ecology and Play among the Okavango Delta Peoples of Botswana." *Human Nature* 15, no. 1 (March 2004): 63–82.

Bolin, Inge. *Growing Up in a Culture of Respect: Child Rearing in Highland Peru*. Austin: University of Texas Press, 2006.

Bowser, Brenda J., and John Q. Patton. "Learning and Transmission of Pottery Style: Women's Life Histories and Communities of Practice in the Ecuadorian Amazon." Pp. 105–29 in *Breaking Down Boundaries: Anthropological Approaches to Cultural Transmission, Learning, and Material Culture*, edited by Miriam T. Stark, Brenda J. Bowser, and Lee Horne. Tucson: University of Arizona Press, 2008.

Broch, Harald B. *Growing Up Agreeably: Bonerate Childhood Observed*. Honolulu: University of Hawaii Press, 1990.

Byrnes, James P. *Minds, Brains, and Learning: Understanding the Psychological and Educational Relevance of Neuroscientific Research*. New York: Guilford, 2001.

Chernela, Janet. "Translating Ideologies: Tangible Meaning and Spatial Politics in the Northwest Amazon of Brazil." Pp. 130–49 in *Cultural Transmission and Material Culture: Breaking Down Boundaries*, edited by Miriam T. Stark, Brenda J. Bowser, and Lee Horne. Tucson: University of Arizona Press, 2008.

Cosminsky, Sheila. "Infant Feeding Practices in Rural Kenya." Pp. 35–54 in *Breastfeeding, Child Health, and Birth Spacing: Cross-Cultural Perspectives*, edited by Valerie Hull and Mayling Simpson. London: Croom Helm, 1985.

Coy, Michael W. "Being What We Pretend to Be: The Usefulness of Apprenticeship as a Field Method." Pp. 115–35 in *Apprenticeship: From Theory to Method and Back Again*, edited by Michael W. Coy. Albany: SUNY Press, 1989.

Crocker, William, and Jean Crocker. *The Canela: Bonding through Kinship, Ritual, and Sex*. New York: Harcourt Brace, 1994.

Defenbaugh, Linda. "Hausa Weaving: Surviving amid the Paradoxes." Pp. 163–79 in *Apprenticeship: From Theory to Method and Back Again*, edited by Michael W. Coy. Albany: SUNY Press, 1989.

Dehyle, Donna. "Constructing Failure and Maintaining Cultural Identity: Navajo and Ute School Leavers." *Journal of American Indian Education* 31 (January 1992): 24–47.

Demuth, Katherine. "Prompting Routines in the Language Socialization of Basotho Children." Pp. 51–79 in *Language Socialization across Cultures*, edited by Bambi B. Schieffelin and Elinor Ochs. Cambridge: Cambridge University Press, 1986.

Dilley, M. Roy. "Secrets and Skills: Apprenticeship among Tukolor Weavers." Pp. 181–98 in *Apprenticeship: From Theory to Method and Back Again*, edited by Michael W. Coy. Albany: SUNY Press, 1989.

Draper, Patricia, and Elizabeth Cashdan. "Technological Change and Child Behavior among the !Kung." *Ethnology* 27, no. 4 (October 1988): 339–65.

Einarsdottir, Jonina. *Tired of Weeping: Mother Love, Child Death, and Poverty in Guinea-Bissau*. Madison: University of Wisconsin Press, 2004.

Elmendorf, Mary L. *Nine Mayan Women: A Village Faces Change.* Cambridge: Schenkman, 1976.

Ember, Carol, and Melvin Ember. "Explaining Corporal Punishment of Children: A Cross-Cultural Study." *American Anthropologist* 107, no. 4 (December 2005): 609–19.

Endicott, Karen Lampell. "Fathering in an Egalitarian Society." Pp. 291–95 in *Father-Child Relations: Cultural and Biosocial Contexts,* edited by Barry S. Hewlett. New York: Aldine, 1992.

Erchak, Gerald M. *The Anthropology of Self and Behavior.* New Brunswick, N.J.: Rutgers University Press, 1992.

Fajans, Jane. *They Make Themselves: Work and Play among the Baining of Papua New Guinea.* Chicago: University of Chicago Press, 1997.

Firth, Raymond. "Education in Tikopia." Pp. 75–90 in *From Child to Adult,* edited by John Middleton. Garden City, N.Y.: Natural History Press, 1970.

Fogel, Allen, Marguerite Barratt Stevenson, and Daniel Messinger. "A Comparison of the Parent-Child Relationship in Japan and the United States." Pp. 35–51 in *Parent-Child Socialization in Diverse Cultures,* edited by Jaipaul L. Roopnarine and D. Bruce Carter. Norwood, N.J.: Ablex, 1992.

Fortes, Meyer. "Social and Psychological Aspects of Education in Taleland and London." Pp. 14–74 in *From Child to Adult: Studies in the Anthropology of Education,* edited by John Middleton. Garden City, N.Y.: Natural History Press, 1938.

Fouts, Hillary N. "Social Contexts of Weaning: The Importance of Cross-Cultural Studies." Pp. 133–48 in *Childhood and Adolescence: Cross-Cultural Perspectives and Applications,* edited by Uwe P. Gielen and Jaipaul L. Roopnarine. Westport, Conn.: Praeger, 2004.

Friedl, Erika. *Children of Deh Koh: Young Life in an Iranian Village.* Syracuse, N.Y.: Syracuse University Press, 1997.

Fung, Heidi. "Becoming a Moral Child: The Socialization of Shame among Young Chinese Children." *Ethos* 27, no. 2 (June 1999): 180–209.

Gallimore, Ronald, Joan Whitehorn Boggs, and Cathie Jordan. *Culture, Behavior, and Education: A Study of Hawaiian-Americans,* vol. 2. Beverly Hills, Calif.: Sage, 1974.

Gaskins, Suzanne. "Cultural Perspectives on Infant-Caregiver Interaction." Pp. 279–98 in *The Roots of Human Sociality: Culture, Cognition, and Human Interaction,* edited by Nicholas J. Enfield and Steven C. Levinson. London: Berg, 2006.

Geertz, Hildred. *The Javanese Family: A Study of Kinship and Socialization.* New York: Free Press, 1961.

Gilmore, David D. "The Manhood Puzzle." Pp. 207–20 in *Gender in Cross-Cultural Perspective*, edited by Caroline B. Brettell and Carolyn F. Sargent. Upper Saddle River, N.J.: Prentice Hall, 2001.

Gladwin, Thomas. *East Is a Big Bird: Navigation and Logic on Puluwat Atoll*. Cambridge, Mass.: Harvard University Press, 1970.

Gladwin, Thomas, and Seymour B. Sarason. *Truk: Man in Paradise*. New York: Wenner-Gren Foundation, 1953.

Goldschmidt, Walter. *The Sebei: A Study in Adaptation*. New York: Holt, Rinehart, and Winston, 1986.

Goodnow, Jacqueline J. "The Socialization of Cognition." Pp. 259–86 in *Cultural Psychology*, edited by James W. Stigler, Richard A. Shweder, and Gilbert Herdt. Cambridge: Cambridge University Press, 1990.

Goody, Esther. "Learning, Apprenticeship, and the Division of Labor." Pp. 233–56 in *Apprenticeship: From Theory to Method and Back Again*, edited by Michael Coy. Albany: SUNY Press, 1989.

———. "Dynamics of the Emergence of Sociocultural Institutional Practices." Pp. 241–64 in *Technology, Literacy, and the Evolution of Society*, edited by David R. Olsen and Michael Cole. Mahwah, N.J.: Erlbaum, 2006.

Gosselain, Olivier P. "Mother Bella Was Not a Bella: Inherited and Transformed Traditions in Southwestern Niger." Pp. 150–77 in *Cultural Transmission and Material Culture: Breaking Down Boundaries*, edited by Miriam T. Stark, Brenda J. Bowser, and Lee Horne. Tucson: University of Arizona Press, 2008.

Gottlieb, Alma. "Luring Your Child into This Life: A Beng Path for Infant Care." Pp. 55–90 in *A World of Babies: Imagined Childcare Guides for Seven Societies*, edited by Judy DeLoache and Alma Gottlieb. Cambridge: Cambridge University Press, 2000.

Greenfield, Patricia M. *Weaving Generations Together: Evolving Creativity in the Maya of Chiapas*. Santa Fe, N.M.: School of American Research Press, 2004.

Guss, David M. "The Enculturation of Makiritare Women." *Ethnology* 21, no. 3 (July 1982): 259–69.

Harkness, Sara, and Charles M. Super. "The Cultural Context of Gender Segregation in Children's Peer Groups." *Child Development* 56, no. 1 (February 1985): 219–24.

———. "East Africa." Pp. 217–39 in *Children in Historical and Comparative Perspective*, edited by Joseph M. Hawes and N. Ray Hiner. Westport, Conn.: Greenwood, 1991.

Herdt, Gilbert. "Sambia Nosebleeding Rites and Male Proximity to Women." Pp. 366–400 in *Cultural Psychology*, edited by James W. Stigler, Richard A. Shweder, and Gilbert Herdt. Cambridge: Cambridge University Press, 1990.

Hern, Warren M. "Family Planning, Amazon Style." *Natural History* 101, no. 12 (December 1992): 30–37.

Hewlett, Barry S., and Michael E. Lamb. "Emerging Issues in the Study of Hunter-Gatherer Children." Pp. 3–18 in *Hunter-Gatherer Childhoods: Evolutionary, Developmental, and Cultural Perspectives*, edited by Barry S. Hewlett and Michael E. Lamb. New Brunswick, N.J.: Transaction/Aldine, 2005.

Hill, Kim, and A. Magdalena Hurtado. *Ache Life History: The Ecology and Demography of a Foraging People*. New York: Aldine de Gruyter, 1996.

Hobart, Angela. "The Shadow Play and Operetta as Mediums of Education in Bali." Pp. 113–44 in *Acquiring Culture: Cross-Cultural Studies in Child Development*, edited by Gustav Jahoda and Ioan M. Lewis. London: Croom Helm, 1988.

Hogbin, H. Ian. *A Guadalcanal Society: The Kaoka Speakers*. New York: Holt, Rinehart, and Winston, 1969.

———. "A New Guinea Childhood: From Weaning till the Eighth Year in Wogeo." Pp. 134–62 in *From Child to Adult*, edited by John Middleton. Garden City, N.Y.: Natural History Press, 1970.

Honawana, Alcinda. *Child Soldiers in Africa*. Philadelphia: University of Pennsylvania Press, 2006.

Hough, Walter. *The Hopi Indians*. Cedar Rapids, Iowa: Torch, 1915.

Howard, Alan. *Learning to Be Rotuman*. New York: Teachers College Press, 1970.

———. "Education in 'Aina Pumehana: The Hawaiian-American Student as Hero." Pp. 115–29 in *Learning and Culture*, edited by Solon T. Kimball and Jacquette H. Burnett, from the proceedings of the 1972 annual meeting of the American Ethnological Society. Seattle: University of Washington Press.

HRAF. "About HRAF." www.yale.edu/hraf/index.html.

Hrdy, Sarah B. *Mothers and Others: The Evolutionary Origins of Mutual Understanding*. Cambridge, Mass.: Belknap, 2009.

Keller, Heidi. *Cultures of Infancy*. Mahwah, N.J.: Erlbaum, 2007.

Kenny, Mary Lorena. *Hidden Heads of Households: Child Labor in Urban Northeast Brazil*. Buffalo, N.Y.: Broadview, 2007.

Kim, Uichol, and So-Hyang Choi. "Individualism, Collectivism, and Child Development: A Korean Perspective." Pp. 227–59 in *Cross-Cultural Roots of Minority Child Development*, edited by Patricia M. Greenfield and Rodney R. Cocking. Hillsdale, N.J.: Erlbaum, 1994.

Lancy, David F. "The Social Organization of Learning: Initiation Rituals and Public Schools." *Human Organization* 34, no. 2 (Summer 1975): 371–80.

———. *Playing on the Mother Ground: Cultural Routines for Children's Development*. New York: Guilford, 1996.

————. "Accounting for the Variability of Mother-Child Play." *American Anthropologist* 109, no. 2 (June 2007): 273–84.

————. *The Anthropology of Childhood: Cherubs, Chattel, and Changelings.* Cambridge: Cambridge University Press, 2008.

Lancy, David F., and M. Annette Grove. "Getting Noticed: Middle Childhood in Cross-Cultural Perspective." *Human Nature* 20, no. 4 (2009 in press).

Langness, Louis L. "Child Abuse and Cultural Values: The Case of New Guinea." Pp. 13–34 in *Child Abuse and Neglect: Cross-Cultural Perspectives,* edited by Jill Korbin. Berkeley: University of California Press, 1981.

Lave, Jean, and Etienne Wenger. *Situated Learning: Legitimate Peripheral Participation.* Cambridge: Cambridge University Press, 1991.

Leavitt, Stephen C. "The Bikhet Mystique: Masculine Identity and Patterns of Rebellion among Bumbita Adolescent Males." Pp. 173–94 in *Adolescence in Pacific Island Societies,* edited by Gilbert Herdt and Stephen C. Leavitt. Pittsburgh: University of Pittsburgh Press, 1998.

Leighton, Dorothea, and Clyde C. Kluckhohn. *Children of the People.* Cambridge, Mass.: Harvard University Press, 1948.

Levin, Paula. "The Impact of Preschool Teaching and Learning in Hawaiian Families." *Anthropology and Education Quarterly* 23, no. 1 (March 1992): 59–72.

LeVine, Robert A. "Ethnographic Studies of Childhood: A Historical Overview." *American Anthropologist* 109, no. 2 (June 2007): 247–60.

Levy, Robert I. *The Tahitians.* Chicago: University of Chicago Press, 1973.

Li, Jin, Lianquin Wang, and Kurt W. Fischer. "The Organization of Chinese Shame Concepts." *Cognition and Emotion* 18, no. 6 (2004): 767–97.

Loudon, John B. "Teasing and Socialization on Tristan da Cunha." Pp. 293–32 in *Socialization: The Approach from Social Anthropology,* edited by Phillip Mayer. London: Tavistock, 1970.

Low, Bobbi S. "Cross-Cultural Patterns in the Training of Children: An Evolutionary Perspective." *Journal of Comparative Psychology* 103, no. 4 (1989): 311–19.

Lutz, Catherine A. "Parental Goals, Ethnopsychology, and the Development of Emotional Meaning." *Ethos* 11, no. 4 (December 1983): 246–62.

MacCormack, Carol P. "Health, Fertility, and Birth in Moyamba District, Sierra Leone." Pp. 105–29 in *Ethnography of Fertility and Birth,* edited by Carol P. MacCormack. Prospect Heights, Ill.: Waveland, 1994.

MacDonald, Katharine. "Cross-Cultural Comparison of Learning in Human Hunting: Implications for Life History Evolution." *Human Nature* 18, no. 4 (2007): 386–402.

Marchand, Trevor H. J. *Minaret Building and Apprenticeship in Yemen.* Richmond, Va.: Curzon, 2001.

Martini, Mary, and John Kirkpatrick. "Parenting in Polynesia: A View from the Marquesas." Pp. 199–222 in *Parent-Child Socialization in Diverse Cultures*, vol. 5, *Annual Advances in Applied Developmental Psychology*, edited by Jaipaul L. Roopnarine and D. Bruce Carter. Norwood, N.J.: Ablex, 1992.

Matthiasson, John S. "But Teacher, Why Can't I Be a Hunter: Inuit Adolescence as a Double-Blind Situation." Pp. 72–82 in *Childhood and Adolescence in Canada*, edited by K. Ishwaran. Toronto: McGraw-Hill Ryerson, 1979.

McNaughton, Peter R. *The Mande Blacksmiths*. Bloomington: Indiana University Press, 1988.

Messing, Simon D. *Highland Plateau Amhara of Ethiopia*. New Haven, Conn.: Human Relations Area Files, 1985.

Morton, Helen. *Becoming Tongan: An Ethnography of Childhood*. Honolulu: University of Hawaii Press, 1996.

Munroe, Lee. "Fatherhood and Effects on Children in Four Cultures." Paper presented at the 34th annual meeting of the Society for Cross-Cultural Research, Santa Fe, New Mexico, February 25, 2005.

Nerlove, Sara B., John M. Roberts, Robert E. Klein, Charles Yarbrough, and Jean-Pierre Habicht. "Natural Indicators of Cognitive Development: An Observational Study of Rural Guatemalan Children." *Ethos* 2, no. 3 (January 1974): 265–95.

Nicolaisen, Ida. "Concepts in Learning among the Punan Bah of Sarawak." Pp. 193–221 in *Acquiring Culture: Cross-Cultural Studies in Child Development*, edited by Gustav Jahoda and Ioan M. Lewis. London: Croom Helm, 1988.

Orellana, Marjorie F. *Translating Childhoods: Immigrant Youth, Language, and Culture*. New Brunswick, N.J.: Rutgers University Press, 2009.

Overing, Joanna. "Personal Autonomy and the Domestication of the Self in Piaroa Society." Pp. 169–92 in *Acquiring Culture: Cross-Cultural Studies in Child Development*, edited by Gustav Jahoda and Ioan M. Lewis. London: Croom Helm, 1988.

Paradise, Ruth, and Barbara Rogoff. "Side by Side: Learning by Observing and Pitching In." *Ethos* 37, no. 1 (March 2009): 102–38.

Peters, John F. *Life among the Yanomami: The Story of Change among the Xilixana on the Mucajai River in Brazil*. Orchard Park, N.Y.: Broadview, 1998.

Philips, Susan U. *The Invisible Culture: Communication in Classroom and Community on the Warm Springs Indian Reservation*. White Plains, N.Y.: Longman, 1983.

Polak, Barbara. Learning by Doing: Am Beispiel der Erdnuß- und Hirseaussaat, unpublished master's thesis, Univeriteit Bayreuth, n.d.

———. "Little Peasants: On the Importance of Reliability in Child Labour." Pp. 125–36 in *Le travail en Afrique noire: Représentations et pratiques à l'époque contermporaine*, edited by Hélène d'Almeida-Topor, Monique Lakroum, and Gerd Spittler. Paris: Karthala, 2003.

Pope-Edwards, Carolyn. "Children's Play in Cross-Cultural Perspective: A New Look at the Six Culture Study." Pp. 81–96 in *Play: An Interdisciplinary Synthesis*, edited by Felicia F. McMahon, Donald E. Lytle, and Brian Sutton-Smith. Lanham, Md.: University Press of America, 2005.

Quinn, Naomi. "Universals of Child Rearing." *Anthropological Theory* 5, no. 4 (December 2005): 477–516.

Raum, Otto Friedrich. *Chaga Childhood: A Description of Indigenous Education in an East African Tribe*. Oxford: Oxford University Press, 1940.

Read, Margaret. *Children of Their Fathers*. New Haven, Conn.: Yale University Press, 1960.

Reichard, Gladys. *Spider Woman: A Story of Navaho Weavers and Chanters*. New York: Macmillan, 1934.

Reichel-Dolmatoff, Gerardo. "Training for the Priesthood among the Kogi of Colombia." Pp. 265–88 in *Enculturation in Latin America*, edited by Johannes Wilbert. Los Angeles: UCLA Latin American Center, 1976.

Richards, Audrey I. *Chisungu*. London: Faber and Faber, 1956.

Riesman, Paul. *First Find Yourself a Good Mother*. New Brunswick, N.J.: Rutgers University Press, 1992.

Rindstedt, Camilla, and Karin Aronsson. "¿Quieres Bañar? Sibling Caretaking, Play, and Perspective-Taking in an Andean Community." Paper presented at 33rd annual meeting of the Jean Piaget Society, Chicago, Illinois, June 2003.

Rival, Laura. "Formal Schooling and the Production of Modern Citizens in the Ecuadorian Amazon." Pp.108–22 in *Schooling the Symbolic Animal: Social and Cultural Dimensions of Education*, edited by Bradley A.U. Levinson. Lanham, Md.: Rowman & Littlefield, 2000.

Roe, Sandra. "A Brief History of an Ethnographic Database: The HRAF Collection of Ethnography." *Behavioral and Social Sciences Librarian* 23, no. 2 (2007): 47–77.

Rogoff, Barbara. *Apprenticeship in Thinking: Cognitive Development in Social Context*. New York: Oxford University Press, 1990.

Rogoff, Barbara, Martha Julia Sellers, Sergio Pirrotta, Nathan Fox, and Sheldon H. White. "Age of Assignment of Roles and Responsibilities to Children: A Cross-Cultural Survey." *Human Development* 19, no. 5 (1975): 353–69.

Rohner, Ronald P., and Manjusri Chaki-Sircar. *Women and Children in a Bengali Village*. Hanover, N.H.: University Press of New England, 1988.

Schieffelin, Bambi B. "Teasing and Shaming in Kaluli Children's Interactions." Pp. 165–81 in *Language Socialization across Cultures*, edited by Bambi B. Schieffelin and Elinor Ochs. Cambridge: Cambridge University Press, 1986.

———. *The Give and Take of Everyday Life: Language Socialization of Kaluli Children*. Cambridge: Cambridge University Press, 1990.

Schlegel, Alice, and Herbert Berry. "Adolescent Initiation Ceremonies: A Cross-Cultural Code." *Ethnology* 18, no. 2 (April 1979): 199–210.

Serpell, Robert. *The Significance of Schooling: Life Journeys in an African Society*. Cambridge: Cambridge University Press, 1993.

Simmons, Leo W., ed. *Sun Chief: The Autobiography of a Hopi Indian*. New Haven, Conn.: Yale University Press, 1942.

Singleton, John. "Japanese Folkcraft Pottery Apprenticeship: Cultural Patterns of an Educational Institution." Pp. 13–30 in *Apprenticeship: From Theory to Method and Back Again*, edited by Michael W. Coy. Albany: SUNY Press, 1989.

Sorenson, E. Richard. *The Edge of the Forest: Land, Childhood, and Change in a New Guinea Protoagricultural Society*. Washington, D.C.: Smithsonian Institution, 1976.

Spencer, Paul. "The Function of Ritual in the Socialization of the Samburu Moran." Pp. 127–57 in *Socialization: The Approach from Social Anthropology*, edited by Philip Mayer. London: Tavistock, 1970.

Spittler, Gerd. *Hirtenarbeit*. Köln: Rüdiger Köppe, 1998.

Takada, Akira. "Mother-Infant Interactions among the !Xun: Analysis of Gymnastic and Breastfeeding Behaviors." Pp. 289–308 in *Hunter-Gatherer Childhoods: Evolutionary, Developmental, and Cultural Perspectives*, edited by Barry S. Hewlett and Michael E. Lamb. New Brunswick, N.J.: Aldine, 2005.

Tanon, Fabienne. *A Cultural View on Planning: The Case of Weaving in Ivory Coast*. Tilburg: Tilburg University Press, 1994.

Toren, Christina. *Making Sense of Hierarchy: Cognition as Social Process in Fiji*. Atlantic Highlands, N.J.: Athlone Press, 1990.

Tronick, Edward Z., R. Brook Thomas, and Magali Daltabuit. "The Quechua Manta Pouch: A Caretaking Practice for Buffering the Peruvian Infant against the Multiple Stressors of High Altitude." *Child Development* 65, no. 4 (August 1994): 1005–13.

Turner, Diane Michalski. "What Happened When My Daughter Became a Fijan." Pp. 92–114 in *Children and Anthropological Research*, edited by Barbara Butler and Diane Michalski Turner. New York: Plenum, 1987.

Tuzin, Donald. *The Voice of the Tambaran: Truth and Illusion in Ilahita Arapesh Religion*. Berkeley: University of California Press, 1980.

Vizedom, Monika, and James P. Zais. *Rites and Relationships: Rites of Passage and Contemporary Anthropology*. Beverly Hills, Calif.: Sage, 1976.

Voget, Fred W. *A History of Ethnology*. New York: Holt, Rinehart, and Winston, 1975.

Wagley, Charles. *Welcome of Tears: The Tapirapé Indians of Central Brazil*. Oxford: Oxford University Press, 1977.

Wallaert-Pêtre, Hélène. "Learning How to Make the Right Pots: Apprenticeship Strategies and Material Culture, a Case Study in Handmade Pottery from Cameroon." *Journal of Anthropological Research* 57, no. 4 (Winter 2001): 471–93.

———. "The Way of the Potter's Mother: Apprenticeship Strategies among Dii Potters from Cameroon, West Africa." Pp. 178–98 in *Cultural Transmission and Material Culture: Breaking Down Boundaries*, edited by Miriam T. Stark, Brenda J. Bowser, and Lee Horne. Tucson: University of Arizona Press, 2008.

Watson-Gegeo, Karen A., and David W. Gegeo. "The Role of Sibling Interaction in Child Socialization." Pp. 54–76. in *Sibling Interaction across Cultures*, edited by Patricia G. Zukow. New York: Springer-Verlag, 1989.

Weisfeld, Glenn E. *Evolutionary Principles of Human Adolescence*. New York: Basic Books, 1999.

Weisner, Thomas S., and Ronald Gallimore. "My Brother's Keeper: Child and Sibling Caretaking." *Current Anthropology* 18, no. 2 (1977): 169–90.

Wenger, Martha. "Work, Play, and Social Relationships among Children in a Giriama Community." Pp. 91–115 in *Children's Social Networks and Social Supports*, edited by Deborah Belle. New York: Wiley, 1989.

Whiting, John W. M. *Becoming a Kwoma*. New Haven, Conn.: Yale University Press, 1941.

Whittemore, Robert Dunster. Child Caregiving and Socialization to the Mandinka Way: Toward an Ethnography of Childhood. Unpublished doctoral dissertation, UCLA, 1989.

Wilbert, Johannes. "To Become a Maker of Canoes: An Essay in Warao Enculturation." Pp. 303–58 in *Enculturation in Latin America*, edited by Johannes Wilbert. Los Angeles: UCLA Latin American Center, 1976.

Wiley, Andrea S. *An Ecology of High-Altitude Infancy*. Cambridge: Cambridge University Press, 2004.

Wober, Mallory M. "Culture and the Concept of Intelligence: A Case in Uganda." *Journal of Cross-Cultural Psychology* 3, no. 4 (December 1972): 327–28.

Yerkes, Robert M., and John D. Dodson. "The Relation of Strength of Stimulus to Rapidity of Habit-Formation." *Journal of Comparative Neurology and Psychology* 18 (1908): 459–82.

Zeitlin, Marian. "My Child Is My Crown: Yoruba Parental Theories and Practices in Early Childhood." Pp. 407–27 in *Parent's Cultural Belief Systems: Their Origins, Expressions, and Consequences*, edited by Sara Harkness and Charles M. Super. New York: Guilford, 1996.

Zelazo, Phillip R., Nancy A. Zelazo, and Sarah Kolb. "'Walking' in the Newborn." *Science* 176, no. 4032 (April 1972): 314–15.

CHAPTER EIGHT

LEARNING FROM OTHER CHILDREN

Ashley E. Maynard and Katrin E. Tovote

Petu', a 9-year-old Mayan girl, is in her family courtyard setting up a small, make-believe soda stand using an old crate and some empty soda bottles. She works quietly, about 20 feet away from her mother and siblings. Her mother is weaving a shawl for one of the girls to wear to the next community-wide fiesta. No one in the family seems to be paying any attention to what Petu' is doing.

After she has gathered all the necessary materials and set up a complete stand, she takes it apart and moves it closer to her family, where she sets the whole thing up again. One of her younger sisters, Chepa, takes this as an invitation and comes over to play with her. Chepa walks up and sticks her hand out as if to pay Petu' for a soda. Petu' takes the "money" and hands Chepa a "soda." Chepa pretends to drink the soda and hands Petu' the empty bottle. Pancho, their 2-year-old brother, has been watching this activity and he leaves his mother's side to go and get a "soda" for himself. When Pancho arrives at the soda stand, Petu' asks him if he wants a soda, using the voice of a market salesperson. Pancho, who is not very talkative yet, sticks his hand out to indicate that he does. Petu' hands him a soda bottle at the same time that a neighbor child, Maruch, who is there spending time with the family, insists that Pancho pay Petu' for the soda. Maruch hands Pancho a leaf to represent money and tells him to pay Petu' for the soda. Pancho then hands Petu' the money and drinks his soda. After he finishes, he hands the soda bottle to Petu', who puts it below the stand and then asks him if he wants another soda. He nods his head yes and she hands him another soda bottle.

Maruch once again helps Pancho by giving him a leaf to pay for the soda. Pancho hands the leaf to Petu' and the routine repeats several times. At one point, Roberto, another neighbor child who is visiting, asks Pancho if he wants a beer, pointing from a distance to an empty beer bottle that is on the stand. Pancho does not respond to this question.

Eventually Pancho moves to the opposite side of the stand, in the traditional position of the seller. He is looking at the bottles under the stand. Petu' takes this opportunity to switch roles. She makes Pancho the seller, and she acts as the buyer. Using the voice of a customer, she tells him that she wants one of his sodas. He is too small to reach over and hand her a soda, so she just takes one and then hands him some play "money." She has to tell him to take the money; he does not ask for it himself. This routine repeats once and then finally Pancho comes around to the front of the stand where he can hand Petu' the sodas himself. The two continue this routine while the other children watch and the mother works on her weaving.

Many children around the world are like Petu', Chepa, and Pancho. They engage in play situations, sometimes involving teaching and learning, and often reflecting adult roles they observe. The children in this example are engaged in pretend play as they mimic a real situation. At the same time, they are teaching a 2-year-old boy how to get involved in selling through play. The family's livelihood comes from selling sodas and other commodities at a market about 2 hours away from their home. Petu', at age 9, is already competent in selling soft drinks. She can figure amounts to charge and make change. In the play situation, she and her friend, Maruch, teach 2-year-old Pancho how to buy and sell soft drinks. In repeating the script over and over, the girls keep Pancho busy and away from his mother, who is working nearby. The mother is not involved in this teaching situation, but she gives approving smiles to the children as they play.

Like Pancho, children around the world spend a lot of time learning from siblings and peers. They can learn cognitive or physical skills, games, how to do chores or work, or normative behavior. In some cultures, children learn how to care for children, and in caring for them, they develop skills in teaching them to do things as they engage them in everyday activities or chores (Maynard 2002). This chapter takes a developmental and ecological perspective to explore a variety of factors that influence the ways that children learn from other children.

When children learn from other children instead of from adults, many factors may influence the course of interactions. These range from age, gender, or status hierarchies, to the basic cognitive or emotional levels of the parties, to the cultural setting. The partial knowledge of child teachers may be just enough for a young learner to pay attention to. That is, more elaborate information provided by an expert might overwhelm a young learner. Children are a closer match to each other in terms of skill level and the range of activities they are interested in. Although adults in some cultures spend time playing with children and teaching them everyday kinds of activities, in many cultures, apart from schoolteachers, adults do not play or teach children directly because they are absorbed in adult work (Gaskins 1999; Lancy 2008), and playing with children is considered inappropriate adult behavior (Gaskins, Haight, and Lancy 2007).

A Cultural Understanding of Siblings and Peers

According to Weisner (1989), in any cultural community, "Siblings always *matter*" (14, his emphasis). Siblings influence each other's learning in important ways, and they may have an altruistic interest in helping each other. On the other hand, unrelated peers provide children with an opportunity to interact with others who may not share the values and practices children first learn at home (Greenfield and Suzuki 1998). Thus peers also seem to always matter. Interactions with other children, whether related or not, are important for a child's social, emotional, and cognitive development.

In many cultures, children's interactions with other children are more prevalent in their day-to-day experiences than their interactions with adults. That is, interactions among children appear to have primacy in many cultures outside the United States and Europe, where adults spend a lot of time caring for or teaching a small number of children. In cultures where children spend a great deal of their time with other children, adults still provide guidance as to proper behavior or how to care for younger siblings (see chapter 7, this volume), but children may rely on siblings and peers for social interaction throughout much of their day (Martini

1994; Weisner 1987; Weisner and Gallimore 1977). Indeed, many studies conducted in non-Western societies indicate that child–adult interaction is much less common than in Western societies (Whiting and Edwards 1988; Zukow 1989b; Zukow-Goldring 2002).

In many cultures, children's interactions with other children begin at birth. Babies may be cared for by other children as well as their mothers. For example, among the Afikpo in Africa, children serve as key personnel in caring for newborns: "when a baby is born it is given, after being washed, to a small child to carry into the house where its mother will spend the next few days. Almost at once it will in part be looked after by quite small children. I have seen a little girl of about five or six carrying a newly born baby over her shoulder, or sitting down and giving it water to drink" (Ottenberg 1968, 80).

Sibling caretaking is nearly universal (Weisner and Gallimore 1977). It is reduced in wealthy strata of complex societies when servants may substitute, in some foraging societies because the infant is always with its mother, and in the modern era of small families. Children have opportunities to interact with peers to varying degrees around the world, depending on, for example, whether they are restricted to their family compounds (and therefore interacting only with kin), whether they are allowed to develop friendship networks with unrelated peers, whether they go to school (where they will meet many unrelated children, usually of both sexes), and whether they work.

Several cross-cultural studies have described siblings as especially effective at socializing each other, in guiding each other in cultural tasks, or in giving verbal or nonverbal didactic help (de León 2002; Dunn 1989; Maynard 2002; Rabain-Jamin, Maynard, and Greenfield 2003; Rogoff et al. 1993; Stewart 1983; Watson-Gegeo and Gegeo 1989; Weisner and Gallimore 1977; Zukow 1989a, 1989b). As they interact with each other, children learn skills that are useful in play situations, for domestic chores, or for other kinds of work. Among the Zinacantec Maya, sibling caretakers teach their younger siblings to do everyday kinds of things, such as caring for baby dolls, making play food and beverages (e.g., coffee, beans, and tortillas), washing, or playing store, as in the opening example of this chapter (Maynard 2002). Older Zinacantec siblings are very adept at deciding what to teach the younger ones, how to teach them, what materials to use, and the like. For example,

Roberto, a 6-year-old boy, has gathered a tortilla press and some dough and brought them near his 2-year-old sister, Carmela. He engages her in pressing tortillas by first doing it himself. He calls attention to each step, "Here I put the dough on, and here I press!" He shows her how to do it and then gives it to her to try. She looks puzzled, so he helps her by situating the dough on the press just right. Then, he closes the top for her, and together they press down on the lever to press the dough. Roberto then opens the press and they look at the round tortilla. "Ay!" exclaims Roberto as he shows Carmela what they have done. They repeat this routine many times.

In another situation, Roberto taught Carmela how to buy and sell items; he set up two store stands, complete with items to sell, and he made her stand in front of one. In yet another situation, Roberto wanted to show Carmela how to read, so he brought out some books and pointed to objects, naming them as he pointed to each one. As the content of what he wanted to teach changed, Roberto showed his skill in adapting to his sister across several kinds of activities.

Observing other children working can be very helpful in learning new skills because the tasks done by children are often less complicated than those done by adults. As in play, children can also give verbal direction in work activities. Tovote (2006) noted that Maya craft sellers on the streets of San Cristóbal de las Casas in Chiapas, Mexico, taught younger siblings how to sell:

Throughout the day, 4-year-old Maria stays close to her older sisters Ana, age 7, and Rosa, age 10. She observes them closely when they offer and sell their Maya craftwork to tourists. Maria herself holds a bunch of homemade bracelets in her hand. Her older sisters approach international and domestic tourists by walking up to or next to them while holding the offered ware (commonly self-made scarves, belts, bracelets) for them to see. They repeat the Spanish phrase "*Cómprale!*" (Buy it!), and seek close body contact with the potential buyers by touching their arms. They usually keep up with the tourists for a few seconds or even a few minutes. During this time Maria does not leave her sisters' side. She also stretches out her little hand to the potential buyer while she seeks to make eye contact. She imitates exactly the words and gestures her older sisters use. She even repeats numbers and prices mentioned by the older girls. However, the way Maria uses the Spanish words makes it obvious that she does not (yet) grasp their full meaning (e.g., "5 for 20 pesos"). However, this is not a problem because once a buyer is willing to buy one of Maria's items the older girls assist Maria in selling. The older girls monitor whether she receives the correct amount of money and also whether she hands back correct change. In between selling to tourists the family members reorganize their products. An older sister shows Maria how to arrange her bunch of bracelets. When the older sisters spot a new potential customer the whole selling procedure (approaching, offering, negotiating) gets repeated, often dozens of times within one day.

The type of learning activity a child is engaged in also depends on what kind of activity is considered appropriate for children in accordance with the local norms and the existing cultural scripts. Western children tend to spend a majority of their time playing and studying (Larson and Verma 1999). Children might be but often do not have to be involved in light household chores. Furthermore, while it is not acceptable for American toddlers to wield sharp objects, it is acceptable for them to learn to ride a Big Wheel or a tricycle. As we will see, children can be effective in teaching each other appropriate behaviors for their cultural setting.

Theoretical Frameworks for Understanding Sibling and Peer Interactions

Whiting and Whiting (1975; see also chapter 3, this volume) provide a comprehensive framework for analyzing and understanding sibling and peer interactions in cultural settings. This model emphasizes the relationships between a child's development and the interrelated nature of the environment, situations, values, people, and institutions, such as school and family, which surround the child.

Cross-cultural analyses have detected a broad range of definitions—arising from the variability in kin and family structures—of "sibling" and "peer" (Gauvain 2001; Parke and Buriel 1998). While Western cultures rely almost exclusively on genetic relationships in their definition of sibling and family, many other societies also include other criteria (Cicirelli 1994; Maynard 2004a; Nuckolls 1993; Watson-Gegeo and Gegeo 1989; Zukow-Goldring 2002). For example, in Pukapuka Atoll in Oceania, members of the same village or church would call each other *taina* (sibling) and rely on each other for support (Hecht 1979, 1981). In many Asiatic, American, and Australian dialects, there are kin terms that differentiate older and younger male and female siblings (Anthropological Institute of Great Britain and Ireland 1872; Greenfield and Childs 1977).

A child's culture influences the nature and extent of peer relationships beyond the home (Gaskins 2006), including interactions with nonrelated children (and adults) in other settings such as public spaces like village squares, streets, markets, public transport, and in educational institutions such as schools, preschools, and day care centers. Peer interactions are a child's first chance to—consciously or unconsciously—carry family-based values and habits to the "outside world" (Greenfield and Suzuki 1998). Some societies discourage cross-gender relationships during childhood (Whiting and Edwards 1988), but in others, mixed-gender interactions are encouraged and can be observed quite frequently (Rogoff 1990). Another area that demonstrates how culture influences peer relationships is the amount of time peers spend together. Whereas in many Western countries children commonly spend a significant part of their day with same-age peers (e.g., in schools, after-school programs, sports clubs), in many Asian countries more time is spent with family members (e.g., helping with chores, visiting relatives) (Larson and Verma 1999).

There are many factors that contribute to and shape sibling and peer learning, including the learning setting and the individual characteristics of the involved parties.

Characteristics of the Learning Setting

Children learn at home, in schools, on the playground, in parks, in grocery stores, in the fields, in sports clubs, in the streets, at work, and so on—whether or not the setting explicitly promotes learning. Setting also influences the kind of learning experiences a child may be engaged in. In formal settings, such as schools, learning is defined as the primary activity, and there are set structures and lessons laid out with goals for what should be learned within a set timeframe. In a formal setting, all should be learning the same material, ideally at the same pace. Formal settings also have explicit roles for teachers. On the other hand, in informal settings,

Figure 8.1. Xunka' and Teresa embroider garments for their father and brother (A. Maynard photo)

such as the sibling play described in the opening vignette, relationships and roles of "teacher" and "student" are negotiated, and students are permitted to learn at an individualized pace, according to what they need to know to do the job they will need to do and according to their developing capabilities.

Various settings for learning can be found in a given society, and children have to learn who can be called on as a teacher and for what tasks across different settings. For example, an Abaluyian village in western Kenya (Weisner 1984) and a small town in north central Italy (New 2008) provide different learning contexts. Among the Abaluyia, a child who seeks guidance is more likely to get help—from adults or peers—if he or she is attempting a chore (Weisner 1984). In northern Italy, infants are constantly under the care of their mothers, and consequently, they don't have much opportunity to interact with peers (New 2008), unlike the Afikpo, mentioned above, who have child caregivers from birth.

The Makeup of the Peer Group

Societies delimit the settings where children are allowed to go, and this may influence whom they get to interact with. Gaskins (1996, 1999) describes the experience of Yucatec Maya children who must play with siblings and leave parents alone to work, while remaining in the family compound. This contrasts with what Martini and Kirkpatrick (1992) found in the Marquesas, where children have many opportunities to interact with un-related peers, afforded by their ability to wander all around their village, to the forest, to the beach, and wherever they choose. Yucatec Maya children learn by watching other children or adults, but they do not seek instruction from adults directly engaged in work activities so as to not interfere with the work. Furthermore, Yucatec children are expected to be able to groom and take care of themselves from a very young age (Gaskins 2000, 2008). Like Yucatec toddlers, Marquesan toddlers also learn to feed and dress themselves. But they move out into the world by following their older siblings, including visiting dangerous (in the eyes of the anthropologists) places such as the boat ramp, elevated bridges, and the stream bed. Older siblings like to take toddlers with them because it gives them a chance to play away from home while fulfilling their role of caregiver. Marquesan toddlers must learn to be self-reliant and nondisruptive in the context of peer groups, a skill they also practice at home with parents.

The size of the peer group is another important factor. In households of industrialized nations, most often there is only one other sibling available. In Gaskins's (1999) field study, Yucatec children's interaction with peers was constrained by the need to hang around the family compound, interacting solely with siblings and other relatives. But in many communities, children are free to join various impromptu social groups, leading to both small and larger group learning activities (Maynard 2004b).

In small-scale non-Western communities in which sibling caretaking is routine, children are more likely to spend time in mixed-age child groups. Mixed-age groups afford different kinds of learning opportunities than same-age groups, where children are more likely to have the same skills. In Western cultures, even informal settings have slowly been formalized. Sandlot baseball with a mixed-age peer group has been replaced by age- and sex-graded and segregated "Leagues." Maynard found that Zinacantec children almost always played in mixed-age groups, which afforded many kinds of models for young children to look up to. In the example of 9-year-old Rosy teaching washing to her younger siblings, below, Rosy gives verbal and nonverbal didactic help to Patricia and Esteban in accordance with her more advanced cognitive and verbal skills. On the other hand, Esteban doesn't say much but does serve as an observational model for Patricia, who watches him closely and copies what he is doing (Maynard 2004b). In James Chisholm's (1983) study of Navajo infancy, the kinds of learning activities children were involved in depended on whether they were in an extended family camp or an isolated nuclear family camp. The children living among extended kin had a greater number and wider variety of caretakers and playmates available, from a wider age range, including their mothers, aunts, older siblings, and cousins. In smaller, isolated camps, children had only their parents and blood siblings as caretakers or playmates.

The Likelihood of Adult Presence and Influence

Depending on norms and habits of a community, adults can be at a distance from, have indirect influence on, or be directly involved in sibling and peer learning. Rogoff (1981) found in a highland Guatemalan community that even though children were often in the presence of an adult, the child and adult did not interact frequently. Child-adult interactions, in fact, dropped significantly with child age: 9-year-olds, for example, interacted significantly more often with siblings and peers in the age range from 7 to 11 years than with adults (50 percent versus 18 percent, respectively; Rogoff 1981). Marquesan children are also often at a distance from caregivers, roaming far from home during the day (Martini and Kirkpatrick 1992). On the other hand, Zinacantec and Yucatec Maya parents have indirect influence on sibling interactions because the children are always within earshot; the parents are able to intervene when a child cries or if there is an argument to settle (de León 2008; Gaskins, 1999). Gaskins (2000) reported that even though Yucatec Maya village children are socially oriented and observe carefully, they rarely initiate contact with adults. Maya children are more likely to communicate with other children unless an adult needs to give them necessary task-oriented directions. In the United States, where mothers are highly involved with child care and sibling caretaking is extremely rare, Corter, Abramovitch, and Pepler

(1983) found that the presence of mothers reduced the total number of sibling interactions and, interestingly, was also associated with aggressive tendencies between the siblings.

Strategies and Trade-offs in Sibling Caretaking

Older children learn how to teach, lead, or control younger children in culturally appropriate ways. Of course, younger siblings must also learn to be cooperative partners. Gaskins's (2006) work with the Yucatec Maya illustrates this point:

> Children, from the time they are very young, are also regularly reminded of their position relative to each of their younger siblings. Children are scolded for not listening to their older siblings and for not taking care of or being generous with their younger ones. . . . Older children are told to fulfill the desires of the younger for no other reason than the little ones are "poor things" and "your younger siblings." At the same time, they are given the authority to order them to do things, and it is expected that they will be obeyed. . . . [I]n play, all children who live in a yard together have the right to enter into any play that is ongoing, even when their entry forces the other children to make significant adjustments in their play. . . . All activities the children engage in must take multi-aged skills and interests into account. (295–6)

All Yucatec children get the opportunity to practice acting as older and as younger siblings. When they act as older siblings, they practice perspective taking and assessing the needs of their younger charges, often putting aside their own desires. When they act as younger siblings, they practice persuading their older siblings, learning to assess when their demands are reasonable and how to best communicate. Rules and skills that are learned in other contexts are thus developed and applied in the sibling context.

In a contrasting case, Rindstedt (2001) shows how teasing, shaming, and threats are used by indigenous sibling caretakers in Ecuador as the means of social control. In one example, a little boy in charge of a toddler girl uses threats to get her to stop crying:

> Geovani tries to stop Miriam's crying by threatening her that her mother is going to vaccinate her. . . . Miriam does not cease crying, though, but

> sobbingly says that her mommy did not bring her along when she left the house. Geovani (rhetorically) asks her to tell him what is the matter, trying to get her to talk, but Miriam does not stop crying. (165–6)

This kind of forceful social control, though not always effective, is sometimes necessary to keep young children clean and away from harm. De León (2008) illustrates how Tzotzil Mayan siblings explain imminent dangers to keep young children away from poisonous bugs. They use their authority in the context of caring for them to keep them safe from harm.

Caretakers must often learn to balance the roles of caretaker and playmate. They must meet the demands for membership in the peer group while maintaining an image of themselves as a good caretaker in the eyes of adults who monitor their behavior. Children may display one style of care in the presence of adults and a different style when only their peers are around. For example, among the Bonerate, Broch (1990) observed:

> The caretaker knows too well that there is no excuse for allowing his charge to cry. The first adult who observes the scene will scold him publicly. . . . Children are no angels, and sometimes when they believe they are unseen they purposely tease their charges. . . . It also seems to make a difference to the caretaker if he has to look after his own sibling or a child from a different household. The youngest children receive somewhat rougher treatment from their own siblings than from other caretakers. One day I observed two children, a boy and a girl, who were looking after their younger siblings. They moved to the edge of the village where the toddlers were teased until they started to cry, to the great amusement of the caretakers. They continued to trouble their charges for a while before they picked them up. Then they returned, hugging the crying youngsters and showing all the villagers how kindly they tried to comfort them! (81)

Minks (2008) observed a similar pattern among the Miskitu. Sibling and peer relations are complicated and can be harmonious or conflictive, hierarchical or egalitarian.

Unlike the mixed-age group where siblings learn how to deal with hierarchies, in settings where children spend a lot of time with same-age peers, they learn how to manage their equal status. In many collectivistic societies, children are expected to display a high degree of sensitivity, cooperation, compliance, and self-control in interaction with peers (Chen 2000; Greenfield and Suzuki 1998), relatively low autonomy and competitiveness, higher mutual sensitivity, and compliance in social interaction. For example, shy, sensitive, and inhibited behavior is desirable in countries such as China that are characterized by Confucian values. Differences in the cultural script become especially evident in how children react to stress or conflict in peer and sibling learning interactions. While most American children react to stress from peers or siblings by either asking them directly to stop their behavior or by showing discomfort (e.g., crying), children in East Asian cultures might rely on a coping strategy called *ren* to deal with stress in interactions with others. *Ren* (translated as "forbearance"), which relies on Confucian values, expresses that a person can move either forward or backward in a difficult situation, and that in certain situations backing off might be more desirable than insisting (Xu et al. 2006). *Ren*, however, is a reciprocal concept, which assumes that the other party also shows *ren* in order to maintain group harmony (Xu et al. 2006). An outsider without this cultural knowledge might misinterpret *ren* as apathy or a lack of interest. Even preschool children socialize each other to reciprocate *ren*.

The Role of Gender

Gender is an often neglected factor in sibling and peer learning interactions. This is surprising insofar as several large-scale cross-cultural studies illustrate significant gender differences in social behavior, including that, at least in the West, children as young as 3 years old tend to play more often with children of their own sex (Barry, Bacon, and Child 1967; Munroe and Munroe 1975/1994; Whiting and Edwards 1988). These preferences for same-sex playmates and other sex-segregated patterns have been shown to increase with age (Maccoby and Jacklin 1987).

Another consistent finding from cross-cultural research is that girls tend to be more nurturant and boys tend to be more physically aggressive (Best 2004). In almost all cultures, girls are socialized to be more nurturing, obedient, and responsible than boys (Barry et al. 1967), which is why girls are more often assigned as sibling caregivers (Weisner and Gallimore 1977; Whiting 1980; Whiting and Whiting 1975). There is also cross-cultural evidence that preadolescent boys compared to girls show higher levels of aggression, competition, and dominance in play interactions (Maccoby 1990). These gender-specific behavioral tendencies have been found in Ethiopia, Switzerland, the United States (Omark, Omark, and Edelmann 1975), the Kalahari (Africa), and England (Konner 1975). Hence, overall learning processes between two or more boys are more likely to be characterized by open displays of power asymmetry, competition, and aggression, while in girls-only learning groups the prevalence of these behavior patterns is less pronounced, or enacted in a more subtle way.

Another important factor is the sometimes rigid assignment of tasks by gender (see also chapter 12, this volume). Gender divisions in "chores" make cross-gender learning activities less likely (Whiting and Edwards 1988). De León (2005) describes a Tzotzil boy growing up in a largely female family eagerly applying himself to the learning of various household skills, including tortilla making, embroidering, and weaving. This occurred in spite of the fact that he was systematically discouraged and reprimanded for his involvement in female tasks (cited in Paradise and Rogoff 2009, 117). However, Maynard (2004c) found for Maya children living in the same village that older boys could teach their baby sisters typical female work in the context of sibling caretaking. However, this "cross-gender" activity was acceptable only when teaching a baby (usually up to age 2 or 2 and a half) to do an important task, such as washing, cooking, or caring for baby dolls (which mimics adult and sibling care of infants). The relative importance of gender differences for a given group should be considered in the study of peer learning interactions.

Peer and Sibling Teaching and Learning and the Influence of Schooling

Large-scale, urban-industrial societies stress structured, decontextualized, child-centered, and formal learning activities (Keller 2007; Maynard 2004b) to transmit a "core" curriculum. By contrast, in the village setting, we see the operation of a "chore" curriculum (see chapter 7, this volume) where peer and sibling learning processes are centered on the acquisition of everyday activities such as carrying water, cooking meals, cleaning, tending flocks, and so on (Lancy 1996; Whiting and Edwards 1988).

In the last few decades, however, schooling has also gained significance in those communities that traditionally emphasized everyday learning. Thus, interesting new questions arise about the interaction of informal (home) and formal (school) communication styles in sibling and peer learning and teaching interactions. As the first children to go to school, siblings are much more familiar with the school style of teaching, unlike their parents, who use traditional models to impart skills. Maynard (2004b), for example, found that indigenous Zinacantec Maya children who go to school regularly blend the traditional Zinacantec model of teaching and learning with school-related teaching and learning experiences when engaged in sibling and peer learning. The Zinacantec model includes observational learning, scaffolding, contextualized talk, bodily closeness between learner and teacher, expectance of obedience, and having multiple models/teachers for the same task. The school model, by contrast, emphasizes verbal instructions, providing more explanations, and teaching with some physical distance. This mixture of teaching styles is illustrated in an exchange Maynard recorded (1999):

> Rosy, a 9-year-old girl who has had a little schooling, sees her 2-year-old sister, Patricia, and 4-year-old brother, Esteban, in the back yard playing with some strings attached to a weaving stick. Rosy enters the scene and places a bucket with a piece of clothing in it between Esteban and Patricia. Then she directs both of them in washing. Esteban expresses that he wants the pants that are in the bucket. Rosy goes to get something else. She returns with another bucket into the frame. Esteban sees that she has the pants as Rosy is putting the bucket in between the two children. Patricia moves the bucket away from Esteban. He says, "Hand me the pants," as he reaches for them. Patricia protests with a baby talk sound. Esteban asks for a bucket from Rosy. She says that they are going to do their washing. Rosy then retreats to watch the washing at a distance and says, "Wash! Wash!" Esteban says, "Let's wash!" And he does the washing action with his threads. He says to Patricia, "Hand me a little water." She protests, saying, "Aaaw," as she looks to the water in her bucket and touches her bucket. Rosy enters to help Patricia wash and says, "Wash Patri!" Rosy then narrates her action of removing the pants from the bucket, "Take out—take out the washing here. Wash! Put soap on your washing here," and she shows the washing movement. She then pretends to put soap on the washing. Xunka' then enters with

a glass of water and says to Rosy, "Look. Look." Rosy tells Xunka', "Give it to him [so that] he can see it," directing Xunka's action. Rosy retreats, to watch the washing from a distance. Rosy then approaches Patricia again to add water to Patricia's bucket, pouring from the big bucket. Esteban continues his washing action, not engaging Patricia. Eventually he knocks over a glass of water, and they all laugh. He asks Xunka' to "Draw some water and bring it back!" Xunka' runs off to get him water. Patricia then looks at what Esteban is doing and imitates the action of washing. Rosy exits the scene completely. Xunka' notices that Rosy has gone and brings water for Patricia and Esteban. "Look at this!" she says, and gives water in a glass to Esteban. She then pours some out of a glass for Patricia. Esteban and Patricia continue washing.

In this example, Rosy blends the more traditional Zinacantec style of teaching, which is characterized by providing very careful, attentive help, with the classroom style, which is characterized by issuing directives and then watching the children follow through from a distance.

Peer Learning in Classrooms

In the earlier Zinacantec case, we saw Rosy blending informal village and formal school strategies. This blending is largely absent in the classroom as anthropologists have documented the conflicts that can arise between school-based and indigenous modes of interaction and learning (Philips 1983). For example, different expectations about the value of peer interaction during lessons can lead to conflicts. This is the case in ethnically diverse classroom settings in individualistic cultures such as in the United States. For example, Adrienne Isaac (1999) conducted ethnographic fieldwork in two classrooms of Latino immigrant children in Los Angeles, California. In one classroom, the teacher had gone through a training program called "Bridging Cultures" (see Trumbull et al. 2001) where she learned about the cultural values of the Latino students, which emphasize collectivistic practices such as collaboration and sharing. This teacher made adjustments in her classroom and lesson plans to allow the children to work together and to create projects in pairs or groups. In the other classroom, the teacher emphasized individualistic values and stressed individual work:

> The children are whispering answers among themselves after one student is called on to respond to the teacher. The teacher then announces to the classroom, "I have heard people whispering and I really don't like it because why? They need to learn by themselves and you really aren't helping them learn. (Trumbull et al. 2001, 34)

Later:

> Brent asks Adrienne (the researcher) for help with his journal writing. David, who was sitting across from Brent at their desk group, tells Adrienne that "nobody is supposed to help him." Brent becomes upset and makes a disappointed expression. David tells Adrienne while Brent listens, "he has to do it by himself." Brent still needs help, however, and asks what the last word on his paper spells. David replies very softly, "glad" as Brent shows him the paper. David looks at Brent's paper more carefully and says "bad, b-a-d," very cautiously in a quiet and nervous voice. (Trumbull et al. 2001, 35)

Isaac noted that in this non–Bridging Cultures class, the children were very conscious of the teacher's do-it-by-yourself values when she was around and showed signs of internal conflict. However, they helped each other freely when she was not around.

While typical U.S. school class environments emphasize individual achievement, autonomous choice, and individual work, many minority and immigrant students come from homes that favor interpersonal relationships over individual performance (Reese et al. 1995). Peer-supported learning and collaborative group activities that reward the group as a whole instead of individuals are effective teaching strategies with students who share a collectivistic background (Greenfield and Suzuki 1998; Trumbull et al. 2001). In Japan, children are expected to rely on their peers to correct them, not the teacher:

> One of the most startling sights for me the first time I saw it was what happens when a student gives an incorrect answer. Other students immediately raise their hands, calling out loudly, "*Chigaimasu!*" "That's wrong!" One of those who called out would then be chosen to give another answer. . . . Teachers routinely and emphatically refrain from giving either positive or negative evaluations of students' answers to

questions or other responses to academic material. Those responses are evaluated, but only by other students. (Benjamin 1997, 45)

According to Benjamin (1997), "Teachers are not available arbiters of correctness, because they fail to act as judges," and "one's peers are reliable guides to academic correctness" (48). Japanese children are placed in groups, or *han*, of about eight children. They learn to rely on each other for social and academic guidance. The fact that *hans* allow the children to successfully teach each other social as well as academic skills at the same time points to the inaccuracy of the widespread Western assumption that formal education and peer assistance or learning are mutually exclusive.

Conclusion

In virtually all societies in the world, regardless of whether they hold a pre- or post-industrialization status, peer and sibling learning interactions help children to practice skills and roles that are essential for their adult life in work, family, or other social settings (Corsaro 1985; Haight and Miller 1993; Vygotsky 1978). Children around the world learn from each other as they engage in sibling caretaking, work, and play with other children. In sibling caretaking, children have the opportunity to learn the perspective-taking and empathy skills involved in providing sensitive care for younger children. Younger children learn to be good at taking direction and being good members of a group led by an elder, eventually learning to lead groups themselves as they become the eldest available. As younger children watch and interact with older children who are working, they are able to learn useful skills. In play with other children, teaching and learning is often not intentional but a part of engaging those with less knowledge or skill in an activity that those with more skill or knowledge want to do. Of course, children's age and culturally defined sex roles play a part in their behavior and the activities they choose to engage in.

Taking an anthropological and cross-cultural vantage is helpful to prevent misinterpretations due to cultural differences. Studying the entire setting of a learning interaction as the basic unit of analysis, rather than individuals, allows a deeper understanding of real-life learning interactions, in which learning is always bidirectional and increases cognitive, social, and emotional functioning for all parties involved (Cicirelli 1975; Maynard 2002, 2004b; Weisner 1989; Zukow-Goldring 2002). Looking at children's learning interactions from a wide angle also brings awareness that learning occurs not only within the framework of specifically arranged educational and child-focused learning settings but also in situations in which the child interacts freely with others as part of everyday activities.

Furthermore, children seem to be able to learn certain skills in situations in which they interact exclusively with one another and are not constrained by adult supervision, curricula, or other instructions (see also chapter 18, this volume). In recent decades, children's opportunities to interact with each other in "adult-free," unstructured settings have dropped significantly. Encounters such as a pack of children engaging in free play in their neighborhood streets or yards, or an older sibling taking care of a younger one without parental supervision, have become less and less common, either because it is perceived as too dangerous for the children to be all by themselves or because a lot of Western middle-class children are equipped with such a tight school and leisure time schedule that there is simply no time for just "hanging out" with other children.

However, perspective-taking, empathy, and communication skills are readily learned from siblings and peers, and unstructured interactions provide the substrate for these skills to develop. Fortunately in recent years, there is increasing awareness that unstructured learning settings for children seem to be a better preparation for the adult working world in many societies, which in the majority of cases emphasizes skills such as communication skills, capacity for teamwork, and the like. It is our hope that the important social and cognitive skills learned in informal settings will find appropriate outlets for expression in formal settings and that schools will become more flexible in their approaches to teaching children the skills and knowledge deemed important by policy-makers who shape school curricula.

Acknowledgments

We are grateful to the editors for their guidance and hard work in helping us with this chapter. We also acknowledge Ben Bergen, Katherine Irwin, and Lori Yancura for their helpful comments.

Bibliography

Anthropological Institute of Great Britain and Ireland. *Journal of the Anthropological Institute of Great Britain and Ireland.* London: Trübner, 1872.

Barry, Herbert, III, Margaret K. Bacon, and Irvin L. Child. "Definitions, Ratings, and Bibliographic Sources of Child-Training Practices of 110 Cultures." Pp. 293–331 in *Cross-Cultural Approaches*, edited by Clellan S. Ford. New Haven, Conn.: HRAF, 1967.

Benjamin, Gail R. *Japanese Lessons.* New York: New York University Press, 1997.

Best, Deborah L. "Gender Roles in Childhood and Adolescence." Pp. 199–228 in *Childhood and Adolescence: Cross-Cultural Perspectives and Application*, edited by Uwe P. Gielen and Jaipaul Roopnarine. Westport, Conn.: Praeger, 2004.

Broch, Harald Beyer. *Growing Up Agreeably: Bonerate Childhood Observed.* Honolulu: University of Hawaii Press, 1990.

Chen, Xinyin. "Social and Emotional Development in Chinese Children and Adolescents: A Contextual Cross-Cultural Perspective." Pp. 229–51 in *Advances in Psychology Research*, vol. 1, edited by Frank Columbus. Huntington, N.Y.: Nova Science, 2000.

Chisholm, James S. *Navajo Infancy: An Ethological Study of Child Development.* Hawthorne, N.J.: Aldine, 1983.

Cicirelli, Victor G. "Effect of Mother and Older Sibling on the Problem-Solving Behavior of the Younger Child." *Developmental Psychology* 11, no. 6 (1975): 749–56.

———. "Sibling Relationships in Cross-Cultural Perspective." *Journal of Marriage and the Family* 56, no. 1 (February 1994): 7–20.

Corsaro, William A. *Friendship and Peer Culture in the Early Years.* Norwood, N.J.: Ablex, 1985.

Corter, Carl, Rona Abramovitch, and Debra J. Pepler. "The Role of the Mother in Sibling Interaction." *Child Development* 54, no. 6 (December 1983): 1599–1605.

de León, Lourdes. "Body and Domestic Space in Zinacantec Socialization." Paper presented at the annual meeting of the Jean Piaget Society, Philadelphia, Pennsylvania, 2002.

———. "Intent Participation and the Nature of Participation Structures: A Look from a Chiapas Mayan Community Everyday Life." Document presented at the Presidential Workshop on Intent Participation, Santa Cruz, California, 2005.

———. "Authority, Attention, and Affect in Directive/Response Sequences in Zinacantec Mayan Siblings." Paper presented at the 107th annual meeting of the American Anthropological Association, San Francisco, California, 2008.

Dunn, Judy. "Siblings and the Development of Social Understanding in Early Childhood." Pp. 106–16 in *Sibling Interaction across Cultures: Theoretical and Methodological Issues*, edited by Patricia G. Zukow. New York: Springer-Verlag, 1989.

Gaskins, Suzanne. "How Mayan Parental Theories Come into Play." Pp. 345–63 in *Parents' Cultural Belief Systems*, edited by Sarah Harkness and Charles Super. New York: Guilford, 1996.

———. "Children's Daily Lives in a Mayan Village: A Case Study of Culturally Constructed Roles and Activities." Pp. 25–61 in *Children's Engagement in the World: Sociocultural Perspectives*, edited by Artin Göncü. New York: Cambridge University Press, 1999.

———. "Children's Daily Lives in a Mayan Village: A Culturally Grounded Description." *Journal of Cross-Cultural Research* 34, no 4 (November 2000): 375–89.

———. "The Cultural Organization of Yucatec Mayan Children's Social Interactions." Pp. 283–309 in *Peer Relationships in Cultural Context*, edited by Xinyin Chen, Doran C. French, and Barry H. Schneider. New York: Cambridge University Press, 2006.

———. "Children's Daily Lives among the Yucatec Maya." Pp. 280–288 in *Anthropology and Child Development: A Cross-Cultural Reader*, edited by Robert A. LeVine and Rebecca S. New. Malden, Mass.: Blackwell, 2008.

Gaskins, Suzanne, Wendy Haight, and David F. Lancy. "The Cultural Construction of Play." Pp. 179–202 in *Play and Development: Evolutionary, Sociocultural, and Functional Perspectives*, edited by Artin Göncü and Suzanne Gaskins. Mahwah, N.J.: Erlbaum, 2007.

Gauvain, Mary. *The Social Context of Cognitive Development*. New York: Guilford, 2001.

Greenfield, Patricia M., and Carla P. Childs. "Understanding Sibling Concepts: A Developmental Study of Kin Terms in Zinacantan." Pp. 335–58 in *Piagetian Psychology: Cross-Cultural Contributions*, edited by Pierre Dasen. New York: Gardner, 1977.

Greenfield, Patricia M., and Lalita Suzuki. "Culture and Human Development: Implications for Parenting, Education, Pediatrics, and Mental Health." Pp. 1059–1109 in *Child Psychology in Practice (Handbook of Child Psychology)*, vol. 4, 5th ed., edited by Irving E. Sigel and K. Ann Renninger. New York: Wiley, 1998.

Haight, Wendy, and Peggy Miller. *The Ecology and Development of Pretend Play*. Albany: SUNY Press, 1993.

Hecht, Julia A. "The Culture of Gender in Pukapuka: Male, Female, and the Mayakitanga 'Sacred Maid.'" *Journal of the Polynesian Society* 86 (1979): 183–206.

———. "The Cultural Contexts of Siblingship in Pukapuka." Pp. 53–77 in *Siblingship in Oceania: Studies in the Meaning of Kin Relations*, edited by Mac Marshall. Ann Arbor: University of Michigan Press, 1981.

Isaac, Adrienne. "How Teachers' Cultural Ideologies Influence Children's Relations inside the Classroom: The Effects of a Cultural Awareness Teacher-Training Program in Two Classrooms." Undergraduate honors thesis, UCLA, 1999.

Keller, Heidi. *Cultures of Infancy*. Mahwah, N.J.: Erlbaum, 2007.

Konner, Melvin. "Relations among Infants and Toddlers in Comparative Perspective." Pp. 99–129 in *Friendship and Peer Relations*, vol. 4, edited by Marc Lewis and Leonard Rosenblum. New York: Wiley, 1975.

Lancy, David F. *Playing on the Mother Ground: Cultural Routines for Children's Development*. New York: Guilford, 1996.

———. *The Anthropology of Childhood: Cherubs, Chattel, and Changelings*. Cambridge: Cambridge University Press, 2008.

Larson, Reed, and Suman Verma. "How Children and Adolescents around the World Spend Time: Work, Play, and Developmental Opportunities." *Psychological Bulletin* 125, no. 6 (1999): 701–36.

Maccoby, Eleanor E. "Gender and Relationships: A Developmental Account." *American Psychologist* 45, no. 4 (1990): 513–520.

Maccoby, Eleanor E., and Carol N. Jacklin. "Sex Segregation in Childhood." Pp. 239–88 in *Advances in Child Development and Behavior*, vol. 20, edited by Hayne W. Reese. New York: Academic, 1987.

Martini, Mary. "Peer Interactions in Polynesia: A View from the Marquesas." Pp. 73–103 in *Children's Play in Diverse Cultures*, edited by Jaipaul Roopnarine, James E. Johnson, and Frank H. Hooper. Albany: SUNY Press, 1994.

Martini, Mary, and John Kirkpatrick. "Parenting in Polynesia: A View from the Marquesas." Pp. 199–222 in *Parent-Child Socialization in Diverse Cultures*, edited by Jaipaul Roopnarine and D. Bruce Carter. Norwood, N.J.: Ablex, 1992.

Maynard, Ashley E. "The Social Organization and Development of Teaching in Zinacantec Maya Sibling Play." Paper presented at the 98th annual meeting of the American Anthropological Association, Chicago, Illinois, 1999.

———. "Cultural Teaching: The Development of Teaching Skills in Maya Sibling Interactions." *Child Development* 73, no. 3 (May 2002): 969–82.

———. "Sibling Interactions." Pp. 229–52 in *Childhood and Adolescence: Cross-Cultural Perspectives and Applications*, edited by Uwe P. Gielen and Jaipaul Roopnarine. Westport, Conn.: Praeger, 2004a.

————. "Cultures of Teaching in Childhood: Formal Schooling and Maya Sibling Teaching at Home." *Cognitive Development* 19, no. 4 (October–December 2004b): 517–36.

————. "Men Don't Make Tortillas: Gender-Role Development in Zinacantec Maya Children." Paper presented at the meetings of the American Psychological Association, Honolulu, Hawaii, 2004c.

Minks, Amanda. "Socializing Rights and Responsibilities: Domestic Play among Miskitu Siblings on the Atlantic Coast of Nicaragua." Paper presented at the 107th annual meeting of the American Anthropological Association, San Francisco, California, 2008.

Munroe, R. Lee, and Ruth H. Munroe. *Cross-Cultural Human Development*. 1975. Prospect Heights, Ill.: Waveland, 1994.

New, Rebecca S. "Child's Play in Italian Perspective." Pp. 213–66 in *Anthropology and Child Development: A Cross-Cultural Reader*, edited by Robert A. LeVine and Rebecca S. New. Malden: Blackwell, 2008.

Nuckolls, Charles W. "An Introduction to the Cross-Cultural Study of Sibling Relations." Pp. 19–41 in *Siblings in South Asia: Brothers and Sisters in Cultural Context*, edited by Charles W. Nuckolls. New York: Guilford, 1993.

Omark, Donald R., Monica Omark, and Murray Edelmann. "Formation of Dominance Hierarchies in Young Children: Action and Perspective." Pp. 289–315 in *Psychological Anthropology*, edited by Thomas Williams. The Hague: Mouton, 1975.

Ottenberg, Simon. *Double Descent in an African Society: The Afikpo Village-Group*. Seattle: University of Washington Press, 1968.

Paradise, Ruth, and Barbara Rogoff. "Side by Side: Learning by Observing and Pitching In." *Ethos* 37, no. 1 (March 2009): 102–38.

Parke, Ross D., and Raymond Buriel. "Socialization in the Family: Ethnic and Ecological Perspectives." Pp. 463–552 in *Handbook of Child Psychology*, vol. 3, *Social, Emotional, and Personality Development*, edited by Nancy Eisenberg. New York: Wiley, 1998.

Philips, Susan U. *The Invisible Culture: Communication in Classroom and Community on the Warm Springs Indian Reservation*. White Plains, N.Y.: Longman, 1983.

Rabain-Jamin, Jacqueline, Ashley E. Maynard, and Patricia Greenfield. "Implications of Sibling Caregiving for Sibling Relations and Teaching Interactions in Two Cultures." *Ethos* 31, no. 2 (2003): 204–31.

Reese, Leslie, Silvia Balzano, Ronald Gallimore, and Claude Goldenberg. "The Concept of *Educación*: Latino Family Values and American Schooling." *International Journal of Educational Research* 23, no. 1 (June 1995): 57–81.

Rindstedt, Camilla. *Quicha Children and Language Shift in an Andean Community*. Unitryck, Sweden: Linköping, 2001.

Rogoff, Barbara. "Adults and Peers as Agents of Socialization: A Highland Guatemalan Profile." *Ethos* 9, no. 1 (April 1981): 18–36.

———. *Apprenticeship in Thinking*. New York: Oxford University Press, 1990.

Rogoff, Barbara, Jayanthi Mistry, Artin Göncü, and Christine Mosier. "Guided Participation in Cultural Activity by Toddlers and Caregivers." *Monographs of the Society for Research in Child Development* 58, 8, Serial No. 236, 1993.

Stewart, Robert B. "Sibling Interaction: The Roles of the Older Child as Teacher for the Younger." *Merrill-Palmer Quarterly* 29, no. 1 (1983): 47–68.

Tovote, Katrin. Unpublished field notes, University of Hawaii, 2006.

Trumbull, Elise, Carrie Rothstein-Fisch, Patricia M. Greenfield, and Blanca Quiroz. *Bridging Cultures between Home and School: A Guide for Teachers*. Mahwah, N.J.: Erlbaum, 2001.

Vygotsky, Lev S. *Mind in Society*. New York: Cambridge University Press, 1978.

Watson-Gegeo, Karen A., and David W. Gegeo. "The Role of Sibling Interaction in Child Socialization." Pp. 54–76 in *Sibling Interaction across Cultures: Theoretical and Methodological Issues*, edited by Patricia G. Zukow. New York: Springer-Verlag, 1989.

Weisner, Thomas S. "Ecocultural Niches of Middle Childhood: A Cross-Cultural Perspective." Pp. 334–69 in *Development During Middle Childhood: The Years from Six to Twelve*, edited by W. A. Collins. Washington, D.C.: National Academic, 1984.

———. "Socialization for Parenthood in Sibling Caretaking Societies." Pp. 237–70 in *Parenting across the Life Span: Biosocial Dimensions*, edited by Jane B. Lancaster, Jeanne Altmann, Alice S. Rossi, and Lonnie R. Sherrod. Hawthorne, N.J.: Aldine, 1987.

———. "Comparing Sibling Relationships across Cultures." Pp. 11–25 in *Sibling Interaction across Cultures: Theoretical and Methodological Issues*, edited by Patricia G. Zukow. New York: Springer-Verlag, 1989.

Weisner, Thomas S., and Ronald Gallimore. "My Brother's Keeper: Child and Sibling Caretaking." *Current Anthropology* 18, no. 2 (June 1977): 169–90.

Whiting, Beatrice B. "Culture and Social Behavior: A Model for the Development of Social Behavior." *Ethos* 8, no. 2 (January 1980): 95–116.

Whiting, Beatrice B., and Carolyn P. Edwards. *Children of Different Worlds: The Formation of Social Behavior*. Cambridge, Mass.: Harvard University Press, 1988.

Whiting, Beatrice B., and John W. M. Whiting. *Children of Six Cultures: A Psychocultural Analysis*. Cambridge, Mass.: Harvard University Press, 1975.

Xu, Yiyuan, Jo Ann Farver, Lei Chang, Lidong Yu, and Zengxiu Zhang. "Culture, Family Contexts, and Children's Coping Strategies in Peer Interactions."

Pp. 264–80 in *Peer Relationships in Cultural Context*, edited by Xinyin Chen, Doran C. French, and Barry H. Schneider. New York: Cambridge University Press, 2006.

Zukow, Patricia G. *Sibling Interaction across Cultures: Theoretical and Methodological Issues*. New York: Springer-Verlag, 1989a.

———. "Siblings as Effective Socializing Agents: Evidence from Central Mexico." Pp. 79–105 in *Sibling Interaction across Cultures: Theoretical and Methodological Issues*, edited by Patricia G. Zukow. New York: Springer-Verlag, 1989b.

Zukow-Goldring, Patricia G. "Sibling Caregiving." Pp. 253–86 in *Handbook of Parenting*, vol. 3, *Status and Social Conditions of Parenting*, 2nd ed., edited by Marc H. Bornstein. Mahwah, N.J.: Erlbaum, 2002.

CHAPTER NINE

LEARNING IN SCHOOLS

Leslie C. Moore

Halima's School Day

Six-year-old Halima sat at her desk, which she shared with another girl and two boys, and listened attentively to her first grade teacher, Mr. Garza. In a loud, clear voice, he began the language lesson, "Bonjour, Papa. Répétez?" Halima and most of her 150 classmates repeated loudly after him the first line of dialogue that he had introduced the day before: "Bonjour, Papa." Mr. Garza said again, "Bonjour, Papa," and the class repeated after him, "Bonjour, Papa." Then Mr. Garza modeled the second line of the dialogue: "Bonjour, mon fils." There was a second of silence. Mr. Garza prompted the class to speak, and several students (but not Halima) produced a repetition of the second line, "Bonjour, mon fils." The teacher approved the repetition and then elicited more of the same: "Très bien. Encore? Bonjour, Papa." The class practiced the two lines of dialogue under Mr. Garza's direction for another 30 minutes, chorally, by row, by desk, and in pairs. On this day, Halima was not one of the children called on to perform the dialogue with a classmate at the front of the classroom. After the language lesson came a mathematics lesson, followed by recess, followed by a writing lesson. All the lessons were conducted entirely in French, while at recess children chatted and shouted in local languages, including Fulfulde, which was Halima's native language and the regional lingua franca. At noon, it was time to go home. Another public elementary school used the same cinder-block classrooms in the afternoon.

Halima walked the kilometer home with her big sister and two boy cousins. She had lunch and a short rest before heading to her Qur'anic school just down the street, around 1:30. Her teacher, Mal Buuba, was not at home when she arrived, but his teenage son was there to supervise the students. Halima took her *alluha* (a wooden tablet on which Qur'anic verses are written for a child to study) from where she had left it the evening before, leaning against the wall of the entryway of Mal Buuba's family compound. She sat down on the gravel-covered ground with her back against the mud wall, crossed her legs, lay her alluha on her lap, and resumed her study of the 108th chapter of the Qur'an. For almost two hours, she practiced her recitation of the *basmalah* (the brief invocation that precedes all but one chapter of the Qur'an) and the three short verses. She repeated the Arabic text over and over in a very loud voice, sometimes bent over her alluha, sometimes sitting up straight. Five other girls from the neighborhood sat along the same wall as Halima, and against the facing wall sat her two boy cousins (who were also in her first grade class) and four other neighborhood boys. Each child recited a different text in a loud voice. Whenever the volume began to fade, Mal Buuba's son commanded them in Fulfulde to recite "with force." At the sound of the call to the afternoon prayer, Halima and the other children stopped reciting, put away their alluhas, and went home. After dinner, Halima returned for the evening session, practicing her recitation for another hour and a half before the call to the night prayer signaled that it was time to go home and go to bed.

Anthropologists in Schools

The scenes above were recorded in Maroua, Cameroon, in 2000. While they illustrate school experiences that are common in much of the world, they do not conform to current Western conceptions of school learning, and most educational researchers ignore such schooling practices and the settings in which they are prevalent. However, anthropologists have conducted many studies in such settings, and their work has expanded and deepened our understanding of how learning is conceptualized, organized, and realized in formal educational contexts. This chapter briefly reviews that literature before returning to the Cameroonian research, which will serve as a case study of the application of anthropology to the study of learning in schools.

Rooted in the work of the 1930s and 1940s on enculturation in non-Western, nonindustrialized societies, the anthropology of education (also known as educational anthropology) emerged as a subfield in the 1950s (Singleton 1999). Much of the early work examined the transmission of culture in school and community settings (e.g., see Gay and Cole 1967; Modiano 1973; Peshkin 1972; Wolcott 1967; and other monographs in the Case Studies in Education and Culture series edited by George and Louise Spindler). In 1970s and 1980s, several ethnographic studies identified differences between "home" and "school" with respect to communicative patterns; cognitive and learning styles; and the values, beliefs, and identities associated with particular ways of learning and knowing (e.g., Au and Jordan 1981; Erickson and Mohatt 1982; Heath 1983; Philips 1983; Tharp and Gallimore 1988). These detailed accounts of home/school discontinuities were offered as (partial) explanations for the disproportionate school failure of ethnic and racial minorities and as arguments for changing the way learning environments were organized in schools. More recently, anthropologists have sought to understand how historical and political forces shape schooling processes; how learning and knowledge are defined differently across contexts; how and why school experiences vary across learners by social categories such as race, class, and gender; and how students and teachers exert their own agency as they appropriate school practices and create new ones by drawing on classroom and community traditions (for several case studies in this vein, see Anderson-Levitt 2003 and Levinson, Foley, and Holland 1996).

Anthropologists of education have illuminated the social organization of schools and classrooms, the values and beliefs that inform schooling and those that are meant to be formed by schooling, and the meanings and consequences of schooling and school practices for individuals and communities. Their studies vary in their relative focus. Some focus on the school and/or the community as a whole in order to understand the complex interplay of policies, values, curriculum, and pedagogy (e.g., Coe 2005; Lomawaiama and McCarty 2006). Others focus on the interactions between teachers and students and among students, locating learning in these culturally organized encounters (e.g., Anderson-Levitt 2002;

Figure 9.1.   Classroom in northern Sudan (V. Blaha photo)

Figure 9.2.   Classroom in northern Sudan (V. Blaha photo)

Schieffelin and Gilmore 1986). And some studies focus on individuals, whose lived experiences and personal narratives are mined for insights into how they participate in and make sense of schooling (or not) (e.g., Cheney 2007; Stambach 2000). Holistic and comparative in perspective, anthropological studies explore how the practices and values of schooling relate to and often conflict with those of other domains of community life. Thus, schools are studied as sites of cultural reproduction and of cultural contact and change.

Many anthropologists have documented the kinds of schooling practices described at the beginning of this chapter. Rote learning and the (nearly) exclusive use of languages that children do not understand well are early and persistent features of schooling throughout the non-Western, nonindustrialized world (Lancy 2008, 313–23). Many scholars have identified these practices as important factors in the low rates of school achievement and completion typical of public schooling in much of the developing world (Anderson-Levitt 2005; Barnett 1979; Bolin 2006; Goody 2006; Hollos and Leis 1989; Hornberger and Chick 2001; Juul 2008; Kulick 1992; Moore 1999; Nash 1970; Watson-Gegeo and Gegeo 1992). The prevalence of rote learning and its persistence in the face of reform are interpreted by many of these scholars as an adaptation to educational policies that privilege the "national" language (often the language of the former colonizers) and to severe underresourcing of many public schools that has lead to overcrowded classrooms, students without textbooks or other materials, and teachers with insufficient training and school language proficiency. While rote learning in public schools is seen by anthropologists as symptomatic of structural problems, rote learning in Qur'anic schools is often described as integral to the tradition (e.g., Eickelman 1985; Fernea 1991; Mommersteeg 1988; Moore 2008; Santerre 1973), even in communities where reform in pedagogy, curriculum, and patterns of participation had occurred or were under way (e.g., Boyle 2004; Brenner 2001; Gade 2004; Wagner 1993).

Cameroon Field Study of Children in Schools

Rote learning is discussed in many anthropological studies of schooling, but few researchers have given it close analytic attention.[1] In my own research, I have sought to understand the organization and significance of rote learning in public and Qur'anic schooling in the Fulbe community of Maroua, Cameroon. My study expands the discussion of home/school discontinuity in two ways. First, I systematically compared two schooling traditions in a single community.[2] Second, I integrated the ethnographic, historical, and interactional discourse analytic approaches that have characterized different strands of anthropological studies of schooling. I worked closely with seven young Fulbe children to document their experiences in their schools and homes (for an example of child-centered ethnography of schooling, see Cheney 2007). I contextualized microanalysis of video-recorded interactions in a holistic study of the community to illuminate the structures of everyday interactions as cultural arrangements, shaped by and in turn shaping community beliefs and values (for a discussion of microethnography, see Philips 1983; Schieffelin and Ochs 1995; also see chapter 10, this volume). I further situated my analysis through broader study of the history and politics of the region, the nation, and the two schooling traditions (for examples of the historical-ethnographic study of schooling, see Coe 2005 and Stambach 2000).

For centuries, rote learning has been part of the educational experience of children around the world. It is foundational to the traditional pedagogies associated with many religious movements (Wagner 1993). Common to all of these traditional pedagogies is the ideology that the achievement of verbatim oral mastery of sacred texts through rote learning is an appropriate and effective way to instill religious orthodoxy and good moral character. Jews memorize Hebrew texts (Drazin 1940), Catholics (pre-Vatican II) memorize Latin texts (Nash 1968), Muslims memorize Arabic texts (Bray 1986), and Hindus and Buddhists memorize Sanskrit texts (Dreyfus 2003). In these traditions, recitation and memorization of sacred texts are valued as acts of piety, discipline, personal transformation, and cultural preservation, whether or not the individual understands the literal meaning of the text.

Built on the foundations of religious education, secular schooling around the world also entails rote learning (Wagner 1983). The recitation and memorization of Greek and Latin texts constituted a large part of curricula in European schools for hundreds of years (Carruthers 1992; Cubberley 1922; Nash 1968). Until the late 1800s, European and North American pedagogical practice stressed textbook memorization and strict discipline, with the former believed to be an important mechanism for instilling and maintaining the latter (Ariès 1965; Cubberley 1922). Rote learning fell out of favor in the West during the 20th century with the advance of the progressive education movement, which stressed learning through doing and methods that encouraged experimentation and independent thinking by learners (Hori 1996). Rote learning came to be characterized as bad for children's creativity, understanding, and enjoyment of learning. Yet it remains a part of schooling all over the world, especially in East Asia (Ho 1994) and among religious fundamentalists in the United States (Wise and Bauer 2004).

Two Schooling Traditions

At the start of this millennium, Qur'anic school and public school in Maroua, Cameroon, were two very different educational institutions, each with its own long and distinct history and tradition of pedagogical practice. The Fulbe established the first Qur'anic schools in northern Cameroon after their jihad of the early 19th century, and Maroua quickly became a center of Islamic education that attracted the sons of the Muslim elite from all over the region (Santerre 1973). The first Western school in Maroua was opened in 1918 by the French colonial administration, and the sons of Fulbe aristocrats were recruited (with limited success) to attend the school in preparation for colonial service (Tourneux and Iyébi-Mandjek 1994). Much changed in Cameroon in the years since the first schools were founded, but the two schooling traditions endured, and Fulbe children participated in both in increasing numbers (Seignobos and Nassourou 2000).[3]

The first several years of Qur'anic schooling were dedicated primarily to the reading, writing, reciting, and partial memorization of the Qur'an in Arabic, which was a sacred language in this community but not one used for everyday communication. The primary lesson objective was the faithful—that is, verbatim, fluent, and reverent—recitation of the text by the novice without assistance. Accurate reproduction of Qur'anic texts was the goal, while comprehension was not. Halima, for example, spent several hours mastering the recitation of four lines from the Qur'an, but the meaning of the text was not explained to her, nor did it occur to her to ask for explanation. Correct rendering of the sounds of the Qur'an constituted the essential first layer of understanding of the sacred text. Subsequent layers of understanding were reserved for the learner who had "finished his Qur'an," that is, recited and written the entire Qur'an without error. A learner might take anywhere from three years to a lifetime to achieve this, and most Maroua Fulbe never did (Santerre 1973).

Public schooling in Cameroon had a structure of cycles, examinations, and diplomas derived from the French educational system (Capelle 1990). The overarching goal of the early grades was for the child to grow accustomed to the school environment and the French language. In the first two or three years, most instructional time was spent on learning to speak, read, and write French, since the vast majority of children came to school with little or no proficiency in French. In language lessons, children repeated utterances modeled by the teacher; copied texts the teacher had written on the blackboard; and memorized songs, poems, and dialogues. Because French was both the target language and the language of instruction, lessons in any subject (civics, hygiene, mathematics, national culture) were conducted in much the same way as language lessons. For example, during the math lesson that followed Halima's language lesson, she and her classmates repeated over and over the addition equations modeled by the teacher, just as they had repeated lines of dialogue. The official expectation was that children develop a basic level of generative competence in French over these first years of schooling; that is, they should come to understand simple French utterances and express themselves simply in French (Ministère de l'Education Nationale 1998). However, most students who started public school in Maroua left school before achieving this level of competence (Iyébi-Mandjek 2000).

In Qur'anic and public schooling, nearly all instruction was in a second language, and second language learning was believed to entail two intertwined processes: the formation of good linguistic habits and the transformation of heart and mind. Teachers in both kinds of school believed that students developed morally and intellectually through the memorization of high-quality linguistic material under the guidance of an expert. For Muslims, the best material was the Qur'an, which was believed to have the power to transform those who committed it to memory (cf. Gade 2004). Similar ideologies have informed French-language instruction in Africa since colonial times. An African became "civilized" (*évolué*) in part through learning French, that is, by acquiring the habits of rational speech and thought—"the French clarity" (*la clarité française*)—that was modeled in the texts they learned by heart (Dauzat 1949).

Qur'anic schooling was believed by Fulbe to provide children with a complete socialization ("*une formation totale*") (Adama and Amadou 1998; Santerre 1973). Some Qur'anic teachers provided instruction in the basic tenets of Islam (e.g., monotheism, Mohammed's status as the final prophet), and a few supervised children's daily prayers. However, Qur'anic school was not only about studying the Qur'an, learning to pray, or learning the basic tenets of the faith. Instilling discipline, respect, and self-control is described as one of the primary goals of Qur'anic school throughout the Muslim world (Bray 1986; Musa Ahmed 1996; Sanneh 1975). According to Tourneux and Iyébi-Mandjek (1994), Qur'anic schooling in Maroua had as its principal objective not the teaching of knowledge, but the inculcation of the values of Muslim society (see also chapter 11, this volume): faith in God, respect for authority and hierarchy, the primacy of the spiritual over the temporal. It was about learning how to *be* Muslim and Fulbe, identities that were considered nearly one and the same.

Like Qur'anic schooling, public schooling was intended to promote and guide children's intellectual, social, and moral development. The child was expected to develop an objective understanding of the world, an individual self-concept, and a Cameroonian identity (Ministère de l'Education Nationale 1998; UNICEF 1993). In both colonial and postcolonial times, public schooling has sought explicitly to promote supra-ethnic identity and to change mentalities from "traditional" or "tribal" viewpoints, which were regarded as impediments to social and economic progress, to more "modern" outlooks and conceptions of the world that favor development. (For an account of how "traditional" culture was used in schools to promote a national identity, see Coe 2005.) Many scholars have argued that the explicit goal of changing mentalities of both colonial and postcolonial educational systems veiled other goals: to train the population for acceptance of and participation in the market economy and the authority of the state apparatus (Atangana 1996; Martin 1982).

Fulbe participation in public schooling was very low until Cameroon's Fulbe president was succeeded in 1982 by a Christian southerner, who ended preferential treatment of Fulbe within the state power structure (Iyébi-Mandjek and Seignobos 2000). At that time, Fulbe authorities began to encourage rather than discourage participation in public schooling, and Fulbe enrollments grew (Santerre 1982b; Tourneux and Iyébi-Mandjek 1994). Fulbe children who attended public school also attended Qur'anic schooling, and such "double schooling" was considered by many to be problematic. Non-Muslim public educators and researchers argued that Qur'anic schooling interfered with students' social, cognitive, and linguistic development by teaching children a passive, nonanalytic learning style and an ethnocentric and superstitious worldview (Santerre 1982a; Tourneux and Iyébi-Mandjek 1994). Many Fulbe claimed that public schooling interfered with children's social, moral, and spiritual development. Time spent in public school was time not spent studying the Qur'an or learning tasks and responsibilities from one's father or mother. Even parents who sent their children to public school expressed concern that children learned things at school—*nasaaraaji* ("things of the whites/people from elsewhere")—that were counter to the norms of Islam and Fulbe culture (Santerre 1982a; Tourneux and Iyébi-Mandjek 1994). Despite the widespread perception of conflict between the traditions, many people noted that there were similarities. As one mother in my study said, at both schools "children have to pay close attention, work hard, and memorize what they need to know."

Rote Learning Reconsidered

In Qur'anic and public schools, rote learning dominated. The primary objective of nearly all lessons was the verbatim memorization and error-free oral rendering of a text in a nonnative language. To this end, teachers modeled speech, and children imitated, rehearsed, and performed it from memory, with little or no comprehension of its meaning. In the course of my comparative study of public and Qur'anic schooling in Maroua, I came to reframe rote learning as guided repetition, a complex and context-sensitive practice for teaching and learning (Rogoff et al. 2007). I identified four phases in guided repetition activities—modeling, imitation, rehearsal, and performance—each of which entails particular rights and obligations for both teacher and student. The guided repetition model emerged from my data analysis, as I came to recognize that public and Qur'anic school activities shared not only the same basic lesson objective but also the same overall sequential structure (for international comparisons of lesson structure, see Alexander 2000 and Anderson-Levitt 2002).

In both schooling traditions, the perceived appropriateness of guided repetition was rooted in similar ideologies of child development and learning. Parents, Qur'anic teachers, and public school teachers all described children in early and middle childhood as excellent and eager imitators and memorizers. Learning through imitation, repetition, and memorization was believed to be well suited to a child between age 6 and puberty, for his or her memory was still clear of distractions and highly impressionable. Parents and Qur'anic teachers spoke of the "virgin memory" (*taaskaare wuule*) of children of this age, while public school teachers referred to their minds as tabulae rasae. Skills and knowledge—or bad habits and incorrect understandings—acquired in this period were believed to be more likely to take root and endure than those introduced at a later age. Thus, according to Qur'anic and public educators, guided repetition was the right approach at the right time.

While guided repetition was used to teach Fulbe children both Qur'anic recitation and French oral expression, it was accomplished in different ways and for different reasons. Some differences were obvious. For example, in Qur'anic school, children learned to recite a sacred text, the faithful reproduction of which was not just the lesson objective but also the long-term educational goal. French language lessons, on the other hand, revolved around the animated performance of a mundane conversation, a carefully selected and scripted subset of linguistic forms, the mastery of which was intended to project the child into generative competence in French. Other differences were less obvious but proved more illuminating. Close, comparative analysis of these two guided repetition activities revealed distinctive interactional patterns in these two activities, and these patterns could be linked to the very different ways of being in the world that children were expected—or at least hoped—to learn through Qur'anic and public schooling.

Distribution of Authority

One of the most important dimensions of difference concerned the distribution of authority to teach. In both schooling traditions, the teacher was the primary modeler and, in the immediate environment, the highest authority on how a text should be rendered. The teacher enlisted the help of children in both settings, but in different ways. Interviews with teachers and parents revealed that these differences in how and how much author- ity was allocated to children to function as peer teachers (see also chapter 8, this volume) were related to participants' beliefs about how children learned, how the text should be treated, and how participants should relate to one another.

In the public school classroom, any student was a potential modeler. While the teacher often relied on a few students he knew to be more capable (many of these children were repeating the first grade), any child who volunteered to model was likely to be given the opportunity to do so. Moreover, children were frequently asked to assess the renderings of other children and to identify and correct errors. The teacher allocated the authority to model, assess, and correct on a turn-by-turn basis. Transcript 1 (table 9.1) illustrates some of these practices.

Public educators believed that children were more interested in other children than they were in the teacher and that teachers should capitalize on this interest. Having peers provide modeling, assessment, and cor- rection was considered good pedagogical practice because peer talk was assumed to be more salient and more memorable for children. Moreover, teachers' elicitations of peer correction and assessment were designed to introduce an element of fun and/or competition and to get children to use French for authentic communicative purposes, both of which were believed to be motivating for children. Practices of distributing authority were also informed by an ideology of equality and equal access. I was told by several teachers that all children were potentially good students and competent speakers of French, and that it is up to the teacher to bring out that potential in each and every child by giving multiple opportuni- ties to play different roles, including that of an authority on academic correctness. (For an analysis of similar evaluation practices in Japanese classrooms, see Benjamin 1997.)

Qur'anic teachers and parents saw no place for peer teaching in the transmission of Qur'anic knowledge. Sacred knowledge and the authority it bestowed were the result of years of devout study (Eisemon 1988; Ries- man and Szanton 1992); thus, the role of expert could not be transferred from day to day, much less turn by turn. Good instruction entailed the

Table 9.1.   Transcript 1: Rehearsal of Dialogue 6 Le cadeau

1	S:	BONJOUR MON FILS J'AI UN CADEAU POURQUOI? Hello my son I have a gift why?
2	T:	((snaps head up from looking at book))
3		UN CADEAU POUR*QUOI*? A gift why?
4	T:	C'EST COMME ÇA? Is it like that? ((makes sweeping gesture with right hand))
5	Class:	NOOOON Noooooo
6	T:	((smiling)) ALORS, C'EST COMMENT? So, how is it?
7	Ss:	⌈ J'AI UN CADEAU POUR *TOI*. I have a gift for you.
8	Ss:	BONJOUR MON FILS J'AI UN CADEAU POUR *TOI*. ⌊ Hello my son I have a gift for you.
9	T:	((smiling)) VOILA. C'EST ÇA. There. That's it.
10		BONJOUR MON FILS J'AI UN CADEAU POUR TOI. Hello my son I have a gift for you.

S = Student, T = Teacher, CAPS = loud, *italics* = emphasis

reverent and individualized transmission of Qur'anic texts to the novice by someone with the religious knowledge and authority to do so. In many schools, a few students who were older and more advanced in their studies were designated as assistant teachers, and they were authorized to supervise children as they rehearsed, to correct their errors, and to administer punishment. Other children were not allowed to occupy themselves with the learning of their peers, although they often did when left unsupervised. Children were still learning the Qur'an and still learning to treat it with proper respect. So there was a significant risk that, either by mistake or by design, a child might model an incorrect rendering or fail to correct an error made by another child.

Table 9.2. Transcript 2: Modeling-Imitation of Verses 1–4, chapter 102
At–Takathur

1	T: Alheekum takasuru	5	T: Hatta zurtumin maqaabira
2	S: Alheekum takafuru	6	S: Hatta zurtu min makaabira
3	T: *Alheekum takasuru*	7	T: Kalla sawfa taalamuuna
4	S: Alheekum taka(s/f)uru	8	S: Kalla sawfa taalamuuna

To recite the Qur'an incorrectly was to turn it into something different from what was revealed to the Prophet by God. Thus, in principle, any error had to be corrected for the sake of the reciter, for anyone listening, and for the Qur'an itself. Teachers usually responded to children's recitation errors by rendering the whole verse as it should have been recited, with no particular emphasis on the error, as transcript 2 (table 9.2) illustrates (I provide no translation of the Arabic because neither teacher nor student understood its meaning).

Qur'anic teachers never imitated a child's error, unlike public school teachers, who routinely did so (as in line 3 of transcript 1). Other children sometimes did this, but only when unsupervised, for a teacher would have punished such blasphemous behavior.

Figure 9.3. Imitation phase in a Maroua Qur'anic school (M. Moritz photo)

Outcomes of Learning by Heart

In the two schooling traditions, different moral and intellectual outcomes were desired, and guided repetition was accomplished in culturally specific ways. Qur'anic schooling was meant to socialize children into reproductive competence in Arabic and into Fulbe and Muslim values of self-control, respect for religious authority and hierarchy, and submission to the word of God. The practice of guided repetition in Qur'anic schools emphasized strict discipline, the authority of the teacher, and reverent renderings of the text. These ways of producing and relating to Arabic texts were essential to competent participation in many community activities, including prayer, religious ceremonies, and healing practices (Moore 2008). Public schooling was meant to create Cameroonian citizens, individuals who could speak and write and think in French as was required in the social, civic, and economic activities of a modern, democratic nation-state. Guided repetition as practiced in the classroom was characterized by more peer interaction, liberal manipulation of the text, and greater fluidity in the roles of expert and novice.

Participation in both Qur'anic and public schooling entailed the use of a nonnative language, and guided repetition was believed by teachers and parents to be essential to second language learning despite its low yields in both kinds of school. In the first few years of Qur'anic schooling, children were expected to learn to reproduce Arabic texts orally and without comprehension, and nearly all Fulbe children learned to do this, albeit at highly varying rates. Some stayed in school long enough to learn to transcribe Arabic texts. A very few "finished their Qur'an," pursued advanced studies, and learned to understand Arabic. Advanced Qur'anic textual knowledge and communicative competence in Arabic were highly valued in the community, and high achievement was widely believed to be God given, a sign of blessing. However, a student who stopped after memorizing a few chapters of the Qur'an was not considered a failure because he had learned as much as he needed to function as a Muslim in the eyes of the community.

In public schooling, the official expectation was that children would quickly learn to understand and express themselves in simple French. However, only a small minority of Mr. Garza's students achieved this level (including Halima and another of the seven focal children in my study), and most who did were in the first grade for the second or third time. Teachers expected such outcomes in classrooms that were overcrowded with children who had little or no prior experience with French, so they focused on teaching as many children as possible to produce French forms correctly and in ways that were appropriate for the ongoing classroom activity. Maroua teachers described these pedagogical goals as both realistic and foundational to all subsequent French language development and academic achievement more generally. Teachers knew that most children would not build on this foundation enough to complete elementary school, but that did not diminish their belief in the value of guided repetition.

Repetition and Change

Understanding that schooling practices are not only culturally and historically rooted but also dynamic is key to an anthropological perspective on learning in schools. Throughout this chapter, I have used the ethnographic past because schooling traditions, like any other tradition, are not static. The educational landscape in Maroua might already be quite different from what I found at the turn of the millennium. Change was in the air when I did my fieldwork, and people's accounts of and responses to change provided additional insights into their ideologies concerning children, learning, and schools.

At the time of my study, there was a growing movement to "modernize" Islamic education in the region. Innovations included collective instruction, instruction in nonreligious subjects, and teaching Arabic both in and out of the context of the Qur'an using techniques that resemble those used to teach French in the public schools. In interviews, Fulbe expressed ambivalence about or even opposition to these innovations. A common objection was that collective instruction could not assure the mastery of each text by every child before the next text was introduced, thus putting some children at risk of reciting with error. Another widespread concern was that treating Arabic "just like any other language" and teaching it to young children who had not yet memorized the Qur'an effectively desacralized the language of the Qur'an and undermined the development of respect for the "Word of God" and the social order in theocratic Fulbe society.

Public education was also undergoing "modernization" at the turn of the millennium. In 1997, Cameroon's Ministry of Education introduced "the new pedagogical approach" (*la nouvelle approche pédagogique* or NAP) (Ministère de l'Education Nationale 1998). Reformers criticized the transmission models that dominated Cameroonian education, claiming that practices such as rote learning inhibited the development of creative and critical thinking, skills that were necessary for the individual's—and the nation's—successful participation in the modern world (Macaire 1993; Ministère de l'Education Nationale 1998). NAP was a more constructivist approach, with the teacher acting less as the source of all information and more as a guide for the student. Maroua teachers considered NAP inappropriate for the early grades (and the rest of the elementary cycle, according to some) because children were not believed to have sufficient competence in the linguistic and behavioral codes of the classroom to take so much responsibility for their own learning.

Another change in progress during my fieldwork was the emergence of guided repetition as a new practice for leading children into the telling of Fulbe folktales (Moore 2006). In addition to telling folktales to an audience of women and children, expert tellers (usually older women) were explicitly teaching folktales to children, and children were using guided repetition among themselves to teach and learn folktales. Child–child folktale socialization often gave rise to stories that did not fully conform to conventions of the oral tradition, such as blending two or more folktales into one, or including real people and places and modern elements like motorcycles. Moreover, such interactions often took place during daylight hours, a violation of the traditional restriction that folktales are told only at night. Several older children told me that they had taught and learned folktales at Qur'anic school when the teacher was not present, and such sites of clandestine peer socialization may have been where the diffusion of guided repetition into the folktale domain began.

The emergence of this new model of folktale socialization was contemporaneous with increased participation by Fulbe children in Qur'anic and public schooling,[4] and it seems likely that there was a relationship between these trends. It may be that Fulbe women, concerned that children busy with their studies were no longer immersed in folktales as in the past, began using a familiar and effective practice for teaching other kinds of oral texts to prevent the loss of the folktale tradition. The innovative use of guided repetition for teaching and learning folktales may have also reflected shifting beliefs and expectations among adults and children regarding the role of younger children in language-centered activities. In guided repetition interactions with adults and with their peers, young children took more vocal, active roles in an activity in which formerly they had played a more passive role until puberty or later. Thus, the folktale tradition was being both sustained and transformed by guided repetition, as children assumed new roles and created new narratives.

Comparing (Learning in) Schools

This chapter opened with a description of the kind of school day that is experienced by millions of children around the world, the sort of schooling practice that is widely deplored but poorly understood by Western researchers and educational reformers. In my study of Qur'anic and public schools, I sought to understand how and why rote learning was done in these two distinct cultural contexts where teaching and learning occurred mostly in nonnative languages. From my ethnography of schooling in this community came the concept of guided repetition. This concept helped me recognize and analyze similarities and differences between the two schooling traditions with respect to teaching and learning practices and the ideologies that informed them. This, in turn, helped me understand the significance of rote learning in this community, its staying power in the face of reform efforts and low educational yields, and its diffusion beyond the schools. In its different forms, guided repetition was believed to play an essential role in children's development of skills and orientations that were fundamental to being and becoming Fulbe, Muslim, and Cameroonian.

In examining the double schooling experience of Halima and her peers in Maroua, we find similarities in practice and ideology between two kinds of schooling that are often contrasted as Western versus non-Western, modern versus traditional, secular versus religious (for a critique of these dichotomies, see Stambach 2004). Both Qur'anic schooling and "Western-style" schooling have spread all over the globe, bringing with them cultural constructions of learning in/and childhood that differed from many practices, values, and beliefs of the communities in which such schooling was adopted or imposed. These schooling traditions have created a "more uniform experience of socialization than in the past" (Anderson-Levitt 2005, 998), but at the same time, schooling is experienced, appropriated, and transformed in different ways in different cultural contexts (Anderson-Levitt 2003). In studying both uniformity and variation in the organization and meaning of schooling cross-culturally, anthropologists have provided important insights into schooling and school learning as social and cultural processes and increased our understanding of how children become cultural beings through their participation in schooling. These contributions come not only from the production of rich ethnographic accounts of a particular kind of schooling in particular communities at particular times, but also from comparisons across individuals, time, space, and schooling traditions.

A Note on Methods

In my study, I combined ethnographic study of the schools and the community with a video-based longitudinal case study design. The study built on my previous work in the region as a researcher (1996 and 1999) and as a Peace Corps volunteer (1992–1994), as well as the extensive research conducted by other scholars on the Fulbe and their language, northern Cameroon, and public and Qur'anic schooling in the region and beyond. In Maroua, I did many hours of observation in both types of schools, as well as participant observation in the homes of Fulbe friends and acquaintances. I hung out with the public school teachers during recess and grading periods. I consulted with local healers who used Qur'anic texts in their remedies. I attended sermons by local Muslim scholars, and I sat in on classes at the provincial Teachers' College. I participated in and documented school events like Youth Day and religious celebrations such as the Feast of Ramadan. I collected secular and Islamic educational materials that were locally available, including textbooks, teachers' guides, local school district reports, booklets on Islam, and audiotapes of sermons by well-known Muslim preachers.

As exhaustive and exhausting as this list of research activities may seem, the case studies were the most labor-intensive part of the study. I tracked seven 6- to 7-year-old Fulbe children over the course of their first year of public school, video recording them at monthly intervals at public school, Qur'anic school, and home, for a total of 90 hours. I also collected, photographed, or photocopied writings and drawings produced by the focal children during this period. Three Fulbe research assistants and I transcribed the video recordings, working first from audio lifts and then working with the video to refine and annotate the transcripts. Once video data collection was complete, I conducted interviews and video playback sessions with public and Qur'anic teachers, Islamic scholars, public education officials, and family members of the focal children. These sessions (which were audio recorded and transcribed) resulted in further annotations of transcripts and a collection of community members' metadiscursive remarks on home and school practices.

Making sense of all my field notes, transcripts, photographs, photocopies, and video and audio recordings was a long process that began in the field and, in fact, continues to this day. As I reviewed my transcripts and video, I created collections of what looked like the "same thing," be it a phase of a lesson or an error correction strategy. After grouping sequences that seemed to be instantiations of the same phenomenon, I sought to identify the features that made me judge them as similar, and this process led to refinement of my categories. The process of creating collections and refining my categories enabled me to identify patterns in pedagogical practice in public and Qur'anic schools, as well as the ideologies that informed them.

Acknowledgments

I am deeply indebted to the children, teachers, and families who participated in my study of schooling in Maroua, Cameroon. My thanks to David Lancy for his editorial support.

Notes

1. Notable exceptions are the cultural psychologists Scribner and Cole (1981a, 1981b), who worked in Liberia and Daniel Wagner (1993), who worked in Morocco.

2. Davis and Davis (1989) discuss but do not compare in detail the two types of schooling.

3. There have been no surveys to provide exact numbers on Fulbe participation in public or Qur'anic schooling, in Maroua or elsewhere in Cameroon, and it is not

possible to determine this simply by looking at enrollment lists. In a survey of 140 Muslim parents in Maroua, Tourneux and Iyébi-Mandjek (1994) found that 100 percent sent their children (boys and girls) to Qur'anic school, 84 percent sent their boys to primary school, and 67 percent sent their girls to primary school. All Fulbe participants in my study asserted that Fulbe were participating more and more in public schooling, as did officials in the schools and in the provincial and division offices of the Ministry of Education. Participants also maintained that more Fulbe boys and girls attended Qur'anic school and for longer than in the past. Seignobos and Nassourou's (2000) count of Qur'anic schools in Maroua showed that the number had increased significantly since Santerre's (1973) study.

4. Judging by participants' retrospective self-reports and the absence of any mention in the extensive work on Fulbe folktales in Cameroon (Baumgardt 1988; Baumgardt and Goggo 2000; Eguchi 1984, 1993; Noye 1971, 1976), I conclude that guided repetition seeped into folktale socialization in the 1990s.

Bibliography

Adama, Hamadou, and Aboubakary Moodibo Amadou. "Itineraires d'Acquisition du Savoir Arabo-Islamitique dans le Nord-Cameroun." *Annales de la Faculté des Arts, Lettres, et Sciences Humaines de l'Université de Ngaoundéré* 3 (1998): 5–38.

Alexander, Robin. *Culture and Pedagogy: International Comparisons in Primary Education*. Malden, Mass.: Blackwell, 2000.

Anderson-Levitt, Kathryn M., ed. *Teaching Cultures: Knowledge for Teaching First Grade in France and the United States*. Cresskill: Hampton, 2002.

——. *Local Meanings, Global Schooling: Anthropology and World Culture Theory*. New York: Palgrave Macmillan, 2003.

——. "The Schoolyard Gate: Schooling and Childhood in Global Perspective." *Journal of Social History* 38, no. 4 (Summer 2005): 987–1006.

Ariès, Philippe. *Centuries of Childhood: A Social History of Family Life*. New York: Vintage Books, 1965.

Atangana, Engelbert. *Cent Ans d'Education Scolaire au Cameroun: Réflexion sur la Nature, les Moyens et les Objectifs de l'Entreprise (1885 à nos jours)*. Paris: L'Harmattan, 1996.

Au, Kathryn H., and Cathie Jordan. "Teaching Reading to Hawaiian Children: Finding a Culturally Appropriate Solution." Pp. 139–52 in *Culture and the Bilingual Classroom: Studies in Classroom Ethnography*, edited by Henry T. Trueba, Grace P. Guthrie, and Katryne H. Au. Rowley, Mass.: Newbury House, 1981.

Barnett, Homer G. *Being a Paluan*. New York: Holt, Rinehart, and Winston, 1979.

Baumgardt, Ursula. "L'Enfant à Travers les Contes Peuls du Cameroun." Pp. 83–114 in *L'Enfant dans les Contes Africains*, edited by Veronika Görög and Ursula Baumgardt. Paris: Conseil International de la Langue Française, 1988.

Baumgardt, Ursula, and Addi Goggo. *Une Conteuse Peule et son Répertoire: Goggo Addi de Garoua, Cameroun: Textes et Analyses*. Paris: Karthala, 2000.

Benjamin, Gail R. *Japanese Lessons*. New York: New York University Press, 1997.

Bolin, Inge. *Growing Up in a Culture of Respect: Child Rearing in Highland Peru*. Austin: University of Texas Press, 2006.

Boyle, Helen. *Quranic Schools: Agents of Preservation and Change*. New York: Routledge Falmer, 2004.

Bray, Mark. "Islamic Education: Continuity and Change." Pp. 79–100 in *Education and Society in Africa*, edited by Mark Bray, Peter B. Clarke, and David Stephens. London: Edward Arnold, 1986.

Brenner, Louis. *Controlling Knowledge: Religion, Power, and Schooling in a West African Muslim Society*. Bloomington: Indiana University Press, 2001.

Capelle, Jean. *L'éducation en Afrique Noire à la Veille des Indépendances (1946–1958)*. Paris: Editions Karthala ACCT, 1990.

Carruthers, Mary. *Book of Memory: A Study of Memory in Mediaeval Culture*. Cambridge: Cambridge University Press, 1992.

Cheney, Kristen E. *Pillars of the Nation: Child Citizens and Ugandan National Development*. Chicago: University of Chicago Press, 2007.

Coe, Cati. *Dilemmas of Culture in African Schools: Youth, Nationalism, and the Transformation of Knowledge*. Chicago: University of Chicago Press, 2005.

Cubberley, Ellwood Patterson. *A Brief History of Education: A History of the Practice and Progress and Organization of Education*. Boston: Houghton Mifflin, 1922.

Dauzat, Alain. *Le Génie de la Langue Française*. Paris: Payot, 1949.

Davis, Susan S., and David A. Davis. *Adolescence in a Moroccan Town: Making Social Sense*. New Brunswick, N.J.: Rutgers University Press, 1989.

Drazin, Nathan. *History of Jewish Education from 515 B.C.E. to 220 C.E. (during the Periods of the Second Commonwealth and the Tannaim)*. Baltimore: Johns Hopkins University Press, 1940.

Dreyfus, Georges B. J. *The Sound of Two Hands Clapping: The Education of a Tibetan Buddhist Monk*. Berkeley: University of California Press, 2003.

Eguchi, Paul Kazuhisa. *Fulfulde Tales of North Cameroon*, vol. 4. Tokyo: Institute for the Study of Languages and Cultures of Asia and Africa, 1984.

———. "'Fulbe-ness' in Fulbe Oral Literature of Cameroon." *Senri Ethnological Studies* 35 (1993): 181–200.

Eickelman, Dale F. *Knowledge and Power in Morocco: The Education of a Twentieth-Century Notable*. Princeton, N.J.: Princeton University Press, 1985.

Eisemon, Thomas. *Benefiting from Basic Education, School Quality, and Functional Literacy in Kenya*. Oxford: Pergamon, 1988.

Erickson, Frederick, and Gerald Mohatt. "Cultural Organization of Participation Structure in Two Classrooms of Indian Students." Pp. 132–74 in *Doing the Ethnography of Schooling: Educational Anthropology in Action*, edited by George Spindler. New York: Holt, Rinehart, and Winston, 1982.

Fernea, Elizabeth. "Muslim Middle East." Pp. 447–70 in *Children in Historical and Comparative Perspective*, edited by Joseph M. Hawes and N. Ray Hiner. Westport, Conn.: Greenwood, 1991.

Gade, Anna M. *Perfection Makes Practice: Learning, Emotion, and the Recited Qur'ān in Indonesia*. Honolulu: University of Hawaii Press, 2004.

Gay, John, and Michael Cole. *The New Mathematics and an Old Culture: A Study of Learning among the Kpelle of Liberia*. New York: Holt, Rinehart, and Winston, 1967.

Goody, Ester N. "Dynamics of the Emergence of Sociocultural Institutional Practices." Pp. 241–64 in *Technology, Literacy, and the Evolution of Society*, edited by David R. Olson and Michael Cole. Mahwah, N.J.: Erlbaum, 2006.

Heath, Shirley Brice. *Ways with Words: Language, Life, and Work in Communities and Classrooms*. New York: Cambridge University Press, 1983.

Ho, David Y. F. "Cognitive Socialization in Confucian Heritage Cultures." Pp. 285–314 in *Cross-Cultural Roots of Minority Child Development*, edited by Patricia M. Greenfield and Rodney R. Cocking. Hillsdale, N.J.: Erlbaum, 1994.

Hollos, Mirada, and Philip E. Leis. *Becoming Nigerian in Ijo Society*. New Brunswick, N.J.: Rutgers University Press, 1989.

Hori, G. Victor Sogen. "Teaching and Learning in the Rinzai Zen Monastery." Pp. 20–49 in *Teaching and Learning in Japan*, edited by Thomas P. Rohlen and Gerald K. LeTendre. Cambridge: Cambridge University Press, 1996.

Hornberger, Nancy H., and J. Keith Chick. "Co-Constructing Safetime in Peruvian and South African Classrooms." Pp. 31–55 in *Voices of Authority: Education and Linguistic Difference*, edited by Monica Heller and Marilyn Martin-Jones. Westport, Conn.: Ablex, 2001.

Iyébi-Mandjek, Olivier. "Enseignement." *Atlas de la Province Extrême-Nord, Cameroun* (CD-Rom), edited by Christian Seignobos and Olivier Iyébi-Mandjek. Paris: Editions de l'Institut de Recherche pour le Développement/Ministère de la Recherche Scientifique et Technique, Institut National de Cartographie, République du Cameroun, 2000.

Iyébi-Mandjek, Olivier, and Christian Seignobos. "Evolution de l'Organisation Politico-Administrative." *Atlas de la Province Extrême-Nord, Cameroun*

(CD-Rom), edited by Christian Seignobos and Olivier Iyébi-Mandjek. Paris: Editions de l'Institut de Recherche pour le Développement/Ministère de la Recherche Scientifique et Technique, Institut National de Cartographie, République du Cameroun, 2000.

Juul, Kristine. "Nomadic Schools in Senegal: Manifestations of Integration or Ritual Performance?" Pp.152–70 in *Designing Modern Childhoods: History, Space, and the Material Culture of Children*, edited by Marta Gutman and Ning de Coninck-Smith. New Brunswick, N.J.: Rutgers University Press, 2008.

Kulick, Don. *Language Shift and Cultural Reproduction: Socialization, Self, and Syncretism in a Papua New Guinean Village*. Cambridge: Cambridge University Press. 1992.

Lancy, David F. *The Anthropology of Childhood: Cherubs, Chattel, and Changelings*. Cambridge: Cambridge University Press, 2008.

Levinson, Bradley A., Douglas E. Foley, and Dorothy C. Holland, eds. *The Cultural Production of the Educated Person: Critical Ethnographies of Schooling and Local Practice*. Albany: SUNY Press, 1996.

Lomawaiama, K. Tsianina, and Teresa L. McCarty. *To Remain an Indian: Lessons in Democracy from a Century of Native American Education*. New York: Teachers College Press, 2006.

Macaire, François. *Notre Beau Métier: Manuel de Pédagogie Appliquée*. Versailles, France: Les Classiques Africaines, 1993.

Martin, Jean-Yves. "Sociologie de l'Enseignement en Afrique Noire." Pp. 545–79 in *La Quête du Savoir: Essais pour une Anthropologie de l'Education Camerounaise*, edited by Renaud Santerre and Celine Mercier-Tremblay. Montréal: Les Presses de l'Université de Montréal, 1982.

Ministère de l'Education Nationale. "Programmes Officiels de l'Enseignement Primaire." Niveau I. Yaounde, Cameroon: Ministère de l'Education Nationale, 1998.

Modiano, Nancy. *Indian Education in the Chiapas Highlands*. New York: Holt, Rinehart, and Winston, 1973.

Mommersteeg, Geert. *In de Stad van de Marabouts*. Amsterdam: Prometheus, 1998.

Moore, Leslie C. "Language Socialization Research and French Language Education in Africa: A Cameroonian Case Study." *Canadian Modern Language Review* 56, no. 2 (December 1999): 329–50.

———. "Changes in Folktale Socialization in a Fulbe Community." Pp. 176–87 in *West African Linguistics: Descriptive, Comparative, and Historical Studies in Honor of Russell G. Schuh*, edited by P. Newman and L. Hyman. Studies in African Linguistics Supplement 11 (2006).

———. "Body, Text, and Talk in Maroua Fulbe Qur'anic Schooling." *Text and Talk* 28, no. 5 (2008): 643–65.

Musa Ahmed. *Sociology of Islamic Education.* Kano, Nigeria: Triumph, 1996.

Nash, Manning. "Education in a New Nation: The Village School in Upper Burma." Pp. 301–13 in *From Child to Adult,* edited by John Middleton. Garden City, N.Y.: Natural History Press, 1970.

Nash, Paul. *Models of Man: Explorations in the Western Educational Tradition.* New York: Wiley, 1968.

Noye, Dominique. Un cas d'Apprentissage Linguistique: L'Acquisition de la Langue par les Jeunes Peuls du Diamare (Nord-Cameroun). Doctoral de Troisième Cycle, 1971.

———. *Blasons Peuls: Eloges et Satires du Nord Cameroun.* Paris: Geuthner, 1976.

Peshkin, Alan. *Kanuri Schoolchildren: Education and Social Mobilization in Nigeria.* New York: Holt, Rinehart, and Winston, 1972.

Philips, Susan U. *The Invisible Culture: Communication in Classroom and Community on the Warm Springs Indian Reservation.* White Plains, N.Y.: Longman, 1983.

Riesman, Paul, and David L. Szanton. *First Find Your Child a Good Mother: The Construction of Self in Two African Communities.* New Brunswick, N.J.: Rutgers University Press, 1992.

Rogoff, Barbara, Leslie Moore, Behnosh Najafi, Amy Dexter, Maricela Correa-Chávez, and Jocelyn Solis. "Children's Development of Cultural Repertoires through Participation in Everyday Routines and Practices." Pp. 490–515 in *Handbook of Socialization: Theory and Research,* edited by Joan E. Grusec and Paul D. Hastings. New York: Guilford, 2007.

Sanneh, Lamin O. "The Islamic Education of an African Child: Stresses and Tensions." Pp. 164–86 in *Conflict and Harmony in Education in Tropical Africa,* edited by Godfry N. Brown and Mervyn Hiskett. London: Allen and Unwin, 1975.

Santerre, Renaud. *Pédagogie Musulmane d'Afrique Noire: L'École Coranique Peule du Cameroun.* Montréal: Presses de l'Université de Montréal, 1973.

———. "Aspects conflictuels de deux systèmes d'enseignement au Nord-Cameroun." Pp. 396–413 in *La Quête du Savoir: Essais pour une Anthropologic de l'Education Camerounaise,* edited by Renaud Santerre, C. Mercier-Tremblay. Montréal: Presses de l'Université de Montréal, 1982a.

———. "Maîtres coraniques de Maroua." Pp. 350–71 in *La Quête du Savoir: Essais pour une Anthropologie de l'Education Camerounaise,* edited by Renaud Santerre, C. Mercier-Tremblay. Montréal: Presses de l'Université de Montréal, 1982b.

Schieffelin, Bambi, and Perry Gilmore. *The Acquisition of Literacy: Ethnographic Perspectives.* Norwood, N.J.: Ablex, 1986.

Schieffelin, Bambi, and Elinor Ochs. "The Microgenesis of Competence: Methodology in Language Socialization." Pp. 251–64 in *Social Interaction, Social Context, and Language*, edited by Dan Isaac Slobin, Julie Gerhardt, Amy Kyratzis, and Jiansheng Guo. Mahwah, N.J.: Erlbaum, 1995.

Scribner, Sylvia, and Michael Cole. *The Psychology of Literacy*. Cambridge, Mass.: Harvard University Press, 1981a.

———. "Unpackaging Literacy." Pp. 71–87 in *Writing: The Nature, Development, and Teaching of Written Communication*, edited by Marcia Farr Whiteman. Hillsdale, N.J.: Erlbaum, 1981b.

Seignobos, Christian, and Abdourhaman Nassourou. "Réligions." In *Atlas de la Province Extrême-Nord, Cameroun*, edited by C. Seignobos and O. Iyébi-Mandjek. Paris: Editions de l'Institut de Recherche pour le Développement/Ministère de la Recherche Scientifique et Technique, Institut National de Cartographie, République du Cameroun, 2000.

Singleton, John. "Reflecting on the Reflections: Where Did We Come From? Where Are We Going?" *Anthropology and Education Quarterly* 30, no. 4 (December 1999): 455–9.

Stambach, Amy. *Lessons from Mount Kilimanjaro: Schooling, Community, and Gender in East Africa*. New York: Routledge, 2000.

———. "Faith in Schools: Toward an Ethnography of Education, Religion, and the State." *Social Analysis* 48, no. 3 (Fall 2004): 92–109.

Tharp, Roland, and Ron Gallimore. *Rousing Minds to Life: Teaching, Learning, and Schooling in Social Context*. New York: Cambridge University Press, 1988.

Tourneux, Henry, and Olivier Iyébi-Mandjek. *L'École dans une Petite Ville Africaine (Maroua, Cameroun)*. Paris: Karthala, 1994.

UNICEF. *Guide Pratique du Maître*. Vanves, France: EDICEF, 1993.

Wagner, Daniel A. "Rediscovering 'Rote': Some Cognitive and Pedagogical Preliminaries." Pp. 179–90 in *Human Assessment and Cultural Factors*, edited by John W. Berry and Sidney H. Irvine. New York: Plenum, 1983.

———. *Literacy, Culture and Development: Becoming Literate in Morocco*. New York: Cambridge University Press, 1993.

Watson-Gegeo, Karen Ann, and David Welchman Gegeo. "Schooling, Knowledge, and Power: Social Transformation in the Solomon Islands." *Anthropology and Education Quarterly* 23, no. 2 (June 1992): 10–29.

Wise, Jessie, and Susan Wise Bauer. *The Well-Trained Mind: A Parent's Guide to Classical Education*. New York: Norton, 2004.

Wolcott, Harry F. *A Kwakiutl Village and School*. New York: Holt, Rinehart, and Winston, 1967.

Part III
LEARNING CULTURAL MEANINGS

CHAPTER TEN
LEARNING COMMUNICATIVE COMPETENCE

Laura Sterponi

Universally, young children are positioned as novices and are expected to progressively acquire a wide array of competencies. This complex and multifaceted apprenticeship process features language both as a central means of knowledge transmission and as a critical target of transmission.[1] In fact, apprenticeship *through* language and apprenticeship *into* language are inseparable dimensions of the process of becoming a competent member of the social group (Cook-Gumperz 1987; Schieffelin and Ochs 1986a, 1986b).

As a simple example, think about the question "What do you say?" This question is used pervasively by American and European middle-class adults in addressing their young children (Ely and Berko-Gleason 1995; Fasulo and Pontecorvo 1999). What it solicits is not a display of linguistic proficiency, but rather a demonstration of cultural competence: the expected response from the child is usually "Thank you" or "Please," which demonstrate politeness; or "I'm sorry" or "I apologize," which demonstrate moral awareness; or "Good morning, Sir," which signals respect. Similar instances of explicit language socialization, such as elicited imitation routines, reformulations, and rhetorical questions have been observed in communities around the world. Prompting practices, in particular, have been documented among the Basotho (Demuth 1986), the Kwara'ae (Watson-Gegeo and Gegeo 1986), the Kaluli (Schieffelin 1986, 1990), the Indo-Guayanese (Sidnell 1997), and the Zinacantec Mayan (de León 1998).

Language use is a form of social action. As such, it is structured by social norms, cultural constructs, beliefs, and ideologies pertaining to language use itself, but also a range of other practices, interpersonal relationships, and individual and group identities. While language development is shaped by neurological and cognitive factors, mastery of one's mother tongue (and similarly of another language) cannot be characterized simply in terms of lexical wealth, semantic complexity, and syntactic virtuosity. Children's communicative development is also molded and organized by sociocultural processes. Grammatical forms are used to carry out social acts and to express opinions. These in turn are connected to social identities and cultural practices, whose meanings reflect and instantiate a community's beliefs and worldview. Thus, in discerning developmental trends in language comprehension and production, the sociocultural matrix of a community's communicative practices has to be taken into account.

Certain patterns of language development that can be observed in young children learning their mother tongue are conundrums if evaluated according to their grammatical properties. In traditional Western Samoan communities, for instance, young children have been documented to master the deictic verb *aumai* ("to bring/give") before the deictic verb *sau* ("to come") (Ochs 1988; Platt 1986). Both verbs are used in imperative constructions to summon others (*sau*) and to demand or request goods (*aumai*), and they are widely used in the social environment in which young children are immersed. If the order of acquisition of these deictic verbs could be predicated on their semantic structure, and on the cognitive load that structure demands for comprehension and production, one would expect *sau* to be mastered before *aumai*.[2] But in Samoan society, the documented order of acquisition can be explained by the hierarchical organization of society, in which physical movement is associated with relatively lower-status individuals. Higher-status persons tend to minimize movements and delegate to lower-status community members actions that require a change of physical location. The deictic verb *sau* is chiefly used to orchestrate those actions and movements. Young children are usually the lowest-ranking people in the household, so while they are frequently summoned with *sau* imperatives, there are few opportunities for them to use the verb appropriately. In contrast, *aumai* is the verb conventionally employed to carry out the act of begging, which is considered an appropriate and indeed expected action for young children to perform (insofar as it implies that the beggar is in a submissive position with respect to the bestower). When this sociocultural context is taken into account, the order of acquisition of the two deictics makes sense.

This chapter discusses language acquisition as a fundamentally cultural process. It draws primarily on the research paradigm of language socialization, which conceives of language acquisition as socialization and contends that the socialization process happens simultaneously *through* language and *into* language (Ochs 1988; Ochs and Schieffelin 1984; Schieffelin 1990; Schieffelin and Ochs 1986a, 1986b). The chapter first examines how culturally specific dispositions differently organize communicative practices and diversely configure communicative competence. Second, it considers child-directed communication and how the language learner is engaged in and exposed to conversational interaction with more competent speakers of the social group. The culture-specific role of child-directed speech in language acquisition is discussed, followed by a further examination of children's positioning in communicative practices and the link between participation structure, socialization, and the expected role of the learner at different developmental stages.

This exploration of the language socialization process continues with an analysis of the relationship between acquisition of discourse practices and identity formation. Special attention is given to narrative as both a social activity and a mode of cognition. Narrative is a powerful resource for apprehending and navigating one's own milieu. The chapter examines its importance both in socializing children to certain socially sanctioned roles and identities and in enabling those same children to construct their own trajectory and a sense of authentic self. The final section reflects on children's agency in the language socialization process: the role of the child in her or his own socialization and in the socialization of others. I argue that the language socialization process is inherently reciprocal and spans a person's lifetime. This argument also sheds light on children's impact on cultural transmission and change.

Sociocultural Dispositions and Communicative Practices

In order to understand the relation of language to sociocultural constructs and processes, and thereby discern the intricacies of acquiring communicative competence, scholars in linguistic anthropology have engaged the semiotic notion of indexicality. Because it is central to understanding what constitutes language competence, a brief discussion of this concept is necessary to provide the context for the more general exploration of language socialization.

Drawing from Charles S. Peirce's (1974) account of the ways in which meaning can be conveyed through signs, linguistic anthropologists have brought to light how members of each speech community associate particular linguistic features—as elementary as morphemes and particles, and more complex grammatical forms or registers—to specific types of speakers or contexts (Agha 2007; Hanks 1990; Ochs 1990; Silverstein 1976). Thus linguistic forms bear indexical meaning: their meaning is based on contextual connections. In turn, the inherent indexical value of linguistic forms is such that every instance of use contributes to reconstituting the relevant context.[3]

A broad spectrum of sociocultural information can be indexed through linguistic forms, notably gender, social status, affective and epistemological stances, ethnicity, and identity. Indexical relationships, however, are more complex than one-to-one direct associations (Ochs 1990; Silverstein 2003). On the one hand, a single linguistic feature may index a wide range of possible social contexts.[4] Deletion of the copula in spoken Standard American English is a case in point: for instance, when someone says "you hungry" instead of "you are hungry," it can index the social status of the person being addressed, such as a child, a foreigner, or an elderly person (Ochs 1990). On the other hand, linguistic forms also occur in patterns, which as a whole index some contextual meaning. Register is a good example of this kind of indexical complexity, being constituted by clustered and patterned linguistic, paralinguistic, and discursive features that as a whole may index (and typify) certain ethnic identities, social roles, or subject positions (Agha 2004). A well-known example of register is baby talk.[5]

Further, indexical meanings may be conveyed through *direct* relations between one or a cluster of linguistic forms and some dimensions of context. Alternatively, certain sociocultural information is conveyed *indirectly*, via the mediation of another indexical relation. Evidential markers, for instance, may index the speaker's epistemic stance, and via a claim of knowledge (or lack thereof), they may index authority and power asymmetry (e.g., Heritage and Raymond 2005; see also chapter 11, this volume).[6]

Finally, indexical relations are noticed, given meaning, and made objects of evaluation, thereby becoming ideologically loaded and pragmatically usable constructs (Silverstein 2003). This ideological layering is captured in Silverstein's concept of *indexical order*, according to which second-order indexicality is generated when first-order indexical variation is "swept up into an ideologically-driven metapragmatics" (Silverstein 2003, 219).

Indexical Relationships and the Organization of Sociocultural Practices: An Illustration

The concept of indexicality provides a useful theoretical framework for understanding the embeddedness of communicative practices in complex sociocultural contexts. An analysis of the act of clarification is offered as an illustration of how everyday routines and conversational exchanges children experience are organized by norms, cultural constructs, beliefs, and ideologies pertaining not solely to language use but also to the pursuit of knowledge, interpersonal relationships, and social order (Ochs 1988). The activity of clarifying one's own or others' talk and behavior is found in all cultures, being undoubtedly a central practice for securing interpersonal intelligibility and attunement. However, what is deemed important to elucidate and the ways in which clarification is pursued vary crossculturally. These differences reflect distinct epistemologies, folk theories of communication, and principles of social order.

Young children's unintelligible utterances and nonverbal behavior are particularly salient targets of clarification among American white middleclass caregivers, while they are more rarely objects of attention and clarification sequences in other communities, such as the Inuit (Crago 1992), the Kaluli (Schieffelin 1990), or the Samoan (Ochs 1988). When infants and young children produce unintelligible verbalizations (or nonverbal actions), American white middle-class caregivers tend to pursue clarification by proffering candidate understandings: *expressed guess strategies* (Ochs 1988) such as "Do you mean X?" or "X? Is that what you're saying?" articulate a clarification for the child to confirm or reject.

In Inuit, Kaluli, and Samoan communities, explicitly inquiring about what someone else is thinking is an undesirable activity. Insofar as clarification may imply guessing the unintelligible communicative intentions of another, such activity is seen as inappropriate. This is especially true when differently ranked individuals (e.g., adults and children) are involved in the clarification activity and the unintelligible utterance is produced by the lower-ranking interlocutor. In these societies, higher-ranking members do not normally accommodate lower-ranking individuals and hence do not attempt to clarify an interlocutor's unclear utterance by guessing its meaning.

When Inuit, Kaluli, and Samoan caregivers do solicit clarification from their children, they most frequently employ *minimal grasp strategies* (Ochs 1988). They display minimal or no apprehension of the child's verbalization (or nonverbal action). Statements of nonunderstanding (e.g., "I don't understand," "I can't understand what you're saying"), *wh-* interrogatives (e.g., "What?" "Who?" "Where?"), quizzical expressions (e.g., "Huh?" or raised eyebrows), as well as explicit requests or directives to repeat the unclear utterance or action (e.g., "Say it again," or "Show me again"), call for the child to take full charge of clearing up unintelligible utterances.

These different cultural approaches to the clarification activity reflect distinct local epistemologies. The preference for a certain kind of response to unintelligibility is informed by tacit assumptions about how knowledge is pursued and what can be accessed as objects of knowledge. In the American white middle-class community studied, deployment of expressed guess strategies instantiates the Socratic method for gaining knowledge (Ochs 1988). Learning and understanding are pursued through articulation and testing of hypotheses. Utilizing this procedure to gain knowledge about the communicative intentions of another also indicates that what is in another's mind is deemed a legitimate and possible object of knowledge. In contrast, ignoring unintelligibility or addressing it through minimal grasp strategies reflects the belief that another's unclear expression cannot be made the object of (verbal) speculation and that knowledge can be gained through repeated exposure.

Different cultural approaches to the clarification activity also reflect distinct folk theories of meaning-making and communication. The aim of expressed guess strategies is to grasp the child's communicative intention, and the child is called on to confirm or disconfirm the interpretation. An utterance or action's correct meaning corresponds to the utterer or actor's intended meaning. In contrast, avoiding speculation about others' thoughts and communicative intentions is linked to a folk theory that emphasizes the consequences of an utterance or action as central to determining the utterance or action's meaning (Schieffelin 1990).

Finally, different cultural approaches to the clarification activity result from different social orders. Expressed guess strategies used to clarify young children's statements are oriented toward and accommodate the child. In offering a possible interpretation of the child's unclear utterance or action, the caregiver takes the perspective of the child; that is, she mobilizes cognitive resources for decentering and articulating a considered guess (Ochs 1982). In a social matrix in which social relationships are closely mapped on hierarchical status, accommodation to the lower-ranking child is inappropriate for the higher-ranking caregiver. Contrariwise, young children are expected to adopt a sociocentric perspective, to notice and accommodate the needs and preferences of higher-ranking persons: for instance, by clarifying their utterances or actions (as well as those of higher-ranking interlocutors).

In summary, clarification is a compelling example of how cognitive and linguistic processes are socioculturally organized. As participants in the clarification activity, young children not only become familiar with the cognitive operations and discourse structures that lead to identification and resolution of unintelligibility; they also learn what can and cannot be accessed as objects of knowledge and valued ways to pursue knowledge. They are socialized into local perspectives on meaning and meaning-making, and into norms and expectations concerning social identities and interpersonal relationships.

Much of social meanings of discourse practices—such as clarification—are constituted and transmitted through indexical relationships that link linguistic forms to acts, stances, roles, identities, and activities. The relation of language to cultural constructs and social order exceeds the semantic domain and is more complex than a one-to-one mapping of form and meaning. It is woven in intricate ways on the axes of multiple orders of indexicality.

LAURA STERPONI

Child-Directed Communication and the
Child as Interlocutor

Theories of language acquisition comprise claims about the nature and role of input in first-language learning (for reviews, see Gallaway and Richards 1994; Snow 1995). Chomsky's initial theorization of the *language acquisition device* was based on an assessment of input as unsystematic, incoherent, and often fallacious (Chomsky 1965). Interestingly, many scholars who criticized innatist theories of language acquisition ended up making claims of universality as well. Baby talk, a specialized register used to address young children, was considered a universal phenomenon, in fact a requirement for children's language acquisition.

In the early 1980s, linguistic anthropologists Elinor Ochs and Bambi Schieffelin (1984) put forward a groundbreaking reconceptualization of baby talk based on their fieldwork in Western Samoa and Papua New Guinea respectively. Ochs and Schieffelin revealed that child-directed speech does not exhibit the same characteristics across cultures; notably, simplification is not universally present. In addition, they observed that features of child-directed speech recurring in different speech communities are differentially frequent.

In light of their fieldwork observations, Ochs and Schieffelin concluded that linguistic simplification is not required for the young child to learn the mother tongue. In fact, Ochs and Schieffelin argued that the notion of input in itself had to be reexamined, in that it implies the need for language to be addressed to the child and to be closely connected to a dyadic model of communication; but it is not the case that everywhere in the world children are spoken to by adults or engaged in dyadic exchanges (Akhtar 2005; Blum-Kulka and Snow 2002; de León 1998).

Ochs and Schieffelin's contribution did not stop at documenting the cultural variability in child-directed speech. Most significantly, they offered an analytic framework that allows us to understand that such variability reflects (that is, is indexical of) distinct systems of beliefs, epistemological orientations, and social orders. For instance, among the Kaluli in Papua New Guinea, infants are considered unable to understand or communicate (Schieffelin 1985, 1990). Mothers do not engage them in dyadic (proto)conversation or take infant vocalizations as precursors of speech endowed with communicative intention. The exposure to language is nevertheless rich, as Kaluli infants are always carried on their mother's body and held facing outward; hence, they are continuously immersed in activities and conversations among adults and older children. In addition, Kaluli mothers often initiate triadic exchanges in which they ventriloquate for their babies using a high-pitched, nasalized voice to engage an older child or adult in conversation. In voicing for their infants, Kaluli mothers use well-formed and unsimplified language.

The Kaluli child is treated as an interlocutor only once she or he begins uttering the words *no* and *bo*, "mother" and "breast" respectively (Schieffelin 1990).[7] At that point, the child becomes the target of explicit language instruction. The most frequent language instructional practice is a prompting routine that consists of offering a model for what the child should say followed by the imperative ɛlɛma ("Say it like that"). No simplification or prosodic alteration is featured in this instructional practice. Indeed, Kaluli caregivers believe that simplification is counterproductive to language acquisition. Learning to talk is a hardening process whose goal implies both mastering "hard words" and overcoming the vulnerability of infancy.

In other cultural groups—such as American and European middle-class communities—newborns are considered intentional communicators, and infants and young children are expected to take on the demanding communicative roles of addressees and speakers. Infants' vocalizations are treated as speech acts (e.g., requests, assessments, complaints) and are often taken up and ratified through repetition or expansion. Indeed, caregivers as well as occasional interlocutors extensively simplify their own linguistic production when talking to children (Ochs and Schieffelin 1984).[8]

In more recent years, Elinor Ochs has returned to an examination of baby talk and has offered an alternative construct for the various ways competent members of different social groups interact verbally and nonverbally with children. Ochs, Solomon, and Sterponi (2005) engage a set of sociocultural dimensions—comprising ideologies, habitats, participation frameworks, activities, and semiotic repertoires—to illuminate the specificities of a community's communicative habitus and in particular child-directed communication. In proposing a multidimensional model of child-directed communication, Ochs and colleagues (2005) extend the range of communicative modalities beyond speech, consider a wider range of communicators (older siblings and other relatives, in addition to the mother).

Ochs and her colleagues suggest that the way different cultures organize child-directed communication "is not neutral with respect to its influence on children's development" (560); that is, it may not maximize the communicative potential of all children. Ochs and colleagues then demonstrate that certain features of Euro-American child-directed communication may hinder the communicative capacities of children with autism spectrum disorders. Specifically, face-to-face body orientation, speech as the primary semiotic medium for the child, and interlocutors' slowed speech tempo and profuse praise, compound the communicative difficulties of children with autism. The case of an Indian woman, mother of a child with severe autism, reported by Ochs and colleagues (2005), shows, however, that the communicative habitus is open to transformation: in trying to overcome major difficulties in the communication with her nonverbal son, Soma Mukhopadhyay challenged commonly held assumptions about autism and adopted an alternative set of child-directed communicative practices attuned to severe autism. These practices—which include side-by-side body orientation, pointing to symbols as the primary semiotic medium for the child, and rapid prompts and restrained praise by the caregiver—allowed the autistic child to communicate extensively with his mother and others.

The Child's Positioning in Communicative Interaction

Previous sections of this chapter have discussed the differential positioning in communicative practices that young children experience in different communities. As the discussion pointed out, theories of language acquisition that presuppose direct input through dyadic simplified verbal interaction do not withstand the evidence of cross-cultural studies. This section further explores the organization of participation in talk when young children are present, and it discusses the link between participation structure, socialization, and expected roles for the child at different developmental stages. Specifically, it examines how the acquisition of communicative competence is closely associated with learning to assume certain subject positions and participant roles and learning to shift among them with different interlocutors and in different activities.

In many cultures, a child's first display of communicative competence is that of attuned listener (e.g., de León 1998, on the Zinacantec Mayans; Gaskins 1996, on the Yucatec Mayans; Schieffelin 1986, on the Kaluli; Toren 1990, on the Fijians). Infants are not recruited as interlocutors, either as speakers or addressees, but are nevertheless engaged in the flow of communication and activities in ways that require them to be attentive—that is, active peripheral participants (see chapter 5, this volume; Lave and Wenger 1991; Rogoff et al. 2003).[9]

As previously mentioned, among the Kaluli, preverbal children are not treated as communicative partners (Schieffelin 1985). However, as early as the first 6 months of life, infants are often involved in triadic interactions with an adult caregiver and an older sibling. An older sibling may be prompted to address rhetorical questions or imperatives to younger brothers or sisters in order to get them to change their course of action. Infants are not expected to respond verbally; in fact, they are not assumed to understand the propositional content of what they are told. The goal of the activity is a behavioral adjustment by the infant, which is usually effectively accomplished.

Among Zinacantec Mayans, infants' vocalizations, gestures, and eye gaze are interpreted as conveying communicative intention, which adults respond to in two ways: either by producing a verbal gloss or by quoting the baby (employing a reported speech frame) (de León 1998). Both speech acts are addressed to other co-present family or community members. Infants are thus considered *protospeakers* long before they begin to talk, but they are not recruited as addressees and speakers in dyadic exchanges. A triadic participation format is more common with children who have begun babbling or uttering words. In elicitation routines, the child is addressed and at the same time invited to speak to a co-present third party.

In dinner conversations among Italian family members, co-present young children (age 3–5 years old) are usually ratified participants and treated as competent interlocutors (Fatigante, Fasulo, and Pontecorvo 1998). Sometimes, however, they are made the topic of talk while being relegated to the more peripheral position of unaddressed recipient or *nonperson* (Benveniste 1996, as cited in Fatigante et al. 1998). Such a change of position is common when dealing with a child's problematic conduct. The child as "dangerous interactant" is thus controlled by casting the child as an unratified participant who can only overhear how others characterize her or his behavior. Alternatively, the adults refer to the child in the third person and metaphorically set the stage for her or him to perform in the way they are talking about. The key of this kind of sequence is usually playful. The child is thus called on to parody her or his own behavior, thereby aligning herself or himself with the characterization the adults have provided verbally.

In summary, children's language learning does not depend on the child being addressed (in simplified or other form) by adults and other competent speakers, or on being treated as an intentional communicator beginning in infancy. Different participant structures recruit children to language socialization practices. These forms of participation and the children's allocations therein vary developmentally and cross-culturally. On the one hand, they are associated with stages of expertise and maturation; on the other, they are related to local theories of socialization and childhood. In this sense, acquiring communicative competence encompasses taking on culturally appropriate subject positions.

Discourse Practices and Identity Formation

The acquisition of communicative competence, being essentially the process of "becoming a speaker of culture" (Ochs 2002), encompasses learning a variety of discourse practices that are part of the community's cultural repertoire. These discourse practices can be conceptualized as social activities and also as modes of cognition and orienting frameworks. As such, their apprehension equips speakers with linguistic and cognitive resources to navigate in their own environments and construct their own trajectory and experience therein.

Narrative is recognized as the most significant and powerful tool for making sense of life experiences as well as for configuring stances and identities (e.g., Bruner 1990, 1993; Mattingly 1998; Morrison 1994; Ochs and Capps 2001; Ricoeur 1984). Ubiquitous across the world's societies, yet culturally stipulated, narrative practices socialize children into a community's worldview and moral perspective, and into expected subject positions, including gendered roles and collective alignments. Cultural and comparative studies have shown that very young children participate in oral narrative activity and that these early stories are already culturally differentiated.

Shirley Brice Heath's (1983) classic study of three communities in the Piedmont Carolinas has revealed that different social groups adopt distinct criteria of tellability and norms for recounting events. More specifically, Heath found that the white working-class community of Roadville, used factual narratives based on personal experiences, with focused attention to detail and truth-value, to convey moral lessons. In contrast, the black working-class Trackton community valued story-tellers who exploited the fictional realm to embellish the narrative and make it more entertaining for the audience. Socialization into these different narrative practices not only configures children's narrative competence differently but also conveys distinct values about what is worth telling and the appropriate framework for interpreting events (see also Preece 1987; Sperry and Sperry 1996).

In exploring the role of narrative practices in the early socialization of Chinese and American children, Peggy J. Miller and colleagues have shown that Chinese parents overwhelmingly employ the recounting of past experiences to remind children of misdeeds and of moral standards. In contrast, American parents utilize stories about their children's past experiences primarily as a medium of entertainment and self-affirmation (Miller, Fung, and Mintz 1996; Miller et al. 1997; see also chapter 11, this volume). Wang and Leichtman's (2000) analysis of the social, emotional, and cognitive features of American and Chinese 6-year-olds' narratives offers congruent findings: Chinese children's stories are more concerned with moral standards and social rules than those produced by American children. In addition, Wang and Leichtman found that in recounting past experiences Chinese children are oriented toward social engagement and interpersonal relationships, whereas their American counterparts show greater orientation toward individual needs, preferences, and lines of action.

Narratives about personal experiences and autobiographical memories are thus culturally specific products, inextricably bound into the community's symbolic and ideological order (Miller, Fung, and Koven 2007; Wang and Brockmeier 2002). Narratives are also instrumental in identity formation: they offer subject positions for children to take on. A community's narrative genres are frameworks that allow members to represent themselves and others in particular ways. At the same time, individuals use narratives to transform their experiences, resist and transcend pre-established identity attributions, and strive for authenticity and self-expression (Bruner 2002; Ochs 2004; Ochs and Capps 2001; Wortham 2001). Indeed, these dynamics of cultural transmission and transformation occur both at the level of the narrated event and the event of narration.

Numerous studies have highlighted how gendered identities are constructed and negotiated through narrative activity. Robin Fivush's research offers a nuanced developmental account of relations between gender, identity, and autobiography in white middle-class families (Fivush 1994; Fivush and Buckner 2003; Fivush et al. 2000). Fivush has found gender differences in the ways girls and boys tell stories about their lives as early as the preschool years. Specifically, preschool girls tend to talk more about the emotional and interactional aspects of their experiences than boys do. By studying spontaneous parent-child conversations about past events, Fivush has been able to connect these early gender differences to the ways mothers and fathers reminisce with their daughters and sons. In those dyadic interactions, mothers and fathers behaved strikingly similarly in engaging differently in narrative with their daughters and sons. With their daughters, both parents talked about emotions and situated events in an interpersonal matrix to a greater extent than with their sons. Although these findings do not indicate that there are monolithic and fixed gender differences in the way males and females talk about past events, the convergence of fathers' and mothers' narrative styles when reminiscing with their daughters and sons is evidence of an early socialization process into culturally appropriate gender roles.

Narrative is also a central tool for the construction of collective identities and a sense of belonging. In her study of narrative renditions of the apparition of Nuestra Señora de Guadalupe in religious education classes, Baquedano-López (2000) shows how teachers use narrative activity to draw children of Mexican descent in Los Angeles into a paradigm of national, albeit diasporic, identity. Baquedano-López's analysis reveals that while the narrative calls for identification with the protagonist, the oppressed Indian who challenges the Spanish clergy, it also represents the master narrative of the Catholic Church in that the ultimate liberating act comes about in the form of divine intervention. In other words, while identification with the protagonist endows children with counterhegemonic storylines that construct an agentive Mexican identity, the narrative also restrains the subversive potential of legitimization of a rebellious character by subsuming his actions within a broader project of collective devotion and redemption.

Narrative activity is also key to the shaping of family identity. In the intimate context of dinnertime, Italian families often engage in co-narration (Fasulo and Pontecorvo 1997; Pontecorvo and Arcidiacono 2007). Most frequently, family members, including young children, revisit past events that feature the family as protagonist. Approximately 30 percent of the co-narrations, however, feature others—that is, individuals not connected by kinship to the participants—as protagonists (Pontecorvo, Amendola, and Fasulo 1994). Both kinds of collective narration contribute to the construction of and socialization into a family identity: in talking about unrelated protagonists, family members take stances and call for people to express opinions about others' behaviors and experiences.

In American white middle-class families (Ochs and Taylor 1992), family narration is less frequently centered on the family as a group. The children are the most frequent protagonists; however, they rarely introduce the narratives themselves. The parents orchestrate the activity, taking on the roles of introducer, primary recipient, and problematizer. In this case, the narrative activity seems to serve as a powerful tool for the construction of the political order of the family (Ochs and Taylor 1992).[10]

Active Apprentice: The Role of the Child in Language Socialization

A fundamental tenet of the language socialization research paradigm is that both adults and children, experts and novices, are engaged in teaching and learning practices as active agents. Young children do not passively internalize cultural knowledge, and cultural apprenticeship does not only happen in childhood (Ochs 1986, 1988).

A convincing illustration of children's agency within and in relation to processes of sociocultural and linguistic apprenticeship is offered by Amy Paugh's (2005) work on language acquisition, use, and shift in

Dominica, West Indies. On that Caribbean island, adults forbid children from speaking Patwa, which is the local creole and the language adults use for informal exchanges and emotionally expressive utterances, in favor of English, the official language and the language of schooling. Still, children often speak Patwa during play with their peers, using it to try out social identities and acts that defy authority and power asymmetries. Paugh argues persuasively that these children are both actively engaged in acquiring communicative competence in an ideologically charged multilingual context and also having an impact on broader processes of language maintenance and shift.

Further evidence of children's agency in language apprenticeship is offered within the research tradition of developmental psycholinguistics. Nancy Budwig (1989, 1990), for instance, has studied the use of self-reference forms by young children acquiring English as a first language. Budwig has observed that the children use personal pronouns ("I" and "me"), and their own names in a systematic but unconventional way, to contrastively mark different agency attributions and degrees of control.

Acknowledging children as agents in the social world, researchers are also compelled to explore how children's actions have implications for others. Children are not only active in their own socialization but are also active socializers of others (Gaskins, Miller, and Corsaro 1992; Pontecorvo, Fasulo, and Sterponi 2001). In many societies, children are responsible for socializing their younger siblings. Linguistic anthropologist Penelope Brown has shown, for example, that in the Tzeltal-speaking Mayan community, children as young as 5 years old are caregivers and employ complex forms of nonliteral language, notably threats and lies, that until very recently had been used on them. In employing those complex forms, children display their ability to consider what others are thinking and manipulate it creatively (Brown 2002).

In Kwara'ae (Solomon Islands), Watson-Gegeo (2001) has observed that as early as when they turn age 3 and begin working regularly, children perform two modal presentations of self: child mode and adult mode. Adult mode is primarily employed in work contexts, where children take on the demeanor of adults and interact with them as equals. By switching between child and adult modes, and by integrating knowledge achieved with peers through pretend play and that attained from adults and firsthand experience, Kwara'ae children "learn about and transform social reality, (re)modeling their culture" (Watson-Gegeo 2001).

Pontecorvo, Fasulo, and Sterponi (2001) have highlighted children's active role in socializing other family members, notably parents, just as they are socialized by them. In other words, while children are engaged in the process of becoming competent members of the social group as children, they are also contributing to the socialization of their parents to culturally specific parental practices (see also Orellana 2009). In Italian families (and likely in many other cultures around the world), children frequently ask their parents for information and explanations (Pontecorvo et al. 2001). In doing so, the children activate a novice-expert framework and assign those roles to themselves and their interlocutors respectively. The addressed parent is thus solicited to display his or her expertise. Such expertise includes knowledge the child lacks, as well as the ability to provide an answer that is intelligible to the child and is culturally appropriate. Moreover, children's questions invoke parents' knowledge as it applies to certain experiences or lines of reasoning with which the children are concerned: parents must package their answers in ways that are responsive to the children's frame of inquiry.

Conclusion

Language and verbal communication are defining features of humanity. Though universal, they are also inherently culturally stipulated. Language acquisition is thus quintessentially a socialization process through which children become *speakers of culture* (Ochs 2002).

This chapter has discussed the relationship between communicative practices and sociocultural structures, in particular the ways this relationship informs the process of language socialization. It described how in different cultures and communities, children experience verbal interaction and come to master communicative competence through different paths and forms of participation. The discussion also highlighted children's agency in language socialization and noted the reciprocal and lifelong character of the process. Indeed, becoming a speaker of culture means learning to speak like a child, a sibling, a parent, a teacher, and many more ways in the different moments of one's life course.

As children take up—*through* language and *with* language—expected social roles and subject positions, they creatively negotiate and manipulate—*through* language and *with* language—their social and existential spaces. Language as both a system and a social practice is continually object and instrument of improvisation and change. Children's role in the transmission and transformation of culture cannot be overstated and should be further explored through multidisciplinary and interdisciplinary endeavors.

Acknowledgments

I am grateful to the editors of the volume, in particular to Suzanne Gaskins for her attentive reading and thoughtful suggestions. In addition, I wish to thank Leslie Moore for her critical advice and support throughout the writing process.

Notes

1. In this chapter, the term *apprenticeship* is used to forefront the situated nature of learning and to focus attention on contexts of acquisition rather than individual mental processes (Rogoff 1990). In this broad sense, the notion of apprenticeship acknowledges the active role of children in organizing learning and socialization but does not necessarily ascribe intentionality or awareness in acquiring cultural knowledge.

2. Unlike *aumai*, *sau* is a noncausative verb (Platt 1986).

3. Not only linguistic signs are inherently indexical, but all kinds of signs can potentially convey information about contextual variables, such as the status or ethnicity of the actor. Goffman (1956), for instance, offers a sharp analysis of "embodied indicators of status and character," which he captured with the notion of demeanor.

4. Ochs (1990) has defined this form of indexical complexity as *collocational indexing* (294).

5. Essential properties of baby talk comprise prosodic features such as high pitch and exaggerated contour, phonological features such as reduplication and special sounds, syntactic features such as parataxis and repetition, lexical features such as hypocorism and kin terms, and discourse features such as question and pronoun shift (Ferguson 1977).

6. Evidential markers express the evidence a speaker has for his or her statement and/or the speaker's degree of confidence in his or her statement (Chafe and Nichols 1986).

7. In many communities around the world, a child's first word is given special attention. Community members often speculate about what that word will be. While there are considerable cross-linguistic similarities in the linguistic characteristics of children's first words (Bornstein et al. 1997; Gentner 1982; Tardif et al. 2008), what the first word means and what this meaning says about the child's presumed nature vary substantially across cultures.

In traditional Western Samoa communities, children are said to utter *tae* as their first word (Ochs 1988). *Tae* means "shit" and is recognized as part of the more complex expression *ai tae*, "eat shit." A curse is thus what Samoan children are expected to utter as their first linguistic act. The expectation and interpretation of children's early vocalization as curse is linked to the cultural concept of the Samoan child's nature as wild, willful, and irreverent. Similarly, among the people of Gapun, Papua New Guinea, infants are considered obstinate and bad-natured (Kulick 1992). The first words attributed to Gapun infants are expressions of dissatisfaction and frustration, such as *oki*, "I'm getting out of here", or *mnda*, "I'm sick of this" (Kulick 1992, 101–2).

8. For an encompassing look at child-rearing practices and parents' cultural belief systems in several cultures, see Harkness and Super (1996).

9. It is worth mentioning that in many cultures, attentive listening is an appropriate behavior not solely for infants but also for older children and adults with certain social statuses (Nicolaisen 1988; Philips 1972).

10. See Aukrust (2002), Beals and Snow (2002), and Georgakopoulou (2002) for additional cross-cultural studies of family narrative and identity formation.

Bibliography

Agha, Asif. "Registers of Language." Pp. 23–45 in *A Companion to Linguistic Anthropology*, edited by Alessandro Duranti. New York: Blackwell, 2004.
———. *Language and Social Relations*. Cambridge: Cambridge University Press, 2007.
Akhtar, Nameera. "The Robustness of Learning through Overhearing." *Developmental Science* 8, no. 2 (March 2005): 199–209.
Aukrust, Vibeke. "'What Did You Do in School Today?' Speech Genres and Tellability in Multiparty Family Mealtime Conversations in Two Cultures." Pp. 55–83 in *Talking to Adults: The Contribution of Multiparty Discourse to Language*

Acquisition, edited by Shoshana Blum-Kulka and Catherine E. Snow. Mahwah, N.J.: Erlbaum, 2002.

Baquedano-López, Patricia. "Narrating Community in Doctrina Classes." *Narrative Inquiry* 10, no. 2 (2000): 1–24.

Beals, Diane E., and Catherine E. Snow. "Deciding What to Tell: Selecting and Elaborating Narrative Topics in Family Interaction and Children's Elicited Personal Experience Stories." Pp. 15–31 in *Talking to Adults: The Contribution of Multiparty Discourse to Language Acquisition*, edited by Shoshana Blum-Kulka and Catherine E. Snow. Mahwah, N.J.: Erlbaum, 2002.

Blum-Kulka, Shoshana, and Catherine E. Snow, eds. *Talking to Adults: The Contribution of Multiparty Discourse to Language Acquisition*. Mahwah, N.J.: Erlbaum, 2002.

Bornstein, Marc H., Linda R. Cote, Sharone Maital, Kathleen Painter, Sung-Yun Park, Liliana Pascual, Marie-Germaine Pêcheux, Josette Ruel, Paola Venuti, and Andre Vyt. "Cross-Linguistic Analysis of Vocabulary in Young Children: Spanish, Dutch, French, Hebrew, Italian, Korean, and American English." *Child Development* 75, no. 4 (July 2004): 1115–39.

Bornstein, M. H, and C. S. Tamis-LeMonda. "Maternal Responsiveness and Infant Mental Abilities: Specific Predictive Relations." *Infant Behavior and Development* 20 (1997): 283–96.

Brown, Penelope. "Everyone Has to Lie in Tzeltal." Pp. 241–275 in *Talking to Adults: The Contribution of Multiparty Discourse to Language Acquisition*, edited by Shoshana Blum-Kulka and Catherine E. Snow. Mahwah, N.J.: Erlbaum, 2002.

Bruner, Jerome. *Acts of Meaning*. Cambridge, Mass.: Harvard University Press, 1990.

———. "The Autobiographical Process." Pp. 38–56 in *The Culture of Autobiography*, edited by Robert Folkenflik. Stanford, Calif.: Stanford University Press, 1993.

———. *Making Stories: Law, Literature, Life*. New York: Farrar, Strauss and Giroux, 2002.

Budwig, Nancy. "The Linguistic Marking of Agentivity and Control in Child Language." *Journal of Child Language* 16, no. 2 (June 1989): 263–84.

———. "A Functional Approach to the Acquisition of Personal Pronouns." Pp. 121–45 in *Children's Language*, vol. 7, edited by Gina Conti-Ramsden and Catherine E. Snow. Hillsdale, N.J.: Erlbaum, 1990.

Chafe, Wallace, and Johanna Nichols, eds. *Evidentiality: The Linguistic Coding of Epistemology*. Norwood, N.J.: Ablex, 1986.

Chomsky, Noam. *Aspects of the Theory of Syntax*. Cambridge, Mass.: MIT Press, 1965.

Cook-Gumperz, Jenny. "Caught in a Web of Words: Some Considerations on Language Socialization and Language Acquisition." Pp. 37–64 in *Children's Worlds and Children's Language*, edited by Jenny Cook-Gumperz, William Corsaro, and Jurgen Streek. Berlin: Mouton de Gruyter, 1987.

Crago, Martha. "Communicative Interaction and Second Language Acquisition: An Inuit Example." *TESOL Quarterly* 26, no. 3 (Autumn 1992): 487–505.

de Léon, Lourdes. "The Emergent Participant: Interactive Patterns in the Socialization of Tzotzil (Mayan) Infants." *Journal of Linguistic Anthropology* 8, no. 2 (December 1998): 131–61.

Demuth, Katherine. "Prompting Routines in the Language Socialization of Basotho Children." Pp. 51–79 in *Language Socialization across Cultures*, edited by Bambi B. Schieffelin and Elinor Ochs. Cambridge: Cambridge University Press, 1986.

Ely, Richard, and Jean Berko-Gleason. "Socialization across Contexts." Pp. 251–70 in *The Handbook of Child Language*, edited by Paul Fletcher and Brian MacWhinney. Cambridge: Blackwell, 1995.

Fasulo, Alessandra, and Clotilde Pontecorvo. "Il Bisogno di Raccontare: Analisi di Narrazioni nel Contesto Familiare." Pp. 180–214 in *Il Sé Narrativo*, edited by Andrea Smorti. Firenze: Giunti, 1997.

———. *Come si Dice? Linguaggio e Apprendimento in Famiglia e a Scuola.* Roma: Carocci, 1999.

Fatigante, Marilena, Alessandra Fasulo, and Clotilde Pontecorvo. "Life with the Alien: Role Casting and Face-Saving Techniques in Family Conversation with Young Children." *Issues in Applied Linguistics* 9, no. 2 (December 1998): 97–121.

Ferguson, Charles A. "Baby Talk as a Simplified Register." Pp. 209–35 in *Talking to Children: Language Input and Acquisition*, edited by Catherine E. Snow and Charles A. Ferguson. Cambridge: Cambridge University Press, 1977.

Fivush, Robyn. "Constructing Narrative, Emotion, and Self in Parent-Child Conversations about the Past." Pp. 136–57 in *The Remembering Self: Construction and Accuracy in the Self-Narrative*, edited by Urlic Neisser and Robyn Fivush. Cambridge: Cambridge University Press, 1994.

Fivush, Robyn, Melissa A. Brotman, Janine P. Buckner, and Sherryl Goodman. "Gender Differences in Parent Child Emotion Narratives." *Sex Roles* 42, nos. 3–4 (February 2000): 233–54.

Fivush, Robyn, and Janine P. Buckner. "Creating Gender and Identity through Autobiographical Narratives." Pp. 149–67 in *Autobiographical Memory and the Construction of a Narrative Self*, edited by Robyn Fivush and Catherine A. Haden. Mahwah, N.J.: Erlbaum, 2003.

Gallaway, Claire, and Brian J. Richards. *Input and Interaction in Language Acquisition.* London: Cambridge University Press, 1994.

Gaskins, Suzanne. "How Mayan Parental Theories Come into Play." Pp. 345–63 in *Parents' Cultural Belief Systems: Their Origins, Expressions, and Consequences*, edited by Sara Harkness and Charles M. Super. New York: Guilford, 1996.

Gaskins, Suzanne, Peggy J. Miller, and William A. Corsaro. "Theoretical and Methodological Perspectives in the Interpretive Study of Children." *New Directions for Child Development* 58 (1992): 5–24.

Gentner, Dedra. "Why Nouns Are Learned before Verbs: Linguistic Relativity versus Natural Partitioning. Pp. 301–34 in *Language Development*, vol. 2, *Language, Thought, and Culture*, edited by Stan A. Kuczaj. Hillsdale, N.J.: Erlbaum, 1982.

Georgakopoulou, Alexandra. "Greek Children and Familiar Narrative in Family Contexts: En Route to Cultural Performances." Pp. 33–53 in *Talking to Adults: The Contribution of Multiparty Discourse to Language Acquisition*, edited by Shoshana Blum-Kulka and Catherine E. Snow. Mahwah, N.J.: Erlbaum, 2002.

Goffman, Erving. "The Nature of Deference and Demeanor." *American Anthropologist* 58, no. 3 (January 1956): 473–502.

Hanks, William F. *Referential Practice: Language and Lived Space among the Maya*. Chicago: University of Chicago Press, 1990.

Harkness, Sara, and Charles M. Super, eds. *Parents' Cultural Belief Systems: Their Origins, Expressions, and Consequences*. New York: Guilford, 1996.

Heath, Shirley B. *Ways with Words*. Cambridge: Cambridge University Press, 1983.

Heritage, John, and Geoffrey Raymond. "The Terms of Agreement: Indexing Epistemic Authority and Subordination in Talk-in-Interaction." *Social Psychology Quarterly* 68, no. 1 (March 2005): 15–38.

Kulick, Don. *Language Shift and Cultural Reproduction: Socialization, Self, and Syncretism in a Papua New Guinea Village*. Cambridge: Cambridge University Press, 1992.

Lave, Jean, and Etienne Wenger. *Situated Learning: Legitimate Peripheral Participation*. Cambridge: Cambridge University Press, 1991.

Mattingly, Cheryl. *Healing Dramas and Clinical Plots: The Narrative Structure of Experience*. Cambridge: Cambridge University Press, 1998.

Miller, Peggy J., Heidi Fung, and Michele Koven. "Narrative Reverberations: How Participation in Narrative Practices Co-Creates Persons and Cultures." Pp. 595–614 in *Handbook of Cultural Psychology*, edited by Shinobu Kitayama and Dov Cohen. New York: Guilford, 2007.

Miller, Peggy J., Heidi Fung, and Judith Mintz. "Self-Construction through Narrative Practices: A Chinese and American Comparison of Early Socialization." *Ethos* 24, no. 2 (June 1996): 237–80.

Miller, Peggy J., Angela R. Wiley, Heidi Fung, and Chung-Hui Liang. "Personal Storytelling as a Medium of Socialization in Chinese and American Families." *Child Development* 68, no. 3 (June 1997): 557–68.

Morrison, Toni. *The Nobel Lecture in Literature.* New York: Knopf, 1994.

Nicolaisen, Ida. "Concepts in Learning among the Punan Bah of Sarawak." Pp. 193–221 in *Acquiring Culture: Cross-Cultural Studies in Child Development,* edited by Gustav Jahoda and Ioan M. Lewis. New York: Croom Helm, 1988.

Ochs, Elinor. "Talking to Children in Western Samoa." *Language and Society* 11, no. 1 (April 1982): 77–104.

———. "From Feelings to Grammar: A Samoan Case Study." Pp. 251–72 in *Language Socialization across Cultures,* edited by Bambi Schieffelin and Elinor Ochs. Cambridge: Cambridge University Press, 1986.

———. *Culture and Language Development.* Cambridge: Cambridge University Press, 1988.

———. "Indexicality and Socialization." Pp. 287–308 in *Cultural Psychology: Essays on Comparative Human Development,* edited by James W. Stigler, Richard A. Shweder, and Gilbert S. Herdt. Cambridge: Cambridge University Press, 1990.

———. "Becoming a Speaker of Culture." Pp. 99–120 in *Language Acquisition and Language Socialization: Ecological Perspectives,* edited by Claire Kramsch. London: Continuum, 2002.

———. "Narrative Lessons." Pp. 269–89 in *A Companion to Linguistic Anthropology,* edited by Alessandro Duranti. Oxford: Blackwell, 2004.

Ochs, Elinor, and Lisa Capps. *Living Narrative: Creating Lives in Everyday Story-telling.* Cambridge, Mass.: Harvard University Press, 2001.

Ochs, Elinor, and Bambi Schieffelin. "Language Acquisition and Socialization: Three Developmental Stories and Their Implications." Pp. 276–320 in *Culture Theory: Essays on Mind, Self, and Emotion,* edited by Richard A. Shweder and Robert A. LeVine. New York: Cambridge University Press, 1984.

Ochs, Elinor, Olga Solomon, and Laura Sterponi. "Limitations and Transformations of Habitus in Child-Directed Communication." *Discourse Studies* 7, nos. 4–5 (2005): 547–83.

Ochs, Elinor, and Carolyn Taylor. "Family Narrative as Political Activity." *Discourse and Society* 3, no. 3 (April 1992): 301–40.

Orellana, Marjorie F. *Translating Childhoods: Immigrant Youth, Language, and Culture.* Piscataway, N.J.: Rutgers University Press, 2009.

Paugh, Amy L. "Multilingual Play: Children's Code-Switching, Role Play, and Agency in Dominica, West Indies." *Language in Society* 34, no. 1 (January 2005): 63–86.

Platt, Martha. "Social Norms and Lexical Acquisition: A Study of Deictic Verbs in Samoan Child Language." Pp. 127–52 in *Language Socialization across Cultures*, edited by Bambi B. Schieffelin and Elinor Ochs. New York: Cambridge University Press, 1986.

Peirce, Charles S. *Collected Papers*. Cambridge, Mass.: Harvard University Press, 1974.

Philips, Susan U. "Participant Structures and Communicative Competence: Warm Springs Children in Community and Classroom." Pp. 370–94 in *Functions of Language in the Classroom*, edited by Courtney B. Cazden, Vera P. John, and Dell Hymes. New York: Columbia Teachers Press, 1972.

Pontecorvo, Clotilde, Silvia Amendola, and Alessandra Fasulo. "Storie in Famiglia: La Narrazione come Prodotto Collettivo." *Età Evolutiva* 47 (1994): 14–29.

Pontecorvo, Clotilde, and Francesco Arcidiacono. *Famiglie all'Italiana*. Milano: Raffaello Cortina Editore, 2007.

Pontecorvo, Clotilde, Alessandra Fasulo, and Laura Sterponi. "Mutual Apprentices: The Making of Parenthood and Childhood in Family Dinner Conversations." *Human Development* 44, no. 6 (2001): 340–61.

Preece, Alison. "The Range of Narrative Forms Conversationally Produced by Young Children." *Journal of Child Language* 14, no. 2 (June 1987): 353–73.

Ricoeur, Paul. *Time and Narrative*, vol. 1. Chicago: University of Chicago Press, 1984.

Rogoff, Barbara. *Apprenticeship in Thinking*. New York: Oxford University Press, 1990.

Rogoff, Barbara, Ruth Paradise, Rebeca M. Arauz-Chávez Maricela, and Cathy Angelillo. "Firsthand Learning through Intent Participation." *Annual Review of Psychology* 54, no. 1 (2003): 175–203.

Schieffelin, Bambi B. "The Acquisition of Kaluli." Pp. 525–93 in *The Crosslinguistic Study of Language Acquisition*, vol. 1, *The Data*, edited by Dan I. Slobin. Hillsdale, N.J.: Erlbaum, 1985.

———. "Teasing and Shaming in Kaluli Children's Interactions." Pp. 165–81 in *Language Socialization across Cultures*, edited by Bambi B. Schieffelin and Elinor Ochs. Cambridge: Cambridge University Press, 1986.

———. *The Give and Take of Everyday Life*. New York: Cambridge University Press, 1990.

Schieffelin, Bambi B., and Elinor Ochs. "Language Socialization." *Annual Review of Anthropology* 15 (1986a): 163–91.

———, eds. *Language Socialization across Cultures*. Cambridge: Cambridge University Press, 1986b.

Sidnell, Jack. "Organizing Social and Spatial Location: Elicitation in Indo-Guayanese Village Talk." *Journal of Linguistic Anthropology* 7, no. 2 (December 1997): 143–65.

Silverstein, Michael. "Shifters, Linguistic Categories, and Cultural Description." Pp. 11–55 in *Meaning in Anthropology*, edited by Keith Basso and Henry Selby. Albuquerque: University of New Mexico Press, 1976.

———. "Indexical Order and the Dialectics of Sociolinguistic Life." *Language and Communication* 23, nos. 3–4 (July–October 2003): 193–229.

Snow, Catherine E. "Issues in the Study of Input: Finetuning, Universality, Individual and Developmental Differences, and Necessary Causes. Pp. 180–93 in *The Handbook of Child Language*, edited by Paul Fletcher and Brian MacWhinney. Cambridge: Blackwell, 1995.

Sperry, Linda L., and Douglas E. Sperry. "The Early Development of Narrative Skills." *Cognitive Development* 11 (1996): 443–65.

Tardif, Twila, Paul Fletcher, Weilan Liang, Zhixiang Zhang, Niko Kaciroti, and Virginia A. Marchman. "Baby's First 10 Words." *Developmental Psychology* 44, no. 4 (2008): 929–38.

Toren, Christina. *Making Sense of Hierarchy: Cognition as Social Process in Fiji.* Atlantic Highlands, N.J.: Athlone, 1990.

Wang, Qi, and Jens Brockmeier. "Autobiographical Remembering as Cultural Practice: Understanding the Interplay between Memory, Self, and Culture." *Culture and Psychology* 8, no. 1 (March 2002): 45–64.

Wang, Qi, and Michelle D. Leichtman. "Same Beginnings, Different Stories: A Comparison of American and Chinese Children's Narrative." *Child Development* 71, no. 5 (September 2000): 1329–46.

Watson-Gegeo, Karen A. "Fantasy and Reality: The Dialectic of Work and Play in Kwara'ae Children's Lives." *Ethos* 29, no. 2 (June 2001): 138–58.

Watson-Gegeo, Karen A., and David W. Gegeo. "Calling-Out and Repeating Routines in Kwara'ae Children's Language Socialization." Pp. 17–50 in *Language Socialization across Cultures*, edited by Bambi B. Schieffelin and Elinor Ochs. Cambridge: Cambridge University Press, 1986.

Wortham, Stanton E. F. *Narratives in Action: A Strategy for Research and Analysis.* New York: Teachers College Press, 2001.

CHAPTER ELEVEN
LEARNING MORALITY

Heidi Fung and Benjamin Smith

Excerpt 1

While adults are engaging in conversation, Didi (at age 3) approaches the researcher's unattended camcorder. As soon as his mother finds out, she yells at him, "Eh, eh, Didi! What has Mama told you? You've never [listened to me]. . . . You cannot [approach Auntie's camcorder]! I'm gonna spank you. You're a child who doesn't obey rules (*bu shou guiju de xiaohaizi*)." By this time, although Didi has left the camcorder, his mother walks up to spank him. He sits down on the floor kicking his feet and crying loudly. Mother continues to upbraid him for being "such a disobedient child" (*bu guai de xiaohaizi*), threatens to abandon him, "We don't want you; you stand here. Let him cry; it doesn't matter. Mom is mad," and makes disparaging comments, "Look how ugly your crying will be on [the researcher's] tape." Didi's sister (at age 5) soon joins in, "Ugly monster, ugly monster, shame on you (*chou ba guai; xiuxiu lian*)." She slides her index finger on her cheek [a shaming gesture mostly applying to children], urges their mother to enforce more public reprimand in front of the researcher), and spanks Didi herself. Their mother immediately stops her. Now leaning on Mom's lap, Didi listens to her lengthy reasoning of the rules (not to disturb a respectful guest's work and infringe upon her property) and why she punished him (for his "not listening to [Mom's] words [*bu tinghua*]").

When Fung was conducting longitudinal observations at young children's homes in Taipei, Taiwan, during the early 1990s, spontaneous events similar to the one above occurred routinely in these middle-class families. In an effort to forestall or to end the transgression, the caregiver often employed various communicative resources to cast the child in an unfavorable light. These events were value-laden and emotionally charged, in which the highlighted affect was shame. In these "events of shame" (Fung 1999, 2006; Fung and Chen 2001, 2002), the caregiver attempted to invoke shameful feelings in the child for what the child had said or done or what she or he failed to do. A number of questions might be raised about such events. What generalized values had been transgressed that prompted a response from the caregiver? Why was shame emphasized so strongly? What was the caregiver trying to teach the child? Who took responsibility for enacting these "events of shame"? Were they ever concerned about the child's well-being or self-esteem or what sense young children might make of these practices? Why did these caregivers employ such heavy-handed disciplinary measures to 3-year-olds? And a final question for researchers: how shall we, as researchers who do not necessarily share the thoughts and values of these parents, best understand and interpret these practices—on their own terms or ours?

Social scientists have long been interested in the topic of the development of morality in children. In psychology, there is a long tradition of studying children's moral development, but its major theories (e.g., the cognitive-developmental approach led by Kohlberg and the distinct-domain approach led by Turiel) tend to downplay culture and cultural learning (Shweder, Mahapatra, and Miller 1987). In this tradition, moral development is seen as individual maturation of cognitive abilities to reason and judge rationally, which does not necessarily require socialization (Gibbs and Schnell 1985). In contrast, the related topic of moral socialization—how culturally specific moral systems are transmitted across generations in societies from adult to child—has been the object of considerable anthropological and cultural psychological research. In shifting the debate toward questions of culture and variability, the sociocultural approach to the acquisition of moral systems reframes the problem of morality itself: whereas the major psychological theorists pursue an approach to morality grounded in accounts of individual moral judgment and rationality, anthropologists and cultural psychologists tend to engage morality as what Zigon (2009) calls a "dispositional or virtue ethics" (79). This means that, in the sociocultural approach, the domain of morality encompasses social practices that create dispositions toward moral virtue. Thus, the problem of moral socialization shifts from questions of individual choice to socially influenced disposition.

The sociocultural approach, however, does tend to exhibit one characteristic weakness: it tends to elide psychosocial questions about the role of children themselves in the moral socialization process. Once a more psychosocial perspective on moral socialization is adopted, the following kinds of questions become necessary: How do children follow the moral value at stake (through self-evaluation and praises or punishment by others)? Does the cultural novice actually learn the moral value being socialized? How does a child's immaturity affect the moral socialization process?

This chapter begins with a review of the dimensions of variability that the sociocultural perspective brings to the study of moral acquisition, illustrated by a number of studies of moral socialization. It then addresses the limitation of the sociocultural approach by analyzing three detailed case studies of moral socialization done by researchers who take into account both the sociocultural context of moral socialization and psychosocial questions about the child's perspective on and participation in processes of moral socialization. The value of this integrated, cultural-developmental approach, including its attention to the concrete detail of everyday interactions, is discussed in the conclusion of the chapter. The argument will be made there that cultural influences on the acquisition of morality are of crucial importance in understanding the nature of children's moral understanding and action, as well as providing a useful window on adult moral systems. This argument implies that the process of transmission of a moral system to immature members of a society needs to be recognized as a complex interplay between sociocultural and psychosocial factors.

The Sociocultural Approach to Moral Socialization

Four key dimensions of the moral socialization process have been shown to exhibit considerable sociocultural variation: (1) the moral values thought to be desirable for cultural novices; (2) understandings about whether such values are socializable; (3) the social actors and institutions that bring about the socialization of cultural novices; and (4) the techniques or interactional strategies that achieve the socialization of cultural novices. In the discussion below of these four dimensions, the research that is reviewed to illustrate existing cultural variation is not always focused exclusively on morality and its socialization, but relevant parts of the larger works are referenced.

The Sociocultural Variability of Moral Values in Socialization

Socioculturally oriented research has amply documented variability in the moral values thought desirable for cultural novices to acquire. Frequently, researchers address some single value or set of values (autonomy, courage, respect, etc.) and argue for its salience within some local cultural world. These virtues are typically investigated in terms of the, as Mahmood (2005) puts it, "repeated performance of actions that entail a particular virtue or vice" (137). This kind of difference is illustrated, then, through a brief discussion of contrastive, value-laden practices in two cultures.

Bolin (2006) argues that the moral world of Quechua-speaking Peruvian peasants centers on the moral value "respect." Within this moral world, one must exhibit respectfulness to one's kin relations (especially older ones) and other fellow villagers—as well as nonhuman entities like animals (e.g., llama, alpaca) and spirits. Respectfulness is immanent in social practices such as sibling caretaking relationships, songs and celebrations dedicated to animals, and rituals of devotion to the spirit world.

In contrast, Fader (2006) argues that Hasidic Jews in New York City aim to cultivate an "autonomy without selfish individualism." In this moral universe, individuals must be able to regulate their "selfish bodily inclinations" through adherence to the commandments of the Torah. An individual's internal locus of moral control is sustainable through the help—and watchful eye—of religious authorities (including divine authority) and caregivers (especially teachers and parents). This form of individual self-regulation is understood to lead to a concern with "fitting in" the community, for example, in the form of pleasing one's caregivers and not challenging authorities.

The Sociocultural Variability of Ideas about the Socializability of Moral Values

Sociocultural research has similarly documented variation in understandings of whether and how certain moral values are thought to be acquirable. Construed narrowly, these are ideas about what Olson and Bruner (1996) call "folk pedagogy," that is, cultural ideas about the process of teaching and learning. More broadly, these understandings can be thought of as cultural beliefs about development and the interventions designed to affect development (e.g., teaching). Oftentimes, these are beliefs that form part of a broader understanding of children or of "immaturity" (see chapter 4, this volume).

Rydstrøm (2001), for example, gives an account of how ideas about moral development condition socialization practices in rural Vietnam. She notes that boys are thought to be *born with* the moral characteristics of their male ancestors (i.e., the honor and reputation of their patriline). Girls, however, must *develop* a sense of respectfulness and harmoniousness through direct training by older female family members. For boys, morality is thought to be a matter of maturation; for girls, it is a matter of socialization.

Lutz (1983), writing about the Micronesian atoll Ifaluk, describes an understanding of moral development dependent on a highly specific kind of "developmental input." In order to ultimately achieve the calm, nonaggressiveness valued on Ifaluk, children must be made to feel *metagu* (a word analogous to "fear") when they are confronted by an adult angry at some childish transgression. This moral system also includes an account of developmental deficiency (252): children who continue to act immaturely are thought to lack sufficient experience with *metagu* (fear).

The Sociocultural Variability of Agents of Moral Socialization

Sociocultural research has provided evidence for variability in the designated agents for moral socialization. While the previous two features discussed were cultural ones about divergent understandings of morality and development, this is a question specifically about social relations: that is, what kind of social actor is actually authorized to bring about a child's moral socialization (e.g., a mother, a father, a teacher, a coach)? This is a question that verges upon wider sociological questions: to what extent do these social actors belong to social institutions (e.g., schools, a village unit) that coordinate a range of material resources (e.g., a curriculum, toys) designed for the socialization of the child?

In her analysis of Euro-American upper-middle-class individualism, Kusserow (2004), for instance, focuses on parents and teachers as the primary agents of socialization. Both seek to inculcate in children a spirit of achievement and the cultivation of a sense of individual uniqueness. Central to this latter concern for both parents and teachers are practices aimed at protecting a child's "psychologized space" (92): a child's bedroom, diary, school cubby, and sense of personal space (around other students) were all regarded as privileged domains of individual privacy. Such spaces were understood to allow for the cultivation of an individuality free from group influence.

Writing of the Buddhist Khmer diaspora in the United States, Smith-Hefner (1999) identifies a much broader pool of legitimate agents of socialization: parents, grandparents, siblings, and a child's mother from a previous life are all understood to play a crucial socializing role. In early childhood, a child's previous-life mother is understood to play an important role in protecting the child from his or her current parents' abuses or their inattention to the character the child has inherited from a previous life. As a child grows older, the current parents and extended family are understood to be increasingly responsible for socializing the child to "know his or her place" within a social hierarchy regimented by age.

The Sociocultural Variability of Moral Socialization Techniques

Sociocultural research has provided evidence for a range of variable techniques or strategies for moral socialization. Frequently, this kind of research has been based on close analysis of the interactions in and through which moral socialization is shown to occur. This has especially been the case among researchers of language socialization (Ochs 1988; Schieffelin 1990; see also chapter 10, this volume) in which language and language use have been analyzed as important media of socialization.

Writing about dinnertime conversations within Italian families, Sterponi (2003) observes the importance of what she calls "account episodes" for Italian moral socialization. In these episodes, caregivers summon children—mostly in the form of questions—to provide accounts of actions regarded as inappropriate (e.g., oversalting food, spitting out food). The real ingenuity of Sterponi's analysis is her close consideration of how the content and construction of a question tend to elicit different kinds of moral accounts from children (e.g., "excuses" or other rhetorical moves). Her close attention to the interactional dynamics of questions and accounts reveals one language-based mechanism through which moral socialization occurs.

In her analysis of socialization among Kaluli people (Papua New Guinea), Schieffelin (1990) notes the importance of one of the Kaluli language's imperative forms for moral socialization. When using this form (*elema*, or "say like this" in Kaluli), caregivers tell a child exactly what to say in a given interaction. While it is used in a variety of contexts, its importance for moral socialization is especially clear in instances in which a caregiver relays to a child utterances that the child can use to help defend her or his food or other possessions from mischievous older children. In doing so, caregivers attempt to have their children conform to the local moral value of reciprocity.

In sum, the above mentioned key dimensions—moral values, ideas about development, socializing agents, and techniques of socialization—constitute a coherent logic of moral socialization in that these four dimensions "make sense" together, and when combined they outline what is needed in an adequate account. For instance, a description of "shaming" as a socialization technique would be incomplete as an account of the total social fact of moral socialization if it did not also include an account of the particular moral value at stake, the ideas about its development, and the social agents and institutions responsible for its socialization. In fact, it is hard to imagine any careful description of a particular technique that did not take into account the other three dimensions.

An Expanded Model of Moral Socialization

In addition to the sociocultural character of moral socialization, there is also the need to examine the role played by children themselves and the mundane mechanisms by which they become "carriers" of moral values over time. In responding to this need, a cultural-developmental approach is suggested, which examines morality "through two lenses" by integrating cross-cultural variation and individual developmental patterns (Jensen 2008). Instead of "starting with presumed physiological universals and 'adding culture on'" (Rosaldo 1983, 136), or conversely, privileging cultural beliefs and practices over individual characteristics and experience, the cultural-developmental approach assumes the individual and cultural contributions to the acquisition of morality to be co-constitutive. One distinguishing strength of this approach has been balancing a concern with the socioculturally specific character of moral socialization with the psychological experiences (cognitive and affective) of the children themselves.

According to Quinn (2005), although cultural models of child-rearing are highly variable in the substance of what is taught, all are designed to "make the child's experience of those lessons constant, to link those lessons to emotional arousal, to connect them to evaluations of the child, as approved or disapproved of, and to prime the child to be emotionally predisposed to learn them. This design ensures that the child is receptive to these lessons, and that the lessons themselves are unmistakable, motivating, and memorable" (477). In other words, the moral socialization process consists not only of cognitive and affective models that guide thoughts and behavior, but also of the ways that practices and activities within which human action is lived out (Weisner 1998). By drawing attention again and again to privileged construals of the child's own experience, the most important and highly emotionally attached people in the child's world create lessons that are unmistakable, motivating, and memorable. The inner mental processes are seen as instantiated in "the custom complex" (Shweder et al. 2006; Whiting and Child 1953) or, to use Bourdieu's (1977) term, "habitus"—the customary discourses and practices guided by the symbolic and behavioral inheritances of the sociocultural group that one belongs to.

To understand fully the process by which children become morally motivated adults requires considering their own agency as they participate in the process. Following child-centered work in anthropology and sociology (see especially Corsaro 2003; James and Prout 1990; Stephens 1995), the approach to studying moral socialization presented in this chapter "do[es] not consider enculturation to represent a passive process in which the child merely absorbs the understandings of his or her culture but rather an active one in which meanings are transformed and created, even as they influence an individual" (Miller 2006, 391). The young moral novices do not simply parrot adult words, nor do they appropriate cultural resources in unaltered forms. Instead, they flexibly and creatively use collective resources to contribute meanings to experience in order to accomplish their own particularity. Due to the child's inborn, well-defined predispositions and the natural capacities to learn and make sense of the world, "it is as accurate to say that [the child] shapes culture as it is to say that culture shapes the child" (Damon 1996, 462). Likewise, Gaskins, Miller, and Corsaro (1992) maintain that "meaning creation through participation in collective cultural routines and practices is anything but passive, especially for children" (11). Once one supplements an account of the cultural specificity of moral systems with an account of children's own experiences organized by those systems, the problem of moral socialization now fully emerges as an inseparably sociocultural and psychosocial fact.

Three Case Studies of an Expanded Model of Moral Socialization

To illustrate the expanded approach outlined above, three case studies of moral socialization will be presented below, all of which address both the sociocultural and psychosocial dimensions of the moral socialization process. While they share this commonality, they differ on many other dimensions, so taken together, they serve as a useful introduction to this approach. The first two, in which Briggs looks at the interactions of an Inuit toddler and her family in Arctic Canada and Smith looks at Aymara playmates' talk in rural Peru, are provided to introduce the potential range of the approach. The third, in which Fung looks at middle-class families in Taipei, Taiwan, will be presented in more detail to give a flavor of the complexity and richness of specificity in the approach. For each, the discussion of the work will address the four dimensions of the sociocultural model of moral socialization outlined above, as well as psychosocial questions about the roles children hold in the process and the ways in which their increasing competence over time structures the means and goals of socialization.

Learning Morality as an Inuit Child

In *Inuit Morality Play* (1998), Jean Briggs gives an extended account of the moral socialization of a single child, called Chubby Maata, among the Inuit of Arctic Canada. Chubby Maata's caregivers want her to become someone who takes her place in an interdependent network of mutually supportive kin (Briggs 1998, 117). The value of nurturance, however, creates certain moral dilemmas that must be recognized: for

269

instance, one must learn who properly belongs within one's network of care; one must appreciate the fact that, if one is not appreciative of others, one makes oneself vulnerable (134–5). In Briggs's analysis, the problems of "interdependence" emerge as sharply as its possibilities.

Chubby Maata does not find it easy to learn these values and their characteristic problems. This is in part because of what it means for Chubby Maata to be a "baby" in Inuit culture. On the one hand, Chubby Maata is a charming, lovable baby (*babykuluk*) whose babyness is sufficient to command love and food. On the other hand, Chubby Maata displays a "lack of understanding," or *silait* behavior (70), of the rules that govern her social world. Both qualities hinder her moral development: she sees herself too easily as an object of care (130–1) and does not yet have the understanding to provide it to others.

The centerpiece of Briggs's analysis is her account of the strategies that Chubby Maata's caretakers use in order to further her moral development. These strategies together comprise a "genre" (Briggs 1998, 8) of playful interaction—characterized by an exaggerated tone and certain recurring phrases—in which Chubby Maata gets presented with the central moral dilemmas of the Inuit virtuous life. More specifically, these dilemmas ("are you a baby?" "who do you like?") serve to dramatize the perils of babyness, helping to push Chubby Maata beyond babyhood and toward an expanded social world.

Chubby Maata's caregivers celebrate her babyness. Chubby Maata's mother, for example, playfully asks her to make the cry of a baby and showers her with hugs and motherly affection as she does so (50–51). This performance also has less desirable consequences, however: while Chubby Maata cries like a baby for her mother, Chubby Maata's sister Rosi playfully attacks her from behind. Chubby Matta's mother explains, "because you're a baby she's attacking you" (42).

Chubby Maata's enactment of babyness drives her socialization in two ways. First, it pushes her toward performing babyness as a social role: she is able to play at being a baby, rather than simply being a baby. In doing so, she has started to build up the tools for how to stop behaving like a baby. It is, after all, just a role to be performed (or not). In addition, Chubby Maata now has one reason for giving up the "baby role": it is her lovability that invites her sister's attack. Babyness brings both love and hostility.

Chubby Maata's social world brings with it other dilemmas that get dramatized through moral play (116): Who matters to her? How should she act toward them? These dilemmas get playfully dramatized. Maata, for instance, a frequent visitor to Chubby Maata's house, asks Chubby Maata if Chubby Maata and her puppy would prefer to come live with Maata. Not dissuaded by Chubby Maata's refusal, Maata scoops up Chubby Maata's puppy and starts to walk home with him. In doing so, Maata poses a difficult question to Chubby Maata. Who matters most to her?

Briggs finds evidence for Chubby Maata's increasing sensitivity to the dilemmas of interdependent social life. In one example, Briggs finds Chubby Maata—after having been scolded for playing with the anthropologist's notes—playfully chanting to herself, "Because I'm not gooood; I'm not goood" (143). While her mother consoles Chubby Maata, telling her that she is a darling baby (and therefore blameless), Chubby Maata continues to (playfully) call herself bad. With this example among others, Briggs argues that Chubby Maata increasingly internalizes the moral landscape of her social world: in this case, Chubby Maata begins to evaluate herself in light of her treatment of others.

Briggs's account addresses all four of the sociocultural dimensions of moral socialization. She identifies "interdependence and mutual support within the group" as the key cultural value that Chubby Maata is being asked to adopt. Her caregivers' productions of challenges for her indicate that they think this value can be taught, although their patience with her stumbles also indicate that they are sensitive to the fact that it is only learned through experience and maturation. A wide range of actors are involved with her socialization, including members of her immediate family and other members of this close-knit community. But it is Briggs's analysis of the strategies used to nudge Chubby Maata along this moral path that is so compelling. Chubby Maata is repeatedly presented with concrete dilemmas that highlight the complexities of interdependence and require her to make choices about her relationships to other people central to her life.

In addition, though, Briggs analyzes the socialization process from a psychosocial perspective. She argues that Chubby Maata, by the end of her longitudinal observations, has begun to internalize the moral perspective that her caregivers are teaching her: she not only increasingly organizes her behavior by those values but also begins to use them in self-evaluation.

Chubby Maata is held responsible for her actions, and until she demonstrates the desired responses to the moral dilemmas presented to her, they continue to be presented to her. So while the impetus for socialization lies with her caregivers, it is thought to be her own responsibility to figure out how to respond to the dilemmas. A central point of Briggs's analysis is that this socialization is targeted at moving Chubby Maata out of one life stage (infancy) into the next stage where she is expected to have begun to master the complexities of interdependent social life. Briggs argues that these developmentally organized strategies are effective in achieving the goal of leading Chubby Maata out of her culturally inappropriate (but developmentally understandable) self-centeredness and into a more balanced interdependence with others.

Learning Morality as an Aymara Child

Benjamin Smith (2008) describes the moral socialization practices of rural Peruvian Aymara speakers. His analysis focuses on the special role that language—in particular, language forms called "stance" forms (see Kockelman 2004; Ochs 1996)—plays in helping children construct gendered moral identities. Stance forms are linguistic structures that allow speakers to make evaluations or take stances on states of affairs; in doing so, they help speakers to situate themselves and their addressees as certain kinds of socially recognizable positions. In English, for example, stance forms like "probably" and "should" help a speaker to make evaluations about likelihood ("He probably will come") and obligation ("He should come"), positioning a speaker as uncertain and morally authoritative, respectively. Stance forms, as children learn to deploy them in mature ways, help them to more fully (and appropriately) participate in interaction.

Aymara boys are socialized to the value of *chacha*-ness or "manliness." Being *chacha* means being tough or unyielding: for example, a young boy washing himself in bone-chilling water urges himself onward, saying, "be a man, be a man"; a young boy perched atop a small cliff overlooking a swimming hole gets urged to just act like a man and jump in. Mundane concerns about being *chacha* are heightened in the boys-only game of marbles: in marbles, boys are understood to enact *chacha*-ness through, among other things, playing against bad luck or *qhincha*—analogous, in some ways, to the connection for adult males between masculinity and the ability to exert tenuous control over the spirit world (Astvaldsson 2002). In this speech community, *qhincha* is understood to be an actual agent that takes the material form of rocks, twigs, or other items that can send a marble veering from its path. While the cultural value of "manliness" suffuses everyday life for boys, the game of marbles is a microcosm where this concern is made explicitly visible as an ongoing interactional spectacle (Barthes 1957).

Young boys below 6 years of age have a tough time being *chacha*. They are understood to be more likely to give in to or to evade the challenges of some task. This is dramatized in marbles very clearly. For instance, they playfully throw their marble instead of striking it with a finger, or they try to remove from the playing field the material things (rocks, twigs) that act as bad luck. The moral transition from early boyhood to boyhood proper is clear: whereas young boys either can't handle or cleverly evade challenges (especially bad luck or *qhincha*), older boys stand up to them. The connection to masculinity is made exceptionally clear: when boys act in ways that count as the evasion of *qhincha*, they get insulted as "gay" or as *qachu* (literally, female animal).

Smith argues that through marbles, boys learn to be *chacha*, and more specifically, that their increasing mastery of a specific kind of stance form facilitates this process. Smith's linguistic focus is on stance forms that help speakers make a specific kind of evaluation: they allow a speaker to evaluate himself as someone who is not in control of his actions, as someone who can no longer be held responsible (see Hill and Irvine 1993). In doing so, these forms help a boy to position himself relative to *qhincha* or bad luck: when a boy is not in control, as implied by use of a stance form, bad luck is.

The stance form called "indirect evidentiality" (see Aikhenvald 2004 on "indirectivity") plays an important role in this socialization process. Indirect evidentiality in Aymara allows speakers to claim that they have no evidence for the assertion they are making (see Hardman 2001). In marbles play, indirect evidentiality gets used to suggest that, at the time of striking the marble, the player had no evidence for the presence of some material artifact that caused a marble to be diverted from its intended path. Jose, for example, after seeing that his marble had been sent veering from its path by a rock earlier claimed to be bad luck, noted, "it turns out the rock was there." In this example, Jose uses evidentiality (translated as "it turns out") to both imply that he had no control over his marble's path and to position himself as being in (manly) confrontation with bad luck. It was *qhincha* (in the form of the rock) that had taken over control of his marble.

While this example shows only the mature usage of this form (in marbles play), the real interest of Smith's project is his analysis of how the increasingly skillful use of these forms helps boys to more fully assume *chacha* as a gendered moral identity. Using evidence from both narrative retelling tasks and marbles play, Smith shows that children below 6–6.5 years of age do not use indirect evidentiality forms in fully mature ways. Before this age, they use these forms to indicate surprise (technically: "mirativity") or in other highly pragmatically constrained ways. As boys acquire these forms, however, they are enabled to portray themselves as out of control and, therefore, in the context of marbles, as being in (manly) confrontation with bad luck (even in defeat).

Smith's account addresses all four of the sociocultural dimensions of moral socialization. He targets the moral value of "manliness" or *chacha*-ness. The moral character of this value is apparent in its broader meaning as toughness, as someone who is capable of playing by the rules even in difficult circumstances. While not brought out in the discussion above, Smith argues that siblings (that is, brothers) are the primary social agents who help bring about the learnable process of becoming a man. Most revealing, however, is Smith's claim about the importance of language form as a socializing mechanism. He shows how Aymara's stance resources help a male child to do the interactional work of manliness.

Smith pays equal attention, however, to the socialization process from the point of view of the boys themselves. While not the focus of this presentation, it is clear—primarily through boyhood insult practices—that boys themselves come to evaluate and regulate marbles play in terms of the moral value of manliness. More striking, however, is Smith's attention to the language-mediated developmental trajectory through which manliness in marbles comes into being. In doing so, Smith reveals the way in which the sociocultural fact of manliness is contingent on the increasing individual capacities for the discursive mobilization of stance.

Learning Morality as a Taiwanese Child

As introduced in the beginning of this chapter, Heidi Fung (Fung 1999, 2006; Fung and Chen 2001, 2002) has contextualized the culture-specific meaning of recurring disciplinary practices with young children in Taiwanese families. While contemporary Taiwan has become increasingly pluralistic and individualistic, the Confucian value of filial piety (*xiao dao*) is still alive and well (see Ho 1996; Hwang 1999; Yeh and Yang 2008). Among other consequences, this value leads parents to want children who are obedient and respectful. Similarly, parents in Wu's (1981) study also expressed concerns about offering too much love and too little discipline to the child. To them, "a most 'abusive' parent is one who does not discipline his or her child, hence 'drowning the child with love (*niai*)'" (154). On the other hand, there are also safeguards against excessive punishment in the family. For instance, when one parent acts as the "black face (*heilian*)" or the bad cop, another (or the elders in the family) often plays the role of "white face (*bailian*)" or the good cop. Strict discipline takes place in the context of a supportive, devoted, and physically close family relationship and is sustained by a strong and prolonged affective tie between parent and child. Thus, there is a "blending of voices," in which a critical voice blends with a voice of loving sentiments.

According to Confucian ideology, "knowing shame (*zhi chi*)" is seen as a virtue, as said in *The Doctrine of the Mean*: "To know shame is to be near courage (*zhi chi jin hu yung*)." It means that if one possesses the moral sense of shame (*chi*), one is able to closely examine and reflect on behaviors and be courageous enough to humbly admit one's own inadequacy or wrongdoing and, hence, amend and improve oneself. Even to this day, the cultural importance of shame is reflected in the rich lexical terms for shame-related notions, including face, criticism, and evaluation. Learning the virtue of shame remains an important part of moral training in Taiwanese childhood.

Working from a corpus of videotaped everyday interactions, spontaneous "events of shame" were identified. In these events, shame is aroused and labeled in response to the young child's breach or transgression, and the moral code is defined and explained. Thus, the child's transgression offers the raw material for the caregiver to work on the process of "socioculturally guided emotional specialization" (Geertz 1959). In this analysis of everyday socializing practices, "emphasis is shifted away from the question of whether a somehow decontextualized emotional experience is 'the same' or 'different' across cultures to that of how people make sense of life's events. What needs to be explored are the particular ways in which cultural meaning and social structure relate to these general characterizations" (Lutz and White 1986, 428).

These events were found to occur regularly during toddlerhood (at a rate of 2.5 events per hour) and were usually carried out in a playful manner (over 60 percent). Through verbal, vocal, paralinguistic, and non-verbal communicative channels, a *prototypical event* (like Excerpt 1 in the introduction) includes the following elements: (1) a precipitating transgression is committed by the child; (2) at least one participant attributes the wrongdoing to the child; (3) at least one participant reprimands the child in an effort to forestall or bring an end to the transgression; (4) through various communicative resources, the participants consciously or unconsciously attempt to provoke the child's feelings of shame by casting the child in an unfavorable light. In addition to the prototypical events (about 80 percent of all events), there are also *nonprototypical events* (about 20 percent), which are similar in every aspect as the prototypical ones except that they occur in the absence of a here-and-now transgression. Moreover, about one-third of the identified events, both prototypical and nonprototypical, encompass more than one episode or subevent that occurred at different times and on multiple occasions (namely, different transgressions or shameful experiences being brought up one after another).

The majority of transgressions are interpreted by the caregiver as breaches of social rules (e.g., inappropriate age and gender behavior, lack of etiquette or politeness, and inappropriate aggressive behavior) but also include property rules and health rules. Many ways are used to induce shame in the child: using explicit labels or markers for shame (e.g., "Shame on you," "You made your mother lose face"); invoking a third party to sit in judgment (e.g., "Auntie (Researcher) is laughing at you," "Go ask your teacher and see if she would approve"); threats of abandonment or ostracism (e.g., "No one wants to befriend with you," "We'll give you away to the neighbor upstairs"); and making disparaging attributions (e.g., "Such a disobedient child"; "How come you're so sissy?"). In addition, there are some common characteristics across all events:

(1) The events always involve a number of people (family members and friends as well as other acquaintances), who play various roles, including a "black face" and a "white face." They also involve nonpresent others (including strangers and imaginary others), who are invoked by the caregiver to sit in judgment of the child's behavior (e.g., "Other kids won't play with you"; "No one dares to marry you [when you grow up]").

(2) In addition to being a shamer or disciplinarian (or the "black face"), the caregiver may also shift her role as a mitigator or protector. In Excerpt 1, the caregiver allowed Didi's sister to shame Didi, but only to

a certain extent and for justifiable reasons. In other times, when addressing the child as an unratified interlocutor (using a third-person instead of second-person pronoun), the caregiver would sympathetically reinterpret the child's shameful experiences from the child's perspective.

(3) As shown in Excerpt 1, any trivial personal or conventional matters (following Turiel's typology [1983; 1997]) could be charged as a moral offense of "not listening to words (*bu tinghua*)." What the caregiver (including Didi's mother) really cares about is the child's capability not only to obey her or his parents but, most importantly, to internalize the rules and norms. Hence, it is the "accumulative offender" or "habitual criminal," but not the "first offender," who would be punished and shamed.

(4) Since the "point" is about the rules and norms, events of shame are future oriented. In addition to a demand for confession, the caregiver projects a better-behaved self who will internalize the rules and not repeat the same mistake again.

These discursive practices inevitably index the asymmetrical power relationship between caregiver and child (with the caregiver having much greater access and control over cultural resources). However, with age, the novice's responses come to incorporate a wider variety of roles, ranging from more passive ones such as complying, confessing, or acceding, to more active ones such as negotiating, provoking, and resisting. By age 4, children have already understood the purpose of events of shame—to teach instead of to harm. And if the caregiver violates the "balanced shaming" rule, the novice may stand up for herself or himself, as shown in Excerpt 2. Throughout my visit time that day, Angu's aunt (the primary caregiver) had been tired and impatient and repeatedly upbraided Angu for a series of past misdeeds, including knocking off a pile of dishes when rushing into the living room (two days earlier on her birthday) and her habitual tendency of spilling food. Frustrated and angry with her aunt, Angu remained cautiously quiet and waited for an auspicious moment in which to upbraid her aunt.

Excerpt 2

Nearly two hours have passed and Aunt has become much more relaxed by now. After a brief teasing debate about who (between Angu and her 5-month-old younger sibling) has made more noises, Angu now seizes the floor and challenges her aunt by pointing index finger to her with eyes rolling: "Why didn't you reason with me nicely? Mama [addressing her aunt], let me ask you a question. When I kicked dishes far away, why were you unreasonable to me (*ni jiu bu jiangli*)? Tell me, hum!" While Aunt is arguing with her, Angu explains that "[It was] because I fell!" Aunt then complains Angu always fails to walk nicely and eat properly. Angu says in a serious tone, "But why didn't you reason with me nicely? It's not that you didn't have Daddy and Mommy. You had Daddy and Mommy before. When you were young, hadn't you spilt?" Aunt laughs and reports that, when she was young, she was well-behaved and had never spilt. Since Angu finds her aunt's claim of childhood perfection incredible, Aunt suggests Angu check with her mother (Aunt's little sister). However, Angu decides to call Aunt's mother (her maternal grandmother) on the phone to get the real scoop on her aunt, but unfortunately no one answers the phone.

With Angu's remarkable level of moral autonomy, instead of construing her own past behavior from her aunt's perspective, she turned the tables on her aunt and forcefully challenged her aunt's moral reasoning. Angu claimed that she had broken the dishes accidentally, not intentionally, and since the aunt was once young herself, she should have been much more sympathetic to Angu's spilling drinks or food. Throughout this exchange, although Angu's aunt did not cede any ground, it is important to note that she recognized Angu's emotion with a smile on her face ("[She] is quarreling with me. Boy, isn't she mad!"). She tolerated Angu's onslaught and never silenced or punished her for speaking her mind. The timing of Angu's retaliation is of interest as well, which demonstrates that attentive listening and observing is an active form of learning.

In this extended case study, Fung identifies two major cultural values that Taiwanese caregivers want to socialize their children into: the virtue of filial piety and knowing shame. The actions of the caregivers strongly indicate that they believe it is possible to teach children about both. Fung describes how through reenacting the past, examining the present, and rehearsing the future, Taiwanese caregivers take advantage of the young novice's rudimentary and psychological sense of shame—the affective disgrace-shame (*xiu*)—to teach them the moral and culturally defined discretion-shame (*chi*).[1] To these caregivers, orchestrating events of shame is a fulfillment of their culturally assigned responsibility for their children's moral education, in line with their belief in filial piety. Finally, Fung identifies the complex and flexible ways that caregivers make the child feel ashamed about a transgression, recognizing that such strategies are only tools to help them think about the perspectives of those with whom they interact. At the same time, she identifies strategies that are available to provide support to children, either during or after "events of shame," especially in the form of the balancing roles of "black face" versus "white face" among adults.

Fung's detailed analysis also illuminates the role of the child in this often intense and emotional socialization process. Even as caregivers hold children to high standards of moral conduct, they also offer them numerous opportunities to actively reflect on their actions by structuring their participation as a good listener and competent learner. This makes sense if one recognizes that the ultimate goal of the socialization is not to enforce appropriate behavior through shaming but to help children develop the ability to be "aware of what others think of them," and that children "are encouraged to act so as to maximize the positive esteem they are granted from others while trying to avoid incurring their disapproval" (Schoenhals 1993, 192). Furthermore, children are being trained to feel shameful if they fail to listen to their conscience ("the voice of one's heart").

While it is not the focus of Fung's study, she provides some evidence that the goals and strategies of Taiwanese moral socialization are quite sensitive to children's age and corresponding development. In Excerpt 1, we see that a 5-year-old can already participate in an event of shaming directed at her younger sibling. In Excerpt 2, we see a 4-year-old being an active participant in negotiating the terms of the event. These are both seen as advances over the typical behavior of 3-year-olds. And by the time these children were teens, there was no trace of any of these sorts of parent-child interactions in front of any outsiders (Fung and Chen 2002). One possible reason is that their parents judged that the teenagers' self-esteem now requires more protection than it did in early childhood, but another might be that they have earned their parents' trust in their ability to courageously self-examine their own acts and behaviors. In either interpretation, the strategies of the parents reflect the development of the children (Fung 2009).

Conclusion

This chapter attempts to understand how one comes to be a culture-specific moral being. By adopting a cultural-developmental approach to moral learning, a sociocultural approach to moral socialization is supplemented with a psychosocial focus. This approach recognizes that not only certain moral values, socializing agents, and teaching techniques might be particularly desirable or highlighted due to "hypercognized" culturally mediated resources and schemas (Levy 1984), but also that individuals actively and creatively appropriate cultural values and symbols and imbue them with emotional saliency and motivational force in order to morally cultivate themselves (Holland 2000).

As illuminated by the above three case studies of moral socialization in the eastern Canadian Arctic, rural Aymara-speaking Peru, and an urban city in Taiwan, this expanded model pays empirical dividends in at least three ways. First, it aims at balancing the socioculturally specific character of moral socialization with the cognitive and affective experiences of young novices themselves. Not only may the socializing practices be emotionally charged, but moral socialization is also driven by the mutual affective ties between young novices and their legitimate socializing agents. Second, one gains leverage on questions about socialization in environments of rapid social change and/or sociocultural heterogeneity: for instance, one may investigate circumstances in which, from a psychosocial perspective, children do not end up learning the moral values that, from a sociocultural point of view, are explicitly endorsed in some cultural community (cf. Kulick 1992; Lancy 2008, 352–69; see also chapters 17 and 18, this volume). And third, one can inquire into whether and to what extent some particular moral socialization values and goals depend on processes of internalization or increasingly sophisticated interactional participation.

In order to truly situate psychosocial development in sociocultural contexts, this expanded model pays particular attention to the concrete detail of interactions and communications that the child engages in everyday life. Although most daily activities are mundane, they are no less significant than the salient and bizarre ones. Through description, evaluation, and negotiation among all participants, these routine practices, as well as the breaches of these practices, serve as the vehicles to reproduce the moral order and bring dialogical elaborations and alternative meanings to the forefront (Much 1997; Shweder and Much 1987; Tappan 1997). Children not only repeatedly participate in situationally specific instantiations of cultural values in recurrent settings, but similar socializing messages can also be repeatedly relayed to them through various channels with or without intent (Harwood, Schölmerich, and Schulze 2000; Miller and Goodnow, 1995). Owing to the children's active role in interaction and strong desire to learn and be accepted, they eventually come to be culture-specific moral beings as well as independent and autonomous thinkers, actors, and meaning-makers. Through examining the mechanisms of this process in close detail, individual psychology and collective culture are revealed to be actively and mutually reconstituted in the tangles of experience and interaction. The end result of this process, as LeVine and New (2008, 3) note, can be understood as "culturally constituted developmental pathways toward maturity for children in a particular community."

Note

1. While the focus of this study is to illustrate the ways in which events of shame are used in family interactions to socialize young children, there is no claim that this model describes all moral socialization. For instance, home is certainly not the only source and site of socialization, and moral teaching takes place, within the home and outside of it, in many instances without transgression or shaming, and in nondisciplinary as well as disciplinary encounters.

Bibliography

Aikhenvald, Alexandra. *Evidentiality*. Oxford: Oxford University Press, 2004.

Astvaldsson, Astvaldur. "Coming to Power: Knowledge, Learning, and Historic Pathways to Authority in a Bolivian Community." Pp. 109–26 in *Knowledge and Learning in the Andes: Ethnographic Perspectives*, edited by Henry Stobart and Rosaleen Howard. Liverpool: Liverpool University Press, 2002.

Barthes, Roland. *Mythologies*. Paris: Editions du Seuil, 1957.

Bolin, Inge. *Growing Up in a Culture of Respect: Child Rearing in Highland Peru*. Austin: University of Texas Press, 2006.

Bourdieu, Pierre. *Outline of a Theory of Practice*. Cambridge: Cambridge University Press, 1977.

Briggs, Jean L. *Inuit Morality Play: The Emotional Education of a Three-Year-Old*. New Haven, Conn.: Yale University Press, 1998.

Corsaro, William A. *We're Friends, Right?: Inside Kids' Culture*. Washington, D.C.: Joseph Henry, 2003.

Damon, William. "Nature, Second Nature, and Individual Development: An Ethnographic Opportunity." Pp. 459–75 in *Ethnography and Human Development:*

Context and Meaning in Social Inquiry, edited by Richard Jessor, Anne Colby, and Richard A. Shweder. Chicago: University of Chicago Press, 1996.

Fader, Ayala. "Learning Faith: Language Socialization in a Hasidic Community." *Language in Society* 35, no. 2 (April 2006): 207–29.

Fung, Heidi. "Becoming a Moral Child: The Socialization of Shame among Young Chinese Children." *Ethos* 27, no. 2 (June 1999): 180–209.

———. "Affect and Early Moral Socialization: Some Insights and Contributions from Indigenous Psychological Studies in Taiwan." Pp. 175–96 in *Indigenous and Cultural Psychology: Understanding People in Context*, edited by Uichol Kim, Kuo-Shu Yang, and Kwang-Kuo Hwang. New York: Springer, 2006.

———. "To Know Shame Is to Be Near Courage: Moral Socialization in Taipei." Pp. 900–901 in *The Child: An Encyclopedic Companion*, edited by Richard A. Shweder, T. R. Bidell, A. C. Dailey, S. D. Dixon, P. J. Miller, and J. Modell. Chicago: University of Chicago Press, 2009.

Fung, Heidi, and Eva Chien-Hui Chen. "Across Time and beyond Skin: Self and Transgression in the Everyday Socialization of Shame among Taiwanese Preschool Children." *Social Development* 10, no. 3 (August 2001): 419–36.

———. "Affect, Culture, and Moral Socialization: Shame as an Example." Pp. 17–48 in *Emotion, Affect, and Culture: Anthropological and Psychological Studies in Taiwanese Society*, edited by Tai-li Hu, Mutsu Hsu, and Kuang-hui Yeh. Taipei: Institute of Ethnology, Academia Sinica, 2002. (in Chinese)

Gaskins, Suzanne, Peggy J. Miller, and William A. Corsaro. "Theoretical and Methodological Perspectives in the Interpretive Study of Children." Pp. 5–23 in *Interpretive Approaches to Children's Socialization*, edited by William A. Corsaro and Peggy J. Miller. San Francisco: Jossey-Bass, 1992.

Geertz, Hildred. "The Vocabulary of Emotion: A Study of Javanese Socialization Process." *Psychiatry* 22 (August 1959): 225–37.

Gibbs, John C., and Steven V. Schnell. "Moral Development 'Versus' Socialization." *American Psychologist* 40, no. 10 (October 1985): 1071–80.

Hardman, Martha James. *Aymara*. Munchen: Lincom Europa, 2001.

Harwood, Robin L., Axel Schölmerich, and Pamela A. Schulze. "Hemogeneity and Heterogeneity in Cultural Belief Systems." *New Directions for Child and Adolescent Development* 87 (Spring 2000): 41–57.

Hill, Jane H., and Judith T. Irvine. *Responsibility and Evidence in Oral Discourse*. Cambridge: Cambridge University Press, 1993.

Ho, David Y. F. "Filial Piety and Its Psychological Consequences." Pp. 155–88 in *The Handbook of Chinese Psychology*, edited by Michael H. Bond. Hong Kong: Oxford University Press, 1996.

Holland, Douglas. "Constructivist Models of Mind, Contemporary Psychoanalysis, and the Development of Culture Theory." *American Anthropologist* 102, no. 3 (September 2000): 538–50.

Hwang, Kwang-Kuo. "Filial Piety and Loyalty: Two Types of Social Identification in Confucianism." *Asian Journal of Social Psychology* 2, no. 1 (April 1999): 163–83.

James, Allison, and Alan Prout. *Constructing and Reconstructing Childhood: New Directions in the Sociological Study of Childhood*. London: Falmer, 1990.

Jensen, Lene A. "Through Two Lenses: A Cultural-Developmental Approach to Moral Psychology." *Developmental Review* 28, no. 3 (September 2008): 289–315.

Kockelman, Paul. "Stance and Subjectivity." *Journal of Linguistic Anthropology* 14, no. 2 (2004): 127–50.

Kulick, Don. *Language Shift and Cultural Reproduction: Socialization, Self, and Syncretism in a Papua New Guinean Village*. Cambridge: Cambridge University Press, 1992.

Kusserow, Adrie. *American Individualisms: Child Rearing and Social Class in Three Neighborhoods*. New York: Palgrave Macmillan, 2004.

Lancy, David F. *The Anthropology of Childhood: Cherubs, Chattel, and Changelings*. Cambridge: Cambridge University Press, 2008.

LeVine, Robert A., and Rebecca S. New. *Anthropology and Child Development: A Cross-Cultural Reader*. Malden, Mass.: Blackwell, 2008.

Levy, Robert I. "Emotion, Knowing, and Culture." Pp. 214–37 in *Culture Theory: Essays on Mind, Self, and Emotion*, edited by Richard A. Shweder and Robert A. LeVine. Cambridge: Cambridge University Press, 1984.

Lutz, Catherine. "Parental Goals, Ethnopsychology, and the Development of Emotional Meaning." *Ethos* 11, no. 3 (Winter 1983): 246–63.

Lutz, Catherine, and Geoffrey M. White. "The Anthropology of Emotions." *Annual Review of Anthropology* 15 (October 1986): 405–36.

Mahmood, Saba. *Politics of Piety: The Islamic Revival and the Feminist Subject*. Princeton, N.J.: Princeton University Press, 2005.

Miller, Joan G. "Insights into Moral Development from Cultural Psychology." Pp. 375–98 in *Handbook of Moral Development*, edited by Melanie Killen and Judith Smetana. Mahwah, N.J.: Erlbaum, 2006.

Miller, Peggy J., and Jacqueline J. Goodnow. "Cultural Practices: Toward an Integration of Culture and Development." Pp. 5–16 in *Cultural Practices as Contexts for Development*, edited by Jacqueline J. Goodnow, Peggy J. Miller, and Frank Kessel. San Francisco: Jossey-Bass, 1995.

Much, Nancy C. "A Semiotic View of Socialization, Lifespan Development, and Cultural Psychology: With Vignettes from the Moral Culture of Traditional

Hindu Households." *Psychology and Developing Societies* 9 (March 1997): 65–106.

Ochs, Elinor. *Culture and Language Development: Language Acquisition and Language Socialization in a Samoan Village.* Cambridge: Cambridge University Press, 1988.

——. "Linguistic Resources for Socializing Humanity." Pp. 407–37 in *Rethinking Linguistic Relativity*, edited by John J. Gumperz and Stephen C. Levinson. Cambridge: Cambridge University Press, 1996.

Olson, David R., and Jerome Bruner. "Folk Psychology and Folk Pedagogy." Pp. 9–27 in *Handbook of Education and Human Development: New Models of Learning, Teaching, and Schooling*, edited by David R. Olson and Nancy Torrance. Oxford: Blackwell, 1996.

Quinn, Naomi. "Universals of Child Rearing." *Anthropological Theory* 5, no. 4 (December 2005): 477–516.

Rosaldo, Michelle Z. "The Shame of Headhunters and the Autonomy of Self." *Ethos* 11, no. 3 (September 1983): 135–51.

Rydstrøm, Helle. "Like a White Piece of Paper: Embodiment and the Moral Upbringing of Vietnamese Children." *Ethnos* 66, no. 3 (November 2001): 394–413.

Schieffelin, Bambi. *The Give and Take of Everyday Life: Language Socialization of Kaluli Children.* Cambridge: Cambridge University Press, 1990.

Schoenhals, Martin. *The Paradox of Power in a People's Republic of China Middle School.* Armonk: M. E. Sharpe, 1993.

Shweder, Richard A., Jacqueline J. Goodnow, Giyoo Hatano, Robert A. LeVine, Hazel R. Markus, and Peggy J. Miller. "The Cultural Psychology of Development: One Mind, Many Mentalities." Pp. 716–92 in *Handbook of Child Psychology*, vol. 1, *Theoretical Models of Human Development*, 6th ed. New York: Wiley, 2006.

Shweder, Richard A., Manamohan Mahapatra, and Joan G. Miller. "Culture and Moral Development." Pp. 1–83 in *The Emergence of Morality in Young Children*, edited by Jerome Kagan and Sharon Lamb. Chicago: University of Chicago Press, 1987.

Shweder, Richard A., and Nancy C. Much. "Determinations of Meaning: Discourse and Moral Socialization." Pp. 197–244 in *Moral Development through Social Interaction*, edited by William M. Kurtines and Jacob L. Gewirtz. New York: Wiley, 1987.

Smith, Benjamin. "The Semiosis of Informal Teaching and the Development of Responsibility in Aymara Childhood." Paper presented at the annual meeting of the American Educational Research Association, New York, March, 2008.

Smith-Hefner, Nancy J. *Khmer American: Identity and Moral Education in a Diasporic Community*. Berkeley: University of California Press, 1999.

Stephens, Sharon. *Children and the Politics of Culture*. Princeton, N.J.: Princeton University Press, 1995.

Sterponi, Laura. "Account Episodes in Family Discourse: The Making of Morality in Everyday Interaction." *Discourse Studies* 5, no. 1 (February 2003): 79–100.

Tappan, Mark B. "Language, Culture, and Moral Development: A Vygotskian Perspective." *Developmental Review* 17, no. 1 (March 1997): 78–100.

Turiel, Elliot. *The Development of Social Knowledge: Morality and Convention*. Cambridge: Cambridge University Press, 1983.

———. "The Development of Morality." Pp. 863–932 in *Handbook of Child Psychology*, edited by William Damon. New York: Wiley, 1997.

Weisner, Thomas S. "Human Development, Child Well-Being, and the Cultural Project of Development." *New Directions for Child and Adolescent Development* 80 (Summer 1998): 69–85.

Whiting, John W. M., and Irvin Child. *Child Training and Personality*. New Haven, Conn.: Yale University Press, 1953.

Wu, David Y. H. "Child Abuse in Taiwan." Pp. 139–65 in *Child Abuse and Neglect: Cross-Cultural Perspectives*, edited by Jill E. Korbin. Berkeley: University of California Press, 1981.

Yeh, Kuang-Hui, and Kuo-Shu Yang. *Filial Piety and the Chinese People: A Psychological Analysis*. Taipei: National Taiwan University Press, 2008. (in Chinese)

Zigon, Jarrett. "Morality and Personal Experience: The Moral Conceptions of a Muscovite Man." *Ethos* 37, no. 1 (March 2009): 78–101.

CHAPTER TWELVE
LEARNING GENDER ROLES

Heather Montgomery

The [central Asian] Yomut have a stated preference for sons and express this preference in many ways. . . . When a son is born it is customary to celebrate. An animal is sacrificed and neighbors invited to feast. After the birth of a son, a member of the local community gives the Moslem call to prayer. This announces to the entire community that a son has been born. No such call is given for a daughter and no celebration is held. . . . When a child dies, neighbors come to offer condolences, and it is customary to say to the bereaved, "May God give you another son!" This is said whether the deceased child was a boy or a girl. When a girl is born, especially if a series of births has produced girls, it is common practice to give the girls a name expressing a wish for a son. Names such as "Boy Needed" (Oghul Gerek) or "Last Daughter" (Songi Qiz) are common for girls. In general, concern for the health and well-being of sons tends to exceed that for girls. . . . If asked whether they prefer sons or daughters, Yomut invariably state a preference for sons. (Irons 2000, 229–230)

The ways in which children learn their gendered roles and identities are fundamental to any anthropological study of childhood. Aside from acknowledging anatomical and physiological differences between boys and girls, cultural directives toward gender begin at, or sometimes even before, birth. Infanticide decisions are often driven by notions about the relative value of boys versus girls, and the increasing use of technology in prenatal testing can mean that decisions are made about children's value and ultimate fate long before they are born. After birth, most societies mark the gender differences between children and highlight them through ceremony and dress, as well as by parents' behavior toward them. As children move into middle childhood, girls may be expected to take on caring and economic responsibilities, and their movements are restricted earlier while their brothers are allowed more freedom. Gender is often highlighted during the transitions to adolescence with rites of passage that further shape and differentiate appropriate roles. How children learn gender roles is, therefore, a vast topic, affecting every aspect of children's lives and every stage of childhood. This chapter examines just three aspects of gender learning: the way that children are taught their relative worth at birth; the impact the sexual division of labor has on their lives in middle childhood; and initiation rituals before and during adolescence. With this focus, the chapter looks at how children learn about gender differences and how these divisions are taught and reinforced throughout their childhoods.

The First Gendered Lesson

As the excerpt that began this chapter suggests, the first gendered lesson learned by both boys and girls concerns their relative value. Festivities occasioned by the birth of a girl in many societies tend to be muted in contrast to the overt celebrations which accompany the birth of a boy, even though girls in middle childhood are often more economically useful than boys (often, but not always). Being identified as female at birth, or even before, may be a death sentence, and there is evidence of preferential female infanticide and of the selective use of prenatal testing and abortion of female fetuses (Dickemann 1979). Most well known are the accounts of Chinese families' preferences for sons. For example, Wolf (1972) writes that, for Hokkien-speaking peasants, "the most crucial decision in a female's life was made in the few moments after she was born. If the family had a surfeit of girls, she was simply allowed to slip into a bucket of water" (54). Even if allowed to live, as Wee (1995) argues about Chinese girls in Singapore, the "preconceived notion that they were a 'useless' burden to their parents was what Chinese female children were born into" (192). From the moment of birth, and in some cases before, therefore, children learn gender and the different, and in many cases unequal, value that is placed on them as girls relative to boys. Their gender determines their different access to resources such as food, parental attention, or medical care, and this sets up a pattern which continues throughout their childhood. Wolf (1972) supplies another telling example:

> She has heard from the time she could understand words that she was a "worthless girl," though the tone may be consoling. The older she gets, however, the more she will be involved in incidents like this one, culled from our child observations. Wan-iu: (a four-year-old girl) was sitting on a small stool near the well. A neighbor came out and said, "Wan-iu:, let Thiam-hok (a two-and-a-half-year-old boy) sit on your stool so he won't get dirty." Wan-iu: pushed him away and said, "No, you can't have my stool. Get away." Wan-iu:'s mother shouted at her angrily, "You are a girl! Give him that stool. I'll beat you to death!" . . . By age five most little girls have learned to step aside automatically for boys. (66–67)

Children born into a society which values boys more than girls will quickly learn that the physical, emotional, or economic support they are likely to receive is highly dependent on their gender, and they will modify their behavior accordingly. They will learn to expect less food and less handling or medical care, to be quieter and less demanding, and to step aside automatically for their brothers. Resources are limited and parents make choices about which children to invest in. Worthman (1999), a biological anthropologist, argues that these decisions are central to understanding gender roles in infancy and the way gender lessons are taught to children (146–7).

That parents give preferential treatment to one sex over another and invest differently in boys and girls has long been a focus of biological and evolutionary studies which claim that this sex bias is more than cultural prescription and involves parents' unconscious strategies to maximize reproductive success. A cornerstone of modern evolutionary biology is parental investment theory, which links the amount of time and energy resources parents invest in offspring to the probability of survivorship and eventual reproduction of those offspring. Worthman (1998) argues that the "differential treatment of children is often legitimated by perceived differences in need or value by sex and becomes integral to the process of gendered social construction of the life course" (38). In certain communities, boys are regularly given more food than girls. This might be analyzed in several ways. For example, evidence suggests that males have higher caloric needs than females in all activity states and at all stages of life and therefore parents are simply responding to their sons' needs. Equally, it may be a sign that girls are less valued than boys and given fewer resources. It might also be the case that giving children different amounts of food may actually create differences, or as Worthman (1998) puts it: "In the process, one could conjecture that such practices may also set males and females on developmentally different tracks in the ontogeny of resource use" (38). Whatever the reasoning behind differential resource allocations, before they can speak or consciously understand, children have already learned important gendered lessons about their relative worth and their respective roles in society.

Trivers and Willard (1973) proposed that parents would invest differentially in their offspring according to their sex, arguing it was more beneficial to parents to invest in the sex that gave them the greatest reproductive benefit in terms of grandchildren. Furthermore, they argued that the physical and social condition of the parents also affected in which children they invested. "In species with a long period of [parental investment] after birth of young [such as humans], one might expect biases in parental behavior toward offspring of different sex, according to the parental condition; parents in better condition would be expected to show a bias toward male offspring" (91). When applied to humans, this hypothesis suggests that in societies in which men may mate with many females, parents in good condition will invest in sons rather than daughters because these sons will also be in better condition and will have a higher chance of mating with multiple women and producing many grandchildren. In contrast, if parents are in poorer condition, both sons and daughters (all other things being equal) are likely to be in poorer condition, but daughters have a higher chance of achieving some sort of mating success than their brothers, who may be outcompeted by other males and have no offspring at all. In such cases, parents may find it worthwhile to invest in daughters rather than sons.

This theory has been much debated ever since, with multiple interpretations of the hypothesis and many different definitions of parental condition (see Cronk 2007 for a summary of these debates). Such a hypothesis has proven useful, however, because it shows that a preference for boys is not universal, and that even when parents express a stated preference for boys over girls, or vice versa, this is not always reflected in their behavior.

Cronk's work among the Mukogodo of Kenya is a good example of this. Although parents express a desire for sons, not daughters, in fact they nurse and hold daughters for longer and take them to local clinics more often, meaning that daughters have a better chance of survival and greater reproductive success in the future. Other groups nearby, higher in the social hierarchy, do not show similar patterns. In analyzing his material, Cronk (2007) puts this discrepancy down to the fact that the Mukogodo are "bottom of the local hierarchy" (28), so that females are more likely to "marry up" than boys, and girls have a greater chance of reproductive success than their brothers. He compares this data to similar studies

Figure 12.1. Prettiest baby contest (E. Lucero photo)

among the Hungarian gypsies, another group at the bottom of rigid local hierarchies, who express a preference for sons and may abort a female fetus if they already have daughters, yet they nurse their daughters longer than they do their sons (Cronk 2007). In both cases, whatever their stated preferences, parents invest in boys and girls differently, based on parental perceptions of the child's reproductive success in the future and the possibility of potential grandchildren. Such choices, evolutionary anthropologists argue, operate on an unconscious level and yet have important implications for how children learn about gender in early childhood.

Gender in Middle Childhood

While gender is clearly a central organizing principle of children's lives from birth, it is in middle childhood that distinct divisions between boys and girls become more pronounced. At this point, children tend to segregate according to gender and spend more time with members of their own sex and age group. Much of the literature from psychology suggests that in middle childhood, there is a universal desire for children to seek out members of their own gender to play with and for a marked division between the sexes to emerge. As Hartup (1983) argues, "Children of all ages associate more frequently with members of their own sex and like them better," and "no observer would question the fact that children avoid the opposite sex in middle childhood and adolescence" (110). Concurring with this, based on comparative data from six different countries, Edwards (2005) claims that "gender segregation was the grand rule of social interactions during middle childhood (age 6–10)" (87). Yet such a pattern is not universal, and elsewhere there is less evidence of such a split. Harkness and Super (1985), for example, have shown that even in the strictly gender-segregated society of the Kipsigis of rural Kenya, children in middle childhood are not separated and do not seem to prefer their own sex as playmates. In several hunter-gatherer societies, such as the !Kung or the Efe, groups of children playing only in same-sex or same-age groups have not been observed, and Konner (2005) claims that multiaged child groups consisting of both boys and girls are one of the features of hunter-gatherer life.

That this segregation is not universal suggests that how and why children separate from the opposite sex is another aspect of gender learning. Although the size of the community needs to be taken into consideration—with small-scale hunter-gatherer communities having small cohorts of children where all ages and sexes play together, while larger cohorts of children do tend to segregate—the most important factor behind this gender segregation is the different economic roles assigned to children. In nonindustrial societies, a very marked sexual division of labor emerges in middle childhood, with girls and boys being assigned very different tasks and assuming very different responsibilities. In learning to labor, children learn gender, and vice versa. Indeed, perhaps one of the safest generalizations to make in studies of children's gender is that girls make the transition from play to work younger than boys and make an economic contribution to the household at an earlier age, whether by undertaking economic work themselves or by freeing up others to do so by providing child care. Furthermore, it is such roles that make larger families possible because, as Lee and Kramer (2002) argue, although children are a net drain on the household, consuming more than they produce, as they become older, their production increases and starts to offset the consumption of younger siblings. By taking on sibling care while young themselves, girls can start to offset the costs of younger children relatively early.

Although the ages at which children are expected to contribute to the household differ, girls are generally expected to take on heavier responsibilities earlier. Edwards (2005) claims "girls spent more of their day doing responsible or productive work, such as childcare, housework, and gardening, while boys spend relatively more of their time playing. These sex differences are seen from age three onwards" (87). Such patterns are repeated elsewhere. Johnson (2000) writes of Fulani girls being expected, by the age of 4, to care for their younger siblings and to fetch water and firewood, and by age 6 to be able to pound grain, produce milk and butter, and sell these alongside their mothers in the market. There is no comparable expectation for boys. In a study of the various tasks carried out by agricultural Giriama children in Kenya, Wenger (1989) found that among children 8–11 years old, girls were observed working approximately 51 percent of the time versus only 20 percent for boys. Furthermore, the terminology used to refer to Giriama children maps onto the gendered division of labor: "A girl, from about 8 years until approximately puberty, is *muhoho wa kubunda*, a child who pounds maize; a boy of this age is a *muhoho murisa*, a child who herds" (99). In other instances, the sexual division of labor in middle childhood is so pronounced that not only are girls' and boys' childhoods totally different but girls' childhoods may effectively end long before those of boys. Chagnon (1968) writes of the Amazonian Yanamamö:

> A girl's childhood ends sooner than a boy's. The game of playing house fades imperceptibly into a constant responsibility to help mother. By the time a girl is ten years old or so, she has become an economic asset to the mother and spends a great deal of time working. Little boys, by contrast, spend hours playing among themselves and are able to prolong their childhood into their late teens if they so wish. By that time a girl has married, and may even have a child or two. (85)

A key issue to emerge from such examples is children's differential geographies and use of space. Not only are girls working harder, but they are also learning to do domestic work in close proximity to their mothers and other adult women. In contrast to boys, who are either expected to carry out tasks such as herding or hunting which take them away from home, or are not expected to help out at all, girls are kept increasingly close to the household, where they become indispensable to, and often inseparable from, their mothers. Because their work is centered in and around the household, their physical freedom to roam is curtailed as they are engaged in domestic duties at home. Even when girls are taking food to markets, they are doing so with their mothers, so that the market becomes an extension of the home. This has clear implications for how children learn gender roles and, in particular, from whom they learn them. Girls are in the company of their mothers and other women of their household for long periods of time and learn their expected gender roles from them, whereas boys do not keep company with their fathers to nearly the same degree and use older siblings or peers as role models to a much greater extent. Lancy (2008) has argued:

> While girls seem firmly attached to their mothers and function from an early age as their assistants, boys are much less often in close proximity to their fathers. . . . And while many of a woman's burdens can be shared with a child, men's work tends to demand physical strength (clearing

bush), finely honed skills (bow-hunting), or erudition—not attributes possessed by little boys. (243)

The restricting of girls to the domestic sphere has further consequences in that it reinforces social pressures to protect girls from inappropriate contact which could "spoil" them. Keeping girls close to the household protects and domesticates their sexuality. In her account of a village in Iran, Friedl (1997) discusses how although girls are viewed as more capable and responsible than boys, particularly in the area of intelligence gathering and finding out what is going on in the neighborhood, they are more restricted in their movements and forbidden from straying far from the house. "Their radius of movement shrinks rapidly, for propriety's sake, just at the age when they become really good at observing and reporting" (8). Boys, in contrast, even at a young age "may be 'turned out in the morning like cows,' as a male teacher said disapprovingly, to come home only to feed and sleep, while a girl is discouraged from leaving the house alone" (148). Such constraints set up a pattern described in many ethnographies in which girls are expected to show early modesty and where they work more, play less, have a greater sense of responsibility, and their freedom to travel is more limited.

Such differences can be partially explained by reference to local notions about the different nature of boys and girls. Analyzing gendered childhoods in the Kerkennah Islands of Tunisia, Platt (1988) noted, "So profound are the differences between males and females thought to be that they begin to manifest themselves before the child is even born. Kerkennis state that male fetuses are active and kicking in the womb, while female fetuses lie still" (273). Throughout childhood, different attributes are assigned to boys and girls, and the roles assigned to them are assumed to complement and reinforce their natural proclivities, so that girls are assumed to be more capable and mature than boys and therefore given greater responsibility earlier. In Tonga, for instance, girls are thought to grasp proper adult behavior earlier than boys. They are perceived as "better" than boys, politer, more mature and well behaved, and are therefore expected to help out with child care and domestic duties earlier (Morton 1996). In Iran, girls are thought to develop reason faster than boys, and this is used to explain why they are more responsible than boys and are able to combine schoolwork with housework in a way in which boys cannot (Friedl 1997).

An important example of the ways in which the supposed innate characteristics of boys and girls lead to different expectations being placed on them is in the realm of sibling care. Although boys in some cases do look after younger children (Henry, Morelli, and Tronick 2005) child care is overwhelmingly assigned to girls because they are assumed to be more nurturing and competent and also because they are the mothers of the future. The perceived nature of girls is thus aligned with overt gender socialization practices so that girls are made responsible for younger children because of their "natural" competence but this "natural" competence is also explicitly taught and tested. Wolf (1972) has commented that girls in rural Taiwan are disciplined much more harshly than their brothers because of their burdens of responsibility. "Obedience training comes earlier for girls than for boys, less by plan than by the accident of role requirements. A child who must be responsible for a younger child's welfare cannot be allowed to disobey on whim" (79).

Other studies have suggested that while the sexual division of labor in childhood may be the product of socialization and an assessment of the relative worth of girls and boys, girls appear to be pre-adapted to provide domestic help. This is shown most clearly in Draper's (1974, 1975, 1997) work on the socialization of !Kung children, where she examined why, in hunter-gatherer societies where young children are expected to take on very few economic roles, behavioral differences between girls and boys continue to exist. She compared two sets of !Kung, one whose members still subsisted through hunting and gathering and another in which the !Kung had settled. In the first group, boys and girls were not differently socialized; neither sex was expected to carry out child care for their siblings nor were they encouraged to accompany their parents on either hunting or gathering trips. Despite this, girls seemed to gravitate to adults, stayed closer to home, and were more tactile, while boys spent more time with their peers and ventured further afield (Draper 1976). In the sedentary group, not only was there more work to be done and mothers needed more help, but the sexual division of labor in childhood was more pronounced, with girls providing much more help to their mothers and being more likely than their brothers to run errands or help prepare food. Boys and girls were still socialized similarly, but girls spent more time closer to home, were in greater contact with adults, and were therefore more likely to be called upon to do chores. Their brothers were less available and less likely to be drafted into domestic work. Draper (1975) concludes, "girls are pre-adapted to succeed . . . under conditions of what we have come to recognize as conventional female sex-role socialization" (613).

The earlier girls are drafted for domestic chores, the sooner gender segregation occurs and the stronger the sexual division of labor which will emerge. In highly segregated societies such as Iran or China, girls are taught domestic skills very early and must make an economic contribution as soon as possible. Friedl (1997) writes that young girls "ought to have mastered household skills at least rudimentarily. . . . This means that a mother has to start training her daughters at an age when boys are under no pressure yet to learn anything at all" (148). In contrast, studies of more egalitarian hunter-gatherer societies have shown that boys and girls are not segregated but play and work in mixed-age and mixed-sex groups for much longer. Neither boys nor girls are expected to help out or to contribute to the household until relatively late, and even when they do contribute, they do so in similar ways. Among the Paraguayan Ache, for instance, older children, both boys and girls, forage for fruits, insect larvae, and small animals within 50 meters of the camp, and both remain with the adult women's group (Hill and Hurtado 1996). Similarly, among the Efe foragers of the Ituri Forest (in the Democratic Republic of Congo), both boys and girls are involved with the care of 1-year-olds, performing many of the same duties, such as playing with them or feeding them, and as they get older providing more skilled care such as comforting or bathing. This care is dependent on the age of the caregiver rather than his or her gender (Henry et al. 2005). Although gendered divisions of labor do occur and by adolescence boys are more likely to be hunting with men than foraging with women, these divisions of labor emerge much later, and hunter-gatherer societies are generally noted for their egalitarianism.

This sexual division of labor has also been seen as part of wider parental investment strategies, which allocate tasks to children based on the totality of the parents' reproductive success and return on all their children, regardless of the inclinations or needs of individuals (Bock 2002a, 2002b). Bock has looked in detail at children's work allocation in multiethnic groups in Botswana and, among other aspects of children's lives, compares boys' work with that of girls (2002a, 2002b). He found that children have very different economic roles, depending on age, gender, levels of growth-based embodied capital (such as size, strength, or coordination), and experience-based embodied capital (e.g., skills or training). Task allocation becomes a trade-off: "Parents can manipulate a child's time allocation to different activities in an attempt to maximize the return on investment across children. It is expected that this manipulation will occur in the trade-off in a child's time budget between non-productive activities that may have a return in the future in the form of experience based embodied capital, such as skill acquisition or formal education, and productive activities to which there is an immediate return" (Bock 2002a, 169).

Bock (2002b) found, for example, that girls were expected to provide child care for younger siblings, but the amount of time they spent doing this depended on the number of younger children needing care and the number of older girls available to look after them. When there are relatively few young children, girls will spend less time looking after them and will be allocated other tasks or encouraged to attend school. Similarly for boys, the amount of time spent herding depends on the size of the herd and also the availability of other help. If the father is absent but the herd size is large, then boys will have to spend more time herding, especially if other boys of a similar age are not around to help. Such data suggest that not only is the sexual division of labor that emerges in early childhood dependent on the perceived differences between boys and girls, but it is also part of wider evolutionary strategies by parents which attempt to maximize the overall return of their children.

Adolescence, Puberty, and Gender

The gender roles constructed by the sexual division of labor are further developed in adolescence to create adult men and adult women capable of personal and social reproduction. Schlegel and Barry (1991) have noted that adolescence is not simply a period of learning new skills and new social roles; it is also about unlearning the dependency and asexuality of childhood. Although the expectations and roles of young people in adolescence differ greatly across cultures, it is clear that social adolescence remains "a universal or nearly universal stage . . . between childhood and full adulthood, characterized by differences from the preceding and following stages in the ways that adolescents behave and are treated" (12). This transitional status is very different for boys and girls.

As Whiting and Whiting (1987) have argued, "while the physiological changes that occur at adolescence are universal to all human populations, the social and cultural reactions to these physical manifestations are not" (xvi). Clearly the social stage of adolescence does coincide approximately with physical puberty, but puberty itself is a highly unstable concept and extremely difficult to define. Worthman (1999) has argued that a wide variety of possible indicators mark the onset of puberty, and while anthropologists have generally taken first menarche to be the first sign of puberty in girls, there may be important markers, such as first breast bud, which are more socially significant. Biological changes need to be given social meaning, and this is the function of initiation rituals. In some cases, these rites start before biological puberty but reach a climax in adolescence, thus preparing the child for life as a gendered adult.

Anthropologists have paid a great deal of attention to initiation and puberty rituals, emphasizing their importance as a way of conveying expectations of bravery in the case of boys and fertility and hard work for girls. Schlegel and Barry (1980) claim that fertility is the primary focus of initiation rites for girls across the world, followed by responsibility and then appropriate sexuality. Girls may well be expected to show bravery during initiation, but this is not the primary focus of the ritual. La Fontaine (1986), in her study of initiation among the Pokot of Ghana, where clitoridectomies are performed as part of initiation rituals, argues that while girls are indeed expected to show courage and fortitude during the operation, its most important function is providing a symbolic break with the past rather than a test of nerve. Before initiation, a girl could have sex without serious social implications. After initiation, sex must take place within, and as a prelude to, procreation—the privilege of adult men and women.

Although genital cutting may be relatively rare in girls' initiations (Brown 1963), it is used here as a dramatic illustration of the ways in which gender roles are aligned with biological sex so that after adolescence a child may move smoothly into adulthood. As Lancy and Grove (chapter 8, this volume) argue, dramatic and painful rites of passage such as circumcision, clitoridectomy, or scarification impress on adolescents a respect for the community's legal and spiritual authorities and its values.

Boddy (1989), working in the Sudan, notes that before circumcision girls and boys are not differentiated, they dress alike and play together, but at circumcision their gender identity is inscribed on their bodies: boys as the future impregnators of women, girls as the potential mothers of men. Female circumcision involves the complete removal of external genitalia and is thought to smooth and purify the outer entrance of the womb. After circumcision, girls are infibulated and the entrance of the vagina is sewn up and has to be opened by a husband on first intercourse and again after each birth. Without circumcision, a girl cannot marry and have children and therefore cannot attain a position of respect when older. Circumcision emphasizes the important role of women as the mothers of men and stresses fertility and the social control of sexuality, all central to the transition to adult womanhood.

Even when genital cutting does not feature in girls' initiation ceremonies, the rites are often painful or involve some sort of ordeal. Markstrom (2008), in her study of initiations, both past and present, among native North Americans describes how, at San Juan Pueblo, girls and boys over the age of 10 were separated and whipped by the chief as a finishing rite. Other groups required long periods of seclusion. Girls fasted, were tattooed, or were walked on by their female relatives. In all these cases, expected gender roles were being conveyed and taught, and the role of women as potential mothers was emphasized and promoted. However, while girls obviously needed to be brave to undergo and withstand the pain of initiation ordeals, and indeed childbirth later on, the importance of bravery was much more pronounced in boys' initiation rituals. Markstrom (2008) gives the example of the *huskanaw* initiation ceremony carried out among the Powhatan. Boys were trained from early in life to be courageous warriors who could withstand multiple hardships. Between the ages of 10 and 15, they were subject to a variety of violent acts, including abductions, beatings, and being forced to ingest dangerous and intoxicating plants. To show apprehension or to flinch from pain was highly shameful, and through conquering their fear and overcoming their ordeal, the boys displayed and performed a socially approved model of masculinity.

Another famous example of the severe initiation rites designed to test boys' strength and endurance is the case of the Sambia in New Guinea, extensively studied by Herdt (1981). He describes a society in which sexual difference and sexual antagonism are central features, and where males live in constant fear of being polluted by women. Women are continually devalued, and part of being a man and learning masculinity is learning to uphold the enmity between men and women and maintaining women's subjugation by men. Sambian boys 7–10 years old undergo particularly brutal masculinizing rituals during initiation, including whipping, beating, forced nose bleeding, and ingestion of other men's semen. Sambian boys have spent almost all of their early lives with their mothers, drinking their breast milk and being socialized by them, but because femininity is devalued and feared, boys are seen as being at risk from these feminine influences, both psychologically and in terms of their physical growth. Boys must thus be socialized away from their mothers and toward the socially approved paths of manhood, and such brutal initiations are part of this. Beatings and nose bleedings teach boys courage and culturally sanctioned stoicism but also purge boys of feminine contaminants, such as breast milk, which they have ingested. Other societies in Papua New Guinea show similar patterns of initiation and share the same ethos concerning gender construction (Favazza 1996; Jilek and Jilek-Aall 1978).

Such examples support Schlegel and Barry's (1979) conclusion that "adolescent initiation ceremonies may be more likely to be held in societies in which gender identity has great social significance" (206) such as the examples discussed in this section. In more egalitarian hunter-gatherer societies, such painful initiation rites are much less common. The lessons boys and girls learn at adolescence build on and reinforce those learned in the rest of childhood. In early and middle childhood, girls are tied to their mothers and the female domain and are intensively socialized as girls, so that adolescence becomes a time of reinforcing these early lessons rather than learning new ones. In contrast, boys tend to associate more intensively with females when young but often grow up with little adult socialization of any kind, so that later they must be resocialized as males, and initiation rituals at adolescence give a powerful symbolic statement of the breakage between the feminized world of their childhood and the masculinized world of their adulthood.

Conclusion

It is very clear from all the ethnographic accounts of children's lives, from the earliest to the most recent, that the childhoods of boys and girls are very different and that, from birth onward, they are treated very differently on account of their sex. Yet discussing gender is not always easy; it is such an integral part of childhood that looking at how children learn gender is as difficult as looking at how they learn to be children. They encounter gender lessons in every interaction from birth onward, in the ways they are handled, in others' responses to them and their own reactions, in how they are dressed, treated, and socialized. However, this chapter has looked at three critical points in the life span—infancy, middle childhood, and puberty—where opportunities to promote gender learning seem plentiful.

Acknowledgments

I acknowledge, with gratitude, the detailed and constructive editorial help provided by David Lancy and John Bock to this chapter.

Bibliography

Bock, John. "Learning, Life History, and Productivity: Children's Lives in the Okavango Delta of Botswana." *Human Nature* 13, no. 2 (June 2002a): 161–98.

———. "Evolutionary Demography and Intrahousehold Time Allocation: Schooling and Children's Labor among the Okavango Delta Peoples of Botswana." *American Journal of Human Biology* 14, no. 2 (March/April 2002b): 206–21.

Boddy, Janice. *Wombs and Alien Spirits: Women, Men, and the Zar Cult in Northern Sudan.* Madison: University of Wisconsin Press, 1989.

Brown, Judith. "A Cross-Cultural Study of Female Initiation Rites." *American Anthropologist* 65, no. 4 (August 1963): 837–53.

Chagnon, Napoleon. *Yanamamö: The Fierce People.* New York: Holt, Rinehart, and Winston, 1968.

Cronk, Lee. "Boy or Girl: Gender Preferences from a Darwinian Point of View." *Reproductive Biomedicine Online* 15, no. 2 (August 2007): 21–30.

Dickemann, Mildred. "Female Infanticide, Reproductive Strategies, and Social Stratification: A Preliminary Model." Pp. 321–67 in *Evolutionary Biology and Human Social Behavior: An Anthropological Perspective*, edited by Napoleon Chagnon and William Irons. North Scituate, Mass.: Duxbury, 1979.

Draper, Patricia. "Comparative Studies of Socialization." *Annual Review of Anthropology* 3 (October 1974): 263–77.

———. "Cultural Pressure on Sex Differences." *American Ethnologist* 2, no. 4 (November 1975): 602–16.

———. "Social and Economic Constraints on Child Life among the !Kung." Pp. 199–217 in *Kalahari Hunter-Gatherers: Studies of the !Kung San and Their Neighbors*, edited by Richard B. Lee and Irven DeVore. Cambridge, Mass.: Harvard University Press, 1976.

———. "Institutional, Evolutionary, and Demographic Contexts of Gender Roles: A Case Study of !Kung Bushmen." Pp. 220–32 in *The Evolving Female: A Life-History Perspective*, edited by Mary Ellen Morbeck, Alison Galloway, and Adrienne L. Zihlman. Princeton, N.J.: Princeton University Press, 1997.

Edwards, Carolyn Pope. "Children's Play in Cross-Cultural Perspective: A New Look at the Six Culture Study." Pp. 81–96 in *Play: An Interdisciplinary Synthesis*, edited by Felicia McMahon, Donald Lytle, and Brian Sutton-Smith. Lanham, Md.: University Press of America, 2005.

Favazza, Armando. *Bodies under Siege: Self-Mutilation and Body Modification in Culture and Psychiatry*. 2nd ed. Baltimore: Johns Hopkins University Press, 1996.

Friedl, Erika. *Children of Deh Koh: Young Life in an Iranian Village*. Syracuse, N.Y.: Syracuse University Press, 1997.

Harkness, Sara, and Charles Super. "The Cultural Context of Gender Segregation in Children's Peer Groups." *Child Development* 56, no. 1 (1985): 219–24.

Hartup, Willard. "Peer Relations." Pp. 103–96 in *Handbook of Child Psychology*, vol. 4, *Socialization, Personality, and Social Development*, edited by E. Mavis Hetherington. New York: Wiley, 1983.

Henry, Paula, Gilda Morelli, and Edward Tronick. "Child Caretakers among Efe Foragers of the Ituri Forest." Pp. 191–213 *in Hunter-Gatherer Childhoods: Evolutionary, Developmental, and Cultural Perspectives*, edited by Barry Hewlett and Michael Lamb. New York: Aldine, 2005.

Herdt, Gilbert. *Guardians of the Flutes: Idioms of Masculinity*. New York: Mc-Graw-Hill, 1981.

Hill, Kim, and Magdalena Hurtado. *Ache Life History: The Ecology and Demography of a Foraging People*. New York: Aldine de Gruyter, 1996.

Irons, William. "Why Do the Yomut Raise More Sons than Daughters?" Pp. 223–36 in *Adaptation and Human Behavior: An Anthropological Perspective*, edited by Lee Cronk, Napoleon Chagnon, and William Irons. New York: Aldine De Gruyter, 2000.

Jilek, Wolfgang, and Louise Jilek-Aall. "Initiation in Papua New Guinea: Psychohygienic and Ethnopsychiatric Aspects." *Papua New Guinea Medical Journal* 21, no. 3 (September 1978): 252–63.

Johnson, Michelle. "The View from the *Wuro*: A Guide to Child Rearing for Fulani Parents." Pp. 171–98 in *A World of Babies: Imagined Childcare Guides for Seven Societies*, edited by Judy DeLoache and Alma Gottlieb. Cambridge: Cambridge University Press, 2000.

Konner, Melvin. "Hunter-Gatherer Infancy and Childhood: The !Kung and Others." Pp. 19–64 in *Hunter-Gatherer Childhoods: Evolutionary, Developmental, and Cultural Perspectives*, edited by Barry Hewlett and Michael Lamb. New York: Aldine, 2005.

La Fontaine, Jean. *Initiation*. Manchester: Manchester University Press, 1986.

Lancy, David F. *The Anthropology of Childhood: Cherubs, Chattel, and Changelings*. Cambridge: Cambridge University Press, 2008.

Lee, Ronald, and Karen Kramer. "Children's Economic Roles in the Maya Family Life Cycle: Cain, Caldwell, and Chayanov Revisited." *Population and Development Review* 28, no. 3 (September 2002): 475–99.

Markstrom, Carol. *Empowerment of North American Indian Girls: Ritual Expressions at Puberty*. Lincoln: University of Nebraska Press, 2008.

Morton, Helen. *Becoming Tongan: An Ethnography of Childhood*. Honolulu: University of Hawaii Press, 1996.

Platt, Katherine. "Cognitive Development and Sex Roles of the Kerkennah Islands of Tunisia." Pp. 271–87 in *Acquiring Culture: Cross-Cultural Studies in Child Development*, edited by Gustav Jahoda and Ioan Lewis. London: Croom Helm, 1988.

Schlegel, Alice, and Herbert Barry. "Adolescent Initiation Ceremonies: A Cross-Cultural Code." *Ethnology* 18, no. 2 (April 1979): 199–210.

———. "The Evolutionary Significance of Adolescent Initiation Ceremonies." *American Ethnologist* 7, no. 4 (November 1980): 696–715.

———. *Adolescence: An Anthropological Inquiry*. New York: Free Press, 1991.

Trivers, Robert, and Dan Willard. "Natural Selection of the Parental Ability to Vary the Sex Ratio of Offspring." *Science* 179, no. 4068 (January 1973): 90–92.

Wee, Vivienne. "Children, Population Policy, and the State in Singapore." Pp. 184–217 in *Children and the Politics of Culture*, edited by Sharon Stephens. Princeton, N.J.: Princeton University Press, 1995.

Wenger, Martha. "Work, Play, and Social Relationships among Children in a Giriama Community." Pp. 91–115 in *Children's Social Networks and Social Supports*, edited by Deborah Belle. New York: Wiley, 1989.

Whiting, John, and Beatrice Whiting. "Foreword." Pp. xiii–xx in *Inuit Youth: Growth and Change in the Canadian Arctic*, edited by Richard Condon. New Brunswick, N.J.: Rutgers University Press, 1987.

Wolf, Margery. *Women and the Family in Rural Taiwan.* Stanford, Calif.: Stanford University Press, 1972.

Worthman, Carol. "Adolescence in the Pacific: A Biosocial View." Pp. 27–54 in *Adolescence in Pacific Island Societies*, edited by Gilbert H. Herdt and Stephen Leavitt. Pittsburgh: University of Pittsburgh Press, 1998.

———. "Evolutionary Perspectives on the Onset of Puberty." Pp. 135–64 in *Evolutionary Medicine*, edited by Wenda Trevathan, Euclid O. Smith, and James Joseph McKenna. Oxford: Oxford University Press, 1999.

Part IV
LEARNING TO MAKE A LIVING

CHAPTER THIRTEEN

SKILL LEARNING FOR SURVIVAL IN NONHUMAN PRIMATES

Kerry Ossi-Lupo

I t's a rare sunny September afternoon in the forests of northeastern Thailand. Nearly all the members of a group of Phayre's leaf monkeys have spread out among the long, thick limbs of an enormous *Afzelia xylocarpa* tree. Most of them are gnawing at their own thick-husked *Afzelia* fruit, a pod nearly as long as a small paperback or databook that encases about five thumb-sized seeds. On one branch, a young juvenile female is not feeding on her own fruit. Instead, she alternates between twisting and tugging on a pod still attached to the tree and chewing at the stem holding it in place. Either she is not strong enough or else, because of her foraging inexperience, she has chosen a fruit that is still too young and too tough to detach. The juvenile gives up and moves over toward a feeding adult only to jump quickly away when that adult lunges at her. She approaches another adult, her mother this time. The young leaf monkey watches attentively as her mother manages to break through to the first seed. It can take quite a while even for an adult female to finish all the seeds in a single pod. As she continues to gnaw and chew, the mother allows her daughter to reach in now and then and grab bits of pulp that drop onto the limb.

This scenario illustrates the daily challenges of being small and inexperienced. These are the challenges that most juvenile primates must tackle as they become more and more independent from their mothers and learn to feed, forage, and interact with other group members on their own. This individual's different choices also serve to illustrate the many options and trajectories any of the other immature group members could follow in coping with the challenges of being juvenile. To return to the example, oftentimes, young leaf monkeys unable to open their own *Afzelia* pods will end up playing together in the broad limbs rather than trying to feed. Or if increasing energetic intake were more of a priority at that time, a juvenile could leave the *Afzelia* for a different, less preferred feeding tree nearby, although such a move would make the individual much more vulnerable to a possible predator attack. Instead, in this case, the young female spent the time observing a more experienced monkey, which may help her to learn similar foraging skills faster. Along the way, she managed to scrounge bits of food she could not have gotten on her own.

More than at any other time in their lives, juvenile primates must engage in a delicate balancing act, making behavioral trade-offs between two critical tasks: reducing risks to improve their own chance of survival and learning skills needed for the future (Pereira and Altmann 1985; see also chapter 2, this volume). At the same time, juveniles must continue putting energy toward their own growth. The stakes are high in finding the right balance because the immature life stage can be a time of relatively great mortality risk (Janson and van Schaik 1993), especially from either predation or starvation.

Surprisingly, field studies of nonhuman primates have rarely focused primarily on juvenile subjects. This history of inattention stems from a number of factors: for one, juveniles tend to be more difficult to observe, follow, and identify than adult subjects in the field (Pereira and Fairbanks 2002). More importantly, juveniles make less than ideal subjects for a number of research topics. For example, primate research commonly explores questions involving determinants or correlates of reproductive success, for which only the longest-term studies (multiple years) could include juveniles, who are, by definition, prereproductive. The tendency to pass over juveniles, however, has slowed opportunities for understanding how early behaviors may already be shaping eventual differences in reproductive success. Different juveniles may utilize different tactics—whether because they are smaller or have a more protective mother or learn tasks more quickly—and these differences may all have consequences that almost certainly carry over into adulthood. As Pereira and Leigh (2003) point out, research focused on adults is the study of the already successful, since it no longer includes those individuals who failed to survive long enough to reach adulthood.

Fortunately, more and more primatologists have begun including juveniles in their work, even making them the primary subjects. Some scientists have tackled their hypotheses in field studies that follow wild subjects in their natural environment while others have focused on captive subjects using controlled experimental methods. Likewise, the research questions include diverse perspectives such as (1) the theoretical (evolutionary) approach asking why primates have such a long juvenile period at all, (2) the more functional and quantifiable aspects such as gaining skills and growing to adult size, and (3) the mechanisms at work in how learning actually takes place. For this last topic, research into social influences has skyrocketed in the past decade or two (reviewed in Fragaszy and Perry 2003; Fragaszy and Visalberghi 2004). But the work has hardly been restricted to juvenile subjects because, among human and nonhuman primates, information not only travels from parents to offspring (vertical transmission) but also between similar-aged and unrelated individuals (horizontal transmission) (Laland and Kendal 2003). Despite our ideas of the ever curious and playful young juvenile, adults may actually be more likely to explore and innovate (Reader and Laland 2001). Thus, studies of social learning or primate intelligence and innovation often span all age groups in order to explore questions of cultural transmission and the spread of novel behaviors (e.g., Fragaszy and Perry 2003; Panger et al. 2002; van Schaik, Deaner, and Merrill 1999; Whiten et al. 1999).

That said, in keeping with the theme of the book, this chapter emphasizes learning during the immature life stage, the time when so many critical skills must be learned even for nonhuman primates. By taking a broader primate perspective, this review first touches on evolutionary explanations for extended juvenility and the adaptive value of learning ability. Next, it examines the functional aspects of the primate juvenile period: what it is juveniles need to learn in order to become competent adults and strategies for surviving until adulthood. Finally, the discussion returns to the ways in which primates go about learning, particularly social influences on learning. The chapter ends as it began, with an example from juvenile Phayre's leaf monkeys in Thailand.

Learning Ability and Life History: The Evolutionary Perspective

One reason to study learning in nonhuman primates is to better understand why this ability might have evolved in our human ancestors. The advantages seem clear. With learning ability comes increased behavioral flexibility, a greater freedom from "preprogrammed" behaviors based on genetic information. As Galef and Laland (2005) put it, with only genetically coded information, natural selection cannot equip individuals with adaptations appropriate for every possible circumstance in a changing environment, but "what natural selection can do is select for information-acquiring systems that permit an individual to adjust its behavior in a broadly adaptive manner to changes in its environment that occur during its life span" (495). It then follows that long-lived species especially, such as primates, will benefit from the flexibility of greater cognitive capacity (Deaner, Barton, and van Schaik 2003), because they will encounter more environmental change and ecological crises in a lifetime (Allman, McLaughlin, and Hakeem 1993), and will also have more opportunities to learn and make use of the information they have learned.

This point homes in on the evolutionary link between primates' relatively larger brain size and their distinctively slow life histories (Charnov and Berrigan 1993; Read and Harvey 1989)—with the latter including not only living longer but also longer gestation, longer intervals between births, and longer juvenile periods. Brain size has long been equated with cognitive ability or ideas of intelligence, and more recent studies have actually tested this and found evidence for a significant relationship between the two (Reader and Laland 2002). In turn, study after study has linked brain size with the timing of primate life histories (Barrickman et al. 2008; life span only: Deaner et al. 2003; Ross 2003). For example, Barrickman and others (2008) found that as brain size increases, so do the durations of gestation, juvenility, and the adult reproductive span. So while the link is clear, explanations for the relationship are still a little murky.

Evolutionary Hypotheses for Extended Immaturity in Primates

Evolutionary explanations have sometimes disagreed as to whether natural selection targeted brain size or life history traits, although more and more seem to favor brain size. Again, Barrickman and others (2008) recently concluded that encephalization led to the slowing of primate life history, largely due to its associated developmental costs and survival benefits. Mortality (death) becomes very costly for long-lived organisms in terms of reproductive success (Janson 2003). But as primates became bigger brained, the greater behavioral flexibility may have allowed individuals to respond better to unexpected ecological crises, such as food shortages, thereby providing a "buffer" against mortality. This cognitive buffering hypothesis (Deaner et al. 2003) suggests that the resulting lower rates of adult mortality should slow life history and, per life history theory, lead to later age at maturity (Charnov 1993).

Other explanations have focused specifically on the immature life stage and on pinpointing possible adaptive benefits of extending it. These benefits would have to be significant enough to outweigh the otherwise obvious costs: for example, the fact that such a delay to the start of sexual maturity increases the risk of dying before reproducing (Pereira 1993). The skill-learning hypothesis suggests that selection favored a longer and slower immature period in which to practice the complex skills that were necessary for adulthood because of the increasing dietary and social complexity that accompanied encephalization (Joffe 1997; described in: Pereira and Altmann 1985). This hypothesis has some weaknesses. Pereira and Fairbanks (2002) point out that if needing time to learn was the driving force behind extended juvenility, then there would be nothing prohibiting juveniles from learning adult skills at larger, adult sizes, especially since that might lower predation and competitive risks. On the other hand, smaller size during this difficult life stage could reduce starvation or malnutrition risks by lowering absolute metabolic requirements (ecological risk-aversion hypothesis: Janson and van Schaik 1993).

To further test the skill-learning hypothesis, some researchers have specifically gauged the timing of the appearance of foraging competence. According to the hypothesis, if immaturity is constrained by skill acquisition, then juveniles should not be fully competent until very close to sexual maturity (i.e., the end of juvenility). Indeed, numerous nonhuman primates show differences between juveniles and adults in diet composition, in foraging efficiency, and in the techniques used to process certain foods (Corp and Byrne 2002; Johnson and Bock 2004; Krakauer 2005; Whitehead 1986). However, several studies have also found that juveniles foraged as competently as adults at ages well before the start of sexual maturity (e.g., gorillas: Watts 1985; squirrel monkeys: Boinski and Fragaszy 1989; Stone 2006; orangutans: van Schaik et al. 2009), which contradicts the hypothesis.

An alternative explanation suggests that if selection had favored bigger brains rather than targeting the timing of immaturity, then lengthened immaturity could simply be a by-product (Bogin 1999; R. Martin 1996) of the fact that larger brain size is energetically expensive (Armstrong 1983). Along these lines, a different constraints-based hypothesis proposes that only a fully mature nervous system can support the complex behaviors of adulthood (Deaner et al. 2003). This maturational constraints hypothesis attributes the delay in development to the fact that larger brains need longer not only to grow but to mature, a process that relies on external or behavioral stimuli and that must follow a fixed sequence (Deaner et al. 2003). Indeed, the timing and length of brain growth per se and of the juvenile period are not correlated (Leigh 2004), and primate brains tend to achieve adult *size* too early—about the time of weaning (Bolter 2004; Leigh 2001), but processes of maturation, such as myelination and dendritic growth, can continue for much longer, especially in the cortex (McKinney 2000).

Skill Learning, Survival, and Growth: The Functional Perspective

As mentioned, the two most basic tasks of any young primate—increasing their odds of survival and learning skills for the future (Pereira and Altmann 1985)—are sometimes, even often, at odds. A baboon example from Johnson and Bock (2004) illustrates the dilemma. When foraging, a juvenile baboon finds and eats figs quickly and easily but takes much longer to find underground roots, which he has a hard time processing. If the juvenile ate only figs, this might provide a nutritional advantage and help him grow faster than other juveniles in the short term, but it comes at the expense of time spent gaining experience with roots. That lack of experience will matter later on when figs and other so-called easy foods are no longer available and the ability to forage for roots becomes an essential skill for a baboon.

Similarly, a chimpanzee is not born knowing how to crack nuts with a rock hammer or to fish for termites. Many primate behaviors are learned either independently or from watching others, and the lengthened immature period allows time to acquire and hone skills before adulthood. Primates, in fact, seem almost uniquely equipped for learning compared to other animals, with their lengthened juvenile periods and their relatively larger brains, which arm them with greater cognitive capacity and behavioral flexibility. The evolution of large primate brains has been attributed to both social and ecological factors (Byrne and Whiten 1988; Milton 1988). A number of comparative analyses that use data from many different primate species have demonstrated that brain size has a positive relationship with group size, the idea being that larger groups require greater social strategizing (Barton 1996; Dunbar 1992). Others have found a similar relationship between brain size and proxies for ecological complexity, such as degree of fruit eating versus leaf eating, home range size, and degree of extractive foraging (Clutton-Brock and Harvey 1980; Gibson 1986). One side note to keep in mind: these socioecological links exist for haplorhine species (tarsiers, monkeys, apes, and humans), but the same relationships do not always hold up among the relatively smaller-brained strepsirhines (Barton 1996), the lemurs and lorises. Nonetheless, the relationship of brain size to both foraging and social complexity has guided investigations into primate learning and intelligence, which have likewise often focused specifically on foraging and social skills.

Learning Social Skills and Forming Relationships

Immaturity is hardly a carefree time for young monkeys and apes. Peers and even some adult group members make good playmates, but they are also competitors for food, future competitors for mates, potential future allies who might provide aid during fights, or alternatively, future aggressors. The complexities of relationships in the adult social network are largely determined by social organization and social structure, which exhibit great variation among primates (Kappeler and van Schaik 2002), including differences in styles of dominance, in the intensity and frequency of aggression or affiliation, and in dispersal patterns. For example, in nonhuman primates, typically males but also females or even both sexes will leave their natal group and immigrate into a new one around the time of sexual maturity (Pusey 1992). These social factors determine, in part, the value of close social bonds and long-term allies, the degree of social tolerance, and in the case of dispersal pattern, those individuals who are more likely to spend their lives together in the same group.

Many primate species not only understand aspects of their own social relationships with others but are also capable of recognizing the various relationships among other group members (Seyfarth and Cheney 1988). That is, an individual knows not only that it is higher ranking than individual B, but also that individual B is higher or lower ranking than individual C. Mastery of such complex social skills requires experience. In their studies of vervet monkeys, Seyfarth and Cheney (1988) found that individuals of all ages could recognize the relationship between two closely related group members, but it was not until they were older than 3 years that subjects could recognize the resemblance between multiple sets of associations that were similar but involved different individuals. Thus, the authors concluded that "knowledge about the social environment is acquired gradually, through levels of increasing complexity" (80).

Sex Differences in Social Behaviors and Partners

During an individual's immaturity, some social relationships provide immediate benefits; for example, proximity to tolerant adults provides access to an experienced model for learning new behaviors, or it might offer protection from fellow group members or predators (Horrocks and Hunte 1993; Pereira 1988). However, early social relationships may serve to develop social bonds that have long-term, even life-long value (Fairbanks 1993; Walters 1987). Based on the consistent patterns of grooming, neighbor proximity, and support and aggression, relationships formed during immaturity have been found to endure into adulthood (Fairbanks 1993). These partner preferences during immaturity, therefore, serve as indicators for the potential long-term value of particular relationships (Fairbanks 1993; Pereira and Altmann 1985; Strier 1993).

Sex differences in juvenile social behavior are prevalent and have been studied in detail to better determine the value of different relationships. For many species, juveniles of the philopatric sex (i.e., the sex that stays and reproduces in the group they were born into) tend to invest significantly more in social relationships particularly with adults (who are also in the group for the long term)—usually either initiating proximity or grooming (Cheney 1978a; O'Brien 1993; Pusey 1990; Strier 1993; Walters 1987). Even from an early age, then, a young female in a female-philopatric species, for example, has a greater interest in integrating herself into the group's social network (e.g., wedge-capped capuchins: O'Brien 1993). Because differences in male and female social behaviors appear well before metabolic or size differences appear (Fragaszy 1990; van Noordwijk et al. 1993), it would seem immature males and females are indeed training or at least preparing for different adult futures (Nikolei and Borries 1997).

Play in nonhuman primates, a behavior almost distinctive to immaturity, also exhibits sex differences. Most of the evidence shows that juvenile males play more frequently, play for longer, and play more roughly (play-fight) than females (cercopithecines: Fairbanks 1993; Nakamichi 1989; gorillas: Maestripieri and Ross 2004). At its peak, play behavior occupies 30 to 40 percent of the time of young male Japanese macaques (Nakamichi 1989).

While it is remotely possible that play provides no adaptive benefit to primates, its prevalence across species as well as the obvious energetic costs and risk of injury imply some counteracting advantage of the play activity (Fagen 1993; see also chapter 6, this volume). Various studies exploring the functional aspects of play have led to a variety of hypotheses proposing its key role in training for motor skills, social skills and relationships, communication, and cognition (Bekoff and Byers 1998; Fagen 1993; Lewis and Barton 2004; Maestripieri and Ross 2004; Martin and Caro 1985). In terms of social skills, play may contribute to learning dominance relationships as well as forming social bonds with preferred play partners (Maestripieri and Ross 2004; Nakamichi 1989, but see Fairbanks 1993). Cheney (1978b) found that juvenile female baboons played most often with infants of high-ranking mothers, a finding that lends some support to the idea of forming relationships with high-value partners (i.e., the high-ranking mothers) but also that females are practicing skills associated with infant care.

This social relationships hypothesis for play, however, has several weaknesses. For example, play partners do not seem to be persistent and long-term as they are among grooming partners (Fairbanks 1993). Other research has found a relationship between the frequency of play and aspects of brain size across primates (e.g., cerebellum size: Lewis and Barton 2004), lending support to an alternative hypothesis—the neural selection model. This model links the timing of play behavior directly to neurological and cognitive development.

Social Rank and Effects on Growth

The social environment also influences growth rates, a very important factor considering that the age at which a young monkey can first conceive (i.e., age at sexual maturity) often depends on having achieved a threshold body size. A juvenile that is large for its age likely reaches sexual maturity earlier than its smaller cohort members (e.g., savannah baboons: Altmann and Alberts 2005). While food availability has a huge impact on growth rates (Altmann and Alberts 2005), an individual's access to food is invariably linked to social factors such as rank. Research with different cercopithecine species—Old World monkeys that typically have dominance hierarchies in which rank is "inherited" from the mother—demonstrated that juveniles whose mothers were higher ranking tended to be larger in body size for their age (Altmann and Alberts 2005; Johnson 2003; Setchell et al. 2001). These studies also found that older mothers who had already had at least one other offspring were more likely to have current offspring that were large for their age. Not all primate species have matrilineal dominance hierarchies, but for those that do, maternal effects last throughout juvenility well after mothers have stopped nursing. These works demonstrate that, under stable hierarchies, the advantage or disadvantage of a mother's rank or experience to an individual's long-term fitness can be significant and altogether separate from the behavioral strategies of the juveniles themselves.

Learning Infant Care

Another common behavioral sex difference for juveniles is the degree of interest or caretaking shown toward infants, usually greater on the part of juvenile females (Fairbanks 1993). Allocare or allomaternal care refers to care given to an infant by an individual other than the mother. While this interest in infants has been cited as a potential means for a young female to establish a relationship with the infant's mother (Cheney 1978a, 1978b), it also provides young females—future mothers—opportunities for gaining experience with infant care. In fact, females who spend more time caring for infants during their own juvenile periods are more likely to successfully raise their own first infant (Fairbanks 1990; Hoage 1977), and that ability to care for infants appears to improve over time (Lancaster

1971). Further evidence for the importance of maternal experience comes from a study of cotton-top tamarins, in which Tardif, Richter, and Carson (1984) found that for mothers who had not had any previous rearing experience at a younger age with younger siblings, mortality for their own infants was 100 percent.

Among most primates, the mother is the primary caregiver for her offspring, but a few species are known to practice paternal care, that is, infant care on the part of fathers or adult males. When adult males regularly exhibit a tendency for paternal care, the expectation would be that juvenile males as well as females should require early experience with infants and thus sex differences should disappear. For the golden lion tamarin, both adult males and females care for infants. And immature behavior follows suit in that both male and female juveniles help to carry infants, although the timing (in terms of the age of infants being carried) was different between sexes and tended to mirror the carrying behavior of like-sexed adults (Hoage 1977). Such findings support, at least indirectly, the idea that juveniles are training, so to speak, for their adult roles.

Learning Ecological Skills

Ecological skills such as ranging, foraging, and predator-avoidance are critical to survival. Without help from the group, an individual unable to identify appropriate foods or where to find them will starve, just as an individual unable to recognize predators or how best to avoid them will likely be eaten. Primates exploit a complex environment (Clutton-Brock and Harvey 1980) in order to consume a high-quality diet. Their dietary niche potentially involves extractive foraging, spatial mapping of the home range, and differentiating plant foods with high nutrient quality as well as high toxicity. Again, developing the competency to exploit such a niche is a crucial task for a young primate, especially after weaning, when an individual can no longer fall back on maternal support. Indeed, dietary variation among even young individuals was shown to predict long-term fitness (Altmann 1991).

During immaturity, however, individuals have a number of possible factors working against them, such as smaller size, lesser strength, incomplete motor development, and inexperience (Boinski and Fragaszy 1989;

319

Corp and Byrne 2002; Johnson and Bock 2004; Post, Hausfater, and Mc-Cuskey 1980). Plentiful evidence for lower foraging efficiency comes from field studies across primate taxa, which have found that young subjects, usually infants, generally tend to take in food more slowly (i.e., lower bite rates), spend more time than adults searching for and finding appropriate foods, take longer to process or access more difficult foods, and even avoid or are forced to exclude particular foods that adults are able to eat (e.g., Corp and Byrne 2002; Fragaszy and Boinski 1995; Johnson and Bock 2004).

The Challenge of Small Size

Because most primates, humans especially, exhibit a long, extended growth period, any disadvantages of small size persist throughout juvenility until closer to sexual maturity, when most individuals approach adult body size (Bercovitch et al. 1998; also see Leigh 1994). While slow growth has been proposed as a means of lowering ecological risks associated with low food availability or reduced intake (Janson and van Schaik 1993; Leigh 1994), being smaller or weaker than others can pose problems for efficient foraging (Fragaszy and Boinski 1995). For one, small size impacts resource access because it determines whether an individual has the necessary strength (manual or jaw strength) to manipulate resources and their substrates (Agostini and Visalberghi 2005), for example, thick-husked fruit.

Chimpanzees in Tanzania eat a particular fruit with a tough outer skin, the *Saba florida* fruit. Researchers have studied in detail how the chimpanzees process this item (Corp and Byrne 2002), a technique that involves at least five stages. As expected, immatures, infants especially, are less adept at the technique. While an individual's level of experience certainly plays some role, the authors also attribute some of the age differences directly to size and strength constraints. For example, immature individuals were less likely than adults to detach fruits from the vine before processing, less likely to carry any detached fruits away to feed, and less likely to detach multiple fruits at the same time—tasks that are all limited by smaller hands and mouths for holding fruits (Corp and Byrne 2002).

Smaller size also reduces competitive ability (Fragaszy and Boinski 1995; Janson and van Schaik 1993). In terms of foraging, this determines an individual's ability to maintain access to a preferred food patch. In general, a much larger individual will often be able to displace a smaller one from a resource. But other elements besides size are at work here, including kinship and rank as well as degree of tolerance, which could enable a small juvenile to feed uninterrupted at a patch from which a full-sized but low-ranking adult might be excluded. Competitive ability will be discussed later as part of the discussion on ecological risks juveniles encounter and the impact on their spatial positioning.

Experience and Skill Development

In the complex ecological niche typical of primates, the roles of skill learning and experience are as important to ecological/foraging competence as size and strength constraints. Keep in mind, however, that in terms of evolutionary hypotheses, at least a few detailed investigations have found that the timing of skill development does not seem to directly constrain the start of maturity in nonhuman primates (squirrel monkeys: Stone 2006; orangutans: van Schaik et al. 2009). Instead, these studies have found that the juveniles of their study species achieve ecological competence well before the age of sexual maturity. But regardless of the evolutionary role of skill acquisition, naïve, inexperienced individuals must practice (and make mistakes along the way) in order to successfully learn complex foraging tasks (e.g., Humle and Snowdon 2008; Krakauer 2005), and a long immature period provides plenty of time in which to hone these ecological skills.

Direct investigation of experience and skill development in wild groups poses difficulties. Because the smallest individuals are also the least experienced, the impact of each can be difficult to disentangle, particularly in field studies or without the control possible in experimental work. Recent research conducted in captivity with immature aye-ayes was designed to do just that—explicitly test and tease apart various constraints on immature foraging skills (Krakauer 2005). Aye-ayes, one of the strepsirhine primates found in Madagascar, are uniquely adapted for specialized foraging: they use their elongated, bony third digit to tap on branches or other wood in order to detect cavities that often contain larvae (Erickson et al. 1998). In an experimental study, Krakauer (2005) found that immature aye-ayes were less efficient at tap foraging than adults, as measured by their ability to locate larval cavities via tapping, gnawing time/ability, and success and speed in extracting larvae. The study compared skill levels over time across (1) immature subjects, (2) naïve adults, and (3) experienced adults to better control for differences in experience, age, and size. Krakauer found strong evidence for experience-based constraint. Both immatures *and* naïve adults were less efficient at gnawing and larval extraction, and both groups demonstrated improved foraging efficiency with repeated exposure to the task (Krakauer 2005).

Like tap foraging, the more complex foraging techniques offer some of the best evidence for experience-based skill development. Foraging for underground or hidden resources, such as larvae, tubers, and roots, requires a certain level of skill not only to extract and process the item but also to initially detect and locate it (Gibson 1986). Other difficult foods include those with physical defenses, such as spines, thorns, or hooks that require tactics for careful removal (Byrne and Byrne 1993), or chemical defenses, which necessitate selective feeding and knowing *what* to eat rather than *how* to eat it.

Some of the most skill-dependent foraging tasks are those that require the use of tools, and these behaviors have been especially well studied because of the obvious similarities with human behavior as well as the rarity among primate taxa in the wild. Chimpanzees are prolific tool users, with a highly diverse set of practices across populations, which includes tasks such as modifying vegetation to fish for termites or ants and using rock hammers and anvils to crack open nuts (Boesch and Boesch 1983; McGrew 1992; Sugiyama 1995; Whiten et al. 1999). Learning to master tasks like nut cracking—whether it's how to choose the best tools or the best techniques for holding and positioning them—takes place over time through observation and practice (Inoue-Nakamura and Matsuzawa 1997). And while infant chimpanzees were already able to perform the basic actions involved in nut cracking, not until several years later could they combine each step in the appropriate order (Inoue-Nakamura and Matsuzawa 1997).

So far, the discussion has focused on skill learning as it pertains to how to eat. But as mentioned, when it comes to plant chemical defenses, young primates must also learn *what* to eat. In general, primates are known to feed selectively, preferring foods with high nutrient or mineral content and avoiding foods high in tannins or toxins, such as certain mature leaves (Glander 1981; Magliocca and Gautier-Hion 2002). Differences in general dietary categories among primates, such as fruit eating versus leaf eating, translate into different risks associated with skill acquisition. For an inexperienced leaf-eating monkey, there can be seemingly small visual differences between an edible leaf and a potentially toxic or indigestible leaf.

In looking at foraging development in more herbivorous species, researchers have found that infants tend to feed synchronously with their mothers (mountain gorillas: Watts 1985; mantled howler monkeys: Whitehead 1986), that is, eating from the same plant item at the same time. Whitehead's findings shed further light on the potential risks involved in learning what to eat; they suggest that young howler monkeys behave differently when feeding on fruits versus leaves, and the latter are more likely to be chemically defended. During bouts of leaf eating, infants were more likely to be in close proximity to an adult female and rarely initiated feeding bouts on leaves without first observing a social partner feeding (Whitehead 1986). However, when it came to fruit, young howlers appeared to be more independent in their feeding behavior. They did not wait for adults to feed first in at least half of the cases, and they were less likely to coordinate their fruit feeding with adults or to feed on the same plant parts (Whitehead 1986). Milton's comparative work (1988) on howler monkeys and spider monkeys corroborated a relationship between basic dietary categories and willingness to experiment regardless of age. She found that both immature and adult spider monkeys (i.e., fruit eaters) were more likely to taste and accept novel foods, while leaf-eating howler monkeys were not.

Ecological Risks and Spatial Tactics for Risk Reduction

Ecological risks generally refer to factors that contribute to the likelihood of death from starvation or predation (Janson and van Schaik 1993), and the broad dietary differences just discussed certainly play a role in determining these risks for both juveniles and adults. For example, a folivorous diet is generally considered to be more predictable across seasons and readily available than a diet of fruits or insects, therefore the risk of starvation should be consistently lower for folivores (Janson and van Schaik 1993; Leigh 1994; Ross and Jones 1999). But ecological risks also depend on species' habitat, for example, whether or not long dry seasons could lead to food shortages, as well as the makeup of the predator community and whether a primate population must contend with aerial predators, terrestrial predators, or both.

In general, smaller, less experienced juveniles tend to face greater ecological risks than adults (Janson and van Schaik 1993). As mentioned previously, immatures are generally at a competitive disadvantage with adults, which means that even if they find and recognize a preferred resource, they may not be able to feed for long before an adult in the group excludes or displaces them from that patch. Not being able to maintain access to a food patch has a substantial impact on foraging success or the rate of intake (Janson 1990; Johnson and Bock 2004). If this competitive disadvantage is severe enough, it may force juveniles to alter their behavior and feed more often on less desirable patches or to feed alone or on the edge of the group in locations more vulnerable to predation (e.g., baboons: Cheney et al. 2004; rank—not age—effects: Hall and Fedigan 1997). Alternatively, the younger juveniles may be able to sacrifice foraging efficiency for the relative safety of the group, depending in part on adult tolerance. Juvenile capuchins, for example, seemed to prefer foraging locations in the most central area of the group where predation risk was determined to be the lowest (Janson 1990).

This spatial tactic has definite protective benefits because foraging with more neighbors presumably lowers predation risk (Hamilton 1971) as well as the time each individual must spend monitoring for predators, since others are also on the lookout (Treves 1998; van Schaik and van Noordwijk 1989). This benefit is especially important for juveniles who likely face greater predation risk in part because their smaller size makes them acceptable prey for a greater number of predators—a small jungle cat that is outweighed by an adult monkey, for example, might find it can still take down a young juvenile. And as for the role of inexperience, juveniles are less likely to detect predators (see van Schaik and van Noordwijk 1989), which means they would have a harder time avoiding those same predators.

Numerous field studies have examined sociospatial patterns, noting which individuals are most often next to the dominant male or most often alone and peripheral. The patterns that emerge for juveniles point to the use of strategies for balancing competitive and predation risks. They also highlight how these risks change over the course of immaturity. While juveniles are still small and their energy demands relatively low, the safety that comes with feeding within the group or near adults might be worth the cost to feeding efficiency (Janson and van Schaik 1993). As juveniles get older and bigger, however, not only does absolute energetic demand increase, but adult tolerance declines and the competitive costs become too great. Pereira (1988) found that as juvenile savannah baboons got older, they approached adult males less often while adults were feeding, and proximity to adult males was associated with reduced feeding rates for older juveniles but not for younger juveniles. These older juveniles also displayed riskier foraging patterns, such as foraging more often without close neighbors.

Social Influences on Learning from Others

The serious risks involved with sociospatial decisions may be mitigated somewhat by social tolerance, which typically is more often extended to infants and young juveniles. Researchers studying capuchin monkeys, for example, have remarked on the high degree of tolerance that adults show especially toward immatures, regularly allowing them to be in close proximity even while feeding (Boinski et al. 2003; Visalberghi and Addessi 2003). The ability to remain nearby when adults are feeding not only lowers predation risks but can also provide opportunities for observing competent adult behavior, and at least for some primate species, adults even tolerate begging or interference such as reaching for a tool or for food (Boinski et al. 2003; Jaeggi, van Noordwijk, and van Schaik 2008; Lonsdorf 2006). This sort of tolerance on the part of an older, often more-experienced group member is one of the keys to the social transmission of information and to social influences on skill learning (Coussi-Korbel and Fragaszy 1995; Fragaszy and Visalberghi 2004; van Schaik et al. 1999). Tolerant social environments are even more important, considering that, unlike in humans, nonhuman primate learning rarely if at all involves active teaching on the part of adults (see also chapter 7, this volume). Even after many years of observing chimpanzee tool use, primatologists either have not observed any evidence of active teaching on the part of chimpanzee mothers or else have seen only rare, anecdotal cases (Boesch 1991; Lonsdorf 2006; Matsuzawa et al. 2001).

In the broadest sense, learning takes place independently via trial and error and practice (e.g., Boinski and Fragaszy 1989; Milton 1993) as well as through social influence (Fragaszy and Visalberghi 2004). Visalberghi and Addessi (2003) explain: "the extent to which monkeys are influenced by social partners depends on what they are learning about" (205), and social learning should be more likely among species adapted to more complex environments (Lefebvre and Giraldeau 1996), like those utilized by many nonhuman primates. In the most obvious example, taking cues from social partners would be extremely valuable when learning about predator avoidance and identification as well as fear behavior because of the grave costs of trial and error in such a life-threatening situation (Laland and Kendal 2003; Visalberghi and Addessi 2003).

But social influences also play a key role in learning about diet and what to eat, as with the howler monkey example described previously (Whitehead 1986). When primate diets include a great diversity of plant or animal matter difficult to distinguish from toxic or indigestible items, then gleaning information from more experienced group members becomes especially important (Visalberghi and Addessi 2003). Complex foraging tasks, such as those involving tools, may require individual practice but would otherwise be extremely difficult to develop (or in fact reinvent) without experienced demonstrators. Termite fishing and nut cracking among chimpanzees both appear to be foraging skills that infants learn through repeated observations of their mothers and other adults (Lonsdorf 2005; Matsuzawa et al. 2001). Lonsdorf (2005) found that infant female chimpanzees spent much more time than infant males at termite mounds observing adults engage in termite fishing (i.e., watching as opposed to practicing). After further study, she found that the females became successful termite fishers themselves more than two years earlier than males, suggesting a powerful role for observation in skill acquisition (Lonsdorf 2005; see also chapter 5, this volume).

Because adults do not actively teach their young, inexperienced individuals may seek out experienced models for observation, even trying to get close enough to take direct cues from what it is they are eating (King 1999). The young of many species show high interest in the food of adults; in support of a learning function rather than simply a nutritional function for this tendency, these cases of food interest occur much more often when the food being eaten is a rare resource or an item otherwise difficult for the immatures to obtain or process on their own (e.g., baboons: King 1999; white-faced capuchins: O'Malley and Fedigan 2005; orangutans: Jaeggi et al. 2008). At the same time, experimental evidence suggests that opportunities for scrounging food scraps from tolerant adults may, in fact, distract immatures from observing how the adult obtained the food and, as a result, delay the process of learning how to access the food on their own (e.g., cotton-top tamarins: Humle and Snowdon 2008). Instead, young subjects who scrounged less were able to learn the foraging task more quickly.

Social factors influence learning in complicated and often indirect ways. For example, among captive capuchin monkeys, individuals were more likely to eat an unknown food if another group member was also feeding nearby, even when the neighbor was not eating the same food (Addessi and Visalberghi 2001). This case demonstrates the process of social facilitation, in which the mere presence of another group member engaging in a particular behavior, such as feeding, is enough to encourage similar activity in the observing individual, thereby "elevating the likelihood of exploration and discovery in relation to the task at hand" (Dindo, Whiten, and De Waal 2009, 419). Social facilitation is just one of several mechanisms by which social learning can operate indirectly among nonhuman primates.

Feeding Efficiency in Phayre's Leaf Monkeys

This section will briefly describe early results from my research on wild juvenile Phayre's leaf monkeys (*Trachypithecus phayrei*) at the Phu Khieo Wildlife Sanctuary (PKWS) in Thailand. For the overall project, data were collected on both adult and juvenile subjects to allow comparisons in exploring four aspects of development—foraging competence, spatial tactics for reducing risks, social investment, and growth. Data were collected for 17 months between October 2006 and May 2008 during all-day follows of three Phayre's leaf monkey groups.

Methods for This and Other Nonhuman Primate Field Studies

At the start of most nonhuman primate fieldwork, one or more study groups are slowly habituated to the presence of human observers over the course of days (rare), months, or years, depending on the particular species

(Williamson and Feistner 2003). Habituation enables researchers to observe study animals from close ranges not only without having the group flee but also, presumably, without them altering their normal behavior. At PKWS, the leaf monkey groups had previously been habituated by other researchers as part of the ongoing project of Drs. Andreas Koenig and Carola Borries.

Often, primatologists will spend time learning to identify each study individual before data collection begins. With certain species or for specific study questions, researchers will trap or dart study subjects at the start of a project, take samples or measurements, and then mark or radio-collar individuals before releasing them to enable identification (Ancrenaz, Setchell, and Curtis 2003; Jolly, Phillips-Conroy, and Muller 2003). Phayre's leaf monkeys possess a number of physical features that vary across individuals, such as their hair crests, the shape of their white muzzles, light rings around their eyes, and the depigmented pattern on their bellies (see figure 13.1). After some time and practice with each group, we used these features to distinguish and identify all 23 juveniles and 31 adults included in the study.

Being able to identify individuals allows for the collection of data via focal sampling, in which a single individual is followed and the behaviors relevant to the research questions are recorded systematically for a set amount of time (Martin and Bateson 1993). Each month, I spent about a week with each group. During that week, I would sample every subject following a preset order for one 20-minute period per time block, which would give me 160 minutes of focal data per individual at the end of the month. The set order of individuals and the even distribution of time blocks are measures taken to avoid incorporating bias. Bias can occur if an observer always samples the individuals that are easiest to locate at the time (e.g., those at lower heights) or from sampling a particular subject most often in the early morning when the group is most active rather than evenly throughout the day.

During the 20-minute samples, I recorded most feeding behaviors (including bites per minute when visibility permitted) and social behaviors continuously, attention status at one-minute intervals, and spatial position such as identities of near neighbors and height in meters at 10-minute intervals. A second observer used another sampling method, scan sampling at 20-minute intervals, to scan the whole group during feeding bouts. In

Figure 13.1. Juvenile male Phayres leaf monkey (K. Ossi-Lupo photo)

order to get a snapshot of who feeds together and on which food items, this observer recorded within a 10-minute period which individuals were feeding and in which trees, their heights, and the identities of their neighbors within 3 meters.

Findings for Feeding Efficiency in Phayre's Leaf Monkeys

Analyses have just started, but some preliminary results from the available subsets of data hint at differences between adult and juvenile

Phayre's leaf monkeys. For feeding, we have examined bite rates as a measure of feeding efficiency. For certain food items, bite sizes were noticeably different across age classes, and rates were adjusted to reflect this. For example, if an adult could eat a whole fruit in one bite but a juvenile regularly took two bites to finish a whole fruit, then the juvenile's bites were counted as half-bites. Bites were counted as either the number of hand-to-mouth movements in a minute for smaller items or the number of whole items eaten for larger foods like fruits (e.g., Barton and Whiten 1993).

A five-month subset of the data was categorized by age group: adults, older juveniles (referred to as J2s) who were 2.5–4 years of age, and young juveniles (J1s) 16–29 months old. Juveniles had significantly slower bite rates across all food categories, suggesting they are less efficient feeders in terms of actual intake. As expected, the J1s consistently had the lowest mean bite rates, then J2s, and then adults (see table 13.1).

It is interesting to note that for the young seeds category, older juveniles' bite rates start to approach those of adults. While this may suggest J2s are nearing adult-level competence for this food type, it leaves open the question of why. Is it a strength-related or experience-based constraint that they may be about to surpass? The leaf monkeys' diet contains a significant proportion of seeds (Suarez 2006), which they must extract from casings that range from relatively thin-shelled pods to thicker, tougher husks. Of course, Phayre's leaf monkeys do not use tools in their foraging like the stone hammers of chimpanzees and capuchin monkeys, but there may be a "best way" to open a pod quickly and still access all the seeds without additional handling. If so, this might require practice and experience to perfect. At the same time, the continual tearing open of presumably fibrous items such as pods and chewing of tough seeds places a greater mechanical demand on these seed eaters (Lucas and Teaford 1994), which certainly depends more on jaw strength than experience.

Table 13.1. Mean Bites per Minute (with Standard Error) across Age Groups of Phayre's Leaf Monkeys

Food Type	Younger Juveniles	Older Juveniles	Adults
Young seeds	7.76 (2.12)	11.12 (2.12)	12.67 (1.84)
Young leaves	9.61 (2.12)	11.29 (1.97)	15.04 (1.65)
Flowers	13.41 (2.12)	14.87 (1.97)	21.43 (1.74)

Future analyses will hopefully be able to better address this open question by examining detailed properties of the foods themselves and then relating measures, such as food toughness, to juvenile differences in feeding behavior (e.g., hominoids: Taylor, Vogel, and Dominy 2008).

Acknowledgments

I would like to thank the editors of this volume, David F. Lancy, John Bock, and Suzanne Gaskins, for the chance to take part in such a useful collaboration, and John Bock in particular for his thoughtful support and helpful suggestions throughout the process. I am grateful for the long-running support and advice of Andreas Koenig and Carola Borries from the very start of my dissertation project. My thanks also go to Amy Lu, Eileen Larney, and Miranda Swagemakers for advice in the field, as well as to the rangers and researchers at PKWS for their wonderful assistance. Thank you also to Wendy Erb, Tim Lupo, and Andreas Koenig for helpful comments on earlier drafts, and to David F. Lancy for his thoughtful editing that much improved this chapter. I gratefully acknowledge financial support for dissertation research on Phayre's leaf monkeys from a National Science Foundation Doctoral Dissertation Improvement Grant (Grant No. BCS-0647837 to A. Koenig and K. Ossi), the L. S. B. Leakey Foundation, the Wenner-Gren Foundation (Grant No. 7639), and the American Society of Primatologists.

Bibliography

Addessi, Elsa, and Elisabetta Visalberghi. "Social Facilitation of Eating Novel Food in Tufted Capuchin Monkeys (*Cebus apella*): Input Provided by Group Members and Responses Affected in the Observer." *Animal Cognition* 4, nos. 3–4 (November 2001): 297–303.

Agostini, Ilaria, and Elisabetta Visalberghi. "Social Influences on the Acquisition of Sex-Typical Foraging Patterns by Juveniles in a Group of Wild Tufted Capuchin Monkeys (*Cebus nigritus*)." *American Journal of Primatology* 65, no. 4 (April 2005): 335–51.

Allman, John, Todd McLaughlin, and Aiya Hakeem. "Brain Weight and Life-Span in Primates." *Proceedings of the National Academy of Sciences of the United States of America* 90, no. 1 (January 1993): 118–22.

Altmann, Jeanne, and Susan C. Alberts. "Growth Rates in a Wild Primate Population: Ecological Influences and Maternal Effects." *Behavioral Ecology and Sociobiology* 57, no. 5 (March 2005): 490–501.

Altmann, Stuart A. "Diets of Yearling Female Primates (*Papio cynocephalus*) Predict Lifetime Fitness." *Proceedings of the National Academy of Sciences of the United States of America* 88, no. 2 (January 1991): 420–3.

Ancrenaz, Marc, Joanna M. Setchell, and Deborah J. Curtis. "Handling, Anaesthesia, Health Evaluation, and Biological Sampling." Pp. 122–39 in *Field and Laboratory Methods in Primatology*, edited by Joanna M. Setchell and Deborah J. Curtis. Cambridge: Cambridge University Press, 2003.

Armstrong, Este. "Relative Brain Size and Metabolism in Mammals." *Science* 220, no. 4603 (1983): 1302–4.

Barrickman, Nancy L., Meredith L. Bastian, Karin Isler, and Carel P. van Schaik. "Life History Costs and Benefits of Encephalization: A Comparative Test Using Data from Long-Term Studies of Primates in the Wild." *Journal of Human Evolution* 54, no. 5 (May 2008): 568–90.

Barton, Robert A. "Neocortex Size and Behavioural Ecology in Primates." *Proceedings of the Royal Society, London B* 263, no. 1367 (February 1996): 173–7.

Barton, Robert A., and Andrew Whiten. "Feeding Competition among Female Olive Baboons, *Papio anubis*." *Animal Behaviour* 46, no. 4 (October 1993): 777–89.

Bekoff, Marc, and John A. Byers, eds. *Animal Play: Evolutionary, Comparative, and Ecological Perspectives*. Cambridge: Cambridge University Press, 1998.

Bercovitch, Fred B., Manuel R. Lebron, H. Samuel Martinez, and Matt J. Kessler. "Primigravidity, Body Weight, and Costs of Rearing First Offspring in Rhesus Macaques." *American Journal of Primatology* 46, no. 2 (1998): 135–44.

Boesch, Christophe. "Teaching among Wild Chimpanzees." *Animal Behaviour* 41, no. 3 (March 1991): 530–2.

Boesch, Christophe, and Hedwige Boesch. "Optimisation of Nut-Cracking with Natural Hammers by Wild Chimpanzees." *Behaviour* 83, nos. 3–4 (1983): 265–86.

Bogin, Barry. "Evolutionary Perspective on Human Growth." *Annual Review of Anthropology* 28, (1999): 109–53.

Boinski, Sue, and Dorothy M. Fragaszy. "The Ontogeny of Foraging in Squirrel Monkeys, *Saimiri Oerstedi*." *Animal Behaviour* 37, no. 3 (March 1989): 415–28.

Boinski, Sue, Robert P. Quatrone, Karen Sughrue, Lara Selvaggi, Malinda Henry, Claudia Stickler, and Lisa M. Rose. "Do Brown Capuchins Socially Learn Foraging Skills?" Pp. 365–90 in *The Biology of Traditions: Models and*

Evidence, edited by Dorothy M. Fragaszy and Susan Perry. Cambridge: Cambridge University Press, 2003.

Bolter, Debra. "Anatomical Growth Patterns in Colobine Monkeys and Implications for Primate Evolution." Doctoral dissertation, University of California, Santa Cruz, 2004.

Byrne, Richard W., and Jennifer M. E. Byrne. "Complex Leaf-Gathering Skills of Mountain Gorillas (*Gorilla g. beringei*): Variability and Standardization." *American Journal of Primatology* 31, no. 4 (1993): 241–61.

Byrne, Richard W., and Andrew Whiten. *Machiavellian Intelligence: Social Expertise and the Evolution of Intellect in Monkeys, Apes, and Humans.* Oxford: Oxford University Press, 1988.

Charnov, Eric L. *Life History Invariants: Some Explorations of Symmetry in Evolutionary Ecology.* Oxford: Oxford University Press, 1993.

Charnov, Eric L., and David Berrigan. "Why Do Female Primates Have Such Long Life Spans and So Few Babies? Or Life in the Slow Lane." *Evolutionary Anthropology* 1, no. 6 (1993): 191–4.

Cheney, Dorothy L. "Interactions of Immature Male and Female Baboons with Adult Females." *Animal Behaviour* 26, no. 2 (May 1978a): 389–408.

———. "The Play Partners of Immature Baboons." *Animal Behaviour* 26, no. 4 (November 1978b): 1038–50.

Cheney, Dorothy L., Robert M. Seyfarth, Julia Fischer, Jacinta C. Beehner, Thore J. Bergman, Sara E. Johnson, Dawn M. Kitchen, Ryne A. Palombit, Drew Rendall, and Joan B. Silk. "Factors Affecting Reproduction and Mortality among Baboons in the Okavango Delta, Botswana." *International Journal of Primatology* 25, no. 2 (2004): 401–28.

Clutton-Brock, Tim H., and Paul H. Harvey. "Primates, Brains, and Ecology." *Journal of Zoology, London* 109 (1980): 309–23.

Corp, Nadia, and Richard W. Byrne. "The Ontogeny of Manual Skill in Wild Chimpanzees: Evidence from Feeding on the Fruit of *Saba florida*." *Animal Behaviour* 139, no. 1 (January 2002): 137–68.

Coussi-Korbel, Sabine, and Dorothy M. Fragaszy. "On the Relation between Social Dynamics and Social Learning." *Animal Behaviour* 50, no. 6 (1995): 1441–53.

Deaner, Robert O., Robert A. Barton, and Carel P. van Schaik. "Primate Brains and Life Histories: Renewing the Connection." Pp. 233–65 in *Primate Life Histories and Socioecology*, edited by Peter M. Kappeler and Michael E. Pereira. Chicago: University of Chicago Press, 2003.

Dindo, Marietta, Andrew Whiten, and Frans B. M. De Waal. "Social Facilitation of Exploratory Foraging Behavior in Capuchin Monkeys (*Cebus apella*)." *American Journal of Primatology* 71, no. 5 (May 2009): 419–26.

Dunbar, Robin I. M. "Neocortex Size as a Constraint on Group Size in Primates." *Journal of Human Evolution* 20 (1992): 469–93.

Erickson, Carl J., Stephen Nowicki, Luke Dollar, and Nathan Goehring. "Percussive Foraging: Stimuli for Prey Location by Aye-Ayes (*Daubentonia madagascariensis*)." *International Journal of Primatology* 19, no. 1 (1998): 111–22.

Fagen, Robert. "Primate Juveniles and Primate Play." Pp. 182–96 in *Juvenile Primates: Life History, Development, and Behavior*, edited by Michael E. Pereira and Lynn A. Fairbanks. New York: Oxford University Press, 1993.

Fairbanks, Lynn A. "Reciprocal Benefits of Allomothering for Female Vervet Monkeys." *Animal Behaviour* 40, no. 3 (September 1990): 553–62.

———. "Juvenile Vervet Monkeys: Establishing Relationships and Practicing Skills for the Future." Pp. 211–27 in *Juvenile Primates: Life History, Development, and Behavior*, edited by Michael E. Pereira and Lynn A. Fairbanks. New York: Oxford University Press, 1993.

Fragaszy, Dorothy M. "Sex and Age Differences in the Organization of Behavior in Wedge-Capped Capuchins, *Cebus olivaceus*." *Behavioral Ecology* 1 (1990): 81–94.

Fragaszy, Dorothy M., and Sue Boinski. "Patterns of Individual Diet Choice and Efficiency of Foraging in Wedge-Capped Capuchin Monkeys (*Cebus olivaceus*)." *Journal of Comparative Psychology* 109, no. 4 (1995): 339–48.

Fragaszy, Dorothy M., and Susan Perry, eds. *The Biology of Traditions: Models and Evidence*. Cambridge: Cambridge University Press, 2003.

Fragaszy, Dorothy M., and Elisabetta Visalberghi. "Socially Biased Learning in Monkeys." *Learning and Behavior* 32, no. 1 (2004): 24–35.

Galef, Bennett G., Jr., and Kevin N. Laland. "Social Learning in Animals: Empirical Studies and Theoretical Models." *Bioscience* 55, no. 6 (2005): 489–99.

Gibson, K. R. "Cognition, Brain Size, and the Extraction of Embedded Food Resources." Pp. 93–103 in *Primate Ontogeny, Cognition, and Social Behaviour*, edited by James G. Else and Phyllis C. Lee. Cambridge: Cambridge University Press, 1986.

Glander, Kenneth E. "Feeding Patterns in Mantled Howling Monkeys." Pp. 231–57 in *Foraging Behavior: Ecological, Ethological, and Psychological Approaches*, edited by A. C. Kamil and T. D. Sargent. New York: Garland STPM, 1981.

Hall, Carolyn L., and Linda M. Fedigan. "Spatial Benefits Afforded by High Rank in White-Faced Capuchins." *Animal Behaviour* 53, no. 5 (May 1997): 1069–82.

Hamilton, W. D. "Geometry for the Selfish Herd." *Journal of Theoretical Biology* 31 (1971): 295–311.

Hoage, R. J. "Parental Care in *Leontopithecus rosalia rosalia*: Sex and Age Differences in Carrying Behavior and the Role of Prior Experience." Pp. 293–305 in *The Biology and Conservation of the Callitrichidae*, edited by D. G. Kleiman. Washington D.C.: Smithsonian Institution, 1977.

Horrocks, Julia, and Wayne Hunte. "Interactions between Juveniles and Adult Males in Vervets: Implications for Adult Male Turnover." Pp. 228–39 in *Juvenile Primates: Life History, Development, and Behavior*, edited by Michael E. Pereira and Lynn A. Fairbanks. New York: Oxford University Press, 1993.

Humle, Tatyana, and Charles Snowdon. "Socially Biased Learning in the Acquisition of a Complex Foraging Task in Juvenile Cottontop Tamarins, *Saguinus oedipus*." *Animal Behaviour* 75, no. 1 (January 2008): 267–77.

Inoue-Nakamura, Noriko, and Tetsuro Matsuzawa. "Development of Stone Tool Use by Wild Chimpanzees (*Pan troglodytes*)." *Journal of Comparative Psychology* 111, no. 2 (1997): 159–73.

Jaeggi, Adrian V., Maria A. van Noordwijk, and Carel P. van Schaik. "Begging for Information: Mother-Offspring Food Sharing among Wild Bornean Orangutans." *American Journal of Primatology* 70, no. 6 (June 2008): 533–41.

Janson, Charles H. "Ecological Consequences of Individual Spatial Choice in Foraging Groups of Brown Capuchin Monkeys, *Cebus apella*." *Animal Behaviour* 40, no. 5 (November 1990): 922–34.

———. "Puzzles, Predation, and Primates: Using Life History to Understand Selection Pressures." Pp. 103–31 in *Primate Life Histories and Socioecology*, edited by Peter M. Kappeler and Michael E. Pereira. Chicago: University of Chicago Press, 2003.

Janson, Charles H., and Carel P. van Schaik. "Ecological Risk Aversion in Juvenile Primates: Slow and Steady Wins the Race." Pp. 57–74 in *Juvenile Primates: Life History, Development, and Behavior*, edited by Michael E. Pereira and Lynn A. Fairbanks. New York: Oxford University Press, 1993.

Joffe, Tracey H. "Social Pressures Have Selected for an Extended Juvenile Period in Primates." *Journal of Human Evolution* 32 (1997): 593–605.

Johnson, Sara E. "Life History and the Competitive Environment: Trajectories of Growth, Maturation, and Reproductive Output among Chacma Baboons." *American Journal of Physical Anthropology* 120 (2003): 83–98.

Johnson, Sara E., and John Bock. "Trade-offs in Skill Acquisition and Time Allocation among Juvenile Chacma Baboons." *Human Nature* 15, no. 1 (2004): 45–62.

Jolly, Clifford J., Jane E. Phillips-Conroy, and Alexandra E. Muller. "Trapping Primates." Pp. 111–21 in *Field and Laboratory Methods in Primatology*, edited by Joanna M. Setchell and Deborah J. Curtis. Cambridge: Cambridge University Press, 2003.

Kappeler, Peter M., and Carel P. van Schaik. "Evolution of Primate Social Systems." *International Journal of Primatology* 23, no. 4 (2002): 707–40.

King, Barbara J. "New Directions in the Study of Primate Learning." Pp. 17–32 in *Mammalian Social Learning: Comparative and Ecological Perspectives*, edited by Hilary O. Box and Kathleen R. Gibson. Cambridge: Cambridge University Press, 1999.

Krakauer, Elissa B. "Development of Aye-Aye (*Daubentonia madagascariensis*) Foraging Skills: Independent Exploration and Social Learning." Doctoral dissertation, Duke University, 2005.

Laland, Kevin N., and Jeremy R. Kendal. "What the Models Say about Social Learning." Pp. 33–55 in *The Biology of Traditions: Models and Evidence*, edited by Dorothy M. Fragaszy and Susan Perry. Cambridge: Cambridge University Press, 2003.

Lancaster, Jane. "Play-Mothering: The Relations between Juvenile Females and Young Infants among Free-Ranging Vervet Monkeys (*Cercopithecus aethiops*)." *Folia Primatologica* 15, (1971): 161–82.

Lefebvre, Louis, and Luc-Alain Giraldeau. "Is Social Learning an Adaptive Specialization?" Pp. 107–25 in *Social Learning in Animals: The Roots of Culture*, edited by Cecelia M. Hayes and Bennett G. Galef Jr. Hillsdale, N.J.: Erlbaum, 1996.

Leigh, Steven R. "Ontogenetic Correlates of Diet in Anthropoid Primates." *American Journal of Physical Anthropology* 94 (1994): 499–522.

———. "Evolution of Human Growth." *Evolutionary Anthropology* 10, no. 6 (2001): 223–36.

———. "Brain Growth, Life History, and Cognition in Primate and Human Evolution." *American Journal of Primatology* 62, no. 3 (March 2004): 139–64.

Lewis, Kerrie, and Robert A. Barton. "Playing for Keeps: Evolutionary Relationships between the Cerebellum and Social Play Behaviour in Non-Human Primates." *Human Nature* 15, no. 1 (2004): 5–21.

Lonsdorf, Elizabeth. "Sex Differences in the Development of Termite-Fishing Skills in the Wild Chimpanzees, *Pan troglodytes schweinfurthii*, of Gombe National Park, Tanzania." *Animal Behaviour* 70, no. 3 (September 2005): 673–83.

———. "What Is the Role of Mothers in the Acquisition of Termite-Fishing Behaviors in Wild Chimpanzees (*Pan troglodytes schweinfurthii*)?" *Animal Cognition* 9, (2006): 36–46.

Lucas, Peter W., and Mark F. Teaford. "Functional Morphology of Colobine Teeth." Pp. 173–204 in *Colobine Monkeys: Their Ecology, Behaviour, and Evolution*, edited by A. G. Davies and J. F. Oates. Cambridge: Cambridge University Press, 1994.

Maestripieri, Dario, and Stephen Ross. "Sex Differences in Play among Western Lowland Gorilla (*Gorilla gorilla gorilla*) Infants: Implications for Adult Behavior and Social Structure." *American Journal of Physical Anthropology* 123 (2004): 52–61.

Magliocca, Florence, and Annie Gautier-Hion. "Mineral Content as a Basis for Food Selection by Western Lowland Gorillas in a Forest Clearing." *American Journal of Primatology* 57, no. 2 (June 2002): 67–77.

Martin, Paul, and Patrick Bateson. *Measuring Behaviour: An Introductory Guide.* Cambridge: Cambridge University Press, 1993.

Martin, Paul, and T. M. Caro. "On the Functions of Play and Its Role in Behavioral Development." Pp. 59–103 in *Advances in the Study of Behavior*, edited by Jay S. Rosenblatt, Colin Beer, Marie-Claire Busnel, and Peter J. B. Slater. Orlando, Fla.: Academic, 1985.

Martin, Robert D. "Scaling of the Mammalian Brain: The Maternal Energy Hypothesis." *News in Physiological Sciences* 11 (1996): 149–56.

Matsuzawa, Tetsuro, Dora Biro, Tatyana Humle, Noriko Inoue-Nakamura, Rikako Tonooka, and Gen Yamakoshi. "Emergence of Culture in Wild Chimpanzees: Education by Master-Apprenticeship." Pp. 557–74 in *Primate Origins of Human Cognition and Behavior*, edited by Tetsuro Matsuzawa. Tokyo: Springer-Verlag, 2001.

McGrew, William C. *Chimpanzee Material Culture: Implications for Human Evolution.* Cambridge: Cambridge University Press, 1992.

McKinney, Michael L. "Evolving Behavioral Complexity by Extending Development." Pp. 25–40 in *Biology, Brains, and Behavior*, edited by Sue Taylor Parker, Jonas Langer, and Michael L. McKinney. Santa Fe, N.M.: School of American Research Press, 2000.

Milton, Katharine. "Foraging Behaviour and the Evolution of Primate Intelligence." Pp. 285–305 in *Machiavellian Intelligence*, edited by Richard W. Byrne and Andrew Whiten. Oxford: Clarendon, 1988.

———. "Diet and Social Organization of a Free-Ranging Spider Monkey Population: The Development of Species-Typical Behavior in the Absence of Adults." Pp. 173–81 in *Juvenile Primates: Life History, Development, and Behavior*, edited by Michael E. Pereira and Lynn A. Fairbanks. New York: Oxford University Press, 1993.

Nakamichi, Masayuki. "Sex Differences in Social Development during the First 4 Years in a Free-Ranging Group of Japanese Monkeys, *Macaca fuscata*." *Animal Behaviour* 38, no. 5 (November 1989): 737–48.

Nikolei, J., and C. Borries. "Sex Differential Behavior of Immature Hanuman Langurs (*Presbytis entellus*) in Ramnagar, South Nepal." *International Journal of Primatology* 18, no. 3 (1997): 415–37.

O'Brien, Timothy G. "Asymmetries in Grooming Interactions between Juvenile and Adult Female Wedge-Capped Capuchin Monkeys." *Animal Behaviour* 46, no. 5 (May 1993): 929–38.

O'Malley, Robert C., and Linda M. Fedigan. "Evaluating Social Influences on Food-Processing Behavior in White-Faced Capuchins (*Cebus capucinus*)." *American Journal of Physical Anthropology* 127 (2005): 481–91.

Panger, Melissa, Susan Perry, Lisa M. Rose, Julie Gros-Louis, Erin Vogel, Katherine MacKinnon, and Mary Baker. "Cross-Site Differences in Foraging Behavior of White-Faced Capuchins (*Cebus capucinus*)." *American Journal of Physical Anthropology* 119 (2002): 52–66.

Pereira, Michael E. "Effects of Age and Sex on Intra-Group Spacing Behaviour in Juvenile Savannah Baboons, *Papio cynocephalus cynocephalus*." *Animal Behaviour* 36, no. 1 (February 1988): 184–204.

——. "Agonistic Interaction, Dominance Relation, and Ontogenetic Trajectories in Ringtailed Lemurs." Pp. 285–305 in *Juvenile Primates: Life History, Development, and Behavior*, edited by Michael E. Pereira and Lynn A. Fairbanks. New York: Oxford University Press, 1993.

Pereira, Michael E., and Jeanne Altmann. "Development of Social Behavior in Free-Living Nonhuman Primates." Pp. 217–309 in *Nonhuman Primate Models for Human Growth and Development*, edited by Elizabeth S. Watts. New York: Alan R. Liss, 1985.

Pereira, Michael E., and Lynn A. Fairbanks. *Juvenile Primates: Life History, Development, and Behavior.* Chicago: University of Chicago Press, 2002.

——. "What Are Juvenile Primates All About?" Pp. 3–12 in *Juvenile Primates: Life History, Development, and Behavior*, edited by Michael E. Pereira and Lynn A. Fairbanks. New York: Oxford University Press, 1993.

Pereira, Michael E., and Steve R. Leigh. "Modes of Primate Development." Pp. 149–76 in *Primate Life Histories and Socioecology*, edited by Peter M. Kappeler and Michael E. Pereira. Chicago: University of Chicago Press, 2003.

Post, David G., Glenn Hausfater, and Sue Ann McCuskey. "Feeding Behavior of Yellow Baboons (*Papio cynocephalus*): Relationship to Age, Gender, and Dominance Rank." *Folia Primatologica* 34 (1980): 170–95.

Pusey, Anne E. "Behavioral Changes at Adolescence in Chimpanzees." *Behaviour* 115, nos. 3–4 (December 1990): 203–45.

——. "The Primate Perspective on Dispersal." Pp. 243–59 in *Dispersal: Small Mammals as a Model*, edited by N. C. Stenseth and W. Z. Lidicker. New York: Springer, 1992.

Read, A. F., and Paul H. Harvey. "Life History Differences among Eutherian Radiations." *Journal of Zoology, London* 219 (1989): 329–53.

Reader, Simon M., and Kevin N. Laland. "Primate Innovation: Sex, Age, and Social Rank Differences." *International Journal of Primatology* 22, no. 5 (October 2001): 787–806.

———. "Social Intelligence, Innovation, and Enhanced Brain Size in Primates." *Proceedings of the National Academy of Sciences of the United States of America* 99, no. 7 (2002): 4436–41.

Ross, Caroline. "Life History, Infant Care Strategies, and Brain Size in Primates." Pp. 266–84 in *Primate Life Histories and Socioecology*, edited by Peter M. Kappeler and Michael E. Pereira. Chicago: University of Chicago Press, 2003.

Ross, Caroline, and Kate E. Jones. "Socioecology and the Evolution of Primate Reproductive Rates." Pp. 73–110 in *Comparative Primate Socioecology*, edited by Phyllis C. Lee. Cambridge: Cambridge University Press, 1999.

Setchell, Joanna M., Phyllis C. Lee, E. Jean Wickings, and Alan F. Dixson. "Growth and Ontogeny of Sexual Size Dimorphism in the Mandrill (*Mandrillus sphinx*)." *American Journal of Physical Anthropology* 115, no. 4 (August 2001): 349–60.

Seyfarth, Robert M., and Dorothy L. Cheney. "Do Monkeys Understand Their Relations?" Pp. 69–84 in *Machiavellian Intelligence*, edited by Richard W. Byrne and Andrew Whiten. Oxford: Clarendon, 1988.

Stone, Anita. "Foraging Ontogeny Is Not Linked to Delayed Maturation in Squirrel Monkeys (*Saimiri sciureus*)." *Ethology* 112, no. 2 (February 2006): 105–15.

Strier, Karen B. "Growing Up in a Patrifocal Society: Sex Differences in the Spatial Relations of Immature Muriquis." Pp. 138–47 in *Juvenile Primates: Life History, Development, and Behavior*, edited by Michael E. Pereira and Lynn A. Fairbanks. New York: Oxford University Press, 1993.

Suarez, Scott A. "Phayre's Leaf Monkeys (*Trachypithecus phayrei*) as Seed Predators in the Phu Khieo Wildlife Sanctuary, Thailand." *American Journal of Physical Anthropology* 129, no. S42 (2006): 173.

Sugiyama, Yukimaru. "Tool-Use for Catching Ants by Chimpanzees at Bossou and Monts Nimba, West Africa." *Primates* 36, no. 2 (April 1995): 193–205.

Tardif, Suzette D., Conrad B. Richter, and Robert L. Carson. "Effects of Sibling-Rearing Experience on Future Reproductive Success in Two Species of Callitrichidae." *American Journal of Primatology* 6, no. 4 (1984): 377–80.

Taylor, Andrea B., Erin R. Vogel, and Nathaniel J. Dominy. "Food Material Properties and Mandibular Load Resistance Abilities in Large-Bodied Hominoids." *Journal of Human Evolution* 55, no. 4 (October 2008): 604–16.

Treves, Adrian. "The Influence of Group Size and Neighbors on Vigilance in Two Species of Arboreal Monkeys." *Behaviour* 135, no. 4 (June 1998): 453–81.

van Noordwijk, Maria A., Charlotte K. Hemelrijk, Louis A. Herremans, and Elisabeth H. M. Sterck. "Spatial Position and Behavioral Sex Differences in Juvenile Long-Tailed Macaques." Pp. 77–85 in *Juvenile Primates: Life History, Development, and Behavior*, edited by Michael E. Pereira and Lynn A. Fairbanks. New York: Oxford University Press, 1993.

van Schaik, Carel P., Robert O. Deaner, and Michelle Y. Merrill. "The Conditions for Tool Use in Primates: Implications for the Evolution of Material Culture." *Journal of Human Evolution* 36, no. 6 (June 1999): 719–41.

van Schaik, Carel P., L. Dunkel, Erin Vogel, and Karin Isler. "Energy Inputs, Not Skill Learning, Determine Age at Maturity in Orangutans and Other Primates." *American Journal of Physical Anthropology* 138, no. S48 (2009): 260 (abstract).

van Schaik, Carel P., and Maria A. van Noordwijk. "The Special Role of Male Cebus Monkeys in Predation Avoidance and Its Effect on Group Composition." *Behavioral Ecology and Xociobiology* 24, no. 5 (1989): 265–76.

Visalberghi, Elisabetta, and Elsa Addessi. "Food for Thought: Social Learning about Food in Feeding Capuchin Monkeys." Pp. 187–212 in *The Biology of Traditions: Models and Evidence*, edited by Dorothy M. Fragaszy and Susan Perry. Cambridge: Cambridge University Press, 2003.

Walters, Jeffrey R. "Transition to Adulthood." Pp. 358–69 in *Primate Societies*, edited by Barbara B. Smuts, Dorothy L. Cheney, Robert M. Seyfarth, Richard W. Wrangham, and Thomas T. Struhsaker. Chicago: Chicago University Press, 1987.

Watts, David P. "Observations on the Ontogeny of Feeding Behavior in Mountain Gorillas (*Gorilla gorilla beringei*)." *American Journal of Primatology* 8, no. 1 (1985): 1–10.

Whitehead, J. M. "Development of Feeding Selectivity in Mantled Howling Monkeys, *Alouatta palliata*." Pp. 105–18 in *Primate Ontogeny, Cognition, and Social Behavior*, edited by James G. Else and Phyllis C. Lee. Cambridge: Cambridge University Press, 1986.

Whiten, Andrew, Jane Goodall, William C. McGrew, Toshisada Nishida, Vernon Reynolds, Yukimaru Sugiyama, Caroline E. G. Tutin, Richard W. Wrangham, and Christophe Boesch. "Cultures in Chimpanzees." *Nature* 399, no. 6737 (1999): 682–5.

Williamson, Elizabeth A., and Anna T. C. Feistner. "Habituating Primates: Processes, Techniques, Variables and Ethics." Pp. 25–39 in *Field and Laboratory Methods in Primatology: A Practical Guide*, edited by Joanna M. Setchell and Deborah J. Curtis. Cambridge: Cambridge University Press, 2003.

CHAPTER FOURTEEN
LEARNING THE ENVIRONMENT

Rebecca K. Zarger

Excerpt from field notes, April 2001

I went with Anthony[1] (11 years old) and his cousin Edgar (6 years old) early in the morning right after breakfast, to check their bird traps. We wound our way through the secondary growth forest behind their house, the two boys running in between the small trees excitedly in their small black rubber boots, with me behind, trying to keep up. They were eager to find out if a bird had been caught overnight and to show me the traps they had built. There wasn't much of a trail, but after about five minutes, we came upon a little clearing in the bush with a small wooden crate-like object on the ground. Their uncle had been helping them build the traps in the bush. . . . The boys put a little bit of corn under the traps, which are constructed like little log cabins out of a very light-weight wood. A stick is propped gingerly by the opening, lifting up one end of the box. When the bird walks inside to eat, the box falls down, trapping it. I got to try one of the little birds they caught . . . *mukuy*, a pigeon-like bird that walks on the ground and not unsurprisingly, tastes like a very tiny chicken. Anthony was going to check these traps at least once a day while he had them, which was for a period of three weeks or so. After that, his father suggested he take a break from trapping birds, because it might be bad luck to be greedy and keep catching more birds in that spot.

Learning to trap birds, or other means of contributing to their household economies, punctuates everyday lived experiences for many children in rural areas around the world. How do children

341

learn such skills? More broadly, how do we become familiar with local ecologies and develop diverse subsistence strategies during childhood? Learning to make a living in any landscape characterizes our human evolutionary history and continues to define humanity in all its diversity and uniqueness as a species. Research into exactly how we go about learning the environment during childhood informs our understanding of a fundamental aspect of the human experience. This discussion begins with an excerpt from my field notes to illustrate several important aspects of what researchers have begun to document about the ways we learn environmental knowledge and practice. The chapter also provides a synthesis of relevant bodies of research. A brief glimpse at the ways early ethnographers attended to the roles the environment and culture play in socialization and child-rearing is a starting point for a historical topography of children's environmental knowledge within the discipline. This overview is followed by a closer look at cognitive and ethnobiological research on learning the environment in childhood—a subfield more recently concerned with documenting children's environmental knowledge. A brief synthesis of relevant theories and methods that are currently emerging across subfields in anthropology contextualizes the final section of the chapter, which focuses on Maya childhoods in southern Belize.

Although the anthropological literature exploring the ways children learn the environment is relatively small, work in this area can benefit from close attention to foundational research by Margaret Mead (*Coming of Age in Samoa*, 1928), Gregory Bateson (*Naven*, 1936), and many other early ethnographers who set the course for subsequent cross-cultural studies of child-rearing, epitomized by the Whitings' Six Cultures Study (Whiting 1963; Whiting and Whiting 1975; see also chapter 3, this volume). Scholars interested in the process of learning the environment have not typically incorporated insights from 20th-century ethnographies on children, child-rearing, and socialization, or the anthropology of childhood. The synopsis provided here of my research with Q'eqchi' Maya children and families in Belize over the last decade illustrates possibilities for bridging these research traditions with theoretical and methodological approaches from ethnobiology and environmental anthropology. The discussion also considers gaps in our understanding and suggests some areas for future inquiry.

How Do Children Learn about the Living World?

Several insights about learning the environment are captured in the short excerpt from my fieldwork that begins this chapter. Scholars working in a variety of disciplines (geography, anthropology, cross-cultural child development, ethnobiology, and human behavioral ecology) have suggested that learning the environment is intimately tied to both play and work (Bock and Johnson 2004; Katz 1989; Lancy 1996; Mead 1928; Tucker and Young 2005; Zarger 2002a). As they learned the intricacies of building bird traps, Anthony and his cousin Edgar consistently blurred the lines between playing at catching birds, playing in the "bush" or forest, and contributing valued meat to their households' next meal. Maya children often engage in the learning process as they go on group outings with other children; either siblings, peers, or cousins. This reflects cultural expectations for sibling caretaking (cf. Weisner and Gallimore 1977) and children contributing to their household economies, but it also has significant implications for our understanding of cultural transmission within this particular domain of knowledge and skills (Zarger 2002a; see also chapter 8, this volume). In addition, such activities tend to be opportunistic and may reflect adult work activities or requests from family members to find certain resources needed in the household. When asked to chop firewood or wash dishes, children in Maya communities in Belize find interesting fruits or berries to snack on along the way, or use wild foods as play objects, oscillating back and forth between working at the requested task and playing on their own or with their peers, a common pattern cross-culturally.

Like the two boys trapping birds, children often venture out in small groups of three to four, beyond the scope of the center of the village or yard, into forested areas, where they guide their own activities away from adult supervision, similar to the pattern observed by Bird and Bliege Bird (2005) for Martu children in Australia. However, adults do exert a distant influence on the process (see also chapter 7, this volume). As we can see in this scenario, the boys' uncle assisted them in building the traps, and Anthony's father decided when the take from their hunting activities had reached a reasonable limit. The two boys interact primarily with their uncle and father throughout the task, which reflects cultural constructions of gender circumscribing daily life and shaping learning contexts. Finally, it is important to note that other types of knowledge and skills, such as learning how to use medicinal plants for healing, would likely be learned in a different modality, as a specialized skill set passed on through more direct instruction, or "scaffolding,"[2] from parent, grandparent, or other relative to the child, requiring more time for mastery during adolescence (Zarger 2002a).

The ability to make generalizations about learning the environment during childhood is still overshadowed by what we have yet to discover. From a small but growing body of research in a variety of settings, it is possible to note several commonalities. However, it is important to note that this discussion draws these similarities together from fairly disparate and isolated bodies of research, influenced by my own research in Belize. Humans have developed many complex ways to represent and understand the biophysical world, a result of a dynamic interplay between the inner and outer worlds of cognition and behavior, perception and action (Atran and Medin 2008; Hutchins 1995; Ingold 2000). During childhood, much of our knowledge of the world we inhabit is learned, shaped by individual cognitive abilities, participation in daily cultural routines (cf. Lancy 1996), and immersion in a local landscape. The experiences that young children have as they come to know the biophysical environment—learning about the way different organisms look, smell, and taste and how they are valued or used by the people around them—are thought to stimulate their imagination and contribute in a profound way to their development (Kahn and Kellert 2002; Nabhan and Trimble 1994; Sobel 2002).

Learning environmental knowledge[3] usually occurs outside of formal school and takes place in the social reproduction of daily life, such as during work and play activities. Acquisition of widely shared knowledge, skills, and practices about local ecologies often relies on informal, experiential, and observational means of "cultural transmission" (Hewlett and Cavalli-Sforza 1986; MacDonald 2007; Ohmagari and Berkes 1997; Ruddle and Chesterfield 1977) or learning in cultural context (Lancy 1996; Stross 1970; Zarger 2002a). Around the globe, most children acquire expertise about their local environment very early in life, concurrent with language acquisition, and adult competency is often obtained by age 12–14 (Hunn 2002; Setalaphruk and Price 2007; Stross 1970; Zarger 2002b). During childhood, it appears that the interactive process of learning about the natural world is simultaneously and variably shaped by cultural expectations, socioeconomic strategies, gender roles, local ecologies, and learning contexts, but more needs to be known about how this takes place. All of these factors vary across individuals, cultural groups, and ecologies, contributing to a particular set of knowledge and skills that adults will need to make a living. Bock (2002) refers to this set of skills as a "basket of competencies," the "composition of which varies temporally and cross-culturally" (168). This is a useful metaphor, as it captures the complexities involved and the ways that skills and knowledge can be added or discarded throughout the life span or between generations.

Scholars and practitioners interested in environmental learning come from diverse research traditions and have used a range of methodological tools and techniques to answer fundamental questions in their research—a selection of those most relevant to this discussion are included here. Generally, research tends to focus inquiry at broad levels: How do children learn skills and knowledge about local environments? What do children know and how do they practice such knowledge? What are common patterns of knowledge and skill acquisition at different ages? Whom do children learn certain skills from—parents, grandparents, siblings, or others? In addition, researchers are now beginning to ask compelling questions which in turn relate to larger, cross-subdisciplinary concerns of the anthropology of childhood and interdisciplinary studies of learning in cultural context.

In order to describe general patterns from what are often very disparate bodies of literature and research traditions, it may be helpful to draw together theory and method to begin to conceptualize the process of learning the environment during childhood. This brief overview looks at three main tenets that are fundamental to constructing a useful theoretical and methodological framework for learning the environment: (1) attending to the ways sociocultural phenomena (such as formal education, gender, politics and power, contingent histories, and globalization) shape the learning process and drive variable distribution of environmental knowledge and practice (Zarger 2002a, 2002b; Zarger and Stepp 2004; Zent 2001); (2) incorporating insights from ethnographic studies of apprenticeship, guided participation, play, and what Ingold calls "enskillment" (Gaskins 1999; Ingold 2000; Lancy 1996; Lave and Wenger 1991; Rogoff 2003)[4] into existing ethnobiological/ethnoecological research on "transmission"; and (3) developing methods for studying the learning

Figure 14.1.   A young boy paddles a wooden dorry across the Moho River, Belize (R. Zarger photo)

process so as to acknowledge the co-construction of daily lives of both children and adults, attempting to triangulate quantitative and qualitative analysis with both cognitive and behavioral data, grounded in rich ethnographies of children's everyday activities. This chapter uses my research with Maya children in Belize to illustrate how these disparate bodies of work can speak to one another, with particular emphasis on the second tenet. Essentially, ethnographic research on situated learning and childhood can help identify the factors that affect learning processes and illustrate the effectiveness of methods such as systematic behavioral observation (particularly evident in research in human behavioral ecology and hunter-gatherer childhoods), while ethnobiology provides theories of content of environmental knowledge, general principles of environmental cognition, and methods suited to environmental data collection such as pile sorts, plant trails, and ethnobotanical collections. When combined, these theoretical and methodological tools allow research in this area to move in productive directions.

Anthropology, Children, and Environment: Early Studies

Although it was not typically singled out as a topic of concern, what is now termed "environmental knowledge" was often one facet among many aspects documented in early anthropological treatments of child-rearing practices and socialization. Descriptions of how children come to know local plants and animals, or the ways they contribute economically to their households, were a component of early studies but certainly not of primary concern (Bronfenbrenner 1977; Hewlett and Cavalli-Sforza 1986; Mead 1930; Ohmagari and Berkes 1997; Pearsall 1950; Ruddle and Chesterfield 1977; J. Whiting 1941).

In *Coming of Age in Samoa*, Mead (1928) writes that young girls' "knowledge of plants and trees is mainly a play one . . . the pandanus provides them with the seeds for necklaces. . . . But once they are regarded as individuals who can devote a long period of time to some consecutive activity . . . now they must learn to recognise these trees and plants for more serious purposes" (17). Mead, in this and other writings, describes the ways children engage in the daily activities that contribute to their development as adults in their societies, and learning about local flora, such as names, uses, and where to find them, is folded into this larger whole. Pearsall (1950) observed that Klamath boys begin to learn to use a bow and arrow when very young, hunting birds and squirrels near their camp. These sorts of observations are common in early ethnographies, often as a part of a chapter on "subsistence" for a given society. Such treatments are largely descriptive, and mention of the environment tends to emphasize modes of production and children learning the skills that they will need as adults.

Cross-Cultural Research on Children and Environment

The mid-20th century marks a transition toward systematic and comparative research on the process of socialization, emphasizing fine-grained behavioral observation, epitomized by the Whitings' Six Cultures Study (Whiting and Whiting 1975). The most significant contribution of the Whitings' legacy is a systematic demonstration of the way sociocultural environments influence children's behavior (Harkness 1992, 108). Studies carried out under this theoretical umbrella also documented cross-cultural patterns for the acquisition of a wide range of specialized skills or techniques such as cultivation, hunting practices, child care, fishing skills, dancing, and cooking (Harkness 1992; Hewlett and Cavalli-Sforza 1988; Jahoda and Lewis 1988; Lancy 1996).

Another relevant body of cross-cultural research includes studies based on the Human Relations Area Files (see also chapters 3, 7, and 15, this volume). In a seminal study, Barry, Child, and Bacon (1959) argue that patterns of socialization are determined by subsistence strategy: for example, comparing pastoralists' and hunter-gatherers' child-rearing practices. Hendrix (1985), who reanalyzed the initial data decades later, notes that critiques of the methods used by Barry and colleagues notwithstanding, the research demonstrates that "societies tend to train boys and girls differently, and that these differences and child training in general are related to the subsistence economy" (260). Welch (1980) also reexamined the role that "type of environment" (measured according to biome type[5]) might play in the relationship between subsistence practices and socialization patterns. He argues that environment type actually exerts *more* influence on child training processes than subsistence.[6] Welch's observation that the physical environment and modes of production exert

significant influence on the structure of society itself bears some similarities to Super and Harkness's (1986) "developmental niche" (discussed
below) although it accords more weight to the biophysical environment.
These studies demonstrate the contributions that children make to their
households through subsistence work and variability of adult expectations
across the categories of age, gender, and mode of production.

Cultural Transmission and the Environment

The 1970s witnessed a diversification in theoretical approaches to socialization and learning, and the term "cultural transmission" came into
use (Tindall 1976). Researchers began to view knowledge as distributed
among individuals in a society, subject to both conservative forces that
ensure continuity and innovation that brings change (see chapter 2, this
volume), and the term was widely applied in ethnographies of education, schooling, and socialization in non-Western contexts. Hewlett and
Cavalli-Sforza's (1986) study of cultural transmission among the Aka
emphasized the acquisition of skills to determine whether transmission
occurs in a "horizontal" (within one generation) or "vertical" (between
generations) pattern by tracking competency across individuals of differing ages (923). Exactly *how* the process of learning occurs was not a
significant part of this or other cultural transmission studies, where the
emphasis is on *what* knowledge or skills individuals can perform.

The work of Mead and other early ethnographers has informed my
research in Belize in several ways, including the need to contextualize
environment with myriad other aspects of social life, such as kinship and
religion, and the value of rich description of activities. Research on child-
rearing is critical to building new theories of learning the environment, as
it has provided empirical insights into the ways parental expectations and
adult roles shape the process. I apply this to my work through interviews
with parents about what children should know about "how to work" by
the time they are adults (Zarger 2002b). Investigations of cultural transmission are also theoretically and methodologically influential for my
research in Belize, as I sort out what individuals know, whom they learn
it from, and at what ages, and to acknowledge the importance of "skills"
in addition to "knowledge" competencies. However, these research traditions provide less guidance on what goes on inside individuals' "heads," or

whether children and adults conceptualize nature in differing ways. Methodologies do not emphasize the content of environmental knowledge in a systematic way. These are tools that ethnobiology and environmental anthropology can contribute.

Knowing Nature: Ethnobiology and Cognitive Approaches to Learning the Environment during Childhood

Environmental anthropology focuses on human-environment relationships, but children, learning, and cultural transmission have been largely ignored (Ohmagari and Berkes 1997; Ruddle 1993). Admittedly, documenting changes in environmental knowledge and skills over time, from generation to generation, is an extremely difficult task. Research timeframes are limited when compared to the dynamic and long-term processes of learning, practicing, and transforming information. A handful of foundational studies defied this trend, including research on traditional food procurement in the Orinoco Delta, Venezuela (Ruddle and Chesterfield 1977) and acquisition of botanical terminology by Tzeltal Maya children (Stross 1969). Hewlett and Cavalli-Sforza's (1986) research with Aka in Africa and Ohmagari and Berkes's (1997) work with Cree women's bush skills quantified cultural transmission by recording individual competency with a specified set of skills. For example, in the case of Cree women, this involved fur preparation, making clothing, or hunting, and for the Aka, making a crossbow and finding honey or vine water. Incorporation of a "skills" component reflects what we know about acquiring expertise about the environment: cross-culturally, learning and doing are typically inseparable. This is an important contribution, but what is not considered is how knowledge and skills are distributed across social groups. Ethnobiological approaches are critical to this effort.

Ethnoscience and Studies of Classification

Research conducted in the field of ethnobiology, or ethnoecology,[7] is an interdisciplinary endeavor with roots in systematic and economic botany, cognitive anthropology, and ethnoscience that has become increasingly systematic and comprehensive since its inception in the 1950s.[8] The goal of "ethnoscience" of the mid-20th century was to develop a systematic way of gaining insight into the cognitive worlds of people from other cultures, thereby also better understanding their behavior and more objectively representing their culture (D'Andrade 1995; Fowler 1977). By the 1990s, over 300 ethnobiological studies from around the world were included in a comparative study of human universals in classifying plants and animals (Berlin 1992). Initially, researchers were interested in documenting the systematicity of what later came to be termed "indigenous knowledge systems," attempting to demonstrate the "fit" between the Linnaean system of classifying natural kinds (itself an ethnobiological system) and the ways indigenous peoples categorized the natural world (Ellen and Harris 2000, 14). Eventually, a focus on acquisition of ethnoecological knowledge and dynamic changes in knowledge over time (Ellen and Harris 2000; Zent 1999, 2001) emerged during the last decade, documenting the extensive knowledge of the biophysical environment which children in many subsistence-based societies share (Hunn 2002; Ross 2002a, 2002b; Zarger 2002a, 2002b).

Initially, research on children in ethnobiology was concerned with confronting generalizations made as a result of dozens of studies of how children categorize natural kinds conducted in the United States with English-speaking populations by developmental psychologists and cognitive scientists (Carey 1985; Johnson and Mervis 1997; Waxman 1999). Very few of these studies employ a cross-cultural perspective, and when they do, industrialized societies are overrepresented (Hewlett and Lamb 2005, 5). However, anthropologists and psychologists have carried out fieldwork with three ethnic groups in the Petén, Guatemala, and Menominee (American Indians) and other "majority culture" social groups in rural Michigan, among other places (Atran 1990; Medin and Atran 1999; Waxman, Medin, and Ross 2007).[9] Significant findings relevant to the present discussion include: the relationships between the ways novices and experts categorize natural kinds such as trees and fish (Medin et al. 1997; Medin et al. 2006); the ways children's reasoning about natural kinds is affected by cultural beliefs; and differences between urban and rural children's inductive reasoning about animal properties (Waxman et al. 2007). As Atran and Medin (2008) note about their cross-cultural test to Carey's (1985) argument that children (in the United States) tend to anthropomorphize animals: "Comparative studies reveal components of biological cognition that vary systematically as a function of cultural milieu and input conditions (intimacy of contact with nature)" (138). Atran and Medin found that anthropocentric reasoning among children was the exception, not the norm, contrary to what Carey earlier proposed (and was largely accepted by developmental psychology) as a universal human characteristic.

As these studies show, a better understanding of development of expertise during childhood will provide a more complete picture of how humans categorize living things. Furthermore, describing the ways we go about learning about the world around us will assist with creating a more nuanced picture of how humans-in-environment think and act, and how this is continually renegotiated by individuals and subsequent generations as they confront changing realities.

Ethnobiological Studies of Children's Environmental Knowledge Acquisition

A small but growing group of researchers in the field of ethnobiology are investigating children's environmental knowledge (see, e.g., Cruz Garcia 2006; Hunn 2002, 2008; Ross 2002a, 2002b; Setalaphruk and Price 2007; Wyndham 2002; Zarger 2002a; Zarger and Stepp 2004; Zent 1999, 2001; Zent and Zent 2004). However, the focus of the majority of this research is not on the *process* of learning as much as documenting the astounding depth of knowledge children have about the biophysical world in non-Western contexts (Hunn 2002) or investigating changes in knowledge over time for the same populations through interviews with adults of differing generations (Ross 2002a, 2002b). These studies benefit from being able to build on past scholarship about the way humans classify, think about, and name natural kinds to begin investigating knowledge in transition and transformation. In order to better understand how children learn the environment, a focus on process, in addition to content, is essential (Zarger 2002a). Integrating method and theory from the anthropology of childhood and studies of learning in cultural context with ethnobiological theories and methods is one way to accomplish this.

Typical methods used in ethnobiology to capture children's environmental knowledge have tended to focus on botanical knowledge variation, using systematic research methods such as consensus analysis (Romney,

Weller, and Batchelder 1986), forest plot interviews (Zent 1999), freelisting and sorting and listing plants or animals (Reyes-García et al. 2007), pile sorts (Zarger 2002b), identifying dried specimens and plant trails (Collins 2001; Hunn 2002, 2008; Wyndham 2004; Zarger 2002b; Zarger and Stepp 2004). Adapting these methods to the unique demands of working with children is sometimes a challenge, but I found in my research that children enjoy pile sorting, plant trails, and drawing activities because they are able to display their knowledge and "teach" the researcher at the same time. Recent studies of ethnobotanical knowledge acquisition employ a varying degree of ethnographic, participant-observation grounded perspectives into their analyses, which are often quantitative measures of knowledge of plant names and uses. Many studies are not as concerned with documenting the behavioral or social contexts of knowledge use and practice (Reyes-García et al. 2007), but others do incorporate this element, recognizing the problems that arise from abstracting knowledge from practice and the context in which it is used (Wyndham 2004; Zarger 2002a).

It is possible to make a few generalizations across studies of learning ethnobiology, but further exploration of them will strengthen the emerging body of work. Contributing to our understanding of developmental patterns in childhood, there appear to be critical time periods for children's knowledge acquisition (ages 5–9) (Zarger 2002b). Furthermore, children exhibit a precocious ability to identify hundreds of species of local flora by middle childhood (Hunn 2002). We also know that children and adults conceptualize and experience the world in different ways, perhaps constituting a "culture of childhood" (Hewlett and Lamb 2005, 18). Support for this notion is found in research that demonstrates that children and adults differ in how they conceptualize common food items known as children's wild "snack foods" (Zarger 2002a). Another important thread focuses on which plants children might learn first, and why, as well as differences in how older and younger children categorize plants and animals. For example, dangerous plants may be more culturally salient and learned first (Wyndham 2004). Older children appear to categorize plants based on utility while younger children focus on morphology, suggesting that cultural information (plant uses) may be layered into biological affordances for distinguishing living kinds from one another (Zarger 2002a). Understanding general patterns for botanical knowledge acquisition will then allow future research to focus on variability across social categories of difference, for example. With regards to methodology, it may be useful to distinguish between "practical" knowledge (skills) and "theoretical" knowledge when studying cultural transmission of ethnobotanical knowledge (Reyes-García et al. 2007). Ultimately, ethnobiology contributes precise methods for documenting distribution and conceptualization of knowledge across individuals, and applying these methods to ethnographically grounded work with children and parents is just beginning. When combined with studies of learning in context, a more holistic picture of learning the environment can emerge; a preliminary outline of the edges of that picture is described in the following section.

Conceptualizing the Process of Learning the Environment: Bringing the Pieces Together

Knowledge such as where to find and trap birds, catch small fish, or locate a tasty snack from a wild plant shape guide children's daily experiences in a particular locale, accumulating over time to sustain a varied and practical understanding of how to "make a living" in that environment. Katz (2004) describes children's learning in the Sudan as "deep, thick, multiple connections between what children [in Howa] did, knew and needed to know [that] resulted in quite elaborate, comprehensive, and workable bodies of knowledge shared more or less by all children ten years and older" (119). By framing environmental knowledge this way, it becomes much more than knowledge; it is also the behaviors associated with this knowledge—the practical "skills" associated with expertise.

Building on Stross (1973), and similar to Katz (2004), I propose a model (Zarger 2002a) of learning environmental knowledge and skills that can be conceptualized as several overlapping spheres of interaction which move through a number of transitions during development: the individual child, cultural routines of daily life, parental and cultural beliefs and expectations, socioeconomic and subsistence strategies, and the local biophysical environment itself. As previously noted, children learn through experience and observation of others. Siblings, cousins, parents, and grandparents are all involved in the informal education of a child into his or her local landscapes. Considering perspectives of children and the adolescents and adults in their lives is critical to creating a synthetic model of learning the environment.

Overwhelming evidence suggests that learning processes in "traditional education systems" are typically experiential or participatory in nature. In some societies, knowledge is transmitted largely through parent-child interaction, as is the case with subsistence knowledge in the Orinoco Delta (Ruddle and Chesterfield 1977) or weaving in Zinacantan (Greenfield, Maynard, and Childs 2000). In other societies, children acquire the bulk of their knowledge through independent observation, participation, or play (Lancy 1996; Zarger 2002a). Acquisition of cultural knowledge and skills, or more broadly socialization, has come to be viewed as an active process—a collaboration between individuals involved in teaching and learning (Rogoff 1990).

Several in-depth, cross-cultural studies of child development that bear out this view of teaching and learning have recently been conducted in the Maya region. These include studies in Tzotzil and Yucatec communities in Mexico (Gaskins 1999; Greenfield et al. 2000) and in Q'eqchi' communities in Belize (Zarger 2002b) which suggest that children guide their own socialization through play, work, and sibling teaching. Informal learning[10] and learning through apprenticeship are also important to building a model of childhood learning of environmental knowledge (Gaskins 1999; Lave and Wenger 1991; Maynard 2002; Rogoff 1990). Research on children's play and work activities illustrates that these activities are critical in the socialization process (Lancy 1996). Daily work activities and cultural expectations overlay a universal human affinity for learning about and categorizing natural kinds (Atran and Medin 2008; Berlin 1992). Parents and researchers agree that children learn environmental knowledge and practice primarily through experience and observation of others (MacDonald 2007; Zarger 2002b). One could argue that siblings, cousins, parents, and grandparents are all "teachers," but learning takes place in the production of daily life.

Although contributions from studies of socialization and child-rearing and ethnobiology are significant for conceptualizing the learning process, another area of research that contributes to a synthesis of theories and methods is human behavioral ecology. This research tradition links cultural and biological aspects of learning the environment through systematic behavioral observation of children's daily activities, contributing to a grow-ing body of literature on hunter-gatherer childhoods in particular ecologies (Hewlett and Lamb 2005; Kramer 2005). Although many aspects remain the same, childhood in economies dominated by hunting and gathering differs in some significant ways from childhood in farm-based economies. For example, food sharing skills and ethics that are highly valued for adults are instantiated in children's play. Kamei (2005) vividly describes how a young Baka boy divided up a spider that he shot as "game" during play into carefully dissected parts for three participants, making it "clear that children exactly recognize adult food-sharing activities and mimic them in their play" (354). In the Okavango Delta, Bock and Johnson (2004) found that households involved in agriculture require more work and less play from children than in foraging or herding ecologies, borne out with their study in a diverse community that encompassed all of these activities (73). All of this work builds on the legacy of cross-cultural studies while inte-grating evolutionary and ecological frameworks and illustrates the pivotal role that specific ecologies play in the learning process. Ethnobiological research could benefit from human behavioral ecology's close attention to the effects that diverse ecologies have on the learning process as well as the need to systematically document daily activities to complement studies of knowledge distribution.

Perhaps one of the most interesting things about the contributions of diverse research traditions across anthropology is the remarkable degree of overlap in broad findings, even given fairly disparate theoretical frames and methods. The fact that generalizations about how children learn the environment are possible speaks to the potential for creating better models of acquisition processes in the future.

Pattern and Process: Learning the Environment during Childhood in Southern Belize

In order to provide a fine-grained vantage point on the process of learn-ing the environment, this section turns to Maya communities in southern Belize, based on ethnographic research I have carried out there over the last decade, including my dissertation research over a period of 18 months and subsequent shorter periods of fieldwork in 2004–2007 and 2009. The village of San Miguel (525 Q'eqchi' and Mopan Maya residents), where the majority of the data were collected, is situated on the eastern slopes of the Maya Mountains, in southern Belize on acres of *milpa* farmlands and secondary forest that produce a diversity of crops and wild plants to meet many of the basic food needs of the community. However, Q'eqchi' have participated in the global economy for at least 200 years in a variety of ways, in a "mosaic" of livelihood strategies (Wilk 1997; Zarger 2009). The most important staple food crop is corn, and cultural identity is strongly tied to its cultivation, preparation, and consumption (Wilk 1997). The landscape is dominated by tropical lowland broadleaf forest, punctuated by craggy limestone hills that jut up out of the flat coastal plain that stretches to the Bay of Honduras on the coast. English is the official language of Belize and used in school settings, and Belizean Creole English is also often spoken. Pressing concerns for many Maya over the last three decades include struggles over land tenure, economic development, indigenous rights, education, and access to health care in the face of globalizing economies and in negotiation with competing interests such as conservation, oil exploration, and extractive timber industries.

It is evident from the study in Belize that children begin to learn subsistence knowledge within the context of their experiences at home, from the time they are infants, concurrent with language acquisition. Brian Stross found a similar pattern in his research on language acquisition in Tzeltal Maya families (Stross 1969, 1973). By age 4, children can identify many of the most common fruits and herbs and will follow older siblings in completing routine subsistence-related tasks. The important transition that occurs between the ages of 5 and 7, when children are expected to begin taking on an increasing amount of work responsibility, also occurs for environmental knowledge (Zarger 2002a, 2002b). The same timeframe and transition have been reported in other studies of botanical knowledge acquisition (Hunn 2002; Stross 1973; Zent and Zent 2004) as well as in studies of subsistence competencies (Bock 2002). Knowledge gradually and steadily increases until early adolescence, when the bulk of environmental knowledge appears to be in place, and individuals take on adult work responsibilities. Child-guided home garden interviews suggest that by the time children are 9 years old, they know 85 percent of Q'eqchi' names for plants in their own home gardens and 50 percent of plants elsewhere (Zarger 2002b). This is similar to the pattern that Hewlett and Cavalli-Sforza (1986) found with Aka children, who mastered most required skills by age 10. A "plant trail" interview with 29 children, who were asked to identify names and uses of over 100 local plants, indicate a noticeable transition that occurs in plant knowledge between the ages of 4 and 7 (Zarger 2002a). This affirms the findings of Rogoff and colleagues (1975), that a significant "jump" in knowledge occurs between age 4 or 5 to age 7, followed by an intense period of acquisition that begins to slow down by the time children move into early adolescence, age 10–12, at which point they gain competency in skills similar to adults.

Local ecologies and cultural landscapes feature prominently as tangible actors in learning the environment during childhood. I found that forested areas around the village provide another rich landscape in which children spend time. Play and peer groups are often "courtyard cousins," as children are sent on errands to collect firewood or wild food resources like mushrooms. As illustrated at the opening of the chapter, young boys trap birds in the forest, providing a supplement to the protein intake of their families. Boys also become quite proficient with homemade slingshots used to stun edible birds out of high branches.

Girls usually do not venture into the forest by themselves, preferring to be accompanied by a male brother or cousin, reflecting distinct gender role socialization patterns (see also chapter 11, this volume) also observed in other Maya communities (Gaskins 1999). I also observed that assuming responsibilities for tasks happens sooner for girls than for boys. While girls 9–12 years old are learning their household responsibilities, boys the same age are still engaged in activities that are closer to play than work, such as trapping birds, swimming in the river, or fishing. This is a generalized pattern cross-culturally (Bock 2002; Lancy 1996).

Siblings pass along extensive information to one another about where to find certain plants and their uses, and how to harvest or cultivate them. Children usually spend a good portion of each day solely in the company of brothers, sisters, and cousins, carrying out daily activities such as household chores, looking for edible snack foods (that most adults might consider inedible), bathing, and playing. Sibling caretaking is a phenomenon that occurs in societies throughout the globe, particularly in non-Western contexts (Weisner and Gallimore 1977), and Q'eqchi' in Belize are no exception. This has important implications for studies of environmental knowledge change.

Based on the primacy of sibling and cousin relationships in the study site, it is likely that transmission of environmental knowledge may depend on sibling or peer teaching, particularly during early childhood. Adults do not normally accompany children on trips to the forested areas near the village or home gardens to collect firewood, herbs, or wild foods. On these trips, children begin to learn to identify useful plants. A mother may give verbal instructions to two or three of her children who are between the ages of 8 and 10. But younger children typically follow along, and toddlers may be picked up and put astride a hip, going along for the adventure as well. A 1-year-old may begin to cry when seeing siblings leaving the house en masse, and for this reason babies are taken along so that the mother and young women may complete their work with fewer distractions.

"Teachers" of particular domains of environmental knowledge and practice appear to vary based on the type of skill in question. Adults are primary teachers on trips to the family farm, which are farther away than younger children may travel on their own (outside the village). In interviews conducted with 44 adults on this topic, almost everyone interviewed stated that they learned plants in the forest by accompanying their mothers and/or fathers to the farm. Grandparents assist with the process of socialization as well. Osborn (1982) notes that Maya grandparents are custodians of agricultural knowledge. Elders are entrusted with remembering who has rights to what land, based on the usufruct system (38). Grandparents, particularly grandmothers, may look after children when their parents are absent for some reason. They may have more nonwork time, and often this is spent engaged with their youngest grandchildren or assisting their daughters or daughters-in-law.

Discussion

The global environmental crisis, including deforestation, climate change, and changing resource use strategies, is affecting human cultures in profound ways. The transmission and acquisition of ethnoecological knowledge may be undergoing dynamic shifts as resource use strategies are also changing, concurrent with globalization. However, these changes are not necessarily even across complex geographies: time-series research with Tzeltal Maya children in Chiapas demonstrates remarkable persistence

359

in children's botanical knowledge across three decades in one community (Zarger and Stepp 2004). Continued alterations to the source of that knowledge—the environment itself—provide challenges for scholars, scientists, and communities interested in the persistence of environmental knowledge. For this reason, more research needs to be conducted on the processes contributing to environmental knowledge continuity and change (Zent 1999, 2001).

Beyond the questions researchers have focused on with regards to what children know and how they learn it, future studies can more fully address the following questions: What do intracultural and intercultural variabilities in knowledge and skills suggest about how social networks and social groups structure learning opportunities during childhood? What may be considered developmental components of the learning process, and what aspects are profoundly shaped by cultural context? How does social and cultural change—such as the complex set of relations often glossed as "globalization"—affect what children know about local ecologies? Research has begun to address these questions, but systematic inquiry would contribute to an emerging tradition.

We know that many complex factors shape the process of learning the environment, in southern Belize as well as in most other places around the world. Globalization in the specific form of conservation and development interventions guides childhood experiences (Katz 2004). In Maya communities in Belize, changing trends in formal schooling, such as mandatory attendance in primary school and more young people pursuing tertiary degrees, are fundamentally impacting how and what children are learning about local landscapes and cultural practices (Zarger 2009). However, this is certainly not a simple matter of exchanging one skill set for another, as an interview in 2009 with Anthony, whose story begins this chapter, illustrates. Anthony is now 19 and recently graduated from high school, a distinction that a decade ago was fairly rare in his community. When I spoke with him about his search for a job and whether he might consider becoming a farmer if he did not find one, he said he was thinking of asking his grandfather about planting corn. Although this wasn't the path he saw for himself when he got his diploma, it was something he now saw value in for many reasons well beyond his control, such as a difficult global economy. I learned a few weeks later that he had accepted a position as a primary school teacher, the job he really wanted.

I wondered if he would still want to cut a plot for his own farm in the fall and whether he would ever teach his own son to trap birds in the nearby woods. Somehow, I think he will.

Acknowledgments

Many people in many places contributed in important ways to the ideas expressed in this chapter, yet any errors are, of course, my own. In particular, I would like to thank Tom Pluckhahn, Don Owen Lewis, the Bardalez family, Rick Wilk, Froyla Tzalam, my family, and many, many families in San Miguel, Big Falls, and Santa Cruz who shared their lives, thoughts, and caldo with me over the last 10 years. Support for this research came from the Inter-American Foundation, Spencer Foundation, Florida International University, the University of South Florida Humanities Institute, and the National Science Foundation (HSD 0827275), with institutional support from the Belize Forest Department and the Belize National Institute of Culture and History (including the Institute for Social and Cultural Research and the Institute of Archaeology).

Notes

1. Throughout this chapter, names of individuals have been changed in order to respect their anonymity.

2. For an overview of the role of scaffolding in socialization, see Gauvain (2005). For an interesting application of theories of scaffolding and "bodily enculturation," see Downey (2008).

3. Definitions of environmental knowledge vary, but scholars generally agree that throughout time, human communities have developed systematic, widely shared, and culturally significant knowledge and practice about the living world in order to make a living in it (Berlin 1992). It is sometimes glossed as "traditional ecological knowledge," or "TEK," but due to the problems and politics of the term *traditional*, its use is avoided here. Berkes (1993) refers to environmental knowledge as, "a cumulative body of knowledge and beliefs, transmitted from one generation to the next, about the relationship of living beings with one another and with their environment" (3).

4. This body of work draws from many theoretical frameworks, but perhaps the most central is the work of Bourdieu and Vygotsky in the formulation of notions of socialization and social reproduction.

5. Welch's study assessed two independent variables in his analysis. One was subsistence type, including societies that rely primarily on either hunting, gathering, fishing, herding, horticulture, or agriculture. The other variable, which he terms "environment type," in fact refers to biomes such as desert, tundra, subtropical bush, temperate grasslands, northern coniferous forests, temperate woodlands, tropical grasslands, and tropical rain forests (Welch 1980, 237).

6. Echoing a similar trend in the subfield of ecological anthropology at the time, Welch (1980) borrows a conceptual device from ecology, observing, "we need to consider that the ecological niche into which a society fits influences the development of all social processes within the society" (241). This can be framed as the application of an approach to understanding human-environment relations that reflects the influence of Julian Steward's (1955) cultural ecology.

7. Ethnoecology as a term was first proposed by anthropologists Charles Frake (1962) and Harold Conklin (1969) and combines theories in linguistics, systematic biology, and psychology to develop a better way to understand a particular cultural group's perceptions and classifications of the natural world.

8. Due to the eclectic nature of the field itself, there is not necessarily a consensus on definitions of *ethnoecology*, and it is at times used interchangeably with *ethnobiology*. However, most researchers define it as the study of the perceptions, beliefs, values, and skills that a group of people has about their local environment. For varying definitions and early applications of the term, see Nazarea (1999), Conklin (1969), Fowler (1977), and Hunn (1989). In practical use, ethnoecology tends to be more encompassing and includes ecological relationships and information about local understandings of climate, landscape change, or navigational techniques, whereas ethnobiology typically refers to studies that are more squarely focused on perceptions and categorization of fauna and flora.

9. For a comprehensive treatment of the suite of studies mentioned briefly here, see Atran and Medin (2008).

10. Informal learning refers to learning that is actually a continuum of observational learning, verbal and bodily instruction, imitation, and guided participation (Greenfield and Lave 1982; Pelisser 1991).

Bibliography

Atran, Scott. *Cognitive Foundations of Natural History: Towards an Anthropology of Science*. Cambridge: Cambridge University Press, 1990.

Atran, Scott, and Douglas L. Medin. *The Native Mind and the Cultural Construction of Nature*. Cambridge: MIT Press, 2008.

Barry, Herbert, III, Irvin Child, and Margaret K. Bacon. "Relation of Child Training to Subsistence Economy." *American Anthropologist* 61, no. 1 (February 1959): 51–63.

Bateson, Gregory. *Naven: A Survey of the Problems Suggested by a Composite Picture of the Culture of a New Guinea Tribe Drawn from Three Points of View*. Stanford, Calif.: Stanford University Press, 1936.

Berkes, Fikret. "Traditional Environmental Knowledge in Perspective." Pp. 1–10 in *Traditional Ecological Knowledge: Concepts and Cases*, edited by Julian T. Inglis. Ottawa: International Development Research Center, Canadian Museum of Nature, 1993.

Berlin, O. Bert. *Ethnobiological Classification: Principles of Categorization of Plants and Animals in Traditional Societies*. Princeton, N.J.: Princeton University Press, 1992.

Bird, Douglas, and Rebecca Bliege Bird. "Martu Children's Hunting Strategies in the Western Desert, Australia." Pp. 129–46 in *Hunter-Gatherer Childhoods: Evolutionary, Developmental, and Cultural Perspectives*, edited by Barry S. Hewlett and Michael E. Lamb. New Brunswick, N.J.: Aldine Transaction, 2005.

Bock, John. "Learning, Life History, and Productivity." *Human Nature* 13, no. 2 (June 2002): 161–97.

Bock, John, and Sara E. Johnson. "Play and Subsistence Ecology among the Okavango Delta Peoples of Botswana." *Human Nature* 15, no. 1 (March 2004): 63–81.

Bronfenbrenner, Urie. "Toward an Experimental Ecology of Human Development." *American Psychologist* 32, no. 7 (1977): 513–31.

Carey, Susan. *Conceptual Change in Childhood*. Cambridge: MIT Press, 1985.

Collins, Darron Asher. "From Woods to Weeds: Cultural and Ecological Transformations in Alta Verapaz, Guatemala." Doctoral dissertation, Tulane University, 2001.

Conklin, Harold C. "An Ethnoecological Approach to Shifting Agriculture." Pp. 221–33. in *Environment and Cultural Behavior: Ecological Studies in Cultural Anthropology*, edited by Andrew P. Vayda. Garden City, N.Y.: Natural History, 1969.

Cruz Garcia, Gisella. "The Mother-Child Nexus. Knowledge and Valuation of Wild Food Plants in Wayanad, Western Ghats, India." *Journal of Ethnobiology and Ethnomedicine* 2 (September 2006): 39.

D'Andrade, Roy. *The Development of Cognitive Anthropology*. Cambridge: Cambridge University Press, 1995.

Downey, Greg. "Scaffolding Imitation in Capoeira: Physical Education and Enculturation in an Afro-Brazilian Art." *American Anthropologist* 110, no. 2 (June 2008): 204–13.

Ellen, Roy, and Holly Harris. "Introduction." Pp. 1–24 in *Indigenous Environmental Knowledge and Its Transformations*, edited by Roy Ellen, Peter Parkes, and Alan Bicker. London: Gordon and Breach, 2000.

Fowler, Catherine S. "Ethnoecology." Pp. 13–16 in *Ecological Anthropology*, edited by Donald L. Hardesty. New York: Wiley, 1977.

Frake, Charles O. "Cultural Ecology and Ethnography." *American Anthropologist* 63, no. 1 (1962): 113–32.

Gaskins, Suzanne. "Play in Perspective: Yucatec Mayan Children's Daily Lives." Paper presented at the annual meeting of the American Anthropological Association, Chicago, Illinois, 1999.

Gauvain, Mary. "Scaffolding in Socialization." *New Ideas in Psychology* 23, no. 3 (December 2005): 129–39.

Greenfield, Patricia, and Jean Lave. "Cognitive Aspects of Informal Education." Pp. 181–207 in *Cultural Perspectives on Child Development*, edited by Daniel A. Wagner and Harold W. Stevenson. San Francisco: W. H. Freeman, 1982.

Greenfield, Patricia M., Ashley E. Maynard, and Carla P. Childs. "History, Culture, Learning, and Development." *Cross-Cultural Research* 34, no. 4 (November 2000): 351–74.

Hansen, Judith Friedman. *Sociocultural Perspectives on Human Learning*. Prospect Heights, Ill.: Waveland, 1979.

Harkness, Sara. "Human Development in Psychological Anthropology." Pp. 102–24 in *New Directions in Psychological Anthropology*, edited by Theodore Schwartz, Geoffrey M. White, and Catherine A. Lutz. Cambridge: Cambridge University Press, 1992.

Hendrix, Lewellyn. "Economy and Child Training Reexamined." *Ethos* 13, no. 3 (Autumn 1985): 246–61.

Hewlett, Barry S., and Luca L. Cavalli-Sforza. "Cultural Transmission among Aka Pygmies." *American Anthropologist* 88, no. 4 (December 1988): 922–34.

Hewlett, Barry S., and Michael E. Lamb. "Emerging Issues in the Study of Hunter-Gatherer Children." Pp. 3–18 in *Hunter-Gatherer Childhoods: Evolutionary, Developmental, and Cultural Perspectives*, edited by Barry S. Hewlett and Michael E. Lamb. New Brunswick, N.J.: Aldine Transaction, 2005.

Hunn, Eugene. "Ethnoecology: The Relevance of Cognitive Anthropology for Human Ecology." Pp. 143–160 in *The Relevance of Culture*, edited by Morris Freilich. New York: Bergin and Garvey, 1989.

————. "Evidence for the Precocious Acquisition of Plant Knowledge by Zapotec Children." Pp. 604–13 in *Ethnobiology and Biocultural Diversity*, edited by John R. Stepp, Felice S. Wyndham, and Rebecca K. Zarger. Athens: University of Georgia Press, 2002.

————. *A Zapotec Natural History: Trees, Herbs, and Flowers, Birds, Beasts, and Bugs in the Life of San Juan Gbee*. Tucson: University of Arizona Press, 2008.

Hutchins, Edwin. *Cognition in the Wild*. Cambridge, Mass.: MIT Press, 1995.

Ingold, Tim. *The Perception of the Environment: Essays on Livelihood, Dwelling, and Skill*. New York: Routledge, 2000.

Jahoda, Gustav, and Ioan M. Lewis. "Child Development in Psychology and Anthropology." Pp. 1–34 in *Acquiring Culture: Cross-Cultural Studies in Child Development*, edited by Gustav Jahoda and Ioan M. Lewis. London: Croom Helm, 1988.

Johnson, Kathy E., and Carolyn B. Mervis. "Effects of Varying Levels of Expertise on the Basic Level of Categorization." *Journal of Experimental Psychology* 126, no. 3 (1997): 248–77.

Kahn, Peter H., and Stephen R. Kellert. *Children and Nature: Psychological, Sociocultural, and Evolutionary Investigations*. Cambridge, Mass.: MIT Press, 2002.

Kamei, Nobutaka. "Play among Baka Children in Cameroon." Pp. 343–62 in *Hunter-Gatherer Childhoods: Evolutionary, Developmental, and Cultural Perspectives*, edited by Barry S. Hewlett and Michael E. Lamb. New Brunswick, N.J.: Aldine Transaction, 2005.

Katz, Cindi. "Herders, Gatherers, and Foragers: The Emerging Botanies of Children in Rural Sudan." *Children's Environments Quarterly* 6, no. 1 (1989): 46–53.

————. *Growing Up Global: Economic Restructuring and Children's Everyday Lives*. Minneapolis: University of Minnesota Press, 2004.

Kramer, Karen. *Maya Children: Helpers at the Farm*. Cambridge, Mass.: Harvard University Press, 2005.

Lancy, David F. *Playing on the Mother-Ground: Cultural Routines for Children's Development*. New York: Guilford, 1996.

Lave, Jean. "The Culture of Acquisition and the Practice of Understanding." Pp. 17–37 in *Situated Cognition: Social Semiotic and Psychological Perspectives*, edited by David Kirshner and James A. Whitson. Mahwah, N.J.: Erlbaum, 1997.

Lave, Jean, and Etienne Wenger. *Situated Learning: Legitimate Peripheral Participation*. New York: Cambridge University Press, 1991.

MacDonald, Katharine. "Cross-Cultural Comparison of Learning in Human Hunting: Implications for Life History Evolution." *Human Nature* 18, no. 4 (December 2007): 386–402.

Maynard, Ashley. "Cultural Teaching: The Development of Teaching Skills in Maya Sibling Interactions." *Child Development* 73, no. 3 (2002): 969–82.

Mead, Margaret. *Coming of Age in Samoa*. New York: New American Library, 1928.

———. *Growing Up in New Guinea: A Comparative Study of Primitive Education*. New York: Morrow, 1930.

Medin, Douglas L., and Scott Atran. "The Native Mind: Biological Categorization and Reasoning in Development and across Cultures." *Psychological Review* 111, no. 4 (2004): 960–83.

———, eds. *Folkbiology*. Cambridge, Mass.: MIT Press, 1999.

Medin, Douglas L., Elizabeth B. Lynch, John D. Coley, and Scott Atran. "Categorization and Reasoning among Tree Experts: Do All Roads Lead to Rome?" *Cognitive Psychology* 32, no. 1 (February 1997): 49–96.

Medin, Douglas L., and Lance J. Rips. "Concepts and Categories: Memory, Meaning, and Metaphysics." Pp. 37–72 in *The Cambridge Handbook of Thinking and Reasoning*, edited by Keith J. Holyoak and Robert G. Morrison. Cambridge: Cambridge University Press, 2005.

Nabhan, Gary Paul, and Stephen Trimble. *The Geography of Childhood: Why Children Need Wild Places*. Boston: Beacon, 1994.

Nazarea, Virginia D. *Ethnoecology: Situated Knowledge/Located Lives*. Tucson: University of Arizona Press, 1999.

Ohmagari, Kayo, and Fikret Berkes. "Transmission of Indigenous Knowledge and Bush Skills among the Western James Bay Cree Women of Subarctic Canada." *Human Ecology* 25, no. 2 (Spring 1997): 197–222.

Osborn, Ann. *Socio-anthropological Aspects of Development in Southern Belize*. Punta Gorda: Belize: Toledo Research and Development Project, 1982.

Pearsall, Marion. *Klamath Childhood and Education*. Anthropological Records. vol. 9, no, 5. Berkeley: University of California Press, 1950.

Pelisser, Catherine. "Anthropology of Teaching and Learning." *Annual Review of Anthropology* 20 (1991): 75–95.

Reyes-García, Victoria, Neus Martí, Thomas McDade, Susan Tanner, and Vincent Vadez. "Concepts and Methods in Studies Measuring Individual Ethnobotanical Knowledge." *Journal of Ethnobiology* 27, no. 2 (September 2007): 182–203.

Rogoff, Barbara. *Apprenticeship in Thinking: Cognitive Development in Social Context*. New York: Oxford University Press, 1990.

———. *The Cultural Nature of Human Development*. Oxford: Oxford University Press, 2003.

Rogoff, Barbara, Martha J. Sellers, Sergio Pirotta, Nathan Fox, and Sheldon H. White. "Age of Assignment of Roles and Responsibilities to Children: A Cross-Cultural Survey." *Human Development* 18 (1975): 353–69.

Romney, A. Kimball, Susan C. Weller, and William H. Batchelder. "Culture as Consensus: A Theory of Culture and Informant Accuracy." *American Anthropologist*, New Series 88, no. 2 (June 1986): 313–38.

Ross, Norbert. "Cognitive Aspects of Intergenerational Change: Mental Models, Cultural Change, and Environmental Behavior among the Lacandon Maya of Southern Mexico." *Human Organization* 61, no. 2 (Summer 2002a): 125–38.

———. "Lacandon Maya Intergenerational Change and the Erosion of Folk Biologic Knowledge." Pp. 585–92 in *Ethnobiology and Biocultural Diversity*, edited by John R. Stepp, Felice S. Wyndham, and Rebecca K. Zarger. Athens: University of Georgia Press, 2002b.

Ruddle, Kenneth. "The Transmission of Traditional Ecological Knowledge." Pp. 17–31 in *Traditional Ecological Knowledge: Concepts and Cases*, edited by Julian T. Inglis. Ottawa: International Development Research Center and International Program on Traditional Ecological Knowledge, 1993.

Ruddle, Kenneth, and R. Chesterfield. *Education for Traditional Food Procurement in the Orinoco Delta*. Berkeley: University of California Press, 1977.

Setalaphruk, Chantita, and Lisa Price. "Children's Traditional Ecological Knowledge of Wild Food Resources: A Case Study in a Rural Village in Northeast Thailand." *Journal of Ethnobiology and Ethnomedicine* 3 (October 2007): 33.

Sobel, David. *Children's Special Places: Exploring the Role of Forts, Dens, and Bush Houses in Middle Childhood*. Detroit, Mich.: Wayne State University Press, 2002.

Steward, Julian H. *Theory of Culture Change: The Methodology of Multilinear Evolution*. Chicago: University of Illinois Press, 1955.

Stross, Brian. "Aspects of Language Acquisition by Tzeltal Children." Doctoral dissertation, University of California, Berkeley, 1969.

———. "Elicited Imitations in the Study of Tenejapa Tzeltal Language Acquisition." *Anthropological Linguistics* 12, no. 9 (December 1970): 319–25.

———. "Acquisition of Botanical Terminology by Tzeltal children." Pp. 107–41 in *Meaning in Mayan Languages*, edited by Munro S. Edmonson. The Hague: Mouton, 1973.

Super, Charles, and Sara Harkness. "The Developmental Niche: A Conceptualization at the Interface of Child and Culture." *International Journal of Behavioral Development* 9, no. 4 (December 1986): 545–69.

Tindall, B. Allan. "Theory in the Study of Cultural Transmission." *Annual Review of Anthropology* 5 (October 1976): 195–208.

Tucker, Bram, and Alyson G. Young. "Growing Up Mikea: Children's Time Allocation and Tuber Foraging in Southwestern Madagascar." Pp. 147–174 in *Hunter-Gatherer Childhoods: Evolutionary, Developmental, and Cultural Perspectives*, edited by Barry S. Hewlett and Michael E. Lamb. New Brunswick, N.J.: Aldine Transaction, 2005.

Waxman, Sandra. "The Dubbing Ceremony Revisited: Object Naming and Categorization in Infancy and Early Childhood." Pp. 233–84 in *Folkbiology*, edited by Douglas L. Medin and Scott Atran. Cambridge, Mass.: MIT Press, 1999.

Waxman, Sandra, Douglas Medin, and Norbert Ross. "Folkbiological Reasoning from a Cross-Cultural Developmental Perspective: Early Essentialist Notions Are Shaped by Cultural Beliefs." *Developmental Psychology* 43, no. 2 (2007): 294–308.

Weisner, Thomas S., and Ronald Gallimore. "My Brother's Keeper: Sibling Caretaking." *Current Anthropology* 18, no. 2 (June 1977): 169–90.

Welch, Michael R. "Environmental vs. Technological Effects on Childhood Socialization Processes: A Cross-Cultural Study." *International Journal of Sociology of the Family* 10 (July–December 1980): 233–42.

Whiting, Beatrice B. *Six Cultures: Studies of Child Rearing*. New York: John Wiley and Sons, 1963.

Whiting, Beatrice B., and John M. Whiting. *Children of Six Cultures: A Psycho-Cultural Analysis*. Cambridge: Harvard University Press, 1975.

Whiting, John W. M. *Becoming a Kwoma*. New Haven, Conn.: Yale University Press, 1941.

Wilk, Richard. *Household Ecology: Economic Change and Domestic Life among the Kekchi Maya in Belize*. Tucson: University of Arizona Press, 1997.

Wyndham, Felice S. "The Transmission of Traditional Plant Knowledge in Community Contexts: A Human Ecosystem Perspective." Pp. 549–60 in *Ethnobiology and Biocultural Diversity*, edited by John R. Stepp, Felice S. Wyndham, and Rebecca K. Zarger. Athens: University of Georgia Press, 2002.

———. "Learning Ecology: Ethnobotany in the Sierra Tarahumara, Mexico." Doctoral dissertation, University of Georgia, 2004.

Zarger, Rebecca K. "Children's Ethnoecological Knowledge: Situated Learning and the Cultural Transmission of Subsistence Knowledge and Skills among Q'eqchi' Maya." Doctoral dissertation, University of Georgia, 2002a.

———. "Acquisition and Transmission of Subsistence Knowledge by Q'eqchi' Maya in Belize." Pp. 593–603 in *Ethnobiology and Biocultural Diversity*, edited by John R. Stepp, Felice S. Wyndham, and Rebecca K. Zarger. Athens: University of Georgia Press, 2002b.

———. "Mosaics of Maya Livelihoods: Readjusting to Global and Local Food Crises." In *Global Food Crisis: Perspectives from Practicing and Applied Anthropologists*, edited by David A. Himmelgreen and Satish Kedia. New York: Wiley, 2009 (in press).

Zarger, Rebecca K., and John R. Stepp. "Persistence of Botanical Knowledge among Tzeltal Maya Children." *Current Anthropology* 45, no. 3 (June 2004): 413–18.

Zent, Stanford. "The Quandary of Conserving Ethnoecological Knowledge: A Piaroa Example." Pp. 90–124 in *Ethnoecology: Knowledge, Resources, and Rights*, edited by Ted Gragson and Ben G. Blount. Athens: University of Georgia Press, 1999.

———. "Acculturation and Ethnobotanical Knowledge Loss among the Piaroa of Venezuela: Demonstration of a Quantitative Method for the Empirical Study of TEK Change." Pp. 190–211 in *On Biocultural Diversity: Linking Language, Knowledge, and the Environment*, edited by Luisa Maffi. Washington, D.C.: Smithsonian Institution, 2001.

Zent, Stanford. "A Genealogy of Scientific Representations of Indigenous Knowledge." Pp. 19–67 in *Landscape, Process, and Power: Re-evaluating Traditional Environmental Knowledge*, edited by Serena Heckler. London: Berghan, 2009.

Zent, Stanford, and Egleé López Zent. "Ethnobotanical Convergence, Divergence, and Change among the Hoti of the Venezuelan Guayana." Pp. 37–78 in *Ethnobotany and the Conservation of Biocultural Diversity*, edited by Thomas J. S. Carlson and Luisa Maffi. Bronx: New York Botanical Garden, 2004.

CHAPTER FIFTEEN
LEARNING TO HUNT

Katharine MacDonald

Hunting has long been seen as playing an important role in human evolution. For example, Washburn and Lancaster (1968, 325) linked hunting to technology, territory size, a division of labor between the sexes, and provisioning of children. More recently, Kaplan and colleagues (2000) proposed that human life history characteristics, including longevity and a long juvenile period, coevolved with increased brain size, lowered adult mortality, and food sharing in the context of a complex foraging niche. In this model, the need to learn complex foraging skills such as hunting, which take a long time to learn but pay off in later life, plays a role in the evolution of distinctive human life history characteristics. The importance of scavenging versus hunting by early hominins continues to be debated (Dominguez-Rodrigo and Pickering 2003), but it is clear that, by a quarter of a million years ago, Neanderthals were successful hunters of large ungulates. In this context, I carried out a cross-cultural study of contemporary children's hunting skills, with the aim of reassessing the broader implications of the archeological evidence. Based on the cross-cultural study, and the paleo-anthropological and archeological record for hunting, I have attempted to form an image of what children's learning and hunting behavior might have been like in the Pleistocene.

Children's hunting skills are relevant to debate on the evolution of a longer human life history and larger brain size, as discussed above. This complex subject is addressed in detail in chapter 2 of this volume, but it is worth noting here that while this article focuses on hunting, a range of ecological and social skills contribute to adult competence among current hunter-gatherers as well as primates (see chapter 13, this volume). Gathered foods, predominantly plants, and aquatic resources make up a large proportion of the diet for some foraging populations (Kelly 1995, 66–73). Success in certain strategies for exploiting plant foods, such as processing mongongo nuts, requires considerable experience (Bock 2002). Social skills could affect the foraging success of juveniles, based on ability to compete for resources or resource patches (Johnson and Bock 2004), cooperatively obtain resources, or get a share of food. A larger brain increases individual fitness by providing more complex cognitive skills that reduce mortality, and this might include skills in social and ecological domains (Barrickman et al. 2008). A number of authors have argued that the social world is the principal challenge shaping primate intelligence (Byrne and Whiten 1988; Humphrey 1976; Joffe 1997; Jolly 1966; Whiten and Byrne 1997). Similarly, hypotheses about the evolution of the long juvenile period emphasize the role of learning about a complex social as well as ecological environment (Ross and Jones 1999, 100). This is supported by comparative studies. Large brains are associated with the ability to find innovative solutions to ecological problems, use tools, map food resources, and employ complex social strategies (reviewed in Barrickman et al. 2008; Reader and Laland 2002).

Methodological Discussion

Analogy with primates and contemporary human populations, particularly hunter-gatherers, plays an important role in interpreting the archeological and fossil record, especially for aspects of behavior for which fossil evidence is limited. In comparing such traits as diet or home range size, hunter-gatherers provide necessary evidence for human behavior in the absence of agriculture (Marlowe 2005, 54). However, for various reasons, reviewed by Marlowe (2005, 54), this analogy is not straightforward. In particular, interaction with agricultural populations has had an impact on hunter-gatherer behavior of varying significance, and contemporary hunter-gatherers have more complex technology than earlier populations. Analogy with hunter-gatherers may be most useful when it is based on an understanding of the processes underlying behavioral variation (Kelly 1995). Evolutionary ecology provides one useful framework for understanding the factors underlying variation in behavior, as well as a source of hypotheses about human evolution. For example, life history models, tested with data on diet and life history from contemporary hunter-gatherers, have been applied to explain the long human juvenile period and life span (Bock 2002; Bock 2005; Kaplan et al. 2000; O'Connell, Hawkes, and Blurton-Jones 1999).

I carried out a cross-cultural study of how children learn hunting skills, with the aim of providing a context for evidence for hunting by Neanderthals, *H. sapiens*, and their immediate ancestors. The ethnological method employed in this study is discussed in chapter 7 of this volume.

Results of Cross-Cultural Study

A cross-cultural review of how children learn hunting skills (MacDonald 2007) revealed a number of interesting patterns. This section summarizes the main results of this study and explores underlying processes which may help us to understand how Pleistocene hunters learned such skills. A wide range of different skills and capabilities are necessary to become a competent hunter, including knowing how to make and use tools and weapons, animal behavior and signs, ability to move quietly, different strategies for capturing prey, and ability to cooperate with other hunters.

Learning to Manufacture and Use Hunting Weapons

In many cases, adults or older children provide hunting weapons for children, often scaled down or toy versions (e.g., MacDonald 2007, 390; Peters 1998, 90). Bock (2005, 127) suggests that by providing tools, parents direct children's activities and help them to forage successfully. However, sometimes small hunting weapons are provided to babies or are unusable. Providing tools may play an additional role in socializing young children to aspire to become good hunters (Peters 1998, 60). Adults occasionally offer advice or provide opportunities for children to practice shooting. Children are often described as playing with miniature hunting weapons, made by themselves or others, or shooting at small prey. In some cases, children participate in games or exercises involving shooting at targets. Children learn to manufacture hunting weapons and traps through observation and practice (MacDonald 2007, 390; Tayanin and

Lindell 1991, 14). Although instruction is limited, children have opportunities to observe older individuals and to become peripherally involved
in the manufacturing process (MacDonald 2007; Tayanin and Lindell
1991). As they grow older, children manufacture a wider range of tool
types with fewer errors, and in later adolescence or adulthood they become
accomplished in manufacturing bows and arrows (Hill and Hurtado 1996,
223; Watanabe 1975). It seems probable that experience contributes to
the ability to successfully manufacture hunting tools.

Ethnographic studies suggest that while young children possess some
skill with a hunting weapon, only older adolescents are fully skilled, and
quantitative studies indicate that strength is the key factor (reviewed in
MacDonald 2007, 391). One such quantitative study of Tsimane hunters
showed that success in target archery corresponds to peaks in strength
around age 20, before the highest values for locating or capturing prey
(Gurven, Kaplan, and Gutierrez 2006). Experience could contribute to
aspects of skill other than marksmanship, including knowing what arrow
point is most suited to specific animals and where an arrow is likely to fall,
as well as cognitive skills relevant to tracking, pursuit, and capture of prey
(Bock and Johnson 2004, 76; Peters 1998, 91–92).

Figure 15.1. Aka boys hunting rats (E. Hagen photo)

Knowledge of Animal Behavior and Signs of Behavior

As reviewed in detail in MacDonald (2007, 391–2), children learn through play hunting or tracking, experience in their play area, and observation and imitation of animals. Based on this early experience, they can locate, identify, and know about the characteristics of plant and animal species before adolescence (see also chapter 14, this volume), but learning continues into adulthood (MacDonald 2007). For example, Yanomamo boys already know the sounds, footprints, and markings of every animal and can call several different bird and animal species when they start to accompany fathers or brothers on forest hunting trips (Peters 1998, 90). While boys about age 10 can identify some animal tracks, men age 40 can identify the highest number (Gurven et al. 2006, 463). Peak identification is later than successful target archery, suggesting a role for experience (Gurven et al. 2006). Knowledge of other aspects of the environment is also important for hunting. Yanomamo boys learn the terrain as well as specific landmarks in the forest on hunting trips (Peters 1998, 61). Children may be given some instruction when they accompany adults, and stories about hunting provide relevant information for children and adults (MacDonald 2007, 392), as well as underscoring the cultural role of hunters (Peters 1998, 138). Adult hunters are described as knowing a great deal about animal behavior (Blurton-Jones and Konner 1976; Liebenberg 1990).

The Role of Experience

There are widespread trends in the ages at which children participate in different hunting activities with different people, as shown in table 15.1 (see also MacDonald 2007, 393–5). Children are often described playing at hunting, generally in the camp, fields, or nearby paths, and may be competent hunters at an early age (MacDonald 2007). For example, Martu children above age 5 often search for and pursue medium-sized lizards, and they are successful hunters from the start, with return rates influenced by walking speed, not experience (Bird and Bliege Bird 2005).

In addition, some children accompany adults on hunting trips when they are about 5 years old (see table 15.1). Children's physical and intellectual development, including height and walking speed, could be important in allowing participation at this age (MacDonald 2007, 393). In

Table 15.1. Ages at Which Children Start Participating in Hunting Activities

Group Name	Lat. (±°)	Age	Activity	People	Prey
Penan	<5	5	Hunting	Father	Any
		9–10	Hunting	Uncles, other adult men	Any
		14–20	Hunting	Siblings/peers	Any
		Adult	Techniques involving stealth, patience, silence		
Aka	<5	5+	Net hunt	Parents	Any
		11 or 12	Hunting		Small game
Bedamuni	<10	5	Checking traps/snares	Father	
		12+	Hunting and fishing	Older adolescent peers	Birds, fish
		12+	Collective hunts	Adult men	Pig
		16–18	Hunting	Solitary	Pig, cassowary
Aboriginal Australians	10–40	Adolescent	Hunting	Adult men	Wallaby and kangaroo
Ju/'hoansi	20	12	Hunting trip	Father, uncles, or older brothers	Mongoose, genet, hare, game birds
Kammu	23	15–18	Kill first buck		Antelope
		10	Setting and checking traps	Adult men	
		12–16	Checking traps, hunting	Father, uncles, elder brothers	
Modoc	40	Adolescent	Hunting	Father	
Kutenai	49.5	6	Hunting	Father	
Eyak	60	Adolescent	Hunting	Father, maternal uncle	
Nunamiut	68	Adolescent	Short hunting trip	Father	
Inupiat	70	Adolescent–after	Hunting trip	Solitary or with peers	Caribou
		12–14	Hunting gun/seal spear	Father	

Source: Katharine MacDonald, "Cross-Cultural Comparison of Learning in Human Hunting: Implications for Life History Evolution," Human Nature 18, no. 4 (December 2007): 394. With kind permission from Springer Science and Business Media.

hunter-gatherer populations, children are generally weaned by age 4, before such expeditions (Konner 2005, 50–51, 57). Children are expected to be able to keep up with adults by age 5 or 6, whether in camp movements or hunting trips (Hill and Hurtado 1996, 222; Konner 2005, 50–51). The ability to keep silent might preclude Penan children's participation in a specific stalking technique, but not other strategies (Puri 1997, 325), and Martu children are described as keeping quiet when accompanying men on hunts (Bird and Bliege Bird 2005, 135).

In some cases, children first go on hunting trips with adults at around age 12 (see table 15.1). Participation might present risks to children's safety, including encountering predators, becoming exhausted or dehydrated, or not being able to keep up and becoming lost (MacDonald 2007, 395). In addition, accompanying children might lower adult returns for hunting. Changes in height and strength in adolescence may remove some of these constraints (Harrison et al. 1993, 339). Martu women comment that children are too slow to keep pace when they are searching and tracking (Bird and Bliege Bird 2005, 135), while Yanomamo boys are already strong enough to quickly pursue wild pigs or monkeys when they join hunting trips (Peters 1998, 90). In addition, children at this stage possess some experience of survival skills (Puri 1997, 400) and knowledge of animal behavior and technology, as well as a good sense of direction (Peters 1998, 90).

Numerous quantitative studies have addressed the role of experience in acquiring hunting skills, leading to different interpretations (Bird and Bliege Bird 2005; Bliege Bird and Bird 2002; Blurton-Jones and Marlowe 2002; Gurven et al. 2006; Kaplan et al. 2000; Walker et al. 2002). While one study demonstrates that children can be competent hunters by age 5 (Bird and Bliege Bird 2005), in several cases maximum hunting success is attained long after men reach adult strength (Gurven et al. 2006; Ohtsuka 1989; Walker et al. 2002). The existence of constraints on children's participation in some hunting activities suggests that we need to consider the interaction between growth and experience, as well as motivation, to understand the development of competent hunting (Bock 2002; Bock 2005).

Social Context

While the role for teaching is limited, other people influence children's acquisition of hunting skills by providing weapons and a model for imitation and by allowing children to accompany them (see table 15.2). Children

Table 15.2. Social Context of Learning Hunting Skills

Role for Adults	Providing First Hunting Weapon	Later Weapon	Teaching Use of Weapon	Accompany on Hunt (First)	Accompany on Hunt (Later)	Manufacturing Skills
Mother	Ju/'hoansi		Ju/'hoansi			Aka
Both parents				Tiwi, Aka		Aka
Older children	Ju/'hoansi, Klamath, Wonie		Ju/'hoansi			
Brother	Bedamuni					
Father	Yamana, Selk'nam, Bedamuni, Wonie, Klamath, Modoc	Ju/'hoansi, Bedamuni, Yamana, Selk'nam	Yamana, Klamath	Nunamiut, Penan, Bedamuni, Inupiat, Modoc, Eyak, Kutenai		
Male relatives	Ju/'hoansi	Wonie		Kammu, Ju/'hoansi, Eyak		Aka
Adults	Kammu, Penan	Kammu				
Adult men		Bedamuni	Penan,		Penan, Bedamuni, Wonie	
Grandparents			Klamath	Penan		Nunamiut

Source: Katharine MacDonald, "Cross-Cultural Comparison of Learning in Human Hunting: Implications for Life History Evolution," *Human Nature* 18, no. 4 (December 2007): 397. With kind permission from Springer Business and Science Media.

often break their small bows (Gusinde 1937, 761), and providing hunting weapons costs manufacturing time and raw materials. However, in many cases these are made out of different and sometimes less costly raw materials, such as rattan rather than bamboo bows (Watanabe 1975). Adults sometimes alter their hunting behavior to allow accompanying children opportunities to practice (MacDonald 2007, 398), and hunters may form groups that are larger than the optimal size in order to teach young people (Smith 1991). By waiting until children acquire a certain level of experience, height, or strength, the negative impact of accompanying children on hunting returns may be reduced.

Adults may therefore face a trade-off. They can accept the costs of training young people to become hunters, including lower current returns. Alternatively, they can avoid such costs and take higher returns by hunting only with experienced individuals but face problems in the future when those children are adults without hunting proficiency. From an evolutionary perspective, this could be problematic. Meat is a useful commodity not only for feeding children and wives but in attracting the attention of potential lovers, ensuring future shares of game from other hunters, and gaining better treatment for offspring (Bird 1999). Based on this, a trade-off occurs across three generations. The older generation might benefit from higher fertility by obtaining higher returns now, but that will not translate into reproductive success for their children and survivorship for their grandchildren unless they spend the time required to train boys to hunt.

This suggests that parents should take the lead in children's hunting education. As shown in table 15.2, relatives play an important role. Fathers and male relatives are generally involved in early hunting expeditions, when the costs may be highest, and the need to teach children survival skills might provide an additional incentive. However, a wide range of people, including brothers, grandparents, cousins, and uncles, and on some occasions nonrelatives, are involved in a child's hunting education (see table 15.2). Hrdy (2005, 70) suggests that nonrelatives might also benefit from helping with child care, by improving their position in a social group, or enhancing the cooperative community in ways that improve future breeding opportunities.

Implications for the Pleistocene

As discussed above, hunting has long been seen as playing an important role in human evolution. However, we need to consider a range of ecological and technological as well as social skills to understand the evolution of human life history and large brain size. This section briefly reviews the evidence for hunting in the broader context of other changes in diet, foraging strategy, brain size, and life history. The fossil and archeological record provides important evidence for models of human evolution. More specifically, the evidence for hunting by hominins, combined with the cross-cultural study already discussed, provides a starting point for discussion of children's hunting in the Pleistocene.

By 2.6 million years ago, hominins were manufacturing stone tools and using them to obtain animal foods (de Heinzelin et al. 1999; Dominguez-Rodrigo et al. 2005; Semaw 2000). Paleozoological analyses from archeological sites dating to 1.8–1.5 million years ago suggest that hominins obtained early access to carcasses, whether by aggressive scavenging or hunting (Dominguez-Rodrigo 1997; Dominguez-Rodrigo and Pickering 2003). Large bifacial tools first appear in the archeological record 1.6 million years ago and have proved to be efficient butchering tools, particularly for large animals (Ambrose 2001; Asfaw et al. 1992; Jones 1980). There is also some evidence for extractive foraging (Backwell and D'Errico 2008; D'Errico and Backwell 2009). Vegetation was influenced by a cooling, drying trend, leading eventually to an expansion of grassland by 1.7 million years ago, with consistently open savannah present after 1.0 million years ago (Cerling 1992; Cerling and Hay 1986; Elton 2008; Sikes 1999). These habitats were rich in large ungulates and high-quality but protected plant foods (Marean 1997). Throughout the Plio-Pleistocene, hominins occupied a wide variety of environments (reviewed in Elton 2008). By 1.8 million years ago, archeological and fossil sites document hominin presence at low latitudes across Eurasia (Dennell and Roebroeks 1996).

A high-quality diet, based on animal products and carbohydrate-rich plant foods, would have been necessary to support the energy requirements of larger bodies and brains, including higher costs for reproduction (Aiello and Key 2002; Aiello and Wheeler 1995; Milton 1999). In one view, an increased emphasis on high-quality but difficult to acquire foods increased the benefits of learning and intelligence and decreased mortality rates, leading to increasing brain size and changes in life history (Kaplan et al. 2000). An alternative perspective highlights the role of hard-working grandmothers provisioning their grandchildren by extractive foraging (O'Connell et al. 1999). A longer juvenile period was incidental to selection for longevity.

Significant changes in the fossil record occurring between 2.5 and 1.8 million years ago include an increase in body size, reduction in sexual dimorphism, increase in absolute and relative brain size, change in limb proportions, and reduction in the size of teeth and jaws (McHenry and Coffing 2000; Wood and Collard 1999a, 1999b). Based on a recent review, the juvenile period and life span of the australopithecines, early *Homo*, and *Homo erectus* were shorter than in modern humans (Robson and Wood 2008). The proportion of older to younger adults in the fossil record increased somewhat in early *Homo* (Caspari and Lee 2004). This provides some support for the view that a larger brain and slower life history evolved in the context of changes in diet and technology.

The fossil record documents the gradual, mosaic evolution of modern humans in Africa and Neanderthals in Europe, although the time-depth of speciation is debated (reviewed by Stringer 2002). An African origin for *Homo sapiens* is consistent with predictions based on intrapopulation genetic studies (Cann, Stoneking, and Wilson 1987; Ingman et al. 2000), while Neanderthal mtDNA supports a long period of divergence (Krings et al. 2000). Brain size increased significantly in the period 600,000–150,000 years ago, and the brain size of classic Neanderthals was slightly smaller than that for early anatomically modern humans taking body size into account (Rightmire 2004; Ruff, Trinkhaus, and Holliday 1997). Increases in absolute brain size combined with a large body size suggest a modern humanlike life history, although the results of recent studies of crown formation times are contradictory (Robson and Wood 2008). Longevity also increased in this time period, but not to the extent seen in recent humans (Caspari and Lee 2004). Increases in body and brain size in this period imply very high reproductive costs, and a high-quality diet and care by individuals other than mothers might have been essential (Aiello and Key 2002).

The first convincing evidence for hunting by hominins comes from the site of Schöningen, Germany, dating to 300,000–350,000 years ago, where multiple wooden spears have been discovered associated with the remains of more than 20 horses (Thieme 1997; Voormolen 2008). After 250,000 years ago, Neanderthals were successfully hunting large herbivores (Gaudzinski-Windheuser and Niven 2009), and some individuals consumed a highly carnivorous diet (Richards et al. 2000). Neanderthal hunting weapons were limited to wooden and perhaps stone-tipped spears (Mazza et al. 2006; Schmitt, Churchill, and Hylander 2003; Shea 2006b; Trinkaus 1997; Villa and Lenoir 2006), and close-range hunting was risky, as evident from Neanderthal skeletons (Berger and Trinkhaus 1995). There is some evidence for Neanderthal exploitation of small prey and marine foods at lower latitudes, focusing on species that could be collected easily (Stiner 2001; Stringer et al. 2008). The record broadly supports a correlation of evidence for hunting as a relatively complex foraging strategy, with larger brain size and slower life histories in this time period (Kaplan et al. 2000); however, the extension of life span is limited.

Between 40,000 and 30,000 years ago, Neanderthals were replaced by modern humans in the fossil record of Europe, accompanied by changes in the archeological record described as the Middle to Upper Palaeolithic transition. Hunting for large herbivores by Upper Palaeolithic humans does not seem to have been dramatically different (Gaudzinski and Roebroeks 2000; Grayson and Delpech 2003). There is evidence in some areas for changes in other aspects of the diet: for example, increasing exploitation of faster moving small game and freshwater fish (Richards 2007; Stiner 2001). More striking innovations include an increase in spatio-temporal variation in tool types and the appearance of ornaments, structures, burial with grave goods, and figurative art (D'Errico 2003). This generally is interpreted in terms of cognitive differences between Neanderthals and humans (e.g., Klein and Edgar 2003). However, some changes in the record, including dietary breadth and investment in technology, can also be explained in terms of responses to population pressure (Henshilwood and Marean 2003, 63), or different energy requirements (Verpoorte 2006).

Learning Hunting Skills in the Palaeolithic

Until late in the Upper Palaeolithic, hunting strategies differed significantly from those practiced by modern hunter-gatherers, most notably in technology. This section explores the effects of these differences and implications for the ontogeny of hunting skill in the period from early evidence of hunting in Germany to the Upper Palaeolithic, with a focus on the Middle Palaeolithic.

Skills and Learning Processes

Since we are dealing with different hominin species, it is possible that these species had differences in learning capacity with implications for skill acquisition; unfortunately, cognition and communication are very hard to study. It is generally assumed that larger brain size has been selected because of the benefits of increased cognitive abilities (Byrne 1995, 213). As discussed above, humans and Neanderthals shared large absolute brain size, while the latter had slightly smaller relative brain size. While 600,000-year-old fossils show morphological characteristics consistent with a human capacity for speech and listening (Martínez, Arsuaga, et al. 2008; Martínez, Rosa, et al. 2004), archeological markers for language are unavailable.

Differences in hunting strategies in the past, particularly in technology, have a number of implications for hunting strategies and for children's learning and participation in hunting activities. Skeletal studies of Neanderthals and early Upper Palaeolithic humans suggest that using a spear involved significant loads on the arm (Schmitt et al. 2003; Trinkaus 1997), and delivering such a weapon probably required considerable strength. Close-range hunting would have been risky, and best carried out in a cooperative group. Drawing on ethnographically documented use of different weapons, Binford (2007, 198–201) argues that hunters using a thrusting spear exploited landscape features and weaknesses of species. Neanderthals do seem to have used features of the landscape in hunting activities, for example, a salt lick (Bratlund 1999). Persistence hunting, or chasing an animal until it is exhausted, is another strategy that could have been practiced in the absence of projectile weapons (Liebenberg 2006, 2008), although Neanderthals faced relatively high costs for locomotion compared with humans (Bramble and Lieberman 2004; Weaver and Steudel-Numbers 2005). ·

Technology

Unlike contemporary hunters, hunters in the Palaeolithic would have needed to acquire skills in stone knapping in addition to hafting and woodworking. Experiments and refitting studies elucidate the sequence of actions used in producing stone tools (Pelegrin 1991; Shennan and Steele 1999). Increasingly complex manufacturing sequences and greater standardization of tools indicate that learners and teachers invested more effort in the acquisition of stone tool manufacturing skills through time (Pelegrin 1991; Shennan and Steele 1999, 375). To produce flakes, Neanderthals carried out a complex series of actions, employing a sophisticated understanding of the knapping properties of stone; however, their tool types varied little in time and space (Mellars 1996, 88, 133). Experiment indicates that modern human children 7–11 years of age have the strength and cognitive skill necessary to produce flaked stone tools (Hawcroft and Dennell 2000). Children would have started to learn to knap flint at this age, after which they would have required some time to acquire full technological competence.

Based on the requirements of hunting technology from this period, and comparison with recent populations, strength was probably key to becoming competent in using a hunting spear, with a limited role for experience. Similarities in the growth period of *H. heidelbergensis*, Neanderthals, and humans suggest that peak strength was attained at a similar age.

Knowledge of Animal Behavior

As regular hunters of large prey, Palaeolithic hunters required knowledge of animal behavior and terrain. Based on the discussion above, knowledge of animal behavior and signs, and other relevant aspects of the environment, may have been learned over a long time period. In deciding which prey to pursue, and working out strategies during the hunt, hunter-gatherers employ extensive knowledge of animal behavior and environmental conditions (Liebenberg 2006, 1018–9). Based on Binford's data, discussed above, knowledge of terrain and animal behavior may have been even more important in this period. Particularly in terrain with thicker vegetation cover, tracking requires a complex process of interpretation of signs and prediction of animal behavior, and this plays a particularly important role in persistence hunting (Liebenberg 2008, 1158). Analogy with recent populations suggests that learning was primarily based on experience, although story-telling could provide an additional source of information.

Strength Constraints and Social Context

Because using a spear and hunting at close range required considerable strength and high risks, it might have been necessary for children to reach a certain level of strength before participating in hunting activities. At the same time, some aspects of hunting competence, including knowledge of animal behavior, were based on experience. Both the strength and experience required to carry out these different components of hunting activities would have been necessary to be a competent hunter (Bock 2002); as a result, peak hunting productivity might have been reached at a late age. Adults would have faced a trade-off between current returns and helping children to learn an important skill, and given the relatively high costs would have allowed children to join hunting groups when they reached a necessary level of strength. Adult hunters would have needed to be extremely productive to compensate for delays in children's productivity (Kaplan et al. 2000). This is interesting in the context of the model of Kaplan and colleagues (2000). Further data are required to reconstruct hominin life histories, especially as a possibly shorter life span would place even higher demands on adults. An important factor may have been the presence of older, more experienced individuals in cooperative hunting groups, whose knowledge compensated for a young hunter's ignorance. Learning to cooperate with a hunting team would be an important part of becoming a competent hunter. In areas where slow-moving small game was abundant, this would have provided a suitable resource for younger children to hunt. In addition, Kuhn and Stiner (2006) suggest that both children and women participated in hunting large game in the past by serving as beaters.

Shennan and Steele (1999) argue that stone tool manufacturing skills were the product of imitative learning, probably aided by active teaching, in the context of increased involvement of fathers in child care. However, as discussed above, children learn to manufacture hunting tools primarily by observation and practice, with opportunities to become peripherally involved in manufacturing, and a variety of people contribute; this is consistent with studies of other craft skills (Kramer 1985, 83). The transmission process may have been equally varied in the past. The social context is nevertheless important for acquisition of complex skills such as tool manufacture, and some changes in social organization and mobility strategies might have implications for opportunities for learning. Shared child care over a longer developmental period could provide children with opportunities to acquire skills and information from a number of adults (Gibson 1999, 360; Shennan and Steele 1999). In addition, mobility strategies in which children and adults traveled together while foraging, then returned to a "home base" (Isaac 1978, 1983) in which multiple activities were carried out, would have provided many opportunities for children to observe stone tool manufacture. One factor in learning to manufacture hunting tools is access to raw materials, whether procured by children themselves or provided by adults. Adults are less likely to give high-quality stone raw materials procured at long distances to children, who might break or lose their tools (Shea 2006a). The majority of stone raw materials were local in the Lower and Middle Palaeolithic (<20km) (Féblot-Augustins 1997) and could have been acquired by children or provided by adults at low cost.

Conclusion

This study helps to build up a picture of children's learning and hunting activities in the Palaeolithic. Further information and studies are needed to improve our understanding of underlying processes and interpretation of the past. There is some potential for testing these suggestions based on the fossil and archeological record, and some questions could be addressed by further ethnographic studies.

The Neanderthal fossil record includes a high proportion of young adults, which Trinkaus relates to high frequencies of trauma and developmental stress indicators (Trinkaus 1995, 137) and suggests that Neanderthal lifestyles led to relatively low life expectancy. According to Pettitt (2000), this "pertains to behavioral shifts occurring on the threshold of adulthood, perhaps to participation in dangerous encounter hunting of medium- and large-size herbivores" (357). Two of the individuals with trauma studied by Berger and Trinkaus (1995) sustained those injuries as juveniles, while the majority of injuries were to prime-aged adults. Schmitt and colleagues (2003) show that there is a difference in the forces experienced by different arms in using a thrusting spear, which may be visible in the skeleton and can be interpreted in terms of reliance on thrusting spears. Early Upper Palaeolithic immature skeletons show levels of humeral asymmetry comparable to that of adults (Cowgill 2009); however, suitable postcranial fossils from earlier periods are rare. The fossil record therefore provides suggestive evidence that hunting was practiced primarily but not entirely by adults, but this evidence is very limited.

Refitting analysis has provided insight into learning processes in the Upper Palaeolithic (e.g., Karlin, Pigeot, and Ploux 1993). Other indicators, including small size, expedience, low-quality raw materials, and specific technological errors, can also be used to identify the contribution of children or unskilled flint knappers in lithic assemblages (Bamforth and Finlay 2008; Shea 2006a; Stapert 2007; see also chapter 16, this volume). This line of research could shed light on children's activities and acquisition of manufacturing skills earlier in the Palaeolithic.

This chapter highlights some questions which could be addressed in ethnographic and archeological studies. Detailed information on the process of learning to manufacture hunting tools, including the roles of practice, observation, and teaching and the time taken to learn, would be relevant. Data on the costs in terms of time and materials of producing hunting tools for children are also of interest. While many experimental studies of stone tool production exist, studies focusing on production by children, and how skill interacts with growth and cognitive development, are rare (but see Hawcroft and Dennell 2000). Experimental studies of spear use have focused on identifying skeletal markers, and it would be interesting to address the effects of strength on successful use. There is little information on children's learning about animal behavior and other aspects of the environment, beyond identification of specific tracks or species. Further study could assess constraints on children's hunting activities, based on the specific risks of different environments, including predators, heat, or difficult terrain, or the specific strategies employed. Empirical studies could assess the return rates for hunting trips with children relative to expected adult returns without children, as well as asking adults when and why they would take children with them.

This study has focused on hunting skill, but ecological competence is dependent on a range of foraging skills as well as social skill. Related studies addressing these other skills could improve understanding of the ontogeny of ecological competence in Pleistocene hunter-gatherers.

KATHARINE MacDONALD

Acknowledgments

This article draws on research carried out as part of the N.W.O. funded project "Thoughtful Hunters" at the Faculty of Archaeology, University of Leiden, the Netherlands.

Bibliography

Aiello, Leslie C., and Catherine Key. "The Energetic Consequences of Being a *Homo Erectus* Female." *American Journal of Human Biology* 14, no. 5 (September 2002): 551–65.

Aiello, Leslie C., and Peter Wheeler. "The Expensive-Tissue Hypothesis: The Brain and the Digestive System in Human and Primate Evolution." *Current Anthropology* 36, no. 2 (April 1995): 199–221.

Ambrose, Stanley H. "Paleolithic Technology and Human Evolution." *Science* 291, no. 5509 (March 2001): 1748–53.

Asfaw, Berhane, Yonas Beyene, Gen Suwa, Robert C. Walter, Tim D. White, Giday WoldeGabriel, and Tesfaye Yemane. "The Earliest Acheulean from Konso-Gardula." *Nature* 360 (December 1992): 732–5.

Backwell, Lucinda, and Francesco D'Errico. "Early Hominid Bone Tools from Drimolen, South Africa." *Journal of Archaeological Science* 35, no. 11 (November 2008): 2880–94.

Bamforth, Douglas B., and Nyree Finlay. "Introduction: Archaeological Approaches to Lithic Production Skill and Craft Learning." *Journal of Archaeological Method and Theory* 15, no. 1 (March 2008): 1–27.

Barrickman, Nancy L., Meredith L. Bastian, Karin Isler, and Carel P. van Schaik. "Life History Costs and Benefits of Encephalization: A Comparative Test Using Data from Long-Term Studies of Primates in the Wild." *Journal of Human Evolution* 54, no. 5 (May 2008): 568–90.

Berger, Thomas D., and Erik Trinkhaus. "Patterns of Trauma among the Neanderthals." *Journal of Archaeological Science* 22, no. 6 (November 1995): 841–52.

Binford, Lewis R. "The Diet of Early Hominids: Some Things We Need to Know before 'Reading' the Menu from the Archaeological Record." Pp. 185–222 in *Guts and Brains: An Integrative Approach to the Hominin Record*, edited by Wil Roebroeks. Leiden: Leiden University Press, 2007.

Bird, Douglas W., and Rebecca Bliege Bird. "Martu Children's Foraging Strategies in the Western Desert, Australia." Pp. 129–46 in *Hunter-Gatherer Childhoods: Evolutionary, Developmental, and Cultural Perspectives*, edited by Barry S. Hewlett and Michael E. Lamb. New Brunswick. N.J.: Transaction, 2005.

Bird, Rebecca. "Cooperation and Conflict: The Behavioral Ecology of the Sexual Division of Labour." *Evolutionary Anthropology* 8, no. 2 (1999): 65–75.

Bliege Bird, Rebecca, and Douglas W. Bird. "Constraints of Knowing or Constraints of Growing? Fishing and Collecting by the Children of Mer." *Human Nature* 13, no. 2 (June 2002): 239–67.

Blurton-Jones, Nicholas G., and Melvin Konner. "!Kung Knowledge of Animal Behavior." Pp. 325–48 in *Kalahari Hunter-Gatherers*, edited by Richard B. Lee and Irven deVore. Cambridge, Mass.: Harvard University Press, 1976.

Blurton-Jones, Nicholas G., and Frank W. Marlowe. "Selection for Delayed Maturity. Does It Take Twenty Years to Learn to Hunt and Gather?" *Human Nature* 13, no. 2 (June 2002): 199–238.

Bock, John. "Learning, Life History, and Productivity: Children's Lives in the Okavango Delta, Botswana." *Human Nature* 13, no. 2 (June 2002): 161–97.

———. "What Makes a Competent Adult Forager?" Pp. 109–128 in *Hunter-Gatherer Childhoods: Evolutionary, Developmental, and Cultural Perspectives*, edited by Barry S. Hewlett and Michael E. Lamb. New Brunswick, N.J.: Transaction, 2005.

Bock, John, and Sara E. Johnson. "Subsistence Ecology and Play among the Okavango Delta People of Botswana." *Human Nature* 15, no. 1 (March 2004): 63–81.

Bramble, Dennis M., and Daniel E. Lieberman. "Endurance Running and the Evolution of Homo." *Nature* 432, no. 7015 (November 2004): 345–52.

Bratlund, Bodil. "Anthropogenic Factors in the Thanatocoenose of the Last Interglacial Travertines at Taubach (Germany)." Pp. 255–62 in *The Role of Early Humans in the Accumulation of European Lower and Middle Palaeolithic Bone Assemblages*, edited by Sabine Gaudzinski and Elaine Turner. Bonn: Habelt, 1999.

Byrne, Richard. *The Thinking Ape*. Oxford: Oxford University Press, 1995.

Byrne, Richard W., and Andrew Whiten. *Machiavellian Intelligence: Social Expertise and the Evolution of Intellect in Monkeys*. Oxford: Oxford University Press, 1988.

Cann, Rebecca L., Mark Stoneking, and Allan C. Wilson. "Mitochondrial DNA and Human Evolution." *Nature* 325, no. 6099 (January 1987): 31–36.

Caspari, Rachel, and Sang-Hee Lee. "Older Age Becomes Common Late in Human Evolution." *Proceedings of the National Academy of Sciences of the United States of America* 101, no. 30 (July 2004): 10895–900.

Cerling, Thure E. "Development of Grassland and Savannas in East Africa during the Neogene." *Palaeogeography, Palaeoclimatology, Palaeoecology* 97, no. 3 (1992): 241–7.

Cerling, Thure E., and Richard L. Hay. "An Isotopic Study of Paleosol Carbonates from Olduvai Gorge." *Quaternary Research* 25, no. 1 (January 1986): 63–78.

Cowgill, Libby W. "The Development of Humeral Strength Asymmetries during Growth: Play, Practice, and Childhood Activity Patterns." *American Journal of Physical Anthropology* 138 (2009): 111.

de Heinzelin, Jean, J. Desmond Clark, Tim White, William Hart, Paul Renne, Giday WoldeGabriel, Yonas Beyene, and Elisabeth Vrba. "Environment and Behavior of 2.5-Million-Year-Old Bouri Hominids." *Science* 284, no. 5414 (April 1999): 625–9.

Dennell, Robin, and Wil Roebroeks. "The Earliest Colonization of Europe: The Short Chronology Revisited." *Antiquity* 70 (September 1996): 535–42.

D'Errico, Francesco. "The Invisible Frontier: A Multiple Species Model for the Origin of Behavioral Modernity." *Evolutionary Anthropology* 12, no. 4 (2003): 188–202.

D'Errico, Francesco, and Lucinda Backwell. "Assessing the Function of Early Hominin Bone Tools." *Journal of Archaeological Science* (2009): 1764–1773.

Dominguez-Rodrigo, Manuel. "Meat-Eating by Early Hominids at the FLK 22 Zinjanthropus Site, Olduvai Gorge (Tanzania): An Experimental Approach Using Cut-Mark Data." *Journal of Human Evolution* 33, no. 6 (December 1997): 669–90.

Dominguez-Rodrigo, Manuel, and Travis Rayne Pickering. "Early Hominid Hunting and Scavenging: A Zooarcheological Review." *Evolutionary Anthropology* 12, no. 6 (2003): 275–82.

Dominguez-Rodrigo, Manuel, Travis Rayne Pickering, Sileshi Semaw, and M. J. Rogers. "Cutmarked Bones from Pliocene Archaeological Sites, at Gona, Afar, Ethiopia: Implications for the Function of the World's Oldest Stone Tools." *Journal of Human Evolution* 48, no. 2 (February 2005): 109–21.

Elton, Sarah. "The Environmental Context of Human Evolutionary History in Eurasia and Africa." *Journal of Anatomy* 212, no. 4 (April 2008): 377–93.

Féblot-Augustins, Jehanne. "Middle and Upper Palaeolithic Raw Material Transfers in Western and Central Europe: Assessing the Pace of Change." *Journal of Middle Atlantic Archaeology* 13 (1997): 57–90.

Gaudzinski-Windheuser, Sabine, and Laura Niven. "Hominin Subsistence Patterns during the Middle and Late Palaeolithic in Northwestern Europe." Pp. 99–112 in *The Evolution of Hominid Diets: Integrating Approaches to the Study of Palaeolithic Subsistence*, edited by Jean-Jacques Hublin and Michael P. Richards. Dordrecht: Springer, 2009.

Gaudzinski, Sabine, and Wil Roebroeks. "Adults Only: Reindeer Hunting at the Middle Palaeolithic Site Salzgitter Lebenstedt, Northern Germany." *Journal of Human Evolution* 38, no. 4 (April 2000): 497–521.

Gibson, Kathleen R. "Cultural Learning in Hominids: A Behavioral Ecological Approach." Pp. 351–66 in *Mammalian Social Learning*, edited by Hilary O. Box and Kathleen R. Gibson. Cambridge: Cambridge University Press, 1999.

Grayson, Donald K., and Françoise Delpech. "Ungulates and the Middle-to-Upper Paleolithic Transition at Grotte XVI (Dordogne, France)." *Journal of Archaeological Science* 30, no. 12 (December 2003): 1633–48.

Gurven, Michael, Hillard Kaplan, and Maguin Gutierrez. "How Long Does It Take to Become a Proficient Hunter? Implications for the Evolution of Extended Development and Long Lifespan." *Journal of Human Evolution* 51, no. 5 (November 2006): 454–70.

Gusinde, Martin. *Die Feuerland-Indianer. Band Ii. Die Yanama.* Mödling bei Wien: Anthropos, 1937.

Harrison, G. Ainsworth, James M. Tanner, David R. Pilbeam, and P. T. Baker. *Human Biology: An Introduction to Human Evolution, Variation, Growth, and Adaptability.* Oxford: Oxford Science, 1993.

Hawcroft, Jenny, and Robin W. Dennell. "Neanderthal Cognitive History and Implications for Material Culture." Pp. 89–99 in *Children and Material Culture*, edited by Joanna S. Derevenski. London: Routledge, 2000.

Henshilwood, Chris, and Curtis W. Marean. "The Origin of Modern Human Behavior: Critique of the Models and Their Test Implications." *Current Anthropology* 44, no. 5 (December 2003): 627–51.

Hill, Kim, and A. Magdalena Hurtado. *Ache Life History: The Ecology and Demography of a Foraging People.* Chicago: Aldine de Gruyter, 1996.

Hrdy, Sarah Blaffer. "Comes the Child before Man: How Cooperative Breeding and Prolonged Postweaning Dependence Shaped Human Potential." Pp. 65–91 in *Hunter-Gatherer Childhoods: Evolutionary, Developmental, and Cultural Perspectives*, edited by Barry S. Hewlett and Michael E. Lamb. New Brunswick, N.J.: Transaction, 2005.

Humphrey, Nicholas K. "The Social Function of Intellect." Pp. 303–17 in *Growing Points in Ethology*, edited by Paul Patrick Gordon Bateson and Robert A. Hine. Cambridge: Cambridge University Press, 1976.

Ingman, Max, Henrick Kaessman, Svante Pääbo, and Ulf Gyllensten. "Mitochondrial Genome Variation and the Origin of Modern Humans." *Nature* 408, no. 6813 (2000): 703–13.

Isaac, Glynn Lloyd. "The Food Sharing Behavior of Proto-Human Hominids." *Scientific American* 238 (April 1978): 90–108.

———. "Bones in Contention: Competing Explanations for the Juxtaposition of Early Pleistocene Artifacts and Faunal Remains." Pp. 3–19 in *Animals and Archaeology*, vol. 1, edited by Juliet Clutton-Brock and Caroline Grigson. Oxford: British Archaeological Reports 163, 1983.

Joffe, Tracey H. "Social Pressures Have Selected for an Extended Juvenile Period in Primates." *Journal of Human Evolution* 32, no. 6 (June 1997): 593–605.

Johnson, Sara E., and John Bock. "Trade-Offs in Skill Acquisition and Time Allocation among Juvenile Chacma Baboons." *Human Nature* 15, no. 1 (March 2004): 45–62.

Jolly, Alison. "Lemur Social Behavior and Primate Intelligence." *Science* 153, no. 3735 (July 1966): 501–6.

Jones, Peter R. "Experimental Butchery with Modern Stone Tools and Its Relevance for Palaeolithic Archaeology." *World Archaeology* 1, no. 2 (1980): 153–75.

Kaplan, Hillard S., Kim Hill, Jane Lancaster, and A. Magdalena Hurtado. "A Theory of Human Life History Evolution: Diet, Intelligence and Longevity." *Evolutionary Anthropology* 9, no. 4 (2000): 156–85.

Karlin, Claudine, Nicole Pigeot, and Sylvie Ploux. "Some Socio-Economic Aspects of the Knapping Process among Groups of Hunter-Gatherers in the Paris Basin Region." Pp. 318–37 in *The Use of Tools by Human and Non-Human Primates*, edited by Arlette Berthelet and Jean Chavaillon. Oxford: Clarendon, 1993.

Kelly, Robert L. *The Foraging Spectrum*. Washington, D.C.: Smithsonian Institution, 1995.

Klein, Richard G., and Blake Edgar. *The Dawn of Human Culture*. New York: Wiley, 2003.

Konner, Melvin. "Hunter-Gatherer Infancy and Childhood: The !Kung and Others." Pp. 19–64 in *Hunter-Gatherer Childhoods: Evolutionary, Developmental, and Cultural Perspectives*, edited by Barry S. Hewlett and Michael E. Lamb. New Brunswick, N.J.: Transaction, 2005.

Kramer, Carol. "Ceramic Enoarchaeology." *Annual Review of Anthropology* 14 (October 1985): 77–102.

Krings, Matthias, Cristian Capelli, Frank Tschentscher, Helga Geisert, Sonja Meyer, Arndt von Haeseler, Karl Grosschmidt, Göran Possnert, Maja Paunovic, and Svante Pääbo. "A View Of Neanderthal Genetic Diversity." *Nature Genetics* 26, no. 2 (October 2000): 144–6.

Kuhn, Steven L., and Mary C. Stiner. "What's a Mother to Do?" *Current Anthropology* 47, no. 6 (December 2006): 953–81.

Liebenberg, Louis. *The Art of Tracking*. Cape Town: David Philip, 1990.

———. "Persistence Hunting by Modern Hunter-Gatherers." *Current Anthropology* 47, no. 6 (December 2006): 1017–25.

———. "The Relevance of Persistence Tracking to Human Evolution." *Journal of Human Evolution* 55, no. 6 (December 2008): 1156–9.

MacDonald, Katharine. "Cross-Cultural Comparison of Learning in Human Hunting: Implications for Life History Evolution." *Human Nature* 18, no. 4 (December 2007): 386–402.

Marean, Curtis W. "Hunter-Gatherer Foraging Strategies in Tropical Grasslands: Model Building and Testing in the East African Middle and Later Stone Age." *Journal of Anthropological Archaeology* 16, no. 3 (September 1997): 189–225.

Marlowe, Frank W. "Hunter-Gatherers and Human Evolution." *Evolutionary Anthropology* 14, no. 2 (March 2005): 54–67.

Martínez, Ignacio, Juan Luis Arsuaga, Rolf Quam, Jose Miguel Carretero, Ana Gracia, and Laura Rodríguez. "Human Hyoid Bones from the Middle Pleistocene Site of the Sima de los Huesos (Sierra de Atapuerca, Spain)." *Journal of Human Evolution* 54, no. 1 (January 2008): 118–24.

Martínez, Ignacio, Manual Rosa, Juan Luis Arsuaga, Pilar Jarabo, Rolf Quam, Carlos Lorenzo, Ana Gracia, Jose Miguel Carretero, Jose Maria Bermúdez de Castro, and Eudald Carbonell. "Auditory Capacities in Middle Pleistocene Humans from the Sierra de Atapuerca in Spain." *Proceedings of the National Academy of Sciences of the United States of America* 101, no. 27 (July 2004): 9976–81.

Mazza, Paul Peter Anthony, Fabio Martini, Benedetto Sala, Maurizio Magi, Maria Perla Colombini, Gianna Giachi, Francesco Landucci, Cristina Lemorini, Francesca Modugno, and Erika Ribechini. "A New Palaeolithic Discovery: Tar-Hafted Stone Tools in a European Mid-Pleistocene Bone-Bearing Bed." *Journal of Archaeological Science* 33, no. 9 (September 2006): 1310–18.

McHenry, Henry M., and Katherine Coffing. "Australopithecus to Homo: Transformations in Body and Mind." *Annual Review of Anthropology* 29 (October 2000): 125–46.

Mellars, Paul. *The Neanderthal Legacy.* Princeton, N.J.: Princeton University Press, 1996.

Milton, Katharine. "A Hypothesis to Explain the Role of Meat-Eating in Human Evolution." *Evolutionary Anthropology* 8, no. 1 (1999): 11–21.

O'Connell, James F., Kristen Hawkes, and Nicholas G. B. Blurton-Jones. "Grandmothering and the Evolution of *Homo erectus.*" *Journal of Human Evolution* 36, no. 5 (May 1999): 461–85.

Ohtsuka, Ryutaro. "Hunting Activity and Aging among the Gidra Papuans: A Biobehavioral Analysis." *American Journal of Physical Anthropology* 80, no. 1 (September 1989): 31–39.

Pelegrin, Jacques. "Les Savoir-faire: Une Très Longue Histoire." *Terrain* 16 (March 1991): 106–13.

Peters, John F. *Life among the Yanomami.* Peterborough, Ontario: Broadview, 1998.

Pettitt, Paul B. "Neanderthal Lifecycles: Developmental and Social Phases in the Lives of the Last Archaics." *World Archaeology* 31, no. 3 (February 2000): 351–66.

Puri, Rajindra Kumar. "Hunting Knowledge of the Penan Benalui of East Kalimantan, Indonesia." Doctoral dissertation, University of Hawaii, 1997.

Reader, Simon M., and Kevin N. Laland. "Social Intelligence, Innovation, and Enhanced Brain Size in Primates." *Proceedings of the National Academy of Sciences of the United States of America* 99, no. 7 (April 2002): 4436–41.

Richards, Michael P. "Diet Shift at the Middle/Upper Palaeolithic Transition in Europe? The Stable Isotope Evidence." Pp. 223–34 in *Guts, Brains, and Human Evolution*, edited by Wil Roebroeks. Leiden: Leiden University Press, 2007.

Richards, Michael P., Paul B. Pettitt, Erik Trinkaus, Fred H. Smith, Maja Paunovic, and Ivor Karavanic. "Neanderthal Diet at Vindija and Neanderthal Predation: The Evidence from Stable Isotopes." *Proceedings of the National Academy of Sciences of the United States of America* 97, no. 13 (June 2000): 7663–6.

Rightmire, G. Philip. "Brain Size and Encephalization in Early to Mid-Pleistocene Homo." *American Journal of Physical Anthropology* 124, no. 2 (June 2004): 109–23.

Robson, Shannen L., and Bernard Wood. "Hominin Life History: Reconstruction and Evolution." *Journal of Anatomy* 212, no. 4 (April 2008): 394–425.

Ross, Caroline, and Kate E. Jones. "Socioecology and the Evolution of Primate Reproductive Rates." Pp. 111–39 in *Comparative Primate Socioecology*, edited by Phyllis C. Lee. Cambridge: Cambridge University Press, 1999.

Ruff, Christopher B., Erik Trinkaus, and Trenton W. Holliday. "Body Mass and Encephalization in Pleistocene *Homo*." *Nature* 387 (May 1997): 173–6.

Schmitt, Daniel, Steven E. Churchill, and William L. Hylander. "Experimental Evidence Concerning Spear Use in Neanderthals and Early Modern Humans." *Journal of Archaeological Science* 30, no. 1 (January 2003): 103–14.

Semaw, Sileshi. "The World's Oldest Stone Artifacts from Gona, Ethiopia: Their Implications for Understanding Stone Technology and Patterns of Human Evolution between 2.6–1.5 Million Years Ago." *Journal of Archaeological Science* 27, no. 12 (December 2000): 1197–214.

Shea, John J. "Child's Play: Reflections on the Invisibility of Children in the Palaeolithic Record." *Evolutionary Anthropology* 15, no. 6 (November–December 2006a): 204–6.

———. "The Origins of Lithic Projectile Point Technology: Evidence from Africa, The Levant, and Europe." *Journal of Archaeological Science* 33, no. 6 (June 2006b): 823–46.

Shennan, Stephen J., and James Steele. "Cultural Learning in Hominids: A Behavioral Ecological Approach." Pp. 367–88 in *Mammalian Social Learning:*

Comparative Ecological Perspective, edited by Hilary O. Box and Kathleen R. Gibson. Cambridge: Cambridge University Press, 1999.

Sikes, Nancy. "Plio-Pleistocene Floral Context and Habitat Preferences of Sympatric Hominid Species in East Africa." Pp. 301–15 in *African Biogeography, Climate Change, and Early Hominid Evolution*, edited by Timothy G. Bromage and Friedemann Schrenk. Oxford: Oxford University Press, 1999.

Smith, Eric A. *Inujjuamiut Foraging Strategies*. Hawthorne, N.J.: Aldine de Gruyter, 1991.

Stapert, Dick. "Neanderthal Children and Their Flints." *PalArch's Journal of Northwest Europe* 1, no. 2 (2007): 16–40.

Stiner, Mary C. "Thirty Years on the 'Broad Spectrum Revolution' and Paleolithic Demography." *Proceedings of the National Academy of Sciences of the United States of America* 98, no. 13 (June 2001): 6993–6.

Stringer, Chris. "Modern Human Origins: Progress and Prospects." *Philosophical Transactions of the Royal Society of London Series B* 357 (2002): 563–79.

Stringer, Chris B., J. Clive Finlayson, R. Nicholas, E. Barton, Yolanda Fernández-Jalvo, I. Cáceres, R. C. Sabin, E. J. Rhodes, Andrew P. Currant, J. Rodriguez-Vidal, F. Giles-Pacheco, and J. A. Riquelme-Cantal. "Neanderthal Exploitation of Marine Mammals in Gibraltar." *Proceedings of the National Academy of Sciences* 105, no. 38 (September 2008): 14319–24.

Tayanin, Damrong, and Kristina Lindell. *Hunting and Fishing in a Kammu Village*. London: Curzon, 1991.

Thieme, Hartmut. "Lower Palaeolithic Hunting Spears from Germany." *Nature* 385 (February 1997): 807–10.

Trinkaus, Erik. "Neanderthal Mortality Patterns." *Journal of Archaeological Science* 22, no. 1 (January 1995): 121–42.

———. "Appendicular Robusticity and the Paleobiology of Modern Human Emergence." *Proceedings of the National Academy of Sciences of the United States of America* 94, no. 24 (November 1997): 13367–73.

Verpoorte, Alexander. "Neanderthal Energetics and Spatial Behavior." *Before Farming* 3, article 2 (2006): 1–6.

Villa, Paola, and M. Lenoir. "Hunting Weapons of the Middle Stone Age and the Middle Palaeolithic: Spear Points from Sibudu, Rose Cottage, and Bouheben." *Southern African Humanities* 18 (2006): 89–122.

Voormolen, Boudewijn. *Ancient Hunters, Modern Butchers: Schöningen 13II-4, a Kill-Butchery Site Dating from the Northwest European Lower Palaeolithic*. Leiden: Faculty of Archaeology, Leiden University, 2008.

Walker, Robert, Kim Hill, Hillard Kaplan, and Garnett McMillan. "Age-Dependency in Hunting Ability among the Aché of Eastern Paraguay." *Journal of Human Evolution* 42, no. 6 (June 2002): 639–57.

Washburn, Sherwood L., and Jane B. Lancaster. "The Evolution of Hunting." Pp. 293–303 in *Man the Hunter*, edited by Richard B. Lee and Irven deVore. Chicago: Aldine, 1968.

Watanabe, Hitoshi. *Bow and Arrow Census in a West Papuan Lowland Community: A New Field for Functional-Ecological Study*. St. Lucia: Anthropology Museum, University of Queensland, 1975.

Weaver, Tim D., and Karen L. Steudel-Numbers. "Does Climate or Mobility Explain the Differences in Body Proportions between Neanderthals and Their Upper Palaeolithic Successors?" *Evolutionary Anthropology* 14, no. 6 (November–December 2005): 218–23.

Whiten, Andrew, and Richard W. Byrne. *Machiavellian Intelligence II: Extensions and Evaluations*. Cambridge: Cambridge University Press, 1997.

Wood, Bernard, and Mark Collard. "The Changing Face of Genus *Homo*." *Evolutionary Anthropology* 8, no. 6 (1999a): 195–207.

———. "The Human Genus." *Science* 284, no. 5411 (April 1999b): 65–71.

CHAPTER SIXTEEN

LEARNING IN AND FROM THE PAST

Patricia L. Crown

Although relatively neglected as a focus of archeological study until the last two decades, children now receive growing attention from archeologists (Kamp 2001a, 2001b, 2002; Lillehammer 1989; Lillie 1997; Moore 1997; Pawleta 2004; Scott 1997; Sofaer Derevenski 1994, 1997). In the study of childhood, archeology offers great time depth and the only glimpse of children's lives in precolonial settings. In turn, anthropology provides archeology with the cross-cultural data, ethnographic descriptions, and theoretical perspectives that aid us in interpreting our data. This chapter reviews some of the many ways archeologists have examined childhood in the past. It then reviews archeological research on crafts learning.

Methods and Issues in the Archeological Study of Childhood

Archeologists use a combination of artifacts (things made by people), ecofacts (remains that tell us about the environment or subsistence), and human remains to learn about the past. They interpret these remains using as many lines of evidence as possible. They may use cross-cultural data, ethnographic or historical documents, informants from indigenous groups, computer modeling, or even their own imaginations to interpret what they find in terms of human behavior. The goals of archeology usually include reconstructing past lifeways, outlining culture histories for different areas, and examining human behavior/culture change in the past.

The earliest archeological research to mention children noted the presence of children in the past in three ways: by recognizing child burials, by interpreting miniature versions of larger objects as toys, and by arguing that poorly made artifacts were the work of children (Judd 1954, 199; Haury 1976). Yet those scholars who identified children in the past did not recognize their potential for addressing issues of broader anthropological interest. Artistic renderings made to reconstruct the past did not consistently or accurately represent childhood either. For instance, while dioramas and book illustrations depict children, pregnant women and nursing infants are notably absent (Kamp and Whittaker 2002, 23–24). However, as an outgrowth of interest in the 1980s in "engendering" the past, some archeologists began to look for other "invisible" people in the archeological record, including children (Baxter 2006a). This now burgeoning research on childhood primarily involves three kinds of data: child burials, images of children, and material culture.[1]

Child Burials

Bioarcheological research on child or subadult burials provides insight into health, diet, disease, and labor in the past (Sobolik 2002; Whittlesey 2002). Studies of pre-adult skeletal material examine stature and growth using measurements of bones (Visser 1998), evidence for dietary breadth using several markers of malnutrition (Blom et al. 2005; Humphrey and King 2000), and the presence of specific diseases through disease markers (Hershkovitz et al. 1997). Adult skeletons can also be used to examine aspects of childhood nutrition and disease, because if the child survives into adulthood, bones often retain specific markers of stress during childhood. Child skeletons can be aged (Olsen, Stermer, and Steinar 1994) and recent developments may allow sexing (Cardoso 2008; Sutter 2003), but adult burials have the advantage of being amenable to more reliable comparisons between males and females. Skeletal material can also provide clues to age at weaning (Schurr 1998), differences in weaning age for males and females in a population (Fink and Merbs 1991), and changes in fertility associated with weaning age (Schurr and Powell 2005; Surovell 2000). Demographic processes such as childhood morbidity trends can be assessed (Bennike et al. 2005; Goodman and Armelagos 1989). Specifically, children's skeletons can be examined for evidence of violence and trauma (Perry 2006; Walker, Cook, and Lambert 1997), infanticide (Bradley 2002; Crist 2005), and child sacrifice (Sillar 1994). The skeleton may reveal markers of stress reflective of workload variation. Such markers can show when children began performing tasks that produce asymmetry (such as hunting with bow and arrow) or specific larger muscle attachments (such as grinding grain). Finally, social practices such as the use of cradle boards, skull binding in childhood to affect particular head shapes, and foot binding all leave traces on skeletal materials (Piper 2002). These studies help us understand parent-offspring relationships, child-rearing practices, and the role of children in society.

Apart from the skeletal materials, archeologists examine child burials to answer a variety of questions about social processes in the past (Olsen 1998). Child burials are particularly important in examining the emergence of social complexity. Assuming that complex societies will have ascribed status, a relatively lavish infant or child burial is considered indicative of such (hereditary) status. High status is determined by the array of artifacts, quality of workmanship, materials used, burial location, and overall energy expenditure across all burials at a site (Crown and Fish 1996; Marangou 1991). When child burials are more lavish than that of most adult burials in the same area, we comfortably interpret the disparity as indicative of ascribed status.

The study of the overall mortuary program at a site often reveals that infants are treated differently than older children at death (Palkovich 1980; Whittlesey 2002). The ethnographic record also confirms that less attention may be paid to infant interment. Typically, children are not considered full members of the community until some specific milestone is reached, such as a naming ceremony or talking (Palkovich 1980; Whittlesey 2002).

Representations of Children and Childhood

Figurines and images of children on artifacts and documents provide another avenue for examining childhood in the past (Beaumont 1994; Scott 1992). They provide critical information on children's appearance, what they wore, their hairstyle and ornamentation, and their activities. There is sculptural and pictorial evidence of age grading, gender markers, and status. Depictions of children in Athenian votive sculpture and vase paintings have been used to explore the stages of childhood and adolescence in 5th century Athens (Beaumont 2000). Hays-Gilpin (2002) traces butterfly hairwhorls, a distinctive hairstyle indicative of the transition to womanhood among the Hopi, on rock art and pottery to 500 C.E. Joyce (2000) has constructed a vivid picture of childhood in early Mesoamerican villages by combing ethnohistoric accounts and examining figurines and images found in codices. Images of children appear in Palaeolithic art, and some researchers suggest that children participated in creating cave art (Roveland 2000).

Children and Material Culture

Material objects made specifically for children are a third data source for archeologists interested in childhood (Sofaer Derevenski 2000). These include infant paraphernalia, such as diapers, cradleboards (Piper 2002), and cradles. Children's play areas are also amenable to study through identification of toys, dolls, and other artifacts (Baxter 2006b; Wilkie 2000), including miniature houses resembling full-scale versions which may have been dollhouses (Brugge 1981, 78). Children's presence in some areas is inferred from the imprints left by small feet (Roveland 2000).

Separating objects of material culture made by children from those made by adults can be difficult. Scholars can only speculate, for example, on whether miniature versions of adult tools were made for or by children and whether they were intended for use in work or play (Marangou 1991; Park 1998; Sillar 1994). One useful clue has been fingerprints, with the small size of fingerprints on some pottery taken as indicative of production by children (Kamp 2001b). Studies that rely on relative skill levels in distinguishing the work of children and adults include work on the knapping of stone tools (Finlay 1997; Grimm 2000; Roux and Bril 2006; Shea 2006) and production of ceramics (Bernbeck 1999; Crown 1999, 2001, 2002, 2007a, 2007b).

Learning Crafts In and From the Past

In most traditional societies, children learn to make crafts as an integral part of their development; indeed, in many societies they are expected to gain all the skills they need to run their own households, including making a variety of objects, by their mid-teens when they may be of marriageable age (Crown 2001, 455; Lancy 2008). Learning crafts entails learning in the context of doing, a lengthy process for most crafts that involves moving toward error-free performance in practice. Over these years, the process of learning leaves a material residue. Learning to weave a blanket, form a pot, or fashion a projectile point leaves production debris along with finished objects. While they are learning, children produce imperfect finished objects that show lower skill levels than objects made by individuals who are experienced. Archeologists compare skill levels of finished objects in attempting to identify the work of learners. This identification is strengthened when production tools, debris, or imperfect finished objects are found with child burials, or when musculoskeletal markers indicate that children were performing repetitive tasks, or when we find images of children performing crafts.

Archeologists rely on studies by educational psychologists of children learning to draw human figures or their awareness of specific art styles to set lower limits on the likely starting point for a child learning a craft. The milestone of holding a drawing tool with a precision grip comes at around age 4, and from this age on, the fine motor skills involved in controlling such tools improve with repeated practice (Biber 1962). Children in pottery-producing cultures must learn to hold paintbrushes properly to decorate vessels. This makes it unlikely that children would learn to decorate pottery before age 4. Likewise, studies indicate that it is not until age 7–9 that children in different cultures fully understand the decorative style characteristic of their group, including the fine points of design symmetry (Dennis 1942, 347; Wilson and Wilson 1984; Wilson and Litgvoet 1992). Such studies provide indications of how the work of child learners would likely look at different ages and how it might differ from the work of an adult.

My own research concentrates on how children learned to make pottery in the past. Becoming a potter requires mastering a sequence of tasks, each involving motor skills, knowledge of materials, tools, and sometimes symbols and rituals. A number of specific tasks are involved in making pottery: collecting clay and other raw materials, including aplastic inclusions (e.g., rock, sand, shell), slip clays, and pigments; processing and mixing the raw materials to make a suitable clay for pottery; forming a vessel; finishing the vessel, including evening walls, slipping, polishing, and perhaps decorating the vessel with a paintbrush and pigment; drying the vessel for an appropriate amount of time; collecting fuel for firing; firing the vessel; adding any postfiring finish. Some of these tasks can be performed at any time of the year by virtually anyone. Others must be completed relatively rapidly or at specific times or may require a high skill level.

The amount of time it takes to learn to make pottery depends on many factors. Contemporary American children may learn in Kindergarten to make small pots by the pinch method, or perhaps even the coil method. Students with continuing interest in pottery may learn to throw pots on a potter's wheel when they are in high school. Wheel throwing is more difficult to learn than pinching clay, partly because it requires greater strength and partly because it requires each hand/arm to perform different but coordinated actions (Roux 1990, 68–70). It is also easier to make a smaller vessel than a larger one; indeed, even in pottery-making communities, many potters never master the largest, most complex forms (Bowser 2000, 227; Kramer 1997, 28). Mastering a simple decoration is much easier than mastering a complex design. Ethnographic studies of novice potters reveal that the learning process can take from a few months to many years (Crown 2007a; David and Kramer 2001; Roux 1990). Potters may not aspire to the highest level of skill until their children are independent and they can devote more time to making pottery (Naranjo 1992).

Learning and teaching frameworks for ceramics (and, indeed, most crafts) generally fall into one of several categories (Schiffer and Skibo 1987, 597; Whiting and Edwards 1988, 16–17). The observation and imitation framework entails a learner watching the actions of a more skilled potter and imitating them; this is generally done without any verbal instruction. Persistent self-instruction involves continuing trial and error. When the learner secures the assistance of a more expert teacher, there may be explicit verbal instruction. Formal apprenticeships generally involve youth learning—over an extended period—from highly skilled individuals (usually not relatives), in exchange for labor or payment (Coy 1989; see also chapter 8, this volume). Because my research concerns societies known as middle-range societies (those that are not as complex as states, but more complex than hunter-gatherer or foraging bands), I examined the learning frameworks for such middle-range societies in the Human Relations Area Files (see chapter 8, this volume). For the 25 pottery-making groups for which observations were available, in 48 percent, children learned pottery production by observation/imitation and trial/error alone; in 24 percent, they received some verbal instruction from adults in domestic contexts; and in 28 percent, they learned through more formal apprenticeships (Crown 2002, 109). This fits with what we know from most ethnographic descriptions of learning in middle-range societies (Bunzel 1929/1972; Crown 1999; DeBoer 1990; Fortes 1938; Goody 1989; Lave and Wenger 1991; Pettitt 1946; Roe 1995, 51; although see Gosselain 1998, 94; Wallaert-Pêtre 2001).

I also drew on historical, ethnographic, and autobiographic accounts of ceramic skill acquisition for southwestern societies during the period 1540 to the present. Historically, Pueblo girls learned to make pottery in domestic contexts by observation/imitation of same-sex adults (Bunzel 1929/1972; Fowler 1977; Hill 1982, 139; Lewis, Mitchell, and Garcia 1990; Stanislawski and Stanislawski 1978; Wyckoff 1985). Girls initiated the learning process, often around age 5–6, by watching and copying adult potters, who were usually relatives. Verbal instruction was rare, although adults sometimes gave brief instructions and often critiqued finished products (Fowler 1977, 29; Hill 1982, 139), but children were discouraged from asking questions. Contemporary Acoma/Laguna potters sometimes give children formed vessels to practice their painting or outline designs for learners to fill in (Olsen 2002, 162, 230), but this level of intervention is rare. The pace of learning was driven by the child's interest and ability, but mastery was expected by age 15 or the threshold of marriage. The published accounts indicate that learning generally followed a sequence from forming vessels, to decorating vessels, to firing vessels.

Learning to Make Pots in the Prehispanic Southwest

My own research explores how children learned to become competent potters in the prehispanic American Southwest. In these areas, sedentary farmers made pottery with painted decorations for use in household and ritual contexts from about 500 to the present. My research examines how knowledge was circulated in these societies, how adults guided learners, how learners accessed technology and knowledge, and the order in which the complex production sequences were mastered. In a survey of eight major U.S. museum collections, I found around 40,000 whole vessels. Of these, I selected 845 for further analysis, including all vessels that appeared to have been made by unskilled individuals. These vessels represent about 3–6 percent of the total vessels of each type examined. The vessels came from seven different culture areas, dating between about 900 and 1450.

I recorded 40 attributes for each vessel, including attributes that assessed skill in vessel painting and forming, vessel technology, vessel life history, and presence of specific learning aids. The latter included faintly incising designs for learners to paint over, providing already formed vessels for learners to decorate, and allowing learners to complete minor details on an otherwise finished design. All these techniques are also attested in ethnographic studies of pottery craft transmission.

My research using archeological collections indicates greater variation in crafts learning in the past than the historical and ethnographic accounts would indicate. This is seen when comparing the results of the study for two culture areas only: the Mimbres area of southwestern New Mexico, with my sample dating between approximately 900–1150; and the Hohokam area of southern Arizona, with my sample dating 700–1100 (Crown 2001). The Hohokam and Mimbres were contemporaneous for part of this time, and assemblages demonstrate interaction between the two groups. While they had different material culture and probably different languages, they did exchange pottery, and perhaps other material items. As far as we know, the materials for making pottery were equally plentiful, equally easy to process, and equally easy to manipulate in the two areas.

Traditionally, Mimbres decorated pots were primarily bowls formed by spiraling thin coils to form the walls and then scraping the coil joins away with a tool. Vessels were then slipped, at least on the interiors, and then painted with iron-based paints. Designs could be either geometric or representational. The pots were then fired in a neutral to reducing atmosphere to achieve black designs on a white background. I compared vessels made by unskilled learners (considered to be children) with those made by skilled potters. The children's vessels included some made by the pinch technique, while the skilled vessels were all made by coiling and scraping. The children made pots that are significantly smaller than those made by adults, with significantly less even wall thicknesses. Children painted fewer motifs per vessel on average, using fatter paintbrushes.

They had to pick up the paintbrush often to achieve a single line and their linework tended to be shaky. Where they painted multiple versions of the same motif, the motifs were often unequal in size. Two bowls have designs classified as "scribbling," with random lines that fail to capture any semblance of traditional Mimbres decoration (see figure 16.1). Children painted Mimbres designs with a high rate of errors; 83 percent of their vessels have 1–10 errors. Many pots show collaboration between skilled adult and learning child. Adults made 50 percent of the vessels decorated by children. On 18 percent of the vessels, a skilled potter painted most of the design, with an unskilled learner finishing a small portion of the design or painting a different wall of the pot. On three vessels, skilled potters faintly outlined designs for learners to paint over, providing a template for the learner to follow (see figure 16.2).

Hohokam potters traditionally formed vessels out of fat coils that were thinned using a wooden paddle to beat the exterior wall, while a stone anvil was placed inside the vessel opposite the paddle. They produced a wider variety of forms and shapes. Designs were painted in hematite pigments on buff-firing clays to create red-on-buff pottery. In the sample of vessels made by unskilled learners, only one pot is formed using a paddle and anvil; the remainder were made by pinching the clay into shape or molding the clay within an existing vessel. Children made significantly smaller vessels in a wide range of shapes, but not as many shapes as adults. Both children and adults painted roughly the same number of types of motifs, but the children had trouble spacing the motifs evenly, so that the last motif was often smaller than the others. Children attempted traditional Hohokam designs, generally without success. As with the Mimbres children, Hohokam children used wide brushes, many brush liftings, and shaky linework in their designs (see figure 16.3). Hohokam child potters made fewer errors than their Mimbres counterparts. Adults made 41 percent of the vessels decorated by children, and they collaborated with children on 6 percent of the designs. However, adults did not provide underlying templates for children to paint.

Several aspects of these results are interesting. Skilled Mimbres potters made few forms with relatively simple technology, but striking designs. When children learned the craft, the emphasis was on the painted designs, so that even from a very young age (as young as 4), Mimbres children were allowed to "decorate" vessels made by adults. The emphasis here seems to

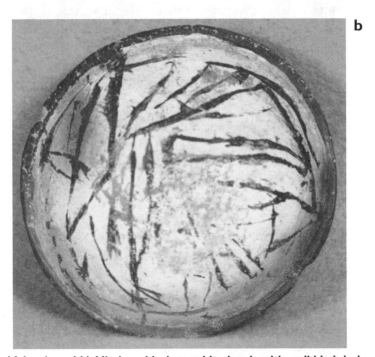

Figure 16.1.   (a and b) Mimbres black-on-white bowls with scribbled designs. (a) Mimbres black-on-white bowl, 35 mm high (Catalog no. 1992.22.402 [11B-508]). (b) Mimbres black-on-white bowl, 58 mm high (Catalog no. 1992.22.1020 [15-B456]). Collection of the Frederick R. Weisman Art Museum at the University of Minnesota, Minneapolis. Transfer, Department of Anthropology, University of Minnesota (M. Tyndall photo).

Figure 16.2. (a and b) Mimbres black-on-white scoop with inset showing spiral with faint outline by skilled potter (barely visible in main photograph by arrow) overpainted by unskilled learner. (Catalog no. 1992.22.869 [15B-300]). Collection of the Frederick R. Weisman Art Museum at the University of Minnesota, Minneapolis. Transfer, Department of Anthropology, University of Minnesota (M. Tyndall photo).

Figure 16.3. (a and b) Hohokam red-on-buff vessels made by unskilled learners. Note numerous brush liftings on (a). On vessel (b), note central series of ticks, which budding potter began by pushing paintbrush from blob up, and then learned while moving around the pot to pull paint from blob down.

(a) Hohokam red-on-buff scoop, 46 mm high (Arizona State Museum Collection, no. 94-134-253). (b) Hohokam red-on-buff jar, 42 mm high (Arizona State Museum Collection, no. 94-134-339). Collections of the Arizona State Museum, University of Arizona(M. Tyndall photo).

have been on learning to paint careful, fine designs. Adults aided in this process by providing finished vessels and templates to follow. Budding potters painted the same range of designs as their elders, from geometric to naturalistic designs of plants and animals. In contrast, Hohokam children began making vessels with nontraditional techniques (pinching) and apparently only mastered the more difficult paddle-and-anvil technique when they had learned the basics of the simpler technology. This may be due to developmental issues, because wielding a paddle and anvil requires greater strength and coordination than pinching or molding a vessel. So the emphasis among the Hohokam seems to have been placed on becoming familiar with the overall technology and designs before attempting to make vessels with the paddle and anvil. Hohokam designs were simpler than Mimbres designs, so that Hohokam children learned to paint a fairly rigid and relatively simple set of standard designs.

The patterning apparent in the sampled vessels indicates that Mimbres children began learning the craft at a younger age than Hohokam children. While both groups of children probably learned by observation and imitation, Mimbres children, with much higher error rates, may have had greater freedom of expression. In contrast, Hohokam children seem to have participated only to the extent that they were capable of doing things appropriately. They began with nontraditional methods and only learned the more difficult forming techniques once they had mastered the rest of the production process.

The Mimbres and Hohokam areas are only two subregions considered in my research program. Other areas and time periods show different patterns in the preferred forms for the earliest fired vessels, the ages at which children began painting vessels based on the motor skills evident in the finished work, the sequence of mastering ceramic technology, the use of traditional methods of forming vessels, the treatment of errors on vessels, and how adults participated in guiding young learners (Crown 2007a). Although my research depends in part on studies in psychology that emphasize *universal regularities* in the stages of development that all humans pass through before adulthood, the results illuminate the *complexity and variety* of ceramic craft learning.

This variability may be linked to the trajectory of change seen in the archeological record (DeBoer 1990; Gosselain 1998; Greenfield 1984). Societies, such as the Hohokam, that emphasize careful replication of adult models tend to have more adult involvement in the training process and are less tolerant of very young, clumsy learners. This pattern ultimately results in slow, gradual change in the archeological record of crafts production. In contrast, societies that emphasize open experimentation and creativity in the training process, such as the Mimbreños, seem to have a different pattern of adult involvement, which leads to more rapid shifts in crafts design and technology (see Wallaert-Pêtre 2001 for a discussion of open and closed learning systems among contemporary African potters).

As discussed earlier, the ethnographic, ethnohistoric, and autobiographical records for indigenous American Southwest groups emphasize only one manner of learning: observation and imitation of skilled same-sex adults. The archeological materials reveal more complex and nuanced ways of learning and teaching in the past, with variation across time and culture areas. In particular, the archeological material shows interaction between skilled adult potters and unskilled children. In some cases, the children may be contributing labor toward finishing pots for adult potters. In other cases, the adult may be "scaffolding" the child's budding abilities and helping them reach a higher level of expertise than they would on their own (Vygotsky 1978). Importantly, vessels made by unskilled learners were not merely "refrigerator art," for 69 percent of the vessels show substantial use wear. Contexts of recovery for the vessels are identical to vessels made by skilled potters. That said, an important future question concerns the possible dependence on child labor in the past. Was making and decorating vessels solely for learning purposes and practice, or was it economically important? At what point were children expected to contribute viable labor to the household and community?

Conclusion

For too long, archeologists assumed that only adults created the past. The hands of children were seen only in the creation of a miniature world of presumed toys. Any deviation from this assumption had to be heavily bolstered by evidence. This viewpoint has been changing, as archeologists recognize that children helped create, break, and reconstitute the archeological record. Learning culturally appropriate behavior and tasks was as critical to a child's survival as it is today. By focusing on the child becoming a skilled craftsperson, we can hope to understand how the processes of learning shaped the material results.

Acknowledgment

Funding for the study of how children learned to become potters in the American Southwest came from the National Endowment for the Humanities (RZ-20362-98), the Wenner-Gren Foundation (Grant #6318), and an American Philosophical Society Sabbatical Fellowship. The vessels discussed are curated at the Arizona State Museum/University of Arizona, Field Museum of Natural History, Museum of New Mexico/Museum of Indian Arts and Culture, Museum of Northern Arizona, Peabody Museum at Harvard University, Smithsonian Institution/National Museum of Natural History Museum Support Center, and the Frederick R. Weisman Art Museum at the University of Minnesota. David Lancy and John Bock provided useful comments on an earlier draft of this paper.

Note

1. Relatively little research has focused on the important issue of how children in the past affected the archeological record (Baxter 2006b; Hammond and Hammond 1981; Shea 2006). Indeed, archeologists have spent more time considering how rodents and dogs alter the archeological record than how children might have. Yet children likely altered the material present in their habitation areas through play, including moving items from one part of the site to another and breaking objects. Archeologists have looked at this issue almost entirely among hunter-gatherer populations (Politis 2005).

Bibliography

Baxter, Jane. "Introduction: The Archaeology of Childhood in Context." Pp. 1–9 in *Childhood in Action: Perspectives on the Archaeology of Childhood*, edited by Jane Baxter. Washington, D.C.: Archeological Papers of the American Anthropological Association, no. 15, 2006a.

——. "Making Space for Children in Archaeological Interpretations." Pp. 77–88 in *Childhood in Action: Perspectives on the Archaeology of Childhood*, edited by Jane Baxter. Washington, D.C.: Archeological Papers of the American Anthropological Association, no. 15, 2006b.

Beaumont, Lesley. "Constructing a Methodology for the Interpretation of Childhood Age in Classical Athenian Iconography." *Archaeological Review from Cambridge* 13, no. 2 (1994): 81–96.

———. "The Social Status and Artistic Presentation of 'Adolescence' in Fifth Century Athens." Pp. 39–50 in *Children and Material Culture*, edited by Joanna Sofaer Derevenski. London: Routledge, 2000.

Bennike, Pia, Mary E. Lewis, Holger Schutkowski, and F. Valentin. "Comparison of Child Morbidity in Two Contrasting Medieval Cemeteries from Denmark." *American Journal of Physical Anthropology* 128, no. 4 (December 2005): 734–46.

Bernbeck, Reinhard. "Structure Strikes Back: Intuitive Meanings of Ceramics from Qale Rostam, Iran." Pp. 90–111 in *Material Symbols: Culture and Economy in Prehistory*, edited by John E. Robb. Occasional paper no. 26. Carbondale: Southern Illinois University, Center for Archaeological Investigations, 1999.

Biber, Barbara. *Children's Drawings: From Lines to Pictures Illustrated*. New York: Bank Street College of Education, 1962.

Blom, Deborah E., Jane E. Buikstra, Linda Keng, Paula Tomczak, Eleanor Shoreman, and Debbit Stevens-Tuttle. "Anemia and Childhood Mortality: Latitudinal Patterning along the Coast of Pre-Columbian Peru." *American Journal of Physical Anthropology* 127, no. 2 (June 2005): 152–69.

Bowser, Brenda. "From Pottery to Politics: An Ethnoarchaeological Study of Political Factionalism, Ethnicity, and Domestic Pottery Style in the Ecuadorian Amazon." *Journal of Archaeological Method and Theory* 7, no. 3 (September 2000): 219–48.

Bradley, Cynthia. "Thoughts Count: Ideology and the Children of Sand Canyon Pueblo." Pp. 169–195 in *Children of the Prehistoric Puebloan Southwest*, edited by Kathryn A. Kamp. Salt Lake City: University of Utah Press, 2002.

Brugge, David. "The Historical Archaeology of Chaco Canyon." Pp. 69–106 in *Archaeological Surveys of Chaco Canyon*, part 2, edited by Alden Hayes, David Brugge, and W. James Judge. Albuquerque: University of New Mexico Press, 1981.

Bunzel, Ruth. *The Pueblo Potter: A Study in Creative Imagination in Primitive Art*. New York: Dover, 1929.

Cardoso, Hugo. "Sample-Specific (Universal) Metric Approaches for Determining the Sex of Immature Human Skeletal Remains Using Permanent Tooth Dimensions." *Journal of Archaeological Science* 35, no. 1 (January 2008): 158–68.

Coy, Michael, ed. *Apprenticeship: From Theory to Method and Back Again*. Albany: SUNY Press, 1989.

Crist, Thomas A. "Babies in the Privy: Prostitution, Infanticide, and Abortion in New York City's Five Points District." *Historical Archaeology* 39, no. 1 (2005): 19–46.

Crown, Patricia. "Socialization in American Southwest Pottery Decoration." Pp. 25–43 in *Pottery and People*, edited by James M. Skibo and Gary Feinman. Salt Lake City: University of Utah Press, 1999.

———. "Learning to Make Pottery in the Prehispanic American Southwest." *Journal of Anthropological Research* 57, no. 4 (Winter 2001): 451–69.

———. "Learning and Teaching in the Prehispanic American Southwest." Pp. 108–24 in *Children in the Prehistoric Puebloan Southwest*, edited by Kathryn A. Kamp. Salt Lake City: University of Utah Press, 2002.

———. "Learning about Learning." Pp. 198–217 in *Archaeological Anthropology: Perspectives on Method and Theory*, edited by James M. Skibo, Michael W. Graves, and Miriam T. Stark. Tucson: University of Arizona Press, 2007a.

———. "Life Histories of Pots and Potters: Situating the Individual in Archaeology." *American Antiquity* 72, no. 4 (July 2007b): 677–90.

Crown, Patricia, and Suzanne Fish. "Gender and Status in the Hohokam Preclassic to Classic Transition." *American Anthropologist* 98, no. 4 (December 1996): 803–17.

David, Nicholas, and Carol Kramer. *Ethnoarchaeology in Action*. Cambridge: Cambridge University Press, 2001.

DeBoer, Warren. "Interaction, Imitation, and Communication as Expressed in Style: The Ucayali Experience." Pp. 82–104 in *The Uses of Style in Archaeology*, edited by Margaret Wright Conkey and Christine Ann Hastorf. Cambridge: Cambridge University Press, 1990.

Dennis, Wayne. "The Performance of Hopi Children on the Goodenough Draw-a-Man Test." *Journal of Comparative Psychology* 34, no. 3 (1942): 341–8.

Fink, Michael, and Charles Merbs. "Hohokam Paleonutrition and Paleopathology of the Salt River Hohokam: A Search for Correlates." *Kiva* 56, no. 3 (1991): 293–317.

Finlay, Nyree. "Kid Knapping: Missing Children in Lithic Analysis." Pp. 203–212 in *Invisible People and Processes: Writing Gender and Childhood into European Archaeology*, edited by Jenny Moore and Eleanor Scott. London: Leicester University Press, 1997.

Fortes, Meyer. "Social and Psychological Aspects of Education in Taleland." Pp. 201–59 in *Time and Social Structure and Other Essays*, edited by Meyer Fortes. London: Athlone, 1938.

Fowler, Carol. *"Daisy Hooee Nampeyo: The Story of an American Indian."* Minneapolis: Dillon, 1977.

Goodman, Alan, and George Armelagos. "Infant and Childhood Morbidity and Mortality Risks in Archaeological Populations." *World Archaeology* 21, no. 2 (October 1989): 225–43.

Goody, Esther. "Learning, Apprenticeship, and the Division of Labor." Pp. 233–55 in *Apprenticeship: From Theory to Method and Back Again*, edited by Michael Coy. Albany: SUNY Press, 1989.

Gosselain, Olivier. "Social and Technical Identity in a Clay Crystal Ball." Pp. 78–106 in *The Archaeology of Social Boundaries*, edited by Miriam T. Stark. Washington, D.C.: Smithsonian Institution, 1998.

Greenfield, Patricia. "A Theory of the Teacher in the Learning Activities of Everyday Life." Pp. 117–38 in *Everyday Cognition: Its Development in Social Context*, edited by Barbara Rogoff and Jean Lave. Cambridge, Mass.: Harvard University Press, 1984.

Grimm, Linda. "Apprentice Flintknapping: Relating Material Culture and Social Practice in the Upper Paleolithic." Pp. 153–71 in *Children and Material Culture*, edited by Joanna Sofaer Derevenski. London: Routledge, 2000.

Hammond, Gawain, and Norman Hammond. "Child's Play: A Distorting Factor in Archaeological Distribution." *American Antiquity* 46, no. 3 (July 1981): 634–6.

Haury, Emil. *The Hohokam: Desert Farmers and Craftsmen*. Tucson: University of Arizona Press, 1976.

Hays-Gilpin, Kelley. "Wearing a Butterfly, Coming of Age: A 1,500 Year Old Pueblo Tradition." Pp. 196–210 in *Children of the Prehistoric Puebloan Southwest*, edited by Kathryn A. Kamp. Salt Lake City: University of Utah Press, 2002.

Hershkovitz, Israel, Bruce M. Rothschild, Bruce Latimer, Olivier Dutour, Georges Léonetti, Charles M. Greenwald, Christine Rothschild, and Lyman M. Jellema. "Recognition of Sickle-cell Anemia in Skeletal Remains of Children. *American Journal of Physical Anthropology* 104, no. 2 (October 1997): 213–26.

Hill, W. W. *An Ethnography of Santa Clara Pueblo New Mexico*. Albuquerque: University of New Mexico Press, 1982.

Humphrey, Louise, and Tania King. "Childhood Stress: A Lifetime Legacy." *Anthropologie: International Journal of the Science of Man* 38, no. 1 (2000): 33–49.

Joyce, Rosemary A. "Girling the Girl and Boying the Boy: The Production of Adulthood in Ancient Mesoamerica." *World Archaeology* 31, no. 3 (February 2000): 473–83.

Judd, Neil. *The Material Culture of Pueblo Bonito*. Smithsonian Miscellaneous Collections, vol. 124. Washington, D.C.: Smithsonian Institution, 1954.

Kamp, Kathryn. "Where Have All the Children Gone? The Archaeology of Childhood." *Journal of Archaeological Method and Theory* 8, no. 1 (March 2001a): 1–34.

———. "Prehistoric Children Working and Playing: A Southwestern Case Study in Learning Ceramics." *Journal of Anthropological Research* 57, no. 4 (Winter 2001b): 427–50.

———. "Working for a Living: Childhood in the Prehistoric Southwestern Pueblos." Pp. 71–89 in *Children of the Prehistoric Puebloan Southwest*, edited by Kathryn A. Kamp. Salt Lake City: University of Utah Press, 2002.

Kamp, Kathryn, and John Whittaker. "*Prehistoric Pueblo Children in Archaeology and Art.*" Pp. 14–40 in *Children of the Prehistoric Puebloan Southwest*, edited by Kathryn A. Kamp. Salt Lake City: University of Utah Press, 2002.

Kramer, Carol. *Pottery in Rajastan: Ethnoarchaeology in Two Indian Cities.* Washington, D.C.: Smithsonian Institution, 1997.

Lancy, David. *The Anthropology of Childhood: Cherubs, Chattel, and Changelings.* Cambridge: Cambridge University Press, 2008.

Lave, Jean, and Etienne Wenger. *Situated Learning: Legitimate Peripheral Participation.* Cambridge: Cambridge University Press, 1991.

Lewis, Lucy, Emma Lewis Mitchell, and Delores Lewis Garcia. "*Daughters of the Anasazi.*" (Video) Interpark. Farmington, N.M.: Film Projects, 1990.

Lillehammer, Grete. "Child Is Born: The Child's World in an Archaeological Perspective." *Norwegian Archaeological Review* 22, no. 2 (1989): 89–105.

Lillie, Malcolm C. "Women and Children in Prehistory: Resource Sharing and Social Stratification at the Mesolithic-Neolithic Transition in Ukraine." Pp. 213–28 in *Invisible People and Processes: Writing Gender and Childhood into European Archaeology*, edited by Jenny Moore and Eleanor Scott. London: Leicester University Press, 1997.

Marangou, Christina. "Social Differentiation in the Early Bronze Age: Miniature Metal Tools and Child Burials." *Journal of Mediterranean Studies* 1, no. 2 (1991): 211–25.

Moore, Jenny. "Conclusion: Visibility of the Invisible." Pp. 251–57 in *Invisible People and Processes: Writing Gender and Childhood into European Archaeology*, edited by Jenny Moore and Eleanor Scott. London: Leicester University Press, 1997.

Naranjo, Tessie. "Social Change and Pottery-Making at Santa Clara Pueblo." Doctoral dissertation, University of New Mexico, 1992.

Olsen, Barbara A. "Women, Children, and the Family in the Late Aegean Bronze Age: Differences in Minoan and Mycenaean Constructions of Gender." *World Archaeology* 29, no. 3 (February 1998): 380–92.

Olsen, Beyer, Eva Margrete Stermer, and Risnes Steinar. "Radiographic Analysis of Dental Development Used in Age Determination of Infant and Juvenile Skulls from a Medieval Archaeological Site in Norway." *International Journal of Osteoarchaeology* 4, no. 4 (December 1994): 299–303.

Olsen, Nancy. "Potters' Choices: The Social Construction of Pottery-Making at Acoma and Laguna Pueblos, New Mexico." Doctoral dissertation, University of New Mexico, 2002.

Palkovich, Ann M. *Pueblo Population and Society: The Arroyo Hondo Skeletal and Mortuary Remains*. Santa Fe: School of American Research Press, 1980.

Park, Robert W. "Size Counts: The Miniature Archaeology of Childhood in Inuit Societies." *Antiquity* 72, no. 276 (June 1998): 269–81.

Pawleta, Michal. "Re-constructing Childhood in Archaeology." *Ethnographisch-archaologische Zeitschrift* 45, nos. 2–3 (2004): 181–97.

Perry, Megan. "Redefining Childhood through Bioarchaeology: Toward an Archaeological and Biological Understanding of Children in Antiquity." Pp. 89–111 in *Childhood in Action: Perspectives on the Archaeology of Childhood*, edited by Jane Baxter. Washington, D.C.: Archeological Papers of the American Anthropological Association, no. 15, 2006.

Pettitt, George A. *Primitive Education in North America*. Berkeley: University of California Publications in American Archaeology and Ethnology, no. 43, 1946.

Piper, Claudette. "The Morphology of Prehispanic Cradleboards: Form Follows Function." Pp. 41–70 in *Children of the Prehistoric Puebloan Southwest*, edited by Kathryn A. Kamp. Salt Lake City: University of Utah Press, 2002.

Politis, Gustavo. "Children's Activity in the Production of the Archaeological Record of Hunter-Gatherers: An Ethnoarchaeological Approach." Pp. 121–43 in *Global Archaeological Theory*, edited by Pedro Paulo Funari, Andrés Zarankin, and Emily Stovel. New York: Springer, 2005.

Roe, Peter. "Style, Society, Myth, and Structure." Pp. 27–76 in *Style, Society, and Person: Archaeological and Ethnological Perspectives*, edited by Christopher Carr and Jill E. Neitzel. New York: Plenum, 1995.

Roux, Valentine. *The Potters Wheel: Craft Specialization and Technical Competence*. New Delhi: Oxford and IBH, 1990.

Roux, Valentine, and Blandine Bril. *Stone Knapping: The Necessary Conditions for a Uniquely Hominid Behaviour*. Cambridge: McDonald Institute Monographs, 2006.

Roveland, Blythe. "Footprints in the Clay: Upper Palaeolithic Children in Ritual and Secular Contexts." Pp. 29–38 in *Children and Material Culture*, edited by Joanna Sofaer Derevenski. London: Routledge, 2000.

Schiffer, Michael B., and James M. Skibo. "Theory and Experiment in the Study of Technological Change." *Current Anthropology* 28, no. 5 (December 1987): 595–622.

Schurr, Mark. "Using Stable Nitrogen-Isotopes to Study Weaning Behavior in Past Populations." *World Archaeology* 30, no. 2 (October 1998): 327–42.

Schurr, Mark R., and Mary Lucas Powell. "The Role of Changing Childhood Diets in the Prehistoric Evolution of Food Production: An Isotopic Assessment." *American Journal of Physical Anthropology* 126, no. 3 (March 2005): 278–94.

Scott, Eleanor. "Images and Contexts of Infants and Infant Burials: Some Thoughts on Some Cross-Cultural Evidence." *Archaeological Review from Cambridge* 11, no. 1 (1992): 77–92.

———. "Introduction: On the Incompleteness of Archaeological Narratives." Pp. 1–11 in *Invisible People and Processes: Writing Gender and Childhood into European Archaeology*, edited by Jenny Moore and Eleanor Scott. London: Leicester University Press, 1997.

Shea, John J. "Child's Play: Reflections on the Invisibility of Children in the Paleolithic Record." *Evolutionary Anthropology* 15, no. 6 (November/December 2006): 212–16.

Sillar, Bill. "Playing with God: Cultural Perceptions of Children, Play and Miniatures in the Andes." *Archaeological Review from Cambridge* 13, no. 2 (1994): 47–64.

Sobolik, Kristin. "Children's Health in the Prehistoric Southwest." Pp. 125–51 in *Children of the Prehistoric Puebloan Southwest*, edited by Kathryn A. Kamp. Salt Lake City: University of Utah Press, 2002.

Sofaer Derevenski, Joanna. "Where Are the Children? Accessing Children in the Past." *Archaeological Review from Cambridge* 13, no. 2 (1994): 7–20.

———. "Engendering Children, Engendering Archaeology." Pp. 192–202 in *Invisible People and Processes: Writing Gender and Childhood into European Archaeology*, edited by Jenny Moore and Eleanor Scott. London: Leicester University Press, 1997.

———, ed. *"Children and Material Culture."* New York: Routledge, 2000.

Stanislawski, Michael B., and Barbara B. Stanislawski. "Hopi and Hopi-Tewa Ceramic Tradition Networks." Pp. 61–76 in *The Spatial Organization of Culture*, edited by Ian Hodder. Pittsburgh: University of Pittsburgh Press, 1987.

Surovell, Todd. "Early Paleoindian Women, Children, Mobility, and Fertility." *American Antiquity* 65, no. 3 (July 2000): 493–508.

Sutter, Richard C. "Nonmetric Subadult Skeletal Sexing Traits: I. A Blind Test of the Accuracy of Eight Previously Proposed Methods Using Prehistoric

Known-Sex Mummies from Northern Chile." *Journal of Forensic Sciences* 48, no. 5 (September 2003): 927–35.

Visser, Edward. "Little Waifs: Estimating Child Body Size from the Historic Skeletal Material." *International Journal of Osteoarchaeology* 8, no. 6 (November/December 1998): 413–23.

Vygotsky, Lev S. *Mind in Society*. Translated by Michael Cole, V. John-Steiner, Sylvia Scribner, and Ellen Souberman. Cambridge, Mass.: Harvard University Press, 1978.

Walker, Phillip L., Della C. Cook, and Patricia M. Lambert. "Skeletal Evidence for Child Abuse: A Physical Anthropological Perspective." *Journal of Forensic Sciences* 42, no. 1 (January 1997): 196–207.

Wallaert-Pêtre, Hélène. "Learning How to Make the Right Pots: Apprenticeship Strategies and Material Culture: A Case Study in Handmade Pottery from Cameroon." *Journal of Anthropological Research* 57, no. 4 (Winter 2001): 471–93.

Whiting, Beatrice B., and Caroline P. Edwards. *Children of Different Worlds: The Formation of Social Behavior*. Cambridge: Harvard University Press, 1988.

Whittlesey, Stephanie. "The Cradle of Death: Mortuary Practices, Bioarchaeology, and the Children of Grasshopper Pueblo." Pp. 152–68 in *Children of the Prehistoric Puebloan Southwest*, edited by Kathryn A. Kamp. Salt Lake City: University of Utah Press, 2002.

Wilkie, Laurie. "Not Merely Child's Play: Creating a Historical Archaeology of Children and Childhood." Pp. 100–14 in *Children and Material Culture*, edited by Joanna Sofaer Derevenski. London: Routledge, 2000.

Wilson, Brent, and Johan Litgvoet. "Across Time and Cultures: Stylistic Changes in the Drawings of Dutch Children." Pp. 75–88 in *Drawing Research and Development*, edited by David Thistlewood. London: Longman, 1992.

Wilson, Brent, and Marjorie Wilson. "Children's Drawings in Egypt: Cultural Style Acquisition as Graphic Development." *Visual Arts Research* 10 (1984): 13–26.

Wyckoff, Lydia. *Designs and Factions: Politics, Religion, and Ceramics on the Hopi Third Mesa*. Albuquerque: University of New Mexico Press, 1985.

Part V
LEARNING IN THE 21ST CENTURY

CHAPTER SEVENTEEN

LEARNING ON THE STREETS: PEER SOCIALIZATION IN ADVERSE ENVIRONMENTS

Jon Wolseth

A Walking Itinerary of the *Zona Colonial*

For nearly two and a half years, I lived in Santo Domingo, Dominican Republic, working street outreach for homeless and near-homeless kids with a Dominican nongovernmental organization (NGO). Although the work was in conjunction with my Peace Corps service, I approached my volunteering as a lesson in making my doctorate in anthropology in some way useful to the world of child welfare services. I attempted to apply ethnographic methods to understanding the realities of street life with the goal of improving upon existing services and helping develop intervention programs sensitive to the needs of the children with whom we worked. Outreach typically included walking through the densely packed streets of the historic Colonial Zone in downtown Santo Domingo at night. The bulk of the kids with whom the organization had constant contact lived and worked in this tourist-heavy area. Through repeated visits to this area, I began to understand the close relationship street kids have with the places they frequent and how much a particular location dictates what types of activities are possible there. In many respects, the ambient qualities of place such as lighting, infrastructure, foot traffic, and pollution shaped the appearance and behavior of the street kids who worked and lived there.

Take, for instance, a typical late Saturday evening walk through part of the Colonial Zone at the end of May. At 2:00 in the morning, the pedestrian mall lost all of the little charm it had during the day. Unlike most of the rest of the city, this part of the Colonial Zone was normally well lit, even well into the early morning. But the street lamps created an artificial halo, a glow that radiated out from the middle and faded into a twilight on the edges near the storefronts. There were few people about—some late-night clubbers returning home, a couple of hamburger vendors, and small bands of street kids. At that hour, the homeless adults were safely on their storefront steps, wrapped in cardboard boxes or blankets or plastic garbage bags. It was the young ones, the kids under 15, who roamed through the Colonial Zone in the early morning. Older homeless kids weren't to be seen. They were looking for money elsewhere, prostituting themselves out along the boardwalk, or stealthily looking for a vulnerable place to rob. Nighttime was busy for street kids.

There was a small group of five in the block ahead of where I was. Some were bootblacks with their homemade wooden shoeshine boxes, seated on top where the customer's shoe would go. Although they would say they were going home that evening if I were to ask, the truth was, it was too late for most of them to get back into their neighborhoods. They lived far from the center of the city and in areas too dangerous to enter at that hour. Two of the five, Alejandro and Manuel, were kids I recognized from our street outreach program.

Alejandro was all dolled up. He had on a long, mauve-colored, quilted women's jacket. Because he was so tiny, the coat reached his heels and looked more like a trench coat than something a snow bunny would wear. With the coat and wearing a pair of aviator glasses he must have lifted off one of the roaming sunglass vendors, Alejandro looked like a mobster. He was the center of attention. Even Manuel, who normally preferred to lead, was under Alejandro's spell.

"Hey *mafioso*," I called out to Alejandro and the group as I passed by, "Careful the tourist police don't catch you horsing around at this hour."

"Jon!" Alejandro called back, detaching himself from the group. The coat billowed out slightly and the tails trailed behind him. Jesus, I thought, he even walks like a mobster. This 13-year-old knows how to act.

Manuel was right behind him. He must have been begging earlier, for he was shoeless and had on a pair of pants so holey they rivaled Swiss cheese. His short frame was covered in a shirt that was two times too long, hanging well below the waist. The combination of the pants, no shoes, and the oversized shirt gave Manuel the look of the perfect mendicant child, like the Little Match Girl or something.

"You guys been hanging out with Julio lately?" I asked, thinking they might know where he'd been sleeping these days.

"No way man, I don't hang out with him," Alejandro replied, "I shine shoes. That's how I make my money. I'm not like him. I don't dumpster dive looking for bottles. That's just nasty. That's for *palomos* and I ain't no *palomo*."

On the streets, you are a *palomo* if you take no care of yourself, have a visible drug addiction—to solvent or glue sniffing with the bottle in hand—and if you dumpster dive, whether it be for food or for collecting bottles. To be called a *palomo*, a kid must look like he has deteriorated in appearance, wearing rags or dirty clothes. Alejandro made that fine social distinction and recognized the kind of path that Julio was on. He wanted no part of it, didn't want to be mistaken for one of those. All *palomos* sleep on the street, but not all kids who sleep on the street are *palomos*. By calling someone else a *palomo*, Alejandro kept up the illusion that his position wasn't that bad.

I extracted myself from the small group and continued on my way down the Conde, past the male hustlers and the female prostitutes who wait outside of Paco's Cafeteria, the 24-hour joint at the very start of the pedestrian mall. Out of the corner of my eye I saw Chulo, one of "our" kids, pimped up in his muscle-bound tank top, looking so much older than his 15 years. He sat at one of the tables just outside of Paco's with another young Dominican and two aging, wrinkled tourists who had bought them beers. My heart fell, deflated at the sight of Chulo with clients. It is one thing to know intellectually what our kids do to survive; it is another to see it happening. The two old guys laughed loudly, their silver heads bobbing up and down, proud of what their $25 would buy them. Chulo caught me looking in his direction and turned his head away. I was furious. I wanted to make a scene, scream at these ugly Americans or Canadians or Germans. Like so many other nights, I turned away and let the indignation and anger wash through me. The worse part was, Chulo would say very little about it, for shame or embarrassment; he did not acknowledge to us how he was making money. If there is no acknowledgement of one's behavior, one can't begin to talk about self-worth, protection, maintaining dignity, or defining boundaries.

Past Parque Independencia, I turned up 11 de Agosto. I crossed over to the sidewalk on the west side to ascend the street. On the next corner, outside a dingy shop, there was a large pile of trash—boxes filled with detritus and loose agglomerates of food waste and other items shoved under the street lamp. There was something moving in the pile and at first I thought it might be a dog, but when the figure looked up, I saw it was human. It was 13-year-old Julio.

"Hey, Julio," I called out as I got nearer. Better to just make my presence known. He turned his head in my direction, back still slightly hunched, and hands holding onto the box he had been rifling through. In his pursed lips was a silly corncob pipe that made him look like a sharecropper.

"Oh! Oh-oh!" Julio recognized my presence without taking the pipe from his mouth.

"What's the what with you?" I greeted him in my best street Spanish.

"Calmer than a clam," he replied, pulling the pipe from his lips. He'd dropped the box. "Lookin' for bottles. I made 150 pesos yesterday in bottles."

I checked out his appearance and thought, Geez, Alejandro was right, he does look like a *palomo*. His clothes were filthy. Even in the low light of the street lamp, I could see the dirt and grime on his jeans, and the maroon t-shirt appeared gray. Julio was fairly dark skinned, but his hands and feet were two shades darker for the filth.

From around the corner there came a tall, lean man just as grimy as Julio. He had an overgrown beard matted on his face, the once curly, kinky hair lying in ropelike patterns. He carried a sack over his shoulder and looked like a thin, black St. Nicholas.

"You find anything little guy?" he asked Julio as he approached.

"Naw, nothin' worth anything."

I made to introduce myself, but the man kept walking past me and muttered, "Let's get goin' then." He turned down the street without another word.

"You hangin' out with him, Julio?" I asked, a bit incredulous that Julio should choose that guy as his street companion.

"Yeah. We collect bottles together. He lets me share his spot down by the cathedral. He's got a way to sneak into that gated park down there."

Julio's choice of friends troubled me. Adults usually meant abuse. "You guys sleep together?" I asked, using an ambiguous construction that could mean anything from having sex to sharing a similar sleeping space.

"Yeah, there in the park. There's lots of space. But we're the only two. Only he knows how to get in through the parking garage next door."

The man had stopped at the corner; he was looking back at us.

"You'd better get going. He's waiting for you. I'll see you tomorrow at the drop-in center, right?"

"Sure. I'll check you later."

He grabbed his own bag of bottles, throwing it over his shoulder, and headed down the street. The bag was so full and Julio so short, the bottles dragged along the pavement, clinking into the night.

Alejandro, Manuel, Chulo, and Julio, while all more or less the same age and from the same general family backgrounds, had discovered four different strategies for making a living on the streets. All four had taken time to move into what had become their primary means of making a living. While they all centered around the same general area of the Colonial Zone, each had found a specialized niche. These specialty niches conditioned their appearance, demeanor, and the skills they acquired.

Alejandro's move into petty thievery, Manuel's identity as a beggar, Chulo's choosing to become a sex worker, and Julio's job as a trash recycler represent particular "career" paths open to youth on the streets of Santo Domingo. Visano (1990) has noted that kids pass through various stages, or careers, on the street. During the passage from newbie to seasoned veteran, a boy or girl learns the appropriate behaviors and dispositions of a street denizen. These young people also learn to value the freedom and independence needed to survive (Beazley 2003). This chapter examines the relationship between urban space and career trajectory for street children. Street career trajectories are conterminous with spatial trajectories. Socialization into the economic, social, and emotional aspects of the street involves relocation, as kids transition from home and neighborhood environments to different locales on the streets and in and out of contact with social welfare agencies (Ennew and Swart-Kruger 2003, 10). When a child leaves home, he or she moves from the more private realm of the home and neighborhood into the more public realm of the street. Because of their marginal social existence, street children can only ever enter into

Figure 17.1.   Taking a break from street outreach activity (J. Wolseth photo)

careers at the social and physical edges of the urban environment. Yet street children learn to master the environment of the city, and through the co-option of public space, they transform their environment.

The streets offer a prime location in which to witness creative adaptation and the development of competency by children. By attending to the acquisition of knowledge about social space among street children, we are better able to see the intelligent ways in which kids build relationships with their environment and the impact that changes to that environment may have on street populations (cf. Ginsburg 2008). Public life on the streets requires that children find their niche through acquiring social skills, information about the urban environment, and if more adept, learning to switch between various street and nonstreet identities. Niche, then, should be understood in both the economic and geographic sense of the term—as both material and cultural phenomenon.

Finding a Niche

Street kids live in public spaces. Because of this public existence, they are consistently under surveillance and forced to interact with the greater public. As Shaw (2007) points out, "Children that live on the street depend on the public for their survival, and they construct their identities in order to take advantage of the expectations and prejudices of their audience. . . . [Their] subjectivity is created through a dialectic of which the public is an important part" (84). In other words, "street child" is only ever a public identity, performed vis-à-vis the social environment of the city and the audience of people who do not share this street identity. Children who are found outside of the private sphere of the home and in public space are exclusively identified with the street, regardless of their living and work situation. (Lucchini 1996, 107).

Place and career combine to shape personal identity. As a means of navigating through the cultural and social strata of urban centers, children on the streets develop detailed cognitive maps, plotting specific opportunities for daily survival. Maps are learned through interaction in public spaces, observation, and accompanying kids who are already established in the city on their daily forays. These cognitive maps organize urban space based on the types of activities permitted there, the kinds of people found in the environment, and the degree of personal safety the location may provide.

Although street children may work in and defend specific territories, they are a highly mobile group, with residence in any one territory fluctuating almost daily. This mobility is an extension of the lives of poor urban and rural children who search for the best possible material and affective conditions. That is, children are placed or place themselves into "circulation" among their natal homes, the local orphanage, and the homes of older siblings, distant relatives, and more well-to-do patrons (Leinaweaver 2007, 2008). Studies of homeless youth populations in the United States show them following defined trajectories among different social service providers on a daily and seasonal basis, both within and between cities (see, e.g., Ruddick 1996; Wolch and Rowe 1992). This pattern of mobility exists in the developing world as well, even though the number of state-supported social services and private NGOs may be fewer or more limited in scope (see Moyer 2004, 125–27). Van Blerk (2005) calls this movement between homeless and nonhomeless spaces "episodic mobility," noting that such movements help shape individual and social identity.

We can see the confluence of activity, space, and identity—niche finding—most clearly in the development of economic strategies in the city. Because their survival depends on interactions with a more affluent public, street kids learn to work the most lucrative zones, such as tourist areas, marketplaces, and upper-class shopping districts. Although they frequent these areas, the work they do belies their social status, as they stoop to shine shoes, beg, sell candies, wash cars, and offer other "convenience" services, such as carrying items to patrons' homes or vehicles. Not all approaches are effective, and there is always the danger that a potential client will be scared off if the child comes on too forcefully, looks too haggard (or not ragged enough), or doesn't show enough deference. The entrepreneurial strategies are often improvised and require little to no start-up costs. There are, however, "best practices" involved in different types of work, as children learn from each other and interactions with their "clients" as to what the most effective way of going about the work might be and where such activity is permitted or most lucrative to practice. This overlap of career, place, and practice is seen in the three street careers of begging, sex work, and pick-pocketing. While I present these careers as separate, street children often combine strategies.

Begging is a performance of identity and follows accepted patterns (Staples 2007). It is closely associated with age: teenagers and young adults are no longer able to garner the pity from passersby (especially tourists) that younger kids do (Aptekar 1988; Goode 1987; Hansson 2003, 5). Hence, routines may develop in which older kids send out and manage younger kids to beg. Begging routines are gendered as well; in Zimbabwe, girls are more successful at begging when they "borrow" an infant that they pretend is their own child or sibling (Rurevo and Bourdillon 2003). In Santo Domingo's *Zona Colonial*, I routinely watched many of the younger kids, like Manuel mentioned above, portray themselves as hungry and orphaned to the general public as they asked for food. They would intentionally wear their most ragged outfits and learned what they considered key English phrases such as "Tengo mucho hungry" and "No family." They shared the money they received from tourists with other members from their cohort to spend on recreational drugs. Some teenagers opted for another strategy: handicapping themselves by tucking one leg up into their pants, they would then sit directly on the cement pavers, hands outstretched in the classic begging posture.

Sex work is a lucrative activity, high-risk but low status, despite its ability to generate access to funds and commodities (Hansson 2003, 8).

Girls who take to the street may enter into sex-for-commodity relationships with foreigners without self-identifying as prostitutes (Kenny 2007, 85). Getting involved in sex work requires a change in appearance. Children who enter the sex trade with the intent of attracting foreign clients must adopt the aesthetic preferences of their clients (cf. Ebigbo 2003, 3). In particular, there may be greater emphasis placed on not looking "street" in order to "pass" in the dominant society. For example, teenage boys in Santo Domingo who, like Chulo, exchanged sex with tourists for commodities took greater care of their appearance, bathing on a more regular basis and pilfering clothing from vendors that would allow them to look more respectable. They also adopted the style of older, nonhomeless male prostitutes to attract a similar foreign client base. These strategies allowed the boys to frequent semirestricted spaces such as hotel lobbies, bars, and pool halls to look for clients—places they would have been excluded from had they not altered their appearance.

Petty thievery is a common economic strategy for street children, whether it be stealing merchandise from vendors, the opportunistic "finding" of unattended items, or the more skillful pickpocketing and bag snatching. In some street environments, specialized vocabulary has developed around these practices, indicating that children learn skills through instruction from experts to novices, as much as through repeated practice. Young (2003), in a drawing exercise with Kampala street boys, elicited surprising evidence as to the socialization of thieving behavior. One 9-year-old boy, in describing the picture he had drawn of bag snatching, replied, "I am timing [waiting to steal] the bag this woman is carrying, to pull it and go with it" (13). Terms describing the manner or way in which the illegal behavior should be carried out, such as "soft touch" and "timing," demonstrate that there are degrees of proficiency involved. Among street boys in the Dominican Republic, boys like Alejandro who are particularly adept at pickpocketing and bag snatching are called *descuidistas*, a local slang term implying that they have developed the fine art of seeing when someone else is being careless (*descuidar*) with their belongings. Becoming proficient as a petty thief involves understanding the different factors of crowds, space, police presence, and potential hiding places. Such skills are often learned accompanying a more experienced child (for further discussion of learning from peers, see chapter 8, this volume) and then honed through trial and error. The fear of being caught increases the pressure to perform agilely.

Begging, sex work, and pickpocketing are three possible careers that involve particular skill sets and knowledge in order for a child to be successful. Street kids readily adapt to their urban environment, exploiting the spatial niches available to them. Careers, too, are fluid, as kids may practice a range of economic strategies without developing an overriding identity as a "beggar," "sex worker," or "thief." Unlike most of the employed population, street kids must be flexible generalists. Some work—and some identities—may be more fixed than others, however, as the moral quality of the place shapes the identity of the people who are found there. For example, rag pickers and garbage dump scavengers exist at the low end of street identities because of their association with dirt (Kenny 2007, 65–68). In Santo Domingo, kids like Julio who collected bottles and took less care in their appearance were considered on a path to becoming part of the more permanent homeless. Their identity as a *palomo* removed them from the possibility of becoming vendors and from interacting with tourists. In spite of their low status, scavengers—as well as bootblacks, windshield washers, and candy sellers—are considered legitimate and respectable workers in the informal sector and see themselves as having greater moral value than those involved in illegal activities.

Mapping spatial and economic niches is part of a broader process of orientation to street life (Beazley 2000). Economic and spatial niches are learned by watching and participating in group life, so street career opportunities, at least initially, may depend on the child's peer group on the street. Part of the adaptation process to street life is the gradual replacement of home ties with street ties and the increasing affiliation with others on the street (Vigil 1988, 2003). The process of finding a career niche as a street child, then, begins with leaving home.

Becoming a Street Kid

Getting to the city and living in public space is not a singular, unproblematic journey for children. The patterns of arrival from and strength of connection with their natal households are complex. While the contributing factors for a specific child are varied, a common denominator is some shift or change in household dynamics that pushes a child to the streets or makes the streets seem a preferable option. For kids from a more rural background, economic pressures within the household may be a particularly acute factor. As Heissler (2008) points out in the context of rural Bangladesh, factors such as access to productive land and social position influence which households are more likely to have children who migrate to urban areas for work. The expectation, however, is that all children who migrate to urban centers will continue to contribute to the family via remittances.

Families in urban and periurban slums also may feel the need to send children to the streets to work. The great majority of "street kids" in northeast Brazil maintain ties to their households, and family members may actually manage their labor (Kenny 2007, 3). Kenny illustrates in detail the exploitative relationship between parents and children. Her stark descriptions belie the more sanguine view of some researchers who highlight the sense of empowerment and autonomy work affords children (see Mickleson 2000).

Living in urban slums allows children to learn streetwise attitudes and dispositions such as verbal finesse, impression management, and a street-tough emotional attitude, to contain and manage levels of interpersonal violence. These skills learned in one's home neighborhood transfer particularly well to the broader urban environment of the city streets. Home neighborhoods also provide an introduction to other, practical skill sets such as learning to spot undercover police as a lookout, problem-solving and math proficiency acquired through being a runner and counter for drug gangs, and entrepreneurial and marketing skills learned by watching older youth involved in the trade of illegal goods (Anderson 1999; Butler 2007; Goldstein 2003; Riaño-Alcalá 2006; Wolseth in press). It may be that those children who are more street oriented in their home neighborhood are at a greater predisposition to venture further out into the city for money-making and recreational opportunities. They may have an advantage in starting mobile street careers such as working as bootblacks and itinerate sellers.

The line between "street child" and "working child" is a contentious and fluid one, not least of all for the individual child (Moyer 2004). As an adaptation to economic and social uncertainty, moving to the street is a process that may evolve slowly. Kids take to the street to work in the informal sector because they are excluded from formal work in businesses and industrial areas (Connolly and Ennew 1996, 134). Still, working in the central city will not necessarily lead to full-time residency on the streets.

What it does indicate, however, is that the majority of kids who spend increasing time on the streets have passed through an introductory stage and, in the process, have identified a variety of street career options.

Assuming an identity as a "street child" requires a period of adjustment. A honeymoon period exists in which kids transition from household and neighborhood ties to street ties, often with the help of a close friend or family member who is already on the streets (Rizzini and Butler 2003, 5). Having contacts on the streets alleviates much of the uncertainty about the possibility for earning a living. It is during this critical stage that children are testing the waters, gaining knowledge and self-confidence before seeking greater independence from their families. Indeed, working on the streets may not be so much an option as a household necessity—as children may be expected to support their families through any means available. All "street kids" undoubtedly begin life working on the streets; choosing to reside there with greater frequency and for longer periods of time is what ultimately leads to the shift in identity.

In recent research, emic definitions of what characterizes a "street kid" have gained more currency. These definitions are preferred to the facile classifications imposed by researchers and policymakers, such as that between being of and being on the street (see Connolly and Ennew 1996 for a discussion of the limitations of etic distinctions). From an emic point of view, the difference between working on the street and being a "street kid" requires a qualitative shift in status. Hecht (1998) notes that the kids he worked with in Recife would only label themselves as "street kids" when they no longer had any ties or contact with their mothers, thus representing their "orphaned" and "abandoned" status. Homeless kids who live with family members on the street, who may look to passersby like "street kids," contest this label by pointing to an accompanying parent (Lucchini 1996).

The process of identifying oneself with the street group may be multiplex, as additional research also demonstrates that the shift from family authority to that of the street group involves some forms of initiation. Research from Brazil and the Dominican Republic, for example, reveals that kids regard their first experience with drug use, be it solvents, marijuana, or crack, as a mark of initiation into street life generally and the peer group specifically (Rizzini and Butler 2003, 17; Wolseth 2009). In Tanzania (Lockhart 2002, 2008) and Indonesia (Beazley 2003), gang rape among boys serves a similar purpose, cementing interdependence and transmitting information about in-group hierarchies in the process (cf. Campos et al. 1994).

Although kids may be street oriented in their neighborhoods, and although this orientation may precipitate a transition into working and living in urban centers, this orientation does not trump the importance of the idea of family as the central institution in their lives. Street relationships are often cast in kin terms, revealing the deep level of continuity kids seek between home life and street life. Stephenson (2006, 166) characterizes the attachment to city space that homeless populations exhibit as ultimately "aimed at re-placement in social structure," substituting their former neighborhood and kin attachments with the social networks available to them on the city streets. It is only through adapting to new sets of socio-spatial relationships that street kids are able to support themselves and cope in their new environment and ultimately make the street their home.

Making the Street Home

The conceptual distinction between "home" and "street" is one that is tied to an ideal model of family life and the social reproduction that occurs within the family (Fass 2005; Kuznesof 2005; Passaro 1996; Premo 2008). If early social role acquisition, including appropriate gender and age norms, takes place within the family structure, living on the street requires that new expectations concerning appropriate roles and behaviors be learned from the street group. While both natal family and street peers socialize children through example, explicit routines, positive reinforcement, and punitive measures, the two do differ in significant ways. Due to the long-term obligations and generational interdependence within kin groups, the investment, guidance, and reliance on children as learners of culture and tradition is greater; there is more at stake for the reproduction of cultural values within the kin group than within the street peer group. In other words, on the streets, kids have to learn more quickly as the repercussions for failure are greater, be more wary of whom to trust, and ultimately keep up with the fast-paced changes in interpersonal relationships occurring daily within the peer group.

The rhetoric and instructional role of "family" is so strong that, across numerous studies, ethnographers report how people living in the street define their social group in familiar or kin terms. Creating fictive kin relationships not only alleviates the emotional attenuation many street kids experience but also provides familiar roles for kids, even if these roles may have slightly different expectations associated with them. For example, in the main pedestrian mall of Moscow, youths recreate complex familiar relationships. Each subcultural group has a number of socially constructed mothers, fathers, and children, with reciprocal exchange expectations paralleling those in the dominant society (Stephenson 2001). Taylor and Hickey (2001) describe the young homeless gang members that live and work in the tunnels under the U.S.-Mexico border at Nogales applying the rhetoric and practices of kin or family to their immediate friends. Similar patterns are found among street youth in Canada and the United States (Hagan and McCarthy 1998). In these instances, the creation of a street family is described as mitigating the alienating effects of life on the street. However, group membership tends to turn over frequently, with the result that one's street family recapitulates the instability of one's natal family. But one can also exercise greater freedom in altering one's street family, as compared to the stifling containment of one's "home." However, by aligning themselves with a particular street group, kids are locked into the economic activities monopolized by the group. The kids in Nogales, for example, teach each other the methods of crossing the border through the tunnels, how to lead others, and ultimately how to take advantage of unsuspecting migrants.

Not all street groups self-consciously reproduce family models. Social organization can also be centered around affiliation with certain occupational choices, drug use, and territorial claims. For example, Goode (1987) in a brief report concerning street children in Colombia, describes the *gallada* as a complex hierarchical set of groups where members pool resources, offer protection, and provide network ties to other groups that may facilitate a child's graduation from begging and shoe shining to criminal activities through apprenticing with an older youth (cf. Aptekar 1988). *Gallada* networks, Goode hints, offer an introduction to other criminal networks throughout the city. Similar social networks, called *turmas*, exist in northeast Brazil, where an ethic of cooperation and companionship prevails (Campos et al. 1994). Such cooperative social organization however, is an idealized and sanitized version of street life that children may perpetuate while, at the same time, telling stories of intergroup violence and instability. In Kampala, for instance, Frankland (2007) notes that young *bayaye*, as street youth are called, understand the limits of sociality. They forge cooperative networks within occupational and geographical groups, but these do not extend across the city to youth in similar situations. At the same time, however, there is general recognition of a shared street experience, as street youth collectively see themselves in opposition to the nation-state. In pointed contrast to Goode's example, Lucchini (1996) asserts that children's groups are fluid and unstable in part due to the scarce economic and food resources available. The social group is too disorderly, Lucchini maintains, for cooperative instruction to occur. Hecht (1998, 45–58) also emphasizes that although street children in Recife rarely roam alone, the groups they form are informal and contrast with the rigid hierarchy and membership of the gangs found in the *favelas*.

The street is a harsh environment where children like those in Lucchini and Hecht's respective studies negotiate survival on a moment to moment basis. The brutal nature of the street undermines sociality and the likelihood of forming relationships with other children (cf. Márquez 1999). Kovats-Bernat (2006) arrives at a similar estimation for the violent social world of Port-au-Prince street children, culminating in sleeping wars (*lage domi*), where rivalry leads to brutal, retaliatory attacks permanently injuring or killing the perceived offender.

The socializing role of the peer group includes, at the very least, an implicit model of behavior, reproducing hierarchy and appropriate ways of interacting with other street denizens. Additionally, peer groups provide a ready-made identity, complete with associated emotional dispositions (Butler 2007). When conditions of conviviality exist—and the acute competition for survival is minimal—friendly instruction between kids will flourish. While there is little evidence to support the existence of formal apprenticing on the streets, kids do create dyadic bonds, often between more and less experienced kids, which are crucial to the integration of new group members (Davies 2008). The transmission of knowledge is often in exchange for services rendered; the privilege of being in the presence of someone who knows the ropes carries a price. Berman (2000) suggests that sexual abuse between more and less experienced kids on the streets in Indonesia is such an accepted part of the scene that newbies normalize it and later expect to be able to abuse others. In the Dominican Republic, more experienced kids often pimp out less experienced ones and requisition the monies earned. Older kids also send younger ones to buy drugs for group consumption, knowing that the younger ones are less likely to be stopped and searched by the police. Through such services and errands, kids gain not only valuable street information but also increased status and reputation within their group (Wolseth 2009).

For some kids, the group may be more of a hindrance as they gain street knowledge. Moving among peer groups or moving in and out of affiliation with a group often entails a change in one's primary career. While Manuel and Alejandro felt they were part of roughly the same group, this group would not include Julio, because of Julio's career choice of being a bottle collector. Likewise, Chulo had graduated from shoe shining into the world of prostitution and hustling, a career that he felt had the potential to remove him from the streets altogether, much like his new primary reference group, the nonhomeless hustlers he had befriended and used to help locate clients. These boys' interactions with the city, too, had changed with their respective career paths. With each new skill set, their cognitive maps changed to reflect their new social position within the urban environment.

Consequences and Suggestions

One of the most important lessons I learned during my time working street outreach in Santo Domingo was that street children, despite the hardships and challenges in their lives, were incredibly well adjusted to the lives they lived. In particular, the relationship between the physical environment of the city and the peer groups they developed to overcome the challenges demonstrated that there was a vibrant subculture created to offset exclusion from broader Dominican society. Peer socialization is an adaptation to difficult environments; some of the behaviors and values may not be healthy, but they have fostered a certain resiliency in body and spirit (see Panter-Brick 2002; Boyden 2003). Aid organizations and those concerned with developing adequate and informed interventions with street child populations would do well to focus their attention on the ways young people fashion the world around them in order to survive (and in some cases thrive) in vulnerable niches. We should turn attention to these positive assets and strengths of street kids, not their deficiencies, in order to build assistance programs that engage with the problems and realities of the street from the perspective of the children themselves (Conticini 2007; Ennew 1994).

As discussed earlier, discovering the child's construction of identity is critical. HIV/AIDS prevention programs aimed at "child prostitutes," for example, must acknowledge that children probably don't identify themselves as sex workers and that they engage in sexual activity for a variety of reasons, not simply in exchange for material goods. Child participants may not view some activities, such as oral sex exchanges or ritualized gang rape, as "sex," but rather as part of being a member of a street group. HIV/AIDS prevention programs would need to address all subcultural aspects of sexual identity and not just those stemming from sex-for-goods/money exchanges.

Attending to identity construction among street children will create better prevention and intervention programs, but the process of fashioning self-understanding must be placed in the geographic context in which it takes place. Despite the resiliency evident in individual children, the relationship between street career, identity, and the physical geography of the city is a fragile one. Any changes in the urban environment such as urban renewal programs, increased policing, or natural disasters have the potential to disrupt the present patterns of a street population. If, as I have suggested, the urban environment conditions street careers, change to that environment will alter the types of career strategies available to kids. This fact was emphasized during my own outreach experience. Two major urban renewal programs on the part of the municipal government reclaimed two parks utilized heavily by street populations for sex work and drug selling. As local authorities moved in to "clean up" the spaces on the edges of the Colonial Zone, the police targeted kids who frequented these areas, attempting to push them out to more marginal areas of the city. However, during the construction phase, the projects created a cottage industry of "appropriating" copper and steel fixtures in order to sell them on the black market. As this opportunity increased the amount of funds available to kids, drug use, especially crack and cocaine use, also increased within the peer group. Once construction was completed, the boom period ended, but heavily addicted kids were willing to take greater risks in other street careers in order to fuel their addiction. Kids who had rarely engaged in sex work began to do so in earnest, but unlike the type of sex-for-commodities exchange that was present before urban renewal, the kids were more likely to participate in sex-for-crack exchanges. This increased their potential risk for infection with a sexually transmitted disease (see Inciardi and Surratt 1998). It also undermined the city's goal of cleaning up the Colonial Zone, as kids became more aggressive in their search for clients in the tourist-trafficked areas created by the renovated parks.

While it is impossible for any outreach or intervention program to foresee all the consequences of radical urban environmental changes to a street kid population, paying close attention to the relationship between environment, behavior, and street knowledge could potentially help local populations better weather such changes. Unfortunately, one of the prevailing prejudices in both research and policy is that "the street" is a poisoned environment, one where children should not be found. While for the long-term health and well-being of individual homeless children this may be true, there are few viable alternatives, given program and monetary restraints. By better understanding "the street," we can design and implement education programs that utilize street knowledge and local cultural practices. In such a manner, we can nurture the solidarity and cooperation found among street populations, highlight why and when exploitation takes place, and, together with young people, create intervention curricula that empower kids to change their lives.

Acknowledgments

I express thanks to the editors of this volume for the opportunity to engage with my research data in a new way and for providing me guidance in thinking through the issues of peer learning on the streets in broader terms. Research for this paper was conducted between November 2004 and November 2006 while I served as a Peace Corps volunteer in the Dominican Republic with the NGO *Niños del Camino* in Santo Domingo. I give special thanks to Adele Williams and Estivaliz Ladrón de Guevara for the chance to serve. My Dominican co-workers Natividad Sosa, Epifanio de Jesús Castillo, Héctor Ramírez, Martha Alcántara, and Dorca Rojas were stalwart companions in the rough and tumble world of the NGO and street outreach. Fellow volunteers Eli Barbado, Núria Perelló, Roberto Palencia, Rúben Gallegos, Isabelle Deneyer, Laura Ibañez, Rachelle Olden, Emily Hoffman, and Mary Rolle offered much-needed emotional and physical support. Most of all, to the hundreds of kids and youths working and living on the streets who let me into their world and their lives, I am indebted for the ways they enriched my life. Pa'lante!

Bibliography

Anderson, Elijah. *Code of the Street: Decency, Violence, and the Moral Life of the Inner City*. New York: Norton, 1999.

Aptekar, Lewis. *Street Children of Cali*. Durham, N.C.: Duke University Press, 1988.

Beazley, Harriet. "Home Sweet Home? Street Children's Sites of Belonging." Pp. 194–212 in *Children's Geographies: Playing, Living, Learning*, edited by Sarah L. Holloway and Gill Valentine. London: Routledge, 2000.

———. "The Construction and Protection of Individual and Collective Identities by Street Children and Youth in Indonesia." *Children, Youth, and Environments* 13, no. 1 (2003). http://colorado.edu/journals/cye.

Berman, Laine. "Surviving on the Streets of Java: Homeless Children's Narratives of Violence." *Discourse and Society* 11, no. 2 (April 2000): 149–74.

Boyden, Jo. "Children under Fire: Challenging Assumptions about Children's Resilience." *Children, Youth, and Environments* 1, no. 1 (2003). http://colorado.edu/journals/cye.

Butler, Udi. "Embodying Oppression: *Revolta* Amongst Young People Living on the Streets of Rio de Janeiro." Pp. 53–74 in *Livelihoods at the Margins: Surviving the City*, edited by James Staples. Walnut Creek, Calif.: Left Coast, 2007.

Campos, Regina, Carlos Mauricio, Marcela Raffaelli, Neal Halsey, Walter Ude, Marilia Greco, Dirceu Greco, Andrea Ruff, and Jon Rolf. "Social Networks and Daily Activities of Street Youth in Belo Horizonte, Brazil." *Child Development* 65, no. 2 (April 1994): 319–30.

Connolly, Mark, and Judith Ennew. "Introduction: Children out of Place." *Childhood* 3, no. 2 (May 1996): 131–45.

Conticini, Alessandro. "Children on the Streets of Dhaka and Their Coping Strategies." Pp. 75–100 in *Livelihoods at the Margins: Surviving the City*, edited by James Staples. Walnut Creek, Calif.: Left Coast, 2007.

Davies, Matthew. "A Childish Culture? Shared Understandings, Agency, and Intervention: An Anthropological Study of Street Children in Northwest Kenya." *Childhood* 15, no. 3 (August 2008): 309–30.

Ebigbo, Peter O. "Street Children: The Core of Child Abuse and Neglect in Nigeria." *Children, Youth, and Environments* 13, no. 1 (2003). http://colorado.edu/journals/cye.

Ennew, Judith. "Parentless Friends: A Cross-Cultural Examination of Networks among Street Children and Street Youth." Pp. 409–28 in *Social Networks and Social Support in Childhood and Adolescence*, edited by Frank Nestman and Klaus Hurrleman. New York: Aldine de Gruyter, 1994.

Ennew, Judith, and Jill Swart-Kruger. "Introduction: Homes, Places, and Spaces in the Construction of Street Children and Street Youth." *Children, Youth, and Environments* 13, no. 1 (2003): 1–21. http://colorado.edu/journals/cye.

Fass, Paula. "Children in Global Migrations." *Journal of Social History* 38, no. 4 (Summer 2005): 937–53.

Frankland, Stan. "No Money, No Life: Surviving on the Streets of Kampala." Pp. 31–52 in *Livelihoods at the Margins: Surviving the City*, edited by James Staples. Walnut Creek, Calif.: Left Coast, 2007.

Ginsburg, Rebecca. "The View from the Back Step: White Children Learn about Race in Johannesburg's Suburban Homes." Pp. 193–212 in *Designing Modern Childhoods: History, Space, and the Material Culture of Children*, edited by Marta Gutman and Ning de Coninck-Smith. New Brunswick, N.J.: Rutgers University Press, 2008.

Goldstein, Donna. *Laughter out of Place: Race, Class, Violence, and Sexuality in a Rio Shantytown*. Berkeley: University of California Press, 2003.

Goode, Judith. *Gaminismo: The Changing Nature of the Street Child Phenomenon in Colombia*. Hanover: Universities Field Staff International. Report—Latin America no. 28, 1987.

Hagan, John, and Bill McCarthy. *Mean Streets: Youth Crime and Homelessness*. Cambridge: Cambridge University Press, 1998.

Hansson, Desirree. "'Strolling' as a Gendered Experience: A Feminist Analysis of Young Females in Cape Town." *Children, Youth, and Environments* 13, no. 1 (2003): 1–19. http://colorado.edu/journals/cye.

Hecht, Tobias. *At Home in the Street: Street Children of Northeast Brazil*. Cambridge: Cambridge University Press, 1998.

Heissler, Karen. "Children's Migration for Work in Bangladesh: The Extra- and Intra-household Factors That Shape 'Choice' and 'Decision-making.'" *Childhoods Today* 2, no. 1 (2008): 1–19. www.childhoodstoday.org.

Inciardi, James A., and Hilary L. Surratt. "Children in the Streets of Brazil: Drug Use, Crime, Violence, and HIV Risks." *Substance Use and Misuse* 33, no. 7 (1998): 1461–80.

Kenny, Mary Lorena. *Hidden Heads of Households: Child Labor in Urban Northeast Brazil*. Buffalo: Broadview, 2007.

Kovats-Bernat, J. Christopher. *Sleeping Rough in Port-au-Prince*. Tallahassee: University Press of Florida, 2006.

Kuznesof, Elizabeth. "The House, the Street, Global Society: Latin American Families and Childhood in the Twenty-First Century." *Journal of Social History* 38, no. 4 (Summer 2005): 859–72.

Leinaweaver, Jessaca. "Choosing the Orphanage: Child Agency on Peru's Margins." *Childhood* 14, no. 3 (August 2007): 375–92.

———. "Improving Oneself: Young People Getting Ahead in the Peruvian Andes." *Latin American Perspectives* 35, no. 4 (July 2008): 60–78.

Lockhart, Chris. "Kunyenga, 'Real Sex,' and Survival: Assessing the Risk of HIV Infection among Urban Street Boys in Tanzania." *Medical Anthropology Quarterly* 16, no. 3 (September 2002): 294–311.

———. "The Life and Death of a Street Boy in East Africa: Everyday Violence in the Time of AIDS." *Medical Anthropology Quarterly* 22, no. 1 (March 2008): 94–115.

Lucchini, Ricardo. *Niños de la Calle: Identidad, Sociabilidad, Droga*. Barcelona: Los Libros de la Frontera, 1996.

Márquez, Patricia. *The Street Is My Home: Youth and Violence in Caracas*. Stanford, Calif.: Stanford University Press, 1999.

Mickelson, Roslyn, ed. *Children on the Streets of the Americas: Globalization, Homelessness, and Education in the United States, Brazil, and Cuba*. London: Routledge, 2000.

Moyer, Eileen. "Popular Cartographies: Youthful Imaginings of the Global in the Streets of Dar es Salaam, Tanzania." *City and Society* 16, no. 2 (December 2004): 117–43.

Panter-Brick, Catherine. "Street Children, Human Rights, and Public Health." *Annual Review of Anthropology* 31, no. 1 (2002): 147–71.

Passaro, Joanne. *The Unequal Homeless: Men on the Streets, Women in Their Place*. New York: Routledge, 1996.

Premo, Bianca. "How Latin America's History of Childhood Came of Age." *Journal of the History of Childhood and Youth* 1, no. 1 (Winter 2008): 63–76.

Riaño-Alcalá, Pilar. *Dwellers of Memory: Youth and Violence in Medellin, Colombia*. Edison, N.J.: Transaction, 2006.

Rizzini, Irene, and Udi Mandel Butler. "Life Trajectories of Children and Adolescents Living on the Streets of Rio de Janiero." *Children, Youth, and Environments* 13, no. 1 (2003). http://colorado.edu/journals/cye.

Ruddick, Susan. *Young and Homeless in Hollywood: Mapping Social Identities*. London: Routledge, 1996.

Rurevo, Rumbidzai, and Michael Bourdillon. "Girls: The Less Visible Street Children of Zimbabwe." *Children, Youth, and Environments* 13, no. 1 (2003). http://colorado.edu/journals/cye.

Shaw, Kurt. *Agony Street: A Reflection on Masochism and Politics on the Street*. Digital Edition. Santa Fe: Shine A Light, 2007. www.shinealight.org.

Staples, James. "Begging Questions: Leprosy and Alms Collection in Mumbai." Pp. 163–85 in *Livelihoods at the Margins: Surviving the City*, edited by James Staples. Walnut Creek, Calif.: Left Coast, 2007.

Stephenson, Svetlana. "Street Children in Moscow: Using and Creating Social Capital." *Sociological Review* 49, no. 4 (November 2001): 530–47.

———. *Crossing the Line: Vagrancy, Homelessness, and Social Displacement in Russia*. Hampshire: Ashgate, 2006.

Taylor, Lawrence J., and Maeve Hickey. *Tunnel Kids*. Tucson: University of Arizona Press, 2001.

Van Blerk, Lorraine. "Negotiating Spatial Identities: Mobile Perspectives on Street Life in Uganda." *Children's Geographies* 3, no. 1 (2005): 5–21.

Vigil, James Diego. "Group Processes and Street Identity: Adolescent Chicano Gang Members." *Ethos* 16, no. 4 (December 1988): 421–45.

———. "Urban Violence and Street Gangs." *Annual Review of Anthropology* 32, no. 1 (2003): 225–42.

Visano, Livy A. "The Socialization of Street Children: The Development and Transformation of Identities." *Sociological Studies of Child Development* 3 (1990): 139–61.

Wolch, Jennifer, and Stacy Rowe. "Mobility Paths of the Urban Homeless." *City and Society* 6, no. 2 (December 1992): 115–40.

Wolseth, Jon. "Good Times and Bad Blood: Violence, Solidarity, and Social Organization on Dominican Streets." In *Youth Violence in Latin America: Gangs and Juvenile Justice in Perspective*, edited by Dennis Rodgers and Gareth Jones. London: Palgrave, 2009.

———. *Jesus and the Gang: Youth, Violence, aand Christianity in Urban Honduras*. Tucson: University of Arizona Press (in press).

Young, Lorraine. "The 'Place' of Street Children in Kampala, Uganda: Marginalisation, Resistance, and Acceptance in the Urban Environment." *Environment and Planning D: Society and Space* 21, no. 5 (2003): 607–28.

CHAPTER EIGHTEEN

CHILDREN'S LEARNING IN NEW SETTINGS

David F. Lancy

In most of the preceding chapters of this book, authors describe patterns of learning by juveniles that are rooted in long-term and relatively stable patterns of biocultural adaptation. In part V, we shift our focus. Wolseth, in chapter 17, provides a vivid case study of children—many from rural villages—learning to adapt to an entirely new ecology: the streets of a large city. This chapter uses a wide-angle lens to briefly examine the many new settings that village children find themselves adapting to. Those settings include schools that have barely taken root in the village, labor, urban streets, and the milieu of the insurgent band. These close-up snapshots provide background for the next section of the chapter, which revisits the six principles enumerated in chapter 1 and provides a wide-angle view of childhood today.

Children Learning in Classrooms

In the late 1960s, I had an opportunity to observe Kpelle children eagerly participating in the new school just built in their village with American aid. However, the pupils' near zero knowledge of English, which was the language of instruction, posed a daunting challenge, compounded by the facts that there were "no books in Kpelle homes to learn from, no library, no *Sesame Street*. Parents, almost all of whom are illiterate, [could not] teach their children what they are expected to learn in school" (Lancy 1975, 378). And the outcome was predictable as eager pupils became frustrated "school leavers," a phenomenon repeatedly documented around the world (Juul 2008, 153; chapter 9, this volume). At the Gapun village school in the Sepik region of Papua New Guinea, Kulick and Stroud (1993) found that children "learn very little during their first two or three years . . . due . . . to their inability to cope with instruction in English. . . . Outside of school . . . literacy skills are almost never used," and after leaving school at age 14–15, "many of these young people may never read and will almost certainly never write again" (32).

In Chillihuani village in the high Andes, where hamlets are dispersed over a valley running from 3,800 and 5,000 meters, children's attendance at school is limited by the harsh climate and the great distance they must walk. The monolingual Quechua children struggle with Spanish as the language of instruction, and the classroom is so overcrowded, many must sit on the floor. In spite of a sympathetic teacher locally, Bolin (2006) notes, generally, Indian children suffer harassment and other forms of abuse at the hands of *mestizo* teachers and students (85–87). Pygmy schoolchildren in Africa are harassed and bullied by children from more powerful Bantu tribes, and Central African government officials speak of them with evident racism and contempt. The obstacles they face mean that, according to a sympathetic teacher, they "sometimes take three to four years to complete a single year of normal schooling" (Raffaele 2003, 132). In Bangladesh, village children begin schooling quite late, having to overcome parental resistance, and their attendance is erratic. Hence, by adolescence, the average student has completed only three years of education (Nath and Hadi 2000).

It is quite common for parents to withhold their children from school or prevent them from doing homework, preferring them to seek employment for wages and/or do housework (de Oliveria 1995, 260). But families may hedge their bets (Bock 2002) and fund schooling for at least some of their children. In Port-au-Prince,

> Ancillary school fees (for books, uniforms, and other supplies) are sufficiently high as to prohibit most poor households from sending all of the family's children to school, despite the fact that primary education is free and compulsory for all children in Haiti. As a result poor families are compelled to make painful decisions about which children will attend school and which will be turned out onto the street to work and thus contribute to the household income. (Kovats-Bernat 2006, 108)

Conflicts between parental and school expectations are legion. Khmer parents can't understand why teachers ask for their "support" but then reject corporal punishment as the best means of obtaining better performance from their children (Smith-Hefner 1993, 139). On Pulap Island (Micronesia), the school atmosphere does mirror village values, but that is not necessarily helpful: for example, "the atmosphere at the school is very lax and permissive . . . cupboards and shelves of the classrooms are in disarray . . . recess lasts two or three times the designated length" (Flinn 1992, 51).

For the forest-dwelling children of the Shipbo tribe in lowland Peru, schooling leads them to a dead end. Occupied with inscrutable classroom lessons, they aren't learning from their environment or community members. They forego the benefits of traditional Shipbo culture, yet they learn so little in school, they carry to town no employable skills (Hern 1992, 36). Because the common folk theory is that children learn best on their own, villagers do not take pains to *teach* the knowledge and skills the children are missing out on (Godoy et al. 2007). In at least one case documented by anthropologists, the Cree did not even take the trouble to change their foraging trips to the weekends to permit the weekday students to tag along and learn to forage. "By the time they finished their schooling, they had become foreigners to Cree tradition, not only by failing to acquire skills and knowledge of the land but also by lacking an appropriate attitude for life on the land. Thus, formal schooling led to the weakening of the existing social system" (Ohmagari and Berkes 1997, 207).

In spite of poor prospects, it is usually the children who initiate and persist with school attendance. If the alternative is lugging around a cranky baby brother or weeding the garden or sticking around home all day helping mother, then spending a few hours in the company of peers, even under otherwise adverse circumstances, might not seem so bad. Guinean students "preferred school to being home, where they would have to do chores . . . the big punishment was to be *bâni* (banished) . . . from school" (Anderson-Levitt 2005, 988). And sometimes a student *does* beat the odds and succeeds, in spite of the obstacles (Hollos 2009). In fact, in interviewing these very ambitious students, many mention the desire to use their education and improved prospects to assist their families (Leinaweaver 2008, 72).

However, the majority will be disappointed and become angry and cynical (Davis and Davis 1989, 141–2). International programs that have for decades promoted universal primary schooling have created "an avalanche of failed aspirations throughout the third world" (LeVine and White 1986, 193), and schools find themselves "in the business of producing failures" (Serpell 1993, 10). Particularly in Africa, frustrated "school leavers" of the 1960s and 1970s became the brutal "child soldiers" of the 1980s and 1990s (Honwana 2005).

The "education gap" between those born into a society that invests in education and those from a society that lacks the cultural or real capital to create successful schools is no longer synonymous with the North-South divide in economic opportunity. The rise of private schooling and transfer of cultural capital (appreciating the importance of storybooks, preschool, homework, computers, exam preparation) to third world elites has replicated this gap in every city and country (e.g., Boum 2008; Falgout 1992; Goody 2006; Kipnis 2001; Stambach 1998).

Child Laborers

Although difficult to assess, it does appear that child labor is increasing at a rapid rate. Millions of children who, in an earlier era, might have been gradually, comfortably, even playfully making their way to adulthood now find themselves virtual slaves, putting in long hours of backbreaking or otherwise physically or emotionally abusive labor. The rise reflects the fact that, in much of the world, carrying capacity has been exceeded and rural families no longer have enough land to support all the surviving children. In an ethnography of the squatter community of Baan Nua in Thailand, Montgomery (2001) found that residents had been forced to relocate because of crowding in their rural homeland. Baan Nua parents find that the best source of income is the prostitution of their children, nearly half of whom had been so employed (Montgomery 2001, 72; see also Rubenson et al. 2005). A second factor is that open markets force producers to pay the lowest wages possible, and children are often as productive as adults but at much lower cost. Mixtec villagers cannot all make a living off the limited amount of arable land, especially to meet new expenses like electricity, manufactured clothing, and taxes. Hence families now participate in an annual migration to the agribusiness-controlled croplands (e.g., tomatoes) in other regions of Mexico and in the United States. The output of a child as young as 8 years old is comparable to that of an adult, and both are paid the same 27 pesos a day (Bey 2003).

In some respects, the Baan Nua children residing with family and Mexican children working alongside their parents are relatively "fortunate." They at least enjoy the protection and guidance of family. In much of West Africa, child slavery is rampant, for example. "In the large Adjame market of Abidjan, Côte d'Ivoire, investigators discovered a 'maid market' wherein young girls were being bought and sold from a ramshackle, corrugated iron, and wood shack" (Bass 2004, 149). This "maid market" is rooted in traditions where poor rural families donate surplus children to better-off urban relatives (Leinaweaver 2008, 60). The girls, "little nieces," serve as maids and in theory have access to improved opportunities, especially improved schooling. However, just as the kin ties may be fictive, the entire promise of "advancement" may be illusory (Jacquemin 2004).

This review could be extended almost indefinitely (Lancy 2008a, 99–105), but what can we say about *learning*? Two things seem self-evident. First, children who are removed from the traditional village setting are *not* learning the panoply of skills, concepts, and expressive culture that construct lifelong membership and survival in a viable *community*. Second, they are employed in the most rudimentary, unskilled, and dangerous jobs where there is little opportunity for learning or *development*. The most comprehensive ethnography of rural children as *laborers* was carried out by Olga Neiuwenhuys (1994) in India's Kerala state. Villagers have two primary sources of income, the fabrication of coir matting (women) and fishing (men). Several things are clear from her analysis. First, children as young as 3 years old are employed. Second, without children's labor input, families could not make ends meet. Third, the skills learned are rudimentary, and girls are kept from learning the more advanced skill of spinning so that they won't be able to compete with the women.

Immigrant Children and Their Families

Throughout this work, children's great capacity for learning and their ability to adapt to an enormous range of cultural conditions have been displayed. As bleak as these contemporary scenes are, it would be remiss on our part not to acknowledge the strength and resiliency children show in adverse circumstances. Kenny (1999) found that Brazilian children "acquire a certain amount of power or confidence in identifying and navigating the social world." While a mother "felt paralyzed when confronted with the bureaucracy of the local health clinic or municipal office . . . and rarely ventured beyond the entrance to the favela," Kenny noted, "children hop on buses and ride them for free, know[ing how to] hustle . . . and spend the better part of the day in [an] urban, informal labor market, amid the dangers, excitement, sights, sounds, and stimuli of life" (379).

The same skills that children apply toward learning the culture of the village can be equally effective in the city, as this example from urban African American communities illustrates. As the afternoon wanes,

> small-drug transactions heightened, and the local "audience" of unsupervised children . . . grew. . . . [One 14-year-old] remarked: "You ought to be out right now. This is when all the peeps [people] is hangin'. *You learn about the streets now. . . . It's good for a young brother to know the streets.* You see everybody, styling and profiling. All the peeps see you. If you want to be seen, this is the time to be out." (Burton and Graham 1998, 16, emphasis added)

Children's adaptability is also revealed in immigrant and refugee families. Orellana's (2001) study of Central American immigrant families in Los Angeles demonstrates how dependent they are on children's rapid learning of the local culture:

> [P]arents in Pico Union take it for granted that children should use their English abilities . . . to translate for them. Furthermore, there are complex English literacy demands for daily life in Los Angeles . . . and parents may need children's help to carry out daily tasks. . . . In many ways *they* are the experts, and their ability to engage successfully with the complex demands of modern life matters for their families' well-being and integration into U.S. society. Children's work facilitates families' access to information and resources. (378)

Many young people migrate without their families (Uehling 2008), and they may well end up on the streets. Clearly, the family structure remains important as the foundation for truly successful adaptation. Just as children are able to assist families, so too, families play a critical role in ensuring that children succeed in school. Specific cases of successful migrant adaptation to the "information society" include: Vietnamese "Boat People" reading to preschoolers (Caplan, Whitmore, and Choy 1991); Central American immigrant parents ensuring that children avoid negative peer influence (Suarez-Orozco 1989); Punjabi families struggling to prevent children from becoming "typical American adolescents" (Gibson 1988).

Escape to the Streets

An extremely thin line separates "street kids" from "poor kids." The Haitian children who are *not* sent to school may be much better off, at least in the short run. Kovats-Bernat's (2006) account of street kids in Port-au-Prince is echoed in numerous recent ethnographies (Evans 2004; Hecht 1998; Kenny 2007; Kilbride, Suda, and Njeru 2000; Márquez 1999). He finds that hustling in the city is relatively lucrative. Children can expect to make "over three times the national daily wage through street labor" (Kovats-Bernat 2006, 108). Initially they may share much of their income with family. But when their contributions are not appreciated (consumed in alcohol by a parent), or worse, they are abused for not bringing home enough, they are likely to spend more and more time with their street family and less and less "at home." Kenny (1999) asserts, "Living with one's family can be one of the riskiest locations for a child . . . where abuse is more abundant than food" (384). This story from a young Brazilian woman is typical:

> I couldn't stand to live at home anymore. My mother liked to hit us, she wouldn't let us go out, we didn't have any freedom. . . . [M]y mother wouldn't let us stay home one single day, we had to work. (Campos et al. 1994, 323)

Still, many children do continue to share their earnings with and visit, even when the family is in a distant village. They do so as a form of social security. In the event of an injury, illness, or the need to escape apprehension for a crime, they have a refuge (Conticini 2007, 87; Kovats-Bernat 2006, 109). Some proportion of street kids may return nightly to their families in a squatter settlement, and indeed, their economic activity

Figure 18.1.   Bookmark seller, Cuernavaca, Mexico (D. Lancy photo)

may be managed by a parent or other family member (Lancy 2008a, 360; Sinervo 2009). However, the majority of children studied by anthropologists live entirely in public.

Street kids are more likely to be male, because girls are both more useful and valued at home and are simultaneously more vulnerable and likely to become "damaged" in the street (Kilbride et al. 2000, 138). And cohorts of street children tend to be unisex. Children who enter the street unaccompanied quickly become attached to older and more experienced peers who readily socialize them to the culture, and that includes a designated *territory*. In the large Kenyan town of Makutano, the children's territory is well known:

> characterized by rubbish, open sewers, mud, and crime . . . .in every way a . . . dangerous area to most inhabitants. To the children, however . . . it is their home, it is a safe, reassuring area buffered away from the dangers of the adult world. (Davies 2008, 320–1)

Children also learn the street slang, terms that only they use and which apply to elements of their culture (Davies 2008, 323). They sport a distinctive wardrobe, such as oversize coats to store or hide their "stuff" (Davies 2008, 324). Another universal aspect of the youth culture is glue-sniffing, which is replaced as a pastime in older children by the use and sale of hard drugs (Márquez 1999, 41).

Along with drugs, promiscuous sex is considered a form of play (Conticini 2007, 88). Resources may be shared, and older, more experienced children look after the "chupapegas . . . the youngest . . . living on the boulevard" (Márquez 1999, 40). These relationships may be of considerable standing and are legitimated when children refer to each other as spouses or siblings (Kilbride et al. 2000, 82–83). On the down side, children are also victimized by the police, merchants, the public, and especially other children. In Port-au-Prince, children engage in *lage domi*:

> ritualized sleeping wars . . . considered by street youths to be a final solution to long-festering animosities that repeatedly emerge. . . . The final violent act is usually a blow . . . while the victim sleeps. . . . Nadès received a slash to the bottom of his feet, which he avenged by burning the foot of his tormentor with molten plastic. (Kovats-Bernat 2006, 130–5)

Intervention programs that remove children from this life-threatening environment have not been conspicuously successful (see chapter 17, this volume). Notable failures are those that "restore" children to the families that drove them away in the first place (Hecht 1998, 110). Russia has

2.5 million street children; however, except in a crisis, those studied by Fujimura (2003, 2005) generally spurn residence in public orphanages in favor of the friendships, freedom, and money they find in the street. Educational and vocational programs are also unattractive. One of Márquez's informants quit the bakery job a nongovernmental organization (NGO) had arranged because he could earn in a day what the bakery paid per week. "He also worked with an NGO for a brief time but found the routine of picking up paper for recycling very boring and skipped work whenever he felt like it" (Márquez 1999, 56).

The remarkable fact is that the culture of the streets also features a sort of "chore curriculum' (see chapters 6, 7, and 17, this volume). Six-year old Reinaldo earned enough to support his mother and six siblings from tips earned guarding parked cars while their owners patronized local bars and restaurants (Kenny 2007, 76). The very young can also learn to become effective beggars:

> Begging styles typically include not only verbal requests but also holding a hand out, pouting, exaggerated smiling, and less frequently, threatening gestures with the face and hands. . . . [S]treet children successfully beg from a full range of givers. . . . Street boys report that children can beg up to the age of 14 years, when they no longer look "innocent." (Kilbride et al. 2000, 70)

Because there is vertical differentiation in the street economy, older residents are willing to train new recruits (Wolseth 2009), teaching them "the tricks of the streets: how to get more money while begging, how to break into cars, how to make master keys" (Márquez 1999, 64). Other sources of money or gifts of food include scavenging for discarded plastic bottles and charcoal to sell, and carrying luggage or running errands (Davies 2008, 318). Children graduate to more lucrative and sophisticated means of earning a living, "forming discrete occupational geographies that make up the nodal points in the networks of the urban economy" (Frankland 2007, 43). Informal sales through unlicensed marketing range from children's toys to hard drugs. Street sellers may be well dressed and fluent in several languages. They may serve as "pilots" or guides: *bayaye* act as intermediaries between the customer and the vendor, leading the way to the market stalls and . . . as guides to sightseers, or directing European sailors and soldiers to prostitutes" (Frankland 2007, 43). Children may thus earn significant sums, finding that they must pay "taxes" to various mafia-like enforcers and police and engage in informal banking to shelter their fortunes (Conticini 2007, 86).

Sex work seems also to be graded. Girls, whose money-earning options are more limited than those for boys,[1] exchange sex for food and small gifts with fellow street kids. When eventually they make themselves available to tourists, "they do not have fixed prices for 'services,' do not identify as sex workers, and do not describe what they do as an 'occupation'" (Kenny 2007, 85). Once they become prostitutes, they may earn more than their male counterparts who are occupied as street sellers and porters (Conticini 2007, 85).

Eventually, street "kids" age out. In Caracas, older youths earn the label *malandro*. These youths take pains to dress well and blend in, earning a living from theft. They "would not be seen as 'street children' causing mischief, but as *malandros* committing serious transgressions. They have outgrown their cute rascal image" (Márquez 1999, 53).

Child Soldiers

There is considerable overlap in the career of a street kid and a child soldier. The popular impression is that child soldiers have been abducted from intact families in rural villages, and that certainly accounts for a significant number, especially in Uganda (Mawson 2004, 133). However, child soldiers seem to be particularly prevalent where the birth rate is high, leading to a very youthful population, and the death rate of adults is high (due mostly to HIV/AIDS), leading to a disproportionately large orphan population (Case, Paxson, and Ableidinger 2004). The poor quality of schooling, noted earlier, and strained relations within families are also contributory. According to Rosen (2005):

> the lack of education and job opportunities ensured an endless supply of . . . unemployable, and alienated youth. Sierra Leone was, and still is, a country filled with unwanted youth. Some portion of this youth were always available to be recruited into any setting—legal or criminal—that offered a hint of economic opportunity. (80)

Furthermore, the experience of life in an urban gang is in many ways indistinguishable from that in a "rebel band." As described by Campos and colleagues (1994), in the city of Belo Horizonte,

> the *turma* is a close-knit group that provides youngsters with support, companionship, and protection. . . . [N]ew members have to steal and prove their willingness to abide by group norms . . . [and] norm breakers are punished, with the ultimate punishment being . . . a ritual involving violence, torture, and gang rape. (324)

Contrast that with Honwana's (2006) findings about the initiation and lifestyle of an Angolan child soldier:

> [According to the soldier,] "We all had to drink two spoons of blood each. They told us that this was important to prevent us from being haunted by the spirits of the people we might kill." . . . [T]ogether with strenuous physical exercise, manipulation of weapons, and the imposition of strict discipline, these practices represent a powerful ritualized initiation into a culture of violence and terror. (62–63)

There is evidence that those who would create juvenile militias recruit directly from urban gangs (Lancy 2008a, 301–2), and demobilized child soldiers readily transform into *mareros* or gang members (Dickson-Gómez 2003, 345). The "education" of a child soldier is, in fact, mostly indoctrination. After all, the current weapon of choice, lightweight, inexpensive assault rifles, "can be carried, stripped, and reassembled by children aged ten years or younger" (Dickson-Gómez 2003, 328).

As we saw with schooled children, the setting in which child soldiers find themselves is noteworthy for what they are *not* learning. "The exaggerated discipline of the guerrilla camps left little room for male adolescents to develop concepts of autonomy and control. They were not given a chance to practice and learn how to be campesino adults, dedicated to subsistence agriculture" (Dickson-Gómez 2003, 344). In Mozambique and Angola, Honwana (2006) notes that communities "are still dealing with the serious disruptions . . . in the life course of young people," that the wars "left a deep moral crisis," and that "the initiation rituals and systematic preparation of young people to become responsible adults ceased. A whole generation was seriously affected" (43).

Our Six Principles Revisited

By way of conclusion, I'd now like to revisit the six general principles enumerated in chapter 1. Our first was that, relative to other species, the *length* of the period of immaturity is elongated due, at least in part, to the need for children to acquire the vast store of information that constitutes culture. In the 21st century, this principle is challenged by a drastic bifurcation of childhood (Lancy 2008b).

In the developed countries, childhood has become dramatically longer, at both ends. That is, anxiety about the child's success in school has promoted an attitude—supported by somewhat dubious scientific evidence—that insists on early cognitive stimulation of the infant. There is a blurring of the distinction between the infant and child stages, brought about, for example, by the use of gestural language ("baby signs") with preverbal children. At the other end of the spectrum, we have "children" remaining at home and continuing as dependents well into their 20s as they finish their education and launch careers. Scholars now label them "emergent adults" (Arnett 2004). By contrast, in developing countries, overpopulation and economic stress have created new conditions whereby children are expected to make an economic contribution at an earlier and earlier age. Kenny (2007) describes poor Brazilian communities where children as young as age 5 are employed producing "much of what Brazilians eat, wear, and sleep in," and that "cacao, gems, minerals, soybean, and grape industries all . . . use cheap (children's) labor" (2). Childhood ends almost before it has begun.

Our second principle is that the end points of learning are culturally defined. In the ethnographic record, one finds considerable variation in village "curricula," especially when comparing pastoralist, forager, and farming communities. For at least the last 100 years, that variability has steadily narrowed. This has occurred because of the reduction in ways that people find to make a living. The population of foragers has shrunk dramatically, and hunting, for example, may now be accomplished with the use of a few tools (outboard motors, rifles) where aboriginal hunters may have used literally hundreds of capture techniques—which children would gradually master (Nelson 1972). A second change that has narrowed expectations has been the global spread of state-sponsored schooling. The content of the curriculum and the methods of instruction, incorporating rote memorization, recitation, learning in a second language, an emphasis on obedience and conformity, and identical curricula for both sexes are just a few of the characteristics associated with schooling throughout the world. Today, "diversity" in learning references relative success in progressing through the hierarchical school system rather than variation in the skill set with which one enters adulthood.

Our third principle identified the universal existence of folk theories or ethnotheories embedded in culture that describe child development and the means by which society is to assist juveniles on the pathway to adulthood. Traditional views have been challenged by the spread of schooling. In particular, the laissez-faire attitude adopted by parents in many societies, accompanied by casual child-tending practices such as sibling care, are now seen as incompatible with the need to prepare children for school and monitor and support their learning of academic subjects (Deyhle 1991; Matthiasson 1979). There is also a growing gap between societies that have entered the demographic transition (Caldwell 1982) and elected to reduce fertility and those that have not. Goddard (1985) describes a poor community in Naples that had, historically, depended on the wages its children earned in shoe factories but where younger couples are electing to have fewer children and to send them to school rather than put them to work. By contrast, in Burkina Faso, high birth rates are maintained in spite of near starvation living conditions. The theory that drives this behavior is "every child is born with its own luck" (Hampshire 2001, 115), and parents believe they have little to contribute to the child's success or failure.

Our fourth principle is that learning is a social process. In the communities studied by anthropologists, children learn from observing and interacting with others. In the 21st century, this is changing. For first world children, knowledge is increasingly packaged in one form of "media" or another. Significant others serve less often as role models and more often as didactic teachers or guides. Schooling, in which one's primary associates are same-age peers, begins at an earlier and earlier age and persists through adolescence. The consequent increase in peer versus adult socialization is a source of scholarly and popular attention (Harris 2009). Schoolchildren still learn in a social context, but that context is an institutional one that is expressly organized to support their learning. For impoverished children who live and/or work outside the home and/or are orphans, learning is also still primarily social, but the cast of potential teachers and role models has changed. Now the child has far less opportunity to observe and interact with a range of neighbors, siblings, and relatives and, instead, is primarily in the company of others of the same sex and nearly the same age—whether living in a modern (e.g., small, nuclear) family or a street family. First and third world children also encounter adults whose roles (teacher, coach, therapist, police, NGO outreach worker) vis-à-vis the child may be quite formal and even aversive.

Our fifth principle focused on the role of the child in taking the initiative to learn her or his culture. Granting children the autonomy to construct their own lessons and learn at their own pace works fine in the traditional village where life skills are practiced and displayed in public. The child's observations, make-believe play, and repetition or practice of fragmentary skill components should lead eventually to mastery. Such "social learning" (chapter 5) has considerably less utility in the "information" society where making a living depends on the long-term acquisition of material that is essentially hidden from view and must be packaged and delivered by experts. On the other hand, in societies where there is rapid cultural change or radical disruptions in the traditional context (war, famine, immigration), children may be expected or required to take even more initiative to learn the "new" culture because traditional socializing agents do not have mastery of it.

The sixth principle identified children as playing two distinct roles. On the one hand, they are to play the role of child, a role partly scripted by society and partly by the child. Indeed, we can expect some degree of conflict between these two scripts. On the other, the child, again collaboratively scripted, occupies the role of an incomplete adult, an adult in the making. In the village, there is the tendency to assign greater value to the second role. The Baining claim to be ashamed rather than proud of their children. They discourage play and other childish behaviors, and they take pains to hurry children along in becoming mature social actors (Fajans 1997). In the information society where the period of dependency and learning has become greatly extended, children are treated as "cherubs" (Lancy 2008a, 2) and their childish, immature behavior is celebrated and prolonged via toys, birthday parties, and targeted media (Clarke 2008). In contrast to third world children risking life and limb, in the first world, children's lives are increasingly constricted. We are so concerned about protecting their *future* prospects, we deny them the chance to *be*. A study conducted in the United Kingdom, for example, showed a dramatic decline in the last 20 years in the number of unaccompanied children permitted to cross the street, go to the cinema, or use public transport (Qvortrup 2005, 8; see also Skenazy 2009).

For children in marginal communities on the urban fringe, neither role sits comfortably. Forced to work, they must relinquish the role of child, but the fact that they've become breadwinners for their families earns them "little increase in autonomy, power, or decision making" (Kenny 2007, 74). That is, their assumption of adult tasks, earning a living, caring for younger kin, and managing a household does not necessarily earn them the status and authority of an adult. The community may still continue to treat them as juvenile (Bissell 2003, 61).

Acknowledgments

Some of the ideas in this chapter were floated at the Re-presenting Childhood and Youth Conference at Sheffield University in 2008, where they provoked a very stimulating discussion. I am grateful to the conference organizers, Allison James in particular. Thanks also to Suzanne Gaskins for several helpful suggestions.

Note

1. Similarly, girls drawn into civil conflicts may have limited choices open to them. In the Liberian conflict, they mostly provided sexual services to the combatants (Utas 2005).

Bibliography

Anderson-Levitt, Kathryn M. "The Schoolyard Gate: Schooling and Childhood in Global Perspective." *Journal of Social History* 38, no. 4 (Summer 2005): 987–1006.

Arnett, Jeffrey J. *Emerging Adulthood: The Winding Road from the Late Teens through the Twenties.* New York: Oxford University Press, 2004.

Bass, Loreta E. *Child Labor in Sub-Saharan Africa.* Boulder, Colo.: Lynne Rienner, 2004.

Bey, Marguerite. "The Mexican Child: From Work with the Family to Paid Employment." *Childhood* 10, no. 3 (August 2003): 287–99.

Bissell, Susan. "The Social Construction of Childhood: A Perspective from Bangladesh." Pp. 47–72 in *Child Labour and the Right to Education in South Asia: Needs versus Rights*, edited by Naila Kabeer, Geetha B. Nambissan, and Ramya Subrahmanian. New Delhi: Sage, 2003.

Bock, John. "Evolutionary Demography and Intrahousehold Time Allocation: School Attendance and Child Labor among the Okavango Delta Peoples of Botswana." *American Journal of Human Biology* 14, no. 2 (March–April 2002): 206–21.

Bolin, Inge. *Growing Up in a Culture of Respect: Child Rearing in Highland Peru*. Austin: University of Texas Press, 2006.

Boum, Aomar. "The Political Coherence of Education Incoherence: The Consequences of Education Specialization in a Southern Moroccan Community." *Anthropology and Education Quarterly* 39, no. 2 (June 2008): 205–23.

Burton, Linda M., and Joan E. Graham. "Neighborhood Rhythms and the Social Activities of Adolescent Mother." *New Directions for Child and Adolescent Development* 82 (Winter 1998): 7–22.

Caldwell, John C. *"The Great Transition": Theory of Fertility Decline*. New York: Academic, 1982.

Campos, Regina, Marcela Raffaelli, Walter Ude, Marilia Greco, Andrea Ruff, Jon Rolf, Carols M. Antunes, Nea Halsey, and Dirceu Greco. "Social Networks and Daily Activities of Street Youth in Belo Horizonte, Brazil." *Child Development* 65, no. 2 (April 1994): 319–30.

Caplan, Nathan, John K. Whitmore, and Marcella H. Choy. *The Children of the Boat People: A Study of Educational Success*. Ann Arbor: University of Michigan Press, 1991.

Case, Anne, Christina Paxson, and Joseph Ableidinger. *Orphans in Africa: Parental Death, Poverty, and School Enrollment*. Princeton, N.J.: Princeton University Center for Health and Wellbeing, Research Program in Development Studies, 2004.

Clarke, Alison J. "Coming of Age in Suburbia: Gifting the Consumer Child." Pp. 253–68 in *Designing Modern Childhoods: History, Space, and the Material Culture of Children*, edited by Marta Gutman and Ning de Coninck-Smith. New Brunswick, N.J.: Rutgers University Press, 2008.

Conticini, Alessandro. "Children on the Streets of Dhaka and Their Coping Strategies." Pp. 75–100 in *Livelihoods at the Margins: Surviving the City*, edited by James Staples. Walnut Creek, Calif.: Left Coast, 2007.

Davies, Matthew. "A Childish Culture? Shared Understandings, Agency, and Intervention: An Anthropological Study of Street Children in Northwest Kenya." *Childhood* 15, no. 3 (August 2008): 309–30.

Davis, Susan Schaefer, and Douglas A. Davis. *Adolescence in a Moroccan Town: Making Social Sense.* New Brunswick, N.J.: Rutgers University Press, 1989.

de Oliveria, Marta Kohl. "The Meaning of Intellectual Competence: Views from a Favela." Pp. 245–70 in *Child Development within Culturally Structured Environments*, vol. 3, *Comparative-Cultural and Constructivist Perspectives*, edited by Jaan Valsiner. Norwood, N.J.: Ablex, 1995.

Deyhle, Donna. "Empowerment and Cultural Conflict: Navajo Parents and the Schooling of Their Children." *Qualitative Studies in Education* 4, no. 4 (1991): 227–97.

Dickson-Gómez, Julia. "Growing Up in Guerilla Camps: The Long-Term Impact of Being a Child Soldier in El Salvador's Civil War." *Ethos* 30, no. 4 (December 2003): 327–56.

Evans, Ruth M. C. "Tanzanian Childhoods: Street Children's Narratives of 'Home.'" *Journal of Contemporary African Studies* 22, no. 1 (January 2004): 69–92.

Fajans, Jane. *They Make Themselves: Work and Play among the Baining of Papua New Guinea.* Chicago: University of Chicago Press, 1997.

Falgout, Suzanne. "Hierarchy vs. Democracy: Two Management Strategies for the Management of Knowledge in Pohnpei." *Anthropology and Education Quarterly* 23, no. 1 (March 1992): 30–43.

Flinn, Juliana. "Transmitting Traditional Values in New Schools: Elementary Education on Pulap Atoll." *Anthropology and Education Quarterly* 23, no. 1 (March 1992): 44–58.

Frankland, Stan. "No Money, No Life: Surviving on the Streets of Kampala." Pp. 31–51 in *Livelihoods at the Margins: Surviving the City*, edited by James Staples. Walnut Creek, Calif.: Left Coast, 2007.

Fujimura, Clementine. "Adult Stigmatization and the Hidden Power of Homeless Children in Russia." *Children, Youth, and Environments* 14, no. 1 (2003). http://colorado.edu/journals/cye.

———. *Russia's Abandoned Children: An Intimate Understanding.* Westport, Conn.: Praeger, 2005.

Gibson, Margaret A. *Accommodation without Assimilation: Sikh Immigrants in an American High School.* Ithaca, N.Y.: Cornell University Press, 1988.

Goddard, Victoria. "Child Labour in Naples: The Case of Outwork." *Anthropology Today* 1, no. 5 (October 1985): 18–21.

Godoy, Ricardo, Craig Seyfried, Victoria Reyes-García, Thomás Huanca, William R. Leonard, Thomas McDade, Susan Tanner, and Vincent Vadez. "Schooling's Contribution to Social Capital: Study from a Native Amazonian Society in Bolivia." *Comparative Education* 43, no. 1 (February 2007): 137–63.

Goody, Ester N. "Dynamics of the Emergence of Sociocultural Institutional Practices." Pp. 241–64 in *Technology, Literacy, and the Evolution of Society*, edited by David R. Olson and Michael Cole. Mahwah, N.J.: Erlbaum, 2006.

Hampshire, Kate. "The Impact of Male Migration on Fertility Decisions and Outcomes in Northern Burkina Faso." Pp. 107–25 in *Managing Reproductive Life: Cross-Cultural Themes in Sexuality and Fertility*, edited by Soraya Tremayne. Oxford: Berghahn, 2001.

Harris, Judith Rich. *The Nurture Assumption: Why Children Turn Out the Way They Do*. New York: Free Press, 2009.

Hecht, Tobias. *At Home in the Street*. Cambridge: Cambridge University Press, 1998.

Hern, Warren M. "Family Planning, Amazon Style." *Natural History* 101, no. 12 (February 1992): 30–37.

Hollos, Marida. "How Pare Children Shape Their Futures." Paper presented at the symposium on Agency and the Role of Children in Genetic and Cultural Transmission, Institute for the African Child Annual Conference, Athens, Ohio, March 2009.

Honwana, Alcinda. "The Pain of Agency: The Agency of Pain." Pp. 31–52 in *Makers and Breakers: Children and Youth in Post Colonial Africa*, edited by Alcinda Honwana and Filip de Boeck. Trenton, N.J.: Africa World, 2005.

———. *Child Soldiers in Africa*. Philadelphia: University of Pennsylvania Press, 2006.

Jacquemin, Mélanie Y. "Children's Domestic Work in Abidjan, Côte d'Ivoire: The Petites Bonnes Have the Floor." *Childhood* 11, no. 3 (August 2004): 383–97.

Juul, Kristine. "Nomadic Schools in Senegal: Manifestations of Integration or Ritual Performance?" Pp. 152–70 in *Designing Modern Childhoods: History, Space, and the Material Culture of Children*, edited by Marta Gutman and Ning de Coninck-Smith. New Brunswick, N.J.: Rutgers University Press, 2008.

Kenny, Mary Lorena. "No Visible Means of Support: Child Labor in Urban Northeast Brazil." *Human Organization* 58, no. 4 (Winter 1999): 375–86.

———. *Hidden Heads of Households: Child Labor in Urban Northeast Brazil*. Buffalo: Broadview, 2007.

Kilbride, Philip, Colette Suda, and Enor Njeru. *Street Children in Kenya: Voices of Children in Search of a Childhood*. Westport, Conn.: Bergin and Garvey, 2000.

Kipnis, Andrew. "The Disturbing Educational Discipline of 'Peasants.'" *China Journal* 46 (July 2001): 1–24.

Kovats-Bernat, J. Christopher. *Sleeping Rough in Port-au-Prince*. Gainesville: University of Florida Press, 2006.

Kulick, Don, and Christopher Stroud. "Conceptions and Uses of Literacy in a Papua New Guinean Village." Pp. 30–61 in *Cross-Cultural Approaches to Literacy*, edited by Brian Street. Cambridge: Cambridge University Press, 1993.

Lancy, David F. "The Social Organization of Learning: Initiation Rituals and Public Schools." *Human Organization* 34, no. 4 (Winter 1975): 371–80.

———. *The Anthropology of Childhood: Cherubs, Chattel, Changelings.* Cambridge: Cambridge University Press, 2008a.

———. "The Long and Short of It: Social Construction of Childhood." Paper presented at 2nd annual international conference sponsored by the Center for the Study of Childhood and Youth, Sheffield University, United Kingdom, 2008b.

Leinaweaver, Jessaca B. "Improving Oneself: Young People Getting Ahead in the Peruvian Andes." Special Issue on Youth, Culture, and Politics in Latin America. *Latin American Perspectives* 35, no. 4 (July 2008): 60–78.

LeVine, Robert A., and Merrie I. White. *Human Conditions.* New York: Routledge and Kegan Paul, 1986.

Márquez, Patricia C. *The Street Is My Home: Youth and Violence in Caracas.* Stanford, Calif.: Stanford University Press. 1999.

Matthiasson, John S. "But Teacher, Why Can't I Be a Hunter: Inuit Adolescence as a Double-Bind Situation." Pp. 72–82 in *Childhood and Adolescence in Canada*, edited by Kenneth Ishwaran. Toronto: McGraw-Hill Ryerson, 1979.

Mawson, Andrew. "Children, Impunity, and Justice: Some Dilemmas from Northern Uganda." Pp. 130–41 in *Children and Youth on the Front Line: Ethnography, Armed Conflict, and Displacement*, edited by Jo Boyden and Joanna de Berry. New York: Berghahn, 2004.

Montgomery, Heather. *Modern Babylon: Prostituting Children in Thailand.* Oxford: Berghahn, 2001.

Nath, Samir R., and Abdullahel Hadi. "Role of Education in Reducing Child Labour: Evidence from Rural Bangladesh." *Journal of Biosocial Science* 32, no. 3 (July 2000): 301–13.

Neiuwenhuys, Olga. *Children's Lifeworlds: Gender, Welfare, and Labour in the Developing World.* London: Routledge, 1994.

Nelson, Richard K. *Hunters of the Northern Ice.* Chicago: University of Chicago Press, 1972.

Ohmagari, Kayo, and Fikret Berkes. "Transmission of Indigenous Knowledge and Bush Skills among the Western James Bay Cree Women of Subarctic Canada." *Human Ecology* 23, no. 2 (June 1997): 197–222.

Orellana, Marjorie Faulstich. "The Work Kids Do: Mexican and Central American Immigrant Children's Contributions to Households and Schools in California." *Harvard Educational Review* 71, no. 3 (Fall 2001): 366–89.

Qvortrup, Jens. "Varieties of Childhood." Pp. 1–20 in *Studies in Modern Childhood: Society, Agency, Culture*, edited by Jens Qvortrup. London: Palgrave, 2005.

Raffaele, Paul. *The Last Tribes on Earth: Journeys among the World's Most Threatened Cultures*. Sydney: Pan Macmillan, 2003.

Rosen, David M. *Armies of the Young: Child Soldiers in War and Terrorism*. New Brunswick, N.J.: Rutgers University Press, 2005.

Rubenson, Birgitta, Le Thi Hanh, Bengt Höjer, and Eva Johansson. "Young Sex-Workers in Ho Chi Minh City Telling Their Life Stories." *Childhood* 12, no. 3 (August 2005): 391–411.

Serpell, Robert. *The Significance of Schooling: Life Journeys in an African Society*. Cambridge: Cambridge University Press, 1993.

Sinervo, Aviva. Appeals of Childhood: Child Vendors, Volunteer Tourists, and Visions of Aid. Unpublished Ph.D. Dissertation. Santa Cruz: UCSC Department of Anthropology, 2009.

Skenazy, Lenore. *Free-Range Kids*. San Francisco: Jossey-Bass, 2009.

Smith-Hefner, Nancy J. "Education, Gender, and Generational Conflict among Khmer Refugees." *Anthropology and Education Quarterly* 24, no. 2 (June 1993): 135–58.

Stambach, Amy. "Education Is My Husband": Marriage, Gender, and Reproduction in Northern Tanzania." Pp. 185–200 in *Women and Education in Sub-Saharan Africa: Power, Opportunities, and Constraints*, edited by Marianne Bloch, Josephine A. Beoku-Betts, and B. Robert Tabachnick. Boulder, Colo.: Lynne Rienner, 1998.

Suarez-Orozco, Marcelo M. *Central American Refugees and U.S. High Schools: A Psycho-social Study of Motivation and Achievement*. Stanford, Calif.: Stanford University Press, 1989.

Uehling, Greta. "Children's Migration and the Politics of Compassion." *Anthropology News* 49, no. 5 (May 2008): 8, 10.

Utas, Mats. "Agency of Victims: Young Women in the Liberian Civil War." Pp. 53–80 in *Makers and Breakers: Children and Youth in Post Colonial Africa*, edited by Alcinda Honwana and Filip de Boeck. Trenton, N.J.: Africa World, 2005.

Wolseth, Jon. "Good Times and Bad Blood: Violence, Solidarity, and Social Organization on Dominican Streets." In *Youth Violence in Latin America: Gangs and Juvenile Justice in Perspective*, edited by Dennis Rodgers and Gareth Jones. New York: Palgrave, 2009.

INDEX

abiding and wide-angled attention, 99

active learners, children as, 94

adolescence: development of capacity, 19; form and timing of human childhood, 11; gender role development, 298; initiation rituals, 299; managing adolescence, 162; maturational process in humans, 15

adults: development of capacity, 19; learning through observation of everyday life, 86; likelihood of adult presence and influence, 190; organisms emerging as adults, 12

adults' role in children's learning: absence of teaching, 145; apprenticeship, 159; chore curriculum, 154; corporal punishment, 152; facilitating craftsmanship, 158; facilitating independence, 148; folklore lessons, 151; formal education, 163; gardening, 157; infants not seen as learners, 146; instruction, 160; managing adolescence, 162; methodology, 167; motivating role, 157; native theories of learning and intelligence, 152; periods of quiescence and passivity, 147; rites of passage, 163; teaching speech, kin terms, and manners, 149; toddler rejection, 148; village learning model, contemporary challenges to, 165; weaning, 148

Amazigh (Berber) girl with self-made clay utensils, *132*

American Ethnological Association, 167

animal behavior, knowledge of, 374, 384

anthropological research: children and the environment, 347; context of learning, 3; cross-cultural study of learning and socialization, 35; evolutionary perspective in social, cultural, and ecological context, 11; parental ethnotheories of children's learning, 65; schools, anthropologists in, 208

apprentice coppersmith, Morocco, *160*

465

ABOUT THE EDITORS
AND CONTRIBUTORS

John Bock is professor of anthropology and coordinator of the Environmental Studies program at Cal State Fullerton. His research interests include the evolution of the human life history, and particularly the juvenile period, the development of ecological competence, and children's growth and development in comparative evolutionary and cross–cultural perspective. He has conducted extensive research in Botswana and New Mexico.

Garry Chick is professor of recreation, park and tourism management and professor of anthropology at Pennsylvania State University. He is a past president of The Association for the Study of Play and the Society for Cross–Cultural Research as well as a fellow of the Academy of Leisure Sciences, the American Anthropological Association, and the Society for Applied Anthropology. His areas of geographical specialization include Mesoamerica, China, and western Pennsylvania. Dr. Chick's topical interests encompass expressive culture, especially adult play and games, leisure and culture, the expressive aspects of technology, time allocation, cross–cultural comparative research, and research methods.

Patricia Crown is distinguished professor of anthropology at the University of New Mexico. Her principal areas of expertise are Southwestern studies and ceramic analysis. Her research has centered on ceramic production and exchange and the economic basis for the emergence of communities in the American Southwest.

Heidi Fung joined the research staff of the Academia Sinica, Institute of Ethnology in Taiwan in 2002 and is now professor at the Institute. She conducts qualitative research on the socialization of shame, construction of self, and the use of narrative.

Suzanne Gaskins is professor of psychology at Northeastern Illinois University. Her research, conducted in a traditional Mayan village in Yucatan, Mexico since 1977, focuses on cultural influences on children's development and their everyday lives. She has studied children's play and work as culturally structured activities and the developmental trajectory of linguistic relativity. She is also interested in the social and cultural organization of informal learning environments, including museums.

Mary Gauvain is professor in the Department of Psychology at UC Riverside. She studies how social and cultural processes contribute to children's acquisition, organization, and use of cognitive skills. Her book, The Social Context of Cognitive Development (2001), describes theory and research on social contributions to cognitive development in four areas—attention, memory, problem solving, and planning.

M. Annette Grove is a graduate student at the Utah State Unversity.

Sara Harkness is a professor of human development and family studies and anthropology at the University of Connecticut. Her research interests include the cultural structuring of human development and health, parents' cultural belief systems, parenting, and cognitive, affective, and social development in early and middle childhood. Her areas of specialization are Africa, Europe, and The United States.

David F. Lancy is professor of anthropology at Utah State University and has done fieldwork in Liberia, Papua New Guinea, and Sweden. He has authored several books on culture and childhood, including, in 2008, *The Anthropology of Childhood: Cherubs, Chattel, and Changelings*.

Katharine MacDonald is a postdoctoral researcher in the Faculty of Archaeology at University of Leiden, the Netherlands. Her general research interests are the evolution of primate intelligence and social learning, comparative approaches to hominin behavior, and responses to environmental change.

Ashley E. Maynard is associate professor and chair of the department of psychology at the University of Hawaii. Her research interests include: the development of teaching in childhood, sibling and peer socialization, cognitive development, schooling and learning in context, ecocultural theory, cultural change and socialization, and activity settings. She conducts interdisciplinary research in Mexico and Hawai'i.

Heather Montgomery is senior lecturer at the Centre for Childhood, Development, and Learning at The Open University, in the United Kingdom. Her research interests center on the anthropology of children and childhood, representations of childhood, the history of childhood, kinship and parenthood, children and sexuality, children and violence, and children's rights.

Leslie C. Moore is assistant professor in the School of Teaching and Learning at The Ohio State University. Her research examines the social and cultural patterning of language and literacy development in communities whose members use multiple languages and participate in multiple schooling traditions. She has worked in northern Cameroon since 1992 and has recently begun work in the Somali community in Columbus.

Robert L. Munroe is emeritus professor of anthropology at Pitzer College. His main area of interest centers on cross–cultural human development.

Kerry Ossi-Lupo is a doctoral student in anthropological sciences, SUNY Stony Brook. Kerry is working on finishing her dissertation research on skill learning, ecological risks, and growth and development in juvenile Phayre's leaf monkeys (Trachypithecus phayrei) at the Phu Khieo Wildlife Sanctuary in Thailand. Her research interests include male affiliation, primate life history variation, the juvenile period in particular, and conservation.

Ruth Paradise is professor-researcher at the Department of Educational Research in the Centro de Investigación y de Estudios Avanzados in

Mexico City. She has studied the learning practices of Mazahua people since the 1980's in Mexico City and the State of Mexico, in family and community settings as well as school settings. Her research focuses on the interactional characteristics of learning and teaching and their relation to the larger sociocultural context, with the aim of better understanding culturally specific ways of expressing autonomy, collaboration, initiative and motivation.

Benjamin Smith is a doctoral student at the University of Chicago. His primary areas of specialization are linguistic anthropology, sex and gender, and childhood. He studies these topics among Aymara-speaking people in the Peruvian Andes.

Laura Sterponi is assistant professor of language and literacy, society and culture at the University of California, Berkeley. She has conducted research on language and literacy socialization in different communities and educational settings. Her work has been published in several journals (including *Childhood*, *Discourse Studies*, *Ethos*, *Human Development*, and *Linguistics and Education*) and languages (English, French, and Italian).

Charles M. Super is professor in the Department of Human Development and Family Studies at the University of Connecticut. His areas of interest center on cultural regulation of human development, particularly biological, cognitive, and emotional development during infancy and childhood and parental and professional ethnotheories of child development and behavior.

Katrin E. Tovote is a PhD candidate in psychology at the University of Hawaii. She has worked and intensified her interdisciplinary and cross–cultural studies in Germany, Spain, Ecuador, Mexico and Hawai'i. Her ecocultural and activity–setting oriented research focuses on the social and cognitive development of children growing up in poverty.

Jon Wolseth is visiting professor in the Department of Sociology, Anthropology, andSocial Work at Luther College. His interests include the anthropology of childhood and youth, interpersonal violence, religious movements, drug use, and street cultures. His areas of specialization are

Central America and the Spanish Caribbean. His monograph *Taking On Violence: Youth, Gangs and Churches in Urban Honduras* will be published by the University of Arizona Press.

Rebecca K. Zarger is assistant professor in the Department of Anthropology, University of South Florida. Drawing from ethnobiology and the anthropology of education and childhood, her research explores the ways subsistence knowledge is learned, taught, and transformed in Q'eqchi' Maya communities in Belize. Other research interests include environmental anthropology, childhood, public engagement in environmental policy, conservation, environmental change, and environmental heritage education.